Chapter 5

Chapter 6

Chapter 7

1810

1820

1830

1846 • Boundary between United States and Canada extended to west coast

1848 • Colony of Vancouver Island created

1840

1870 • North-West Territories created
• Scrip process begins

1871 • Treaty process begins
• Canadian Pacific Railway Company formed

1873 • Laws of St. Laurent
• North West Mounted Police (NWMP) formed
• Pacific Scandal

1879 • National Policy

1850 • Douglas Treaties

1858 • Colony of British Columbia formed

1850

1860 • Cariboo Gold Rush

1864 • Tsilhqot'in Uprising

1866 • Colonies of Vancouver Island and British Columbia join

1860

1871 • British Columbia enters Confederation

1870

1880 • CPR Syndicate formed

1884 • Riel returns to the Northwest
• Métis Bill of Rights created

1885 • Northwest Uprising
• Riel executed
• CPR completed

1885 • CPR completed Head Tax created

1880

1896 • Manitoba Schools Question
• Campaign for immigration to the West

1897 • Yukon Gold Rush

1890

1901 • First wireless message sent across Atlantic

1903 • Alaska Boundary dispute settled

1907 • Anti-Asian riots in Vancouver

1908 • Continuous Passage Act enacted

1900

1910

1914 • *Komagata Maru* incident
• First World War begins

1920

HORIZONS CANADA'S EMERGING IDENTITY

second edition

Michael Cranny

Graham Jarvis

Garvin Moles

Bruce Seney

PEARSON

ISBN 10: 0-13-504046-9
ISBN 13: 978-0-13-504046-1

Project Team
Publisher: Susan Cox
Research & Communications Managers: Aerin Guy, Patti Henderson
Managing Editor: Gaynor Fitzpatrick
Developmental Editors: Cara James, Christel Kleitsch
Coordinating Editor: Martha Malic
Production Editor: Allana Barron
Copyeditor: Susan Ginsberg
Fact Check: Christine Higdon
Art Coordination: Carolyn E. Sebestyen
Production Coordinators: Maria Miceli, Sharlene Ross
Manufacturing Manager: Jane Schell
Cover & Interior Design: Alex Li
Composition: David Cheung
Maps: Crowle Art Group
Index: Axis Indexing Service
Permissions/Photo Researchers: Indu Arora, Karen Hunter

Cover image: Albert Normandin/Masterfile

Printed and bound in the U.S.A.

7 8 9 10   CC   14 13 12 11

PEARSON

Acknowledgements

Pearson Education would like to thank the educators who helped to shape *Horizons: Canada's Emerging Identity*, 2nd edition through discussions, surveys, focus groups, and review comments.

Contributing Writers

Dean Cunningham
Tom Morton
Alan Sears

Program Advisors and Reviewers

Jenise Boland
Dean Cunningham
Tom Morton
Joan Parsonson

Teacher Reviewers

Jocelyn Beaton
Larry Calvert
Roland Case
Leah Christensen
Barb Izard
Janet Ruest
Barry Walker
Russel Willey

Contents

What does it mean when someone tells you that "you can't judge a book by its cover?" They are asking you to think critically about something and to not take it at face value.

Understanding Critical Thinking

Critical thinkers are open-minded. They ask questions and communicate with others to form an opinion. They gather relevant information and use criteria, which are the standards or tests used while making a judgement, to guide their responses. Being a critical thinker can help you create an opinion or decide on an option based on good reasons.

In *Horizons*, you will study the geography, history, and economy of Canada. How might critical thinking apply to social studies?

- It can be easier to remember the facts of an event when you learn them in order to make a decision or solve a problem.

- It can help you apply critical thinking outside of the classroom.

- It can help your future: employers value people who think critically.

- Thinking deeply about issues is part of being a good citizen.

How do you know you are applying critical thinking skills? As you work through *Horizons*, use the chart below as a checklist to keep on track.

When I draw conclusions or interpret information	• I base them on evidence • I check to see if they are consistent • I base them on assumptions I can state
When I use evidence to support my claims	• I check that my evidence is clear, accurate, and relevant • I use sufficient evidence • I also consider evidence that opposes my position
When I base my claims on assumptions	• I clearly identify my assumptions and determine if they are justifiable • I consider how my assumptions shape my point of view
When I use concepts or ideas that others may not understand or may interpret differently	• I identify key concepts and explain them clearly • I consider alternative concepts • I make sure I am using concepts with precision
When I come to a definite final conclusion	• I search for negative as well as positive implications • I consider all possible consequences

Critical Thinking in History and Geography

Most historians and geographers agree that there are certain big ideas that need to be grasped in order to understand social studies. One way to approach the big ideas is to ask critical thinking questions. Here are some examples.

Questions to ask while studying history:

- How did things get to be as they are today?

- What groups of people am I a part of? What are their origins?

- How should we judge the actions of others in the past?

- Are things getting better or are they getting worse?

- What stories about the past should I believe? On what grounds?

- Which stories should we tell? What about the past is significant enough to pass on to other generations?

- What can we do to make the world a better place?

Questions to ask while studying geography:

- What is a place like?

- Why is a place located where it is?

- How are we connected to places?

- How are we connected to the environment?

- What is our responsibility to the environment?

Understanding the Critical Thinking Icon

In *Horizons*, a Critical Thinking Icon will appear at the start of each chapter. Several parts of the icon will be highlighted, showing you which critical-thinking elements are the focus of the chapter. These elements are meant to guide you in your critical examinations of the people, places, and events you will study in the text.

However, it is important to remember that each element of the Critical Thinking Icon can be applied to any issue or subject you wish to study. On pages viii–ix, you will see examples of how each element of the icon can be applied to a specific issue—in this case, communications technology. Each element within the icon focuses on a different area of critical inquiry. Think of this example as a framework for increasing your understanding on any issue that you may come across, both at school and in your everyday life.

Using the Critical Thinking Icon

Significance

- Which had the most influence on Canada: the telephone or the Internet?

- What has made Blackberry technology so significant?

Judgements

- Should censorship of the Internet be allowed?

- Can communication technology be used to improve people's lives?

Cause and Consequence

- Why was the Internet developed?

- How might blogs and social networks influence how students learn?

Significance

Judgements

Cause and Consequence

Patterns and Change

Evidence

Perspectives

Patterns and Change
- How has telephone technology changed in the past twenty years?
- Why might the invention of the cell phone be a turning point in the history of communication?

Evidence
- How reliable is information from the Internet?
- What sources should I use?

Perspective
- How might the Internet help us understand the perspectives of people living in other countries?
- How do the ways people communicate reflect their perspectives?

A Note on Perspective

When Marco Polo travelled to China in the 13th century, he visited Sumatra, an island in what is now Indonesia. He encountered an animal he had never seen before: a rhinoceros. Polo wrote that he had seen "unicorns, which are scarcely smaller than elephants. They have a single large black horn in the middle of the forehead." Today, we may see this as a misunderstanding. However, we all see the world based on our experiences. When we come across something new, as Marco Polo did, we often interpret it according to what we already know. From Polo's perspective, an animal with one horn was a unicorn.

To begin to understand others, we need to recognize their perspective of the world. *Perspective* is a point of view that people share. What should we remember about perspectives during our studies?

Perspectives Can Be Different

Recognizing that perspectives may be different than our own is the starting point for understanding how others view the world. Beyond this, we need to recognize that although people's ideas from another time or place may seem unfamiliar, their perspective may make sense to them. We cannot necessarily judge people from the past, for example, with our present-day perspectives. Recognizing that people's perspectives are formed by their experiences and knowledge is the beginning to understanding.

One Group Can Hold Many Perspectives

In any given culture and in any given time, people hold a variety of values and beliefs. Just like today, differing perspectives in the past were normal. For example, many people in British North America did not want to form a united Canada; some preferred joining the United States, while others wanted to remain independent. Seeing a variety of perspectives in any group will open up our understanding of the past.

Perspectives Can Change

Over time, you may find that your perspectives on issues or events may change as you study further or learn more about the perspectives of others. Recognizing perspectives can not only help us to understand others, it may be essential for getting along in a culturally diverse country such as Canada. Social studies should give us practice moving beyond our own perspectives and taking seriously the perspectives of others.

Becoming Active Citizens

Have you ever sat in social studies class and asked yourself, "Why are we learning this stuff?" It's a good question—there are many reasons for studying history and geography. One reason is to learn about being thoughtful and responsible citizens.

Being a thoughtful and responsible citizen has nothing to do with becoming a legal citizen of Canada. Let's consider the terms *thoughtful* and *responsible* separately.

Being Thoughtful Citizens

Canadians face many issues, such as how we can protect the environment while still creating opportunities for work and recreation. Solutions to issues like these are often worked out through discussion. Sometimes people express opinions on issues without using the critical thinking skills discussed in this book. Their opinions are not based on evidence, and they have not taken other perspectives into account.

Social studies will help you to be more thoughtful about issues. For example, First Nations' land claims are important issues in British Columbia and Canada. Finding a fair solution to these claims requires deliberation among those who understand the history of First Nations in Canada, and the issues surrounding natural resources in the areas being claimed. Thoughtful citizens understand both history and geography.

Being Responsible Citizens

Sometimes people need to take action to make a difference. Every day, people make the decision to become involved to find fair solutions. It can be a small thing, such as recycling, or a larger undertaking such as running for public office, or volunteering at an organization. Responsible citizens do not only talk, they also take action to change things.

In social studies, you will learn about other citizens who changed Canada and British Columbia. You will also be asked to think about your responsibility to be agents of change and to consider what you can do to help improve society.

What steps can you take to make a difference in your community?

UNIT 1

The Geography of Canada

This unit helps you investigate these questions.

- What physical and natural forces have shaped Canada?

- Why is Canada a country of such great natural diversity?

- How have physical and natural forces shaped the culture and identity of Canadians?

- How have communities in Canada adapted to, and been affected by, geographical changes?

Natural forces. Plate tectonics—movements within and on the earth's crust—formed the mountains of Canada. Mount Robson is the highest mountain in the Rockies. It was eroded and sculpted by glaciers into the landscape we see today. Do you think mountains like this one might change in the future?

Nature's highways. Melting water from glaciers and rivers shaped the landscapes of Canada. Aboriginal peoples, and later fur traders and explorers, used the rivers to travel across the country.

Changes. The geography of Canada was changed as colonization spread from the Atlantic Ocean to the Pacific Ocean. As newcomers grew in number, the landscape was changed even further. Will these changes continue?

A smaller world. Modern communication has bridged the distances of what early explorers called "the great lone land." The identity of Canadians has been shaped by Canada's size and landscape. As the country "shrinks" as a result of new technology, will an identity so closely linked to the land be lost?

1 Canada: Making Connections

Chapter Outcomes

In this chapter, you will examine the geography of Canada. By the end of the chapter, you will

- identify and understand the five themes of geography

- identify the different physical and natural regions of Canada

- analyze the processes that formed Canada's regions

- describe the effect of climate and physical geography on Canada's population distribution

- describe the formation of the cultural landscape

- evaluate the impact of human actions on the environment

- describe the impact of natural and artificial boundaries

Significance • Patterns and Change • Judgements • CRITICAL INQUIRY • Evidence • Cause and Consequence • Perspectives

Examine the two images shown here. Do they define "Canada" to you? Why or why not? Now read the quotation below. How does it relate to your image of Canada? Give examples of times when Canada's geographic diversity was a challenge for you, your family, or someone you know.

How does studying Canada's geography help us understand how the land has shaped us, and how we have shaped the land?

In this chapter, you will study Canada's regions, climates, and cultural landscapes. You will be introduced to issues, such as climate change, that may have a great effect on Canada's future. For many, the identity of Canada is linked to the vast size and physical diversity of this country. As you follow Canada's historical, economic, and cultural development in *Horizons*, knowledge of geography will help you to better understand the reasons behind these developments.

Key Terms

geographic perspective	geology
latitude	topography
longitude	plate tectonics
Global Positioning System (GPS)	seismic
sustainable	climate
globalization	ecosystem
Geographic Information System (GIS)	cultural landscapes

...if some countries have too much history, we have too much geography.

—Prime Minister Mackenzie King, House of Commons, June 18, 1936

The Five Themes of Geography

▶ **How can an understanding of location, place, regions, movement, and interaction help us study geography?**

DID YOU KNOW...

Modern geography includes the study of both physical geography (including climate, landscapes, and oceans) and human geography (including culture, communities, and transportation).

Although you might think that geography is something you only need to deal with in class, it is really a part of your everyday life. When you travel across town, when you text message or e-mail a friend, or when you read a headline about world trade, you are taking part in the broad area of study called geography.

Geography explores how people interact with the world around them. It involves climate, geology, economics, biology, history, and more. What would your family consider if you were moving to a new town? The climate, the size of the town, and types of jobs and recreational activities that are available might be concerns. These are also questions a geographer would ask. Geographers also study how humans interact with each other, and how they affect and are affected by the land. These are themes you will study throughout this text.

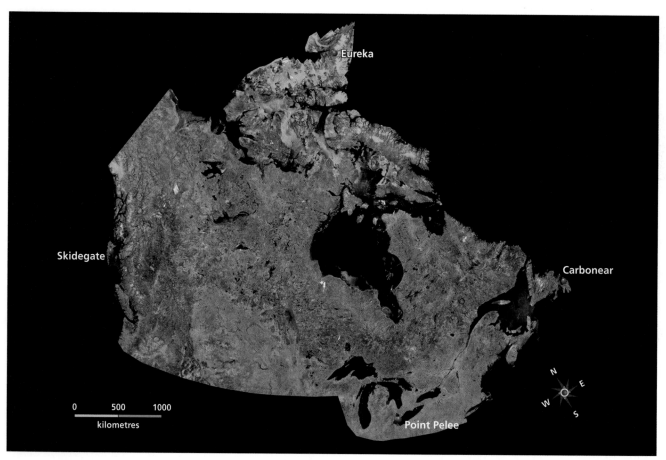

FIGURE 1–1 "Canada, which we tend to think of as a thin ribbon of city lights stretched out along the forty-ninth parallel, is as high as it is wide. It's as far from Eureka, on Ellesmere Island, to Point Pelee in Ontario… as from Carbonear to Skidegate" (Peter Gzowski, journalist). How would you describe Canada to someone not familiar with this country?

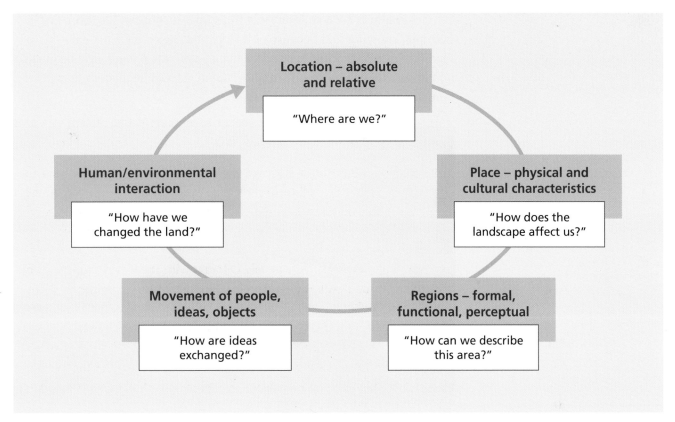

FIGURE 1–2 The five themes of geography provide a framework that allows you to select and organize information.

Geography begins with posing questions and gathering information. The five themes of geography are a convenient way to help you gather and organize this information. You can then examine the information and draw conclusions from your questions, making the five themes a valuable tool in helping you to develop a **geographic perspective**. Looking for patterns in the events, problems, or issues presented in *Horizons* helps you study the behaviour of people in their environments both in the past and in the present.

geographic perspective a way of looking at and understanding the world

Location

Why do we need to know where people or places are located? Knowing the location of people or places is usually the first step in the process of a geographic study. Absolute locations are very precise, in terms of position on the globe. For example, Kelowna, British Columbia, is located at 49 degrees north **latitude** and 119 degrees west **longitude**. Relative locations are described by time, direction, or distance from one place to another: Kelowna is approximately 400 km east of Vancouver, 600 km west of Calgary, 110 km north of the United States border, and 1100 km south of the Yukon border.

latitude the distance of any point north or south of the equator, measured up to 90 degrees

longitude the distance of any point east or west of the Prime Meridian, measured up to 180 degrees

Geographers are also interested in the significance of location. For example, knowing that because of its location, Kelowna is the gateway to the Okanagan Valley and serves as a transportation, service, and business hub gives us much more information about the city, its history and development, and the people who live there.

Global Positioning System (GPS)
a system of satellites and portable receivers able to pinpoint each receiver's location anywhere on earth

FIGURE 1–3 A **Global Positioning System (GPS)** allows you to find a location with amazing accuracy. GPS is used by researchers and map-makers to pinpoint exact locations. It is used to survey land, explore for resources, track wildlife, and fight fires. Receivers are now common in cars, and are used by hikers and boat owners, and in sports. They are also popular as personal tracking devices.

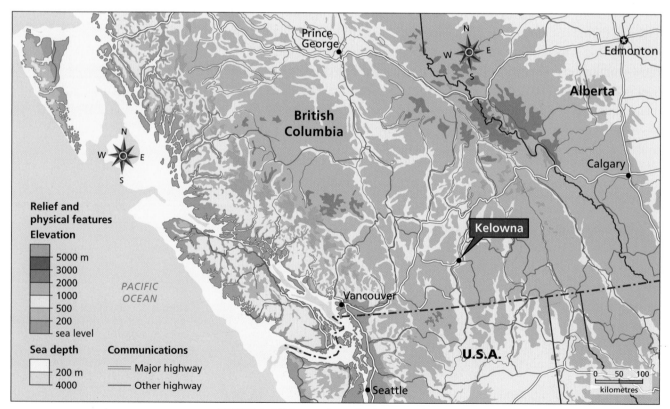

FIGURE 1–4 This map shows the location of Kelowna. Why is Kelowna the transportation and service hub of the region? What other centres in the region have a significant location in terms of their economic role or regional influence?

Geographically, Canada is ideally located to participate in the global economy of the 21st century. On the Pacific and Atlantic coastlines, Canada's transportation connections with Europe, Asia, and Latin America are well-established. The ports of Prince Rupert and Vancouver are the closest major North American ports to China, South Korea, and Japan. Halifax is North America's closest harbour to Europe, and is ice free year round. International airports in Vancouver, Halifax, and Newfoundland and Labrador open up connections to Asia and Europe. Together, these airports serve approximately 50 million passengers a year.

By land, Canada is connected to one of the largest consumer markets in the world—the United States. Trucking and railway freight carriers transport millions of dollars worth of goods across the border every year.

Canada is also large enough to cover many time zones. This can allow business transactions to happen around the clock: business people can access European markets from midnight until noon, and then link with Asian economies from noon to midnight.

- How might Canada's ideal location affect the country's economic future?

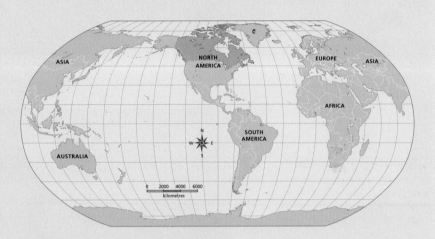

FIGURE 1–5 Canada is at the centre of this map of the world. How does this perspective support the idea that Canada has an ideal location? How else might Canada's position be represented on a map?

Place: Physical and Cultural Landscapes

How do the physical characteristics of a place affect how people live? Landforms, bodies of water, soil, and mineral deposits can bring advantages, disadvantages, or both. For example, Prince Rupert, British Columbia, is in a mountainous area on the coast and has heavy rainfall, but also has abundant forests and access to the ocean.

Nearly every human activity leaves its mark on the environment. The visible results of human activity are known as the "cultural landscape." People affect the landscape in different ways. For example, in the Prince Rupert area, the Tsimshian First Nation removed bark from standing trees to make blankets, clothing, and fishing nets. The long-term effect of this **sustainable** activity is that the trees survived, and the forest stood for centuries. Later, as more people came to the area, the physical environment underwent dramatic alterations as the forest was cleared for timber and to build roads, ports, and buildings. You will learn more about resource management in British Columbia in later chapters.

sustainable an activity that maintains an ecological balance by avoiding the depletion of a natural resource

FIGURE 1–6 Laxspa'aws (Pike Island) is a small island near Prince Rupert. Although archeological evidence shows that the island has been the home of the Tsimshian Nation for thousands of years, its environment remains intact.

FIGURE 1–7 Examine this view to determine how people have modified and adapted to the physical environment of Prince Rupert. How does this compare with the image above? Is one better than the other? Why?

Regions

How can geographers organize information about different areas? Regions are areas that have common characteristics, such as government, landforms, or climate. They are the basic unit of study in geography, and you will learn about several different types of regions in this chapter. You use the idea of "region" when you say you will travel to "the coast," "the interior," "South Asia," or "the Middle East." In this text, you will be introduced to topics such as climate change, the building of communities, the political growth of Canada, and Canada's changing economy. All of these topics can be studied as regional issues.

WEB LINK ● ● ● ● ● ● ● ● ● ● ●
Tour Canada from space. Look at the Pearson Web site to learn more.

FIGURE 1–8 Examine this satellite image and list the regions you might divide it into. Are there regions that you already know about that can be found in this image? After you read the table on this page, look at the image and your regions again. Has anything changed?

Types of Regions

	Definition	Examples
Formal regions	Based on official boundaries, such as cities and provinces. Can also include areas that share physical or climatic similarities. These regions are usually widely accepted.	St. Lawrence Lowlands, Greater Victoria Regional District
Functional regions	Based on connections created by an activity such as communication or trade flows. These regions can only exist as long as the activity or duty exists.	The distribution area of a newspaper, North American Free Trade Agreement countries
Perceptual regions	Determined by people's attitudes and feelings. This type of region usually has meaning only to individuals who have a "mental map" of it as a region.	"up north," "the interior"

Geography studies how places and people relate to each other—but how might geographers deal with instant worldwide communication? What parts of the world do *you* connect with every day?

The rapid growth of the Internet and other communication systems, such as satellite phones, has influenced political boundaries, communities, and the movement of people, ideas, and objects. The speed of communication has helped bring about what many have called the "death of distance." Geographers are concerned with what links people and places together, and they must now look at the way people interact in cyberspace. One example of this would be the study of communities that exist only online.

When Canadian philosopher Marshall McLuhan coined the phrase "global village" in the early 1960s, long before the Internet existed, it was a popular new concept. Why did the term hold such interest? McLuhan was describing a future world in which technology could cross barriers between nations and regions of the world.

Today, McLuhan's phrase is still well-known, and the "global village" he predicted is real, showing itself not only in the instant sharing of information and the creation of online communities, but in many international agreements and trade that happens between countries worldwide, including Canada.

Have all aspects of the global village been positive? This is another question being asked by geographers. Protecting the environment, for example, is no longer just a local issue. The environment of the entire planet can be affected by the actions of its global citizens. But perhaps cyberspace can help bridge those barriers—solutions about climate change, for example, will need the cooperation of all nations.

- Is this cooperation possible? How can aspects of the global village help the environment?

- What are the advantages and disadvantages of online communication? Should it be regulated by governments and individuals? Why or why not?

WEB LINK ●● ● ● ● ● ● ● ● ● ● ● ● ● ● ●

Go to the Pearson Web site to learn more about Marshall McLuhan and his theories about media, culture, and language.

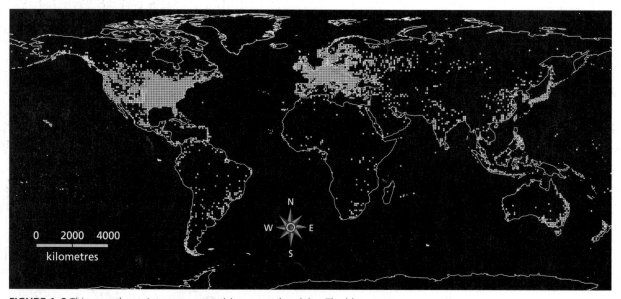

FIGURE 1–9 This map shows Internet connectivity across the globe. The blue areas have the most intense activity, followed by orange, and then yellow. Areas with no colour have no connectivity. Explain the patterns that can be seen here.

FIGURE 1–10 The Gulf States are centres of finance, recreation, and tourism. In the malls, such as in this one in Dubai (which has an indoor ski hill), you can see the mingling of ideas from around the world. Find the Gulf States in an atlas. How does their location make them a link between East and West?

Movement of People, Ideas, and Objects

How do people interact in the 21st century? Modern technology allows people to interact no matter where they are. Even people in the most remote locations can be in contact with others. **Globalization** has created a world of rapid movement and interaction, and ever-faster communication. So, not only are people and goods moving, but ideas are as well. Fads, fashions, and ideas can spread quickly throughout the world.

globalization the process of economic, technological, political, and cultural forces creating a single, global society

Human/Environmental Interaction

What brings about changes in the natural landscape? Humans depend on the environment and adapt to it, but they also change it dramatically to suit their needs and wants. Geographers are especially interested in knowing how the actions of people change the natural environment. For example, how do dams, roads, industry, and housing developments change an environment? How have land-use decisions affected our ability to buy locally grown food? How has information technology changed where people work? How does the moving of an industrial plant from one community to another affect the people in these two communities?

FIGURE 1–11 As this community's population increased, housing began to replace farmland. This dramatically changed the environment. Have changes like this occurred in your community? Why?

ACTIVITIES

1. Summarize in your own words the main idea from each of the five themes of geography.

2. Brainstorm a list of the ways people (from the earliest inhabitants to today) have affected the landscape in your area. What were the long- and short-term effects of these activities on the environment?

Using and Understanding Maps

You may typically use maps as a means of finding directions, and today those types of maps are readily available on the Internet. Maps can be one of the best ways to share information about a place or region, showing climate, population, or political boundaries, and they can show how places have changed over time. Maps also show us something about those who made them—their perspective, their purpose in sharing information, and what they think is important.

What all maps have in common is that they are a visual representation of an area. They all use symbols, sometimes explained in a legend, to display information. A compass rose may be included to show north, south, east, and west. Maps also use scale to indicate distance—an important feature if you need to decide the best way to travel.

As you use this text, part of your study will involve maps. Some will show geographical information, while others will show historical, cultural, political, or economic information. To interpret a map, you may ask some or all of these questions:

- What kind of map is it? What can it be used for?

- Who created the map, and when?

- What do we know about the creator from examining the map?

- How was the map created? Where did the information come from?

- Who would use this map?

- Are there any symbols on the map? What do they mean?

- Have there been changes to the area since the map was drawn? What do these changes tell us?

- What is the significance of the map?

Geographic Information System (GIS) an information system that stores, analyzes, and presents geographic data

FIGURE 1–12 Satellites gather information on oceans, soils, land use, pollution, and weather. This information can then be translated onto maps using a **Geographic Information System (GIS)**. This satellite image shows the destruction of forests in British Columbia by the Mountain pine beetle (in red). How might a map of this information be useful for industries, community members, or the government?

In your studies, you will come across many types of maps. Some may even be combinations of types. Practise identifying and interpreting maps by looking at the maps on this page. What do they show? What might they be used for? Use the questions on the previous page as a guide if necessary.

FIGURE 1–13 Political Maps

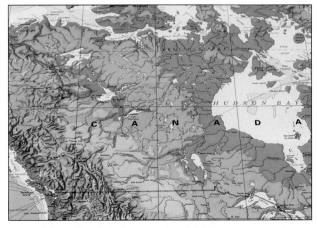

FIGURE 1–14 Physical/Topographical Maps

FIGURE 1–15 Historical Maps

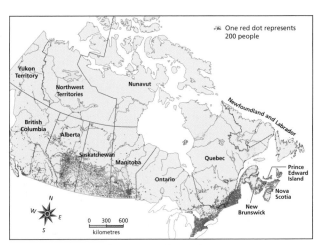

FIGURE 1–16 Special-Purpose/Thematic Maps

APPLY IT

1. Choosing one type of map from above, draw a map of your school and its surroundings. Use different sources of information to construct your map.

2. Refer to the five themes of geography on pages 6–13. How might maps be used in the study of each theme?

3. In groups, use the Web link to access maps at Natural Resources Canada. Choose one of the categories listed under "Explore Our Maps." Present a report to the class on the maps in that category and their uses.

Perspectives

4. How does a map reflect the world view of the map-maker? Consider issues such as perspective, values, economics, and beliefs.

The Physical Regions of Canada

▶ **How can Canada be divided into physical regions?**

With the second-largest land mass of any country, Canada has a great variety of landscapes. Its mountains, plains, massive Canadian Shield, and northern lands made development a challenge; however, the lowlands, rivers, and valleys of southern Canada proved relatively easy to travel through and were therefore suitable for development.

The physical geography of Canada is defined by the regions shown in the map below. Each of these regions has very different **geological** features, landforms, climate, and vegetation. Each was formed by different geological processes.

geology the study of the earth's crust to learn its origin, history, and structure

topography the shape and structure of the surface features of a place or region

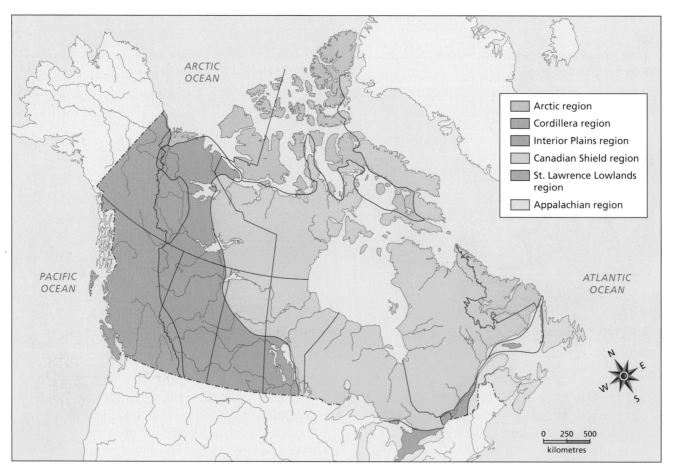

Legend:
- Arctic region
- Cordillera region
- Interior Plains region
- Canadian Shield region
- St. Lawrence Lowlands region
- Appalachian region

FIGURE 1–17 The physical regions of Canada are based mostly on the type of rock found in that region, and on the **topography**. Why is looking at regions a useful way to analyze geographic factors?

How did ice and snow shape Canada as we know it today? In Canada, about a million years ago, the climate became very cold. The amount of snow falling in Canada's North began to exceed the amount that melted in the spring. Eventually, the buildup of snow in the North reached 3 km in depth. As the snow accumulated, weight and pressure turned it to ice. As even more snow fell and pressure increased, the ice began to move out from the centre of the ice sheets, covering more and more of the land. At its greatest extent, the ice sheets, or continental glaciers, covered most of North America.

As the ice sheets moved, they shaped the land. Pushing away the top level of soil, the ice scraped a large area down to bare rock, creating the Canadian Shield.

In some cases, the ice sheets deposited rocks and debris, leaving ridges called moraines. They also carved deep fjords, and left behind large boulders, called glacial erratics, which can be found throughout Canada.

When the climate warmed, the ice began to melt. About 10 000 years ago, great amounts of meltwater flowed, flooding the land, shaping valleys and ridges, and filling low areas to form lakes.

- Would you expect current changes in climate to lead to similar dramatic changes in the future? Why or why not?

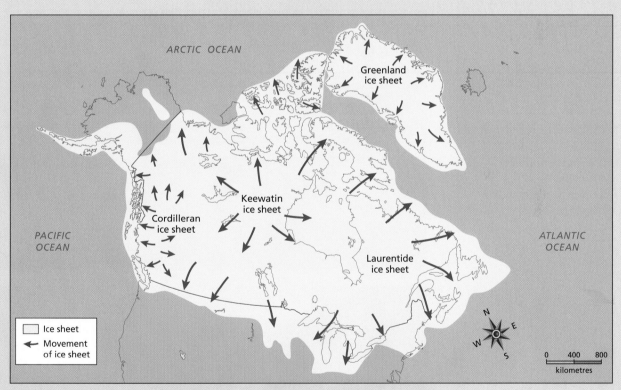

FIGURE 1–18 During the last ice age, ice sheets and glaciers covered most of Canada. Some areas of the Yukon escaped glaciation because of a lack of snow. Compare this map to a physical map of North America. What evidence can be seen of glacial activity? Can you see evidence of the ice age in your area?

The Appalachian Region

The Appalachian region is an extension of the Appalachian mountains, which begin in the southeastern United States and end in the Maritime provinces of Canada. It has a varied landscape of rolling hills, valleys, small mountains, highlands, and coastal fjords—what is left of an older mountain range worn down by glaciers and by millions of years of erosion.

The **sedimentary rocks** of the Appalachians were deposited at a time when the area was heavily forested. The rock layers gradually covered the vegetation, and over time these layers became large deposits of coal. Non-metallic minerals such as gypsum are also found in the rock layers. **Igneous rock** is present as a result of ancient volcanic activity, as is **metamorphic rock**, which is formed by heat and pressure. These actions formed metallic minerals such as iron, lead, and zinc.

Deposits of coal and minerals, rich fishing resources, vast forests, and farmland encouraged the creation of numerous communities along the coast and in the river valleys of the Appalachian region. Ports developed in natural harbours and have linked the region to trade and shipping for hundreds of years.

sedimentary rock rock made up of layered deposits that have fused together

igneous rock rock formed from molten material, such as lava

metamorphic rock rock changed from its original form through heat and pressure

FIGURE 1–19 These two images show the varied landscape of the Appalachian region. With some of the resources of the region in decline, what action might people take to protect those resources?

The Canadian Shield Region

The Canadian Shield makes up nearly half of Canada's land surface. In geological terms, shield formations are among the oldest areas in the world. These shields are hard, rigid blocks, surrounded by younger continental landforms. The Canadian Shield stretches from the Arctic Islands south to the United States border and east across Labrador.

The Shield was once a volcanic mountain range. Over millions of years, weathering and erosion—especially the action of glaciers—have worn the land down to a landscape of flat, bare rock, lakes, and wetlands. Travel is difficult in this terrain, and the thin soils make it unsuitable for agriculture. Most areas of the region are sparsely populated.

Much of the rock of the Shield has been changed into metamorphic rock by heat and pressure. This process also created many valuable minerals, such as copper, gold, lead, diamonds, platinum, and nickel, making the Shield one of the world's richest areas for mining. Small mining centres such as Timmins in Ontario, Val-d'Or in Quebec, and Thompson in Manitoba were one-industry towns built in isolated areas to extract the mineral wealth of the Shield.

FIGURE 1–20 The worn-down landscape of the Shield is evident in this historic photo of Cobalt, Ontario. Why might the geography of the Shield prevent the growth of larger communities and mining centres, even though there are rich mineral deposits?

FIGURE 1–21 Hydroelectricity is another valuable resource in the Shield region, where its many rivers provide seemingly endless power. This dam is in James Bay, Quebec. What is the impact of using water as a resource in the Shield? Is it a better option than other sources of power? Why or why not?

The Arctic Region

The Arctic region includes plains, lowlands, and mountains. Pressure at the northeastern edge of the Canadian Shield pushed up the sedimentary rock to form a range of **fold mountains**. These mountains, called the Innuitian Mountains, extend more than 1000 km across the northern islands of the Arctic region. Since they are similar to the Appalachians, they likely contain the same minerals. Little exploration of mineral resources has taken place due to the region's remote location and harsh climate. However, the mineral wealth of this region may not remain untapped. An increased rate in the melting of sea ice has been noticed in recent years—possibly due to climate change—and open waters will mean greater opportunities for transportation and exploration.

The Innuitian Mountains cover much of the islands of the eastern Arctic, and lowlands cover the islands of the western Arctic. The lowlands are composed of sedimentary rock. They are similar to the Great Lakes–St. Lawrence Lowlands, and have deposits of oil and natural gas. Melting sea ice has also made this resource more accessible. The possibility of increased shipping of oil and gas through Arctic waters has raised concerns for the environment among the Inuit, who rely on the region's wildlife for food and clothing. The same fears are held by the Canadian government and environmentalists.

fold mountains mountains formed by sedimentary rock being pushed together by forces within the earth and folded into mountains and valleys

DID YOU KNOW...
Diamond mining has recently become one of the more profitable resource industries in the Arctic region.

FIGURE 1–22 Devon Island, in Nunavut, is part of the Innuitian mountain range. What natural resources might be found here? Consider what would happen with reduced ice and snow cover.

FIGURE 1–23 The Mackenzie River delta, in the Northwest Territories, provides a habitat for migrating birds and beluga whales. The river has been, and continues to be, a source of food and transportation for the people who live there. Natural gas has also been found in the delta. What challenges might lie ahead for the people and wildlife in this area?

The St. Lawrence Lowlands

The St. Lawrence Lowlands are between Lakes Huron, Erie, and Ontario, and extend along the banks of the St. Lawrence River to Quebec City. This region was formed mainly by the retreating ice sheets that covered most of Canada during the last ice age. The ice sheets pushed soils from the Shield onto the area where the lowlands are today. As the ice sheets melted, giant lakes formed—lakes much larger than today's Great Lakes.

When the lakes drained to their present size, the old shoreline of the larger lakes remained as bluffs. Between the old shorelines and the present lakes, fertile areas of well-drained sandy soils were left behind. These areas now make up the rich agricultural land around Lake Ontario and the St. Lawrence River. The fertile land allowed First Nations people, such as the Huron, to practise a stable agricultural economy, and later European immigrants established farms and orchards. Today, orchards of apples, peaches, pears, and cherries provide a profitable business for farmers. Vineyards and wineries are also developing in the region.

Although the Lowlands are the smallest region in Canada, they are home to about half of Canada's population. Access to the Great Lakes and the St. Lawrence River has provided for the transportation of goods and raw materials in and out of Canada, and industry has thrived in the region.

FIGURE 1–24 The flat, rolling valleys of the St. Lawrence Lowlands contain rich soils that make the area suitable for farming. This orchard is in the Niagara region. Why might this region be among the first areas of Canada colonized by Europeans?

FIGURE 1–25 The St. Lawrence River runs from the the Great Lakes to the Atlantic Ocean. Why do you think some of Canada's largest cities can be found in this region?

The Interior Plains

In Canada, the Interior Plains region stretches from the Canadian Shield to the Cordillera mountains. The Interior Plains were formed as soils carried by rivers from the Canadian Shield were deposited at its edge. These deposits formed horizontal layers of sedimentary rock, which became large areas of mostly flat land, rolling hills, and river valleys.

Millions of years ago, when the area had a tropical climate and was covered by water, occasional flooding left remains of plants and animals. Over time, these remains were pressed between sedimentary layers to form large deposits of **fossil fuels**, such as oil and natural gas, and **evaporites** such as potash.

The wide, flat spaces and grasslands were ideal for grazing animals such as bison, and provided food and a way of life for the First Nations of the region. Later, the grasslands were changed by cattle ranches and vast farms. Other areas of the region were covered by parkland and boreal forests. Major cities such as Edmonton, Saskatoon, and Calgary developed on the banks of the many rivers that criss-cross the region.

The region's agricultural economy has been seriously affected by drought during the last century. The "Dirty Thirties," as the 1930s became known, saw the ruin of crops due to drought. Large areas were so dry that wind blew the soil away, creating huge dust storms.

> ## Did You Know...
>
> Increased European immigration to the plains brought overhunting and loss of habitat, which left the bison nearly extinct. This would have a devastating effect on the First Nations and Métis people of the plains, as you will read in later chapters.

FIGURE 1–26 Wind, rain, and river water continue to expose the sedimentary layers deposited millions of years ago. In some parts of Alberta, diverse deposits of fossils have created a booming tourist industry and have attracted paleontologists from around the world.

FIGURE 1–27 The Interior Plains include not only flat prairie and farmland, but also rivers, lakes, and forests. Together, these natural resources provided a rich environment for both the First Nations people who moved throughout the region and the immigrants who farmed and raised cattle. Why do you think the two lifestyles had difficulty existing side by side?

The Cordillera

The Cordillera region of Canada is made up of parallel mountain ranges separated by a series of plateaus, trenches, and valleys in British Columbia and the Yukon. This diverse landscape, which also includes dormant volcanoes, glaciers, and ice fields, is part of a vast chain of mountains that stretches from Alaska to Chile.

The Rocky and Coast mountain ranges, along with British Columbia's Interior Plateau, are the youngest landforms in Canada. They were formed when **plate** collision caused the earth's crust to buckle, pushing and folding volcanic rock into mountains. This plate movement, called **plate tectonics**, also caused the formation of plateaus, valleys, and trenches. Erosion from rivers and glaciers created the rugged, mountainous landscape seen today.

As in the Canadian Shield, geological processes left rich mineral deposits, such as copper, gold, and coal. Mining remains a major industry in the Cordillera, along with forestry. Sediments carried downstream by rivers were deposited in valleys. These deposits formed the rich, fertile soils of areas like the Fraser River Valley, which today has several land uses—agricultural, industrial, and recreational. Major cities such as Vancouver also developed along the Fraser River. Before the building of roads and railways, the river was a vital transportation route for Aboriginal peoples and Europeans who came later.

plate a slab of the earth's crust; plates are underneath all continents and oceans, regularly moving away from and toward each other

plate tectonics forces and movement within and on the earth's crust that form its features, such as mountain ranges and ocean basins

FIGURE 1–29 The jagged peaks of Mount Waddington, British Columbia's highest mountain, are typical of the Coast Range.

FIGURE 1–28 This rockslide on the Sea-to-Sky Highway cut off the route between Vancouver and Whistler. Examine this image. How does the physical landscape shown here affect human activity? How does human activity affect the land?

DID YOU KNOW...

The rich deposits of gold and coal in this region resulted in booms of activity in the 19th and 20th centuries. This activity helped develop British Columbia as a province.

Canada's west coast is where two tectonic plates collide, making it the most active **seismic** area in Canada. Every year small quakes occur along the Juan de Fuca **subduction zone**, off the coast of Vancouver Island. As Vancouver Island is pushed against the mainland, tension builds along its west coast. When that tension is released, the earth will shift. Most quakes are too small to be felt. The strongest recent tremors were recorded in Courtenay in 1946, registering 7.3 on the **Richter scale**.

Scientists think we are overdue for a major earthquake—the "Big One." Evidence of earlier earthquakes has been found in coastal sediment layers that are greatly disturbed. Research shows that a major earthquake may have occurred around 1700. Some scientists fear that the pressure of the past 300 years may be released in a mega-quake.

- Should action be taken in your community to prepare for a major earthquake? For example, should the government restrict development in particularly risky areas? Why or why not?

seismic relating to earthquakes or other vibrations of the earth's crust

subduction zone a long region with a trench, where a descending tectonic plate is pushed down into the earth

Richter scale a measure of the power of earthquakes

FIGURE 1–30 Signs like this one in British Columbia warn people that they are in a low-lying coastal area that could be affected by a tsunami. Evacuation routes are also marked.

DID YOU KNOW...

Oral histories of some coastal First Nations, such as the Quileute and the Cowichan, tell that a major earthquake occurred in 1700. A great shaking of the land and huge waves hitting Vancouver Island are described. An entire village of the Pachena Bay First Nation was destroyed by the wave. Japanese reports of a tsunami in the same year agree with this oral history.

ACTIVITIES

1. Draw a chart that compares and contrasts the six physical regions of Canada. Points of comparison may include geological features, climate, vegetation, and geological process.

2. Explain how the location and abundance of certain resources affected the history of each region.

3. Use a population map of Canada to determine which physical region has the largest population. Which region has the smallest? Give two reasons for the difference.

4. Use one of the five themes of geography to create a short presentation on the physical regions of Canada.

5. Based on what you have learned about the physical regions of Canada so far, predict why people might be drawn to live and work in those regions. Check your answers and modify them if necessary as you continue in this chapter.

The Climates of Canada

▶ **What creates different climates in Canada, and what impact does climate have on human activity?**

On a daily basis, we pay attention to wind, clouds, rain, and sunshine. These changing conditions, from day to day and month to month, are what we call weather. In fact, most Canadians would agree that weather is what we tend to talk about the most.

Weather patterns seen in an area from year to year are known as the **climate** of that area. Knowing the climate of a region helps us to answer questions that may arise as you use this text. How have the climates of Canada affected where people live? Why do people choose one area over another? How is a region affected by climate change?

Most of Canada lies above 49 degrees latitude. Inland areas experience a **continental climate**, with some extreme temperature changes and low **precipitation**. Coastal areas are moderated by a **maritime climate**, with mild temperatures and high precipitation. The Atlantic coast has a harsher climate than coastal British Columbia. In that region, wind blowing off the land creates greater differences in temperature, rain, and snow than on the west coast.

climate the temperatures, humidity, rainfall, and atmospheric conditions of a region over long periods of time

continental climate the climate of a continent's interior

precipitation climate rain, snow, hail, and fog

maritime climate a coastal climate

Temperature

Conditions that can affect temperature in Canada's regions are explained in the table below.

Latitude	The higher the latitude, the lower the intensity of the sun's rays. As a result, there is a greater seasonal variation in the length of day and night. These conditions can affect farming, since crops need long days and warm seasons.
Altitude	The higher the altitude, the colder the temperature. Mountainous or hilly areas generally experience colder temperatures, which is why snow can still appear on mountains in the summer.
Distance from the sea	The surface of land heats and cools more quickly than water. A large land mass such as Canada can be very hot in summer and very cold in winter. By contrast, temperatures in areas such as the west coast of Canada are moderated by the ocean, creating less of a difference between summer and winter temperatures.
Wind direction	In Canada, prevailing winds (those that usually come from one direction) are from the west or the north. West coast communities have the mildest winter temperatures as a result of warm westerly winds coming off the ocean.
Ocean currents	Ocean currents are either warm or cold, depending on where they come from. Ocean currents warm or heat the air, which is then blown onto land. The west coast, with a warm current, has a mild climate. Newfoundland and Labrador, next to a cold ocean current, has much harsher winters.

Precipitation

Canada's precipitation—rain, snow, hail, and fog—varies by region. The amount of precipitation received by an area is largely determined by its distance from the sea and by the prevailing winds. Precipitation is also affected by temperatures, topography, and masses of cool and warm air. Heavy precipitation is often seasonal, as shown by Figure 1–31 below.

Changes in Canada's precipitation levels are attributed to climate change. Some areas of Canada have seen an increase in rain and snow, which can lead to flooding, while other areas have experienced drought.

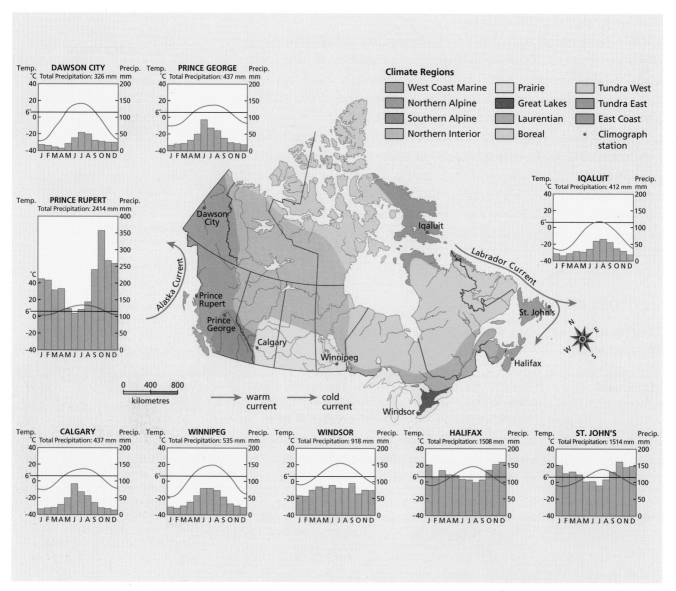

FIGURE 1–31 The climate regions of Canada. The climographs included show average monthly temperature with a line graph, and average monthly precipitation with a bar graph. Discuss the relationship between location and temperature and precipitation levels for Calgary, Windsor, and Iqaluit. Can any of the locations shown on the map be described as having a typically Canadian climate? Why, or why not?

FIGURE 1–32 While heavy rain or hail can cause great damage, a lack of precipitation can be a serious problem as well. This farmer in Alberta cannot grow hay to feed his cattle, and watering holes in pastures have dried out. Dry conditions can also increase the risk of forest fire, and low water levels in rivers and lakes affect fish and other wildlife. What could be the long-term effect of less rain in Canada? More rain?

WEB LINK ● · · · · · · · · · · · · · · · · · · ·

Natural Resources Canada and Environment Canada have information on Canada's climate. Check the Pearson Web site.

Climate Change

Over the past 200 years, the world became more industrialized and burned massive amounts of fossil fuels—coal, oil, and natural gas—which then trapped greenhouse gases in the atmosphere. The "greenhouse effect" is now seen as the cause of the overall warming of the earth's climate. The rate of warming also seems to be increasing. The Intergovernmental Panel on Climate Change, established by the World Meteorological Organization and the United Nations Environment Programme, is the main world body studying the science of climate change. According to the panel's 2007 report, 11 of the last 12 years have been among the warmest years since 1850. Climate change affects the world's temperature and precipitation patterns, and because of our northerly location, will especially affect Canada.

The rise in temperature is being seen in all parts of Canada, and each year brings more evidence of the effects of climate change, particularly in the Arctic region. Melting and crumbling permafrost has damaged homes, buildings, and roads. Ice roads, commonly used in the winter months to truck supplies to isolated communities, are melting earlier in the spring than they used to. An increase in melting sea ice means that polar bears will spend more time on land and less time travelling and hunting on pack ice. Therefore, their contact with humans will increase, perhaps with devastating results. Also, without ice to hunt on, the bears could starve.

FIGURE 1–33 This satellite image shows Hurricane Juan approaching the coast of Nova Scotia in September 2003. Juan was one of the most powerful and damaging hurricanes to hit Canada. Some scientists believe that increased warming of ocean waters and air will result in more hurricanes every year. How might this affect people in the Maritime provinces?

WEB LINK ● ● ● ● ● ● ● ● ● ● ●

For information on climate change
and the threats to Canada, visit the
Pearson Web site.

Along with changes in the Arctic, drier summers on the Prairies, flooding and storms in eastern Canada, plunging survival rates for spawning salmon in British Columbia, unusual weather conditions, and an increase in pests such as the mountain pine beetle are just some of the threats this country faces. However, Canada also remains on the list of countries that are the highest global emitters of greenhouse gases. While there are differences of opinion among governments and organizations as to the best ways to reduce global warming, all agree that targets must be set. You will learn more about the effects of climate change and threats to Canada's environment and economy in later chapters of *Horizons*.

FIGURE 1–34 Quickly melting snow and rain causes rapid rises in river levels. In Golden, British Columbia, this farm was flooded by the rising waters of the Columbia River. The B.C. provincial government announced in 2008 that it would spend $16 million on flood protection measures. Do you think these precautions are necessary? Why?

ACTIVITIES

1. Examine the climographs in Figure 1–31 to identify and explain which locations have the following: highest rainfall, lowest precipitation, lowest monthly temperature, highest monthly temperature, and the greatest range in temperature between summer and winter.

2. Explain in what ways, and why, the east and west coasts of Canada have different climates. Theorize how these different climates affect daily life in those regions.

3. Prince Rupert, Edmonton, and St. John's are at approximately the same latitude, yet have different climates. What are the main reasons the climate of each city is different from the other two?

4. Which of the five conditions that affect temperature do you think has the greatest impact on your community? Explain your thinking.

5. List three impacts climate change has had on your community. In what ways has it affected you and your family?

6. In groups, discuss possible solutions to prevent further global warming. Think about what you could do at the local level, and explore what local organizations may already be doing. Present your best solution to the class.

7. Use an organizer to explore how the study of climate might relate to each of the five themes of geography.

Canada's Natural Regions

▶ **How do people affect the natural regions of Canada?**

Natural regions are areas where animals and plants live in relation to each other and to the non-living parts of the environment. The natural environment of Canada is made up of a number of these large **ecosystems**, or biomes, each with its own type of vegetation and animal species.

A biome contains smaller ecosystems—natural areas where the life cycles of plants, animals, and other organisms are linked to each other and to their physical surroundings. Smaller ecosystems are in turn made up of habitats, or places where plants and animals have adapted to certain conditions (for example, a wetland). Because all elements in the ecosystem are dependent on each other, altering one part of the system or introducing something new sets off a chain reaction. For example, draining a wetland has a dramatic impact on the plants and animals that exist in that habitat.

ecosystem an ecological community of plants and animals together with its environment, extending over an area

DID YOU KNOW...

Rats were introduced into Haida Gwaii (Queen Charlotte Islands) in the last century by coastal trading ships. The rats quickly reduced the number of nesting birds, forcing the government to introduce a control program.

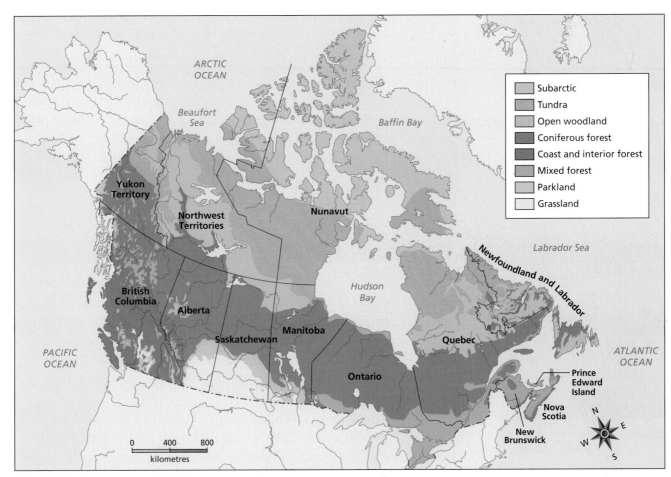

FIGURE 1–35 Much of Canada is covered by boreal forest. Natural vegetation is determined by temperature and precipitation, soil, the slope of the land, and drainage. Why do you think grasslands and lowlands, in particular, might show the effects of human activity?

The Natural Regions of Canada	
Subarctic	Many swampy areas of scattered coniferous trees mixed with tundra vegetation. Along with some Arctic wildlife are caribou, lemmings, and snowy owls.
Tundra	A treeless landscape of permafrost with mostly low shrubs, mosses, and lichens. Polar bears, seals, walruses, muskox, and Arctic foxes survive in this harsh climate.
Open woodland	An area of scattered evergreen trees, shrubs, and grass. Animal species living in this region can include caribou, martens, bears, geese, beaver, and lynx.
Coniferous forest	Evergreens such as spruce, fir, pine, and aspen are the most common. This region has deer, moose, black bears, and many fur-bearing animals, as well as hawks, eagles, and various types of wild ducks. Soils are not very fertile.
Coast and interior forest	This is primarily a coniferous forest region. The coast region trees show greater growth because of a wet and mild climate. The higher slopes of mountains above the treeline have tundra and Arctic vegetation. Some southern interior valleys have short grass and plants. Unsettled areas are home to abundant wildlife: cougars, mountain sheep, bears, moose, and birds.
Mixed forest	Made up of softwood trees, such as hemlock and cedar, as well as hardwood trees such as maple, birch, oak, and ash. This region has the same wildlife as the coniferous region. Soil is more fertile in mixed forests than in coniferous forests.
Parkland	A transition zone between the dry southern prairies and the coniferous forest, this region has long grasses and clumps of aspen and cottonwood trees. Wildlife from the coniferous forest and grasslands are found here.
Grassland	This is an area of short grasses with not enough moisture for trees. Antelope, gophers, and wild fowl are the main animals. Bison, until hunted to near extinction, were the largest animals. Soils are far more fertile than in the forest regions.

FIGURE 1–36 The Athabasca River is fed by melting glaciers, and areas of Alberta rely on the meltwater during dry summers. What might happen as climate change shrinks the glaciers?

The Effect of Human Activities

Are there places in Canada where it is possible to see how the land looked before European colonization? This may be true for some parts of northern Canada, but it is not for many of the natural regions of eastern Canada and the southern Prairie Provinces. Although First Nations living in these regions did little to alter the ecosystems, the arrival of Europeans, and later immigration and industrialization have at times drastically altered natural regions.

Enjoying an abundance of water in most parts of Canada, many Canadians are unconcerned about threats to water quality and quantity. However, a growing number of people are taking an interest in the health of this vital resource—particularly due to the effects of climate change on stream flows and the water levels in lakes.

Water quality is becoming a major issue in both southern and northern Alberta. In southern Alberta, most of the natural prairie has been replaced by grain farming and cattle operations. **Runoff** from farms and pollution from animal **feedlots** are a threat to soil and water quality. Feedlots also place a huge drain on local water supplies; one animal can drink up to 57 litres of water a day, and there are thousands of animals in feedlots.

Northern Alberta has had massive development of oil and gas deposits, particularly in the oil sands. As the world demand for oil increases, so has the expansion of this project, leading to a booming economy and great wealth for Alberta. In fact, including the Alberta oil sands, Canada's oil reserves are the second-largest in the world—second only to Saudi Arabia.

However, with the boom comes the burden of dealing with the environmental costs and health risks to people. Effects on land and water are on a large scale, with acres of muskeg and boreal forest transformed into open pit mines in order to expose the layers of oil-laden sands. To produce one cubic metre of oil, about 4.5 cubic metres of water must be used. This water is diverted from the Athabasca River, and in a year, the oil sands production will consume more water than a small city. During this process, the water becomes contaminated and must be stored in ponds. In 2008, more than 500 ducks died in a storage pond when the system that was designed to keep them away failed.

While all residents in the region are exposed to health risks, it is the Cree, Dene, and Métis whose health is most at risk due to their traditional reliance on fish, moose, and other local foods. Toxic materials released in the mining process accumulate and become concentrated in the flesh of animals. Balancing the costs to the environment with the economic benefits from the tar sands is a problem for Albertans.

runoff pesticides, herbicides, and other materials that drain from fields into rivers, lakes, and groundwater

feedlot an enclosed area where large herds of cows are fed and raised

DID YOU KNOW...

The United Nations Environment Programme has identified Alberta's oil sands as one of the 100 key global environmental "hotspots."

WEB LINK ● · · · · · · · · · · · · · · · ·
On the Pearson Web site, read about other perspectives on the Alberta oil sands.

FIGURE 1–37 The Athabasca oil sands in northern Alberta are expanding. If the planned projects are completed, nearly 3000 km² of forest could be cleared, and roads and pipelines will be built. Do the economic benefits of the oil sands outweigh the environmental costs? Why or why not?

The people of Fort Chipewyan, a tiny community on the shores of Lake Athabasca, are particularly vulnerable to pollutants travelling down the Athabasca River and settling in the fine sediment of Lake Athabasca. The lake is a traditional place for hunting and fishing, and the communities of Cree, Dene, and Métis live mostly on a diet based on local wildlife and fish. They have noticed an alarming increase in fish with severe mutations downstream from the oil sands. First Nations communities in this area have expressed concern about how development is affecting their drinking water. People have complained to government and health authorities about an alarming increase in a variety of cancers and other diseases.

The Alberta government and the corporations involved say that the rapid increase in development has made it difficult to control the growth of projects and provide protection for the environment. Take a look at two different views on the development of the tar sands.

> *Year round water quality and quantity as well as aquatic habitats will be maintained in the Athabasca River. This includes the critical spring floods in the Athabasca River Delta that directly benefit fish and wildlife populations. The proposed MOSS (Mineable Oil Sands Strategy) allows for rerouting of some tributaries of the Athabasca River under certain conditions, which include ensuring that water quality is maintained within the remainder of the altered stream; water quality from altered drainage meets environmental standards before the water enters the Athabasca River;... the loss of fish habitat is properly replaced.*
>
> —**Alberta Government Mineable Oil Sands Strategy, 2007**

> *The Mikisew Cree have asked many questions during the hearing for oil sands projects. The concern... has been the quality and quantity of water in the Athabasca River. The Mikisew Cree have noted that prior to the 1960s, one could drink the river water, but now no one would consider the thought. After participating in... hearings since 2003... (we) still do not know the cumulative impacts of oil sands mining on the Athabasca River water quality. The panel have concluded that the impacts of each project will be negligible, but the First Nations realize that the incremental impacts of each successive project are significant. Community knowledge suggests that contaminants from oil sands' facilities extend to Lake Athabasca.*
>
> —**Mikisew Cree First Nation submission to Alberta Government Oil Sands Consultation, 2007**

WHAT DO YOU THINK?

1. Do you accept the government's assurances regarding water quality and quantity? Why, or why not?

2. What advice would you give the Mikisew First Nation in responding to the Alberta government's assurances?

ACTIVITIES

1. Make a list of the possible impacts of one of the following on an ecosystem: a road built through wilderness; a music festival held in a rural, agricultural area.

2. Write a report card on Canada's land-use policy. Think of climate change, water use, and other issues you consider important.

3. Use the information from the table on page 30 to describe the biome in which you live.

4. How does the theme of human/environmental interaction help us understand aspects of the natural regions of Canada?

WHO
Owns the Arctic?

by John Dwyer

Some countries... see these passages as international waters and challenge Canada's claim that the Northwest Passage is part of our territorial waters.

I f someone asked you who owned the Arctic, what would your answer be? Many assume that Canada's northern boundaries include the high Arctic, as well as the North Pole. Some Canadian maps even show this. But is this accurate? Take a look at the map below. How many other countries may also lay claim to the Arctic?

Although the Inuit have long made their home in this region, the Arctic has also been seen as a barren wasteland. In the 21st century, this has changed, as more sea ice begins to melt. Water that is usually blocked by ice year round is now open. This has cleared the way for ships and people, and the discovery of oil and valuable minerals is making the world take notice.

Now, this issue of sovereignty—a country's authority or power within its boundaries—has been opened in the Arctic. Countries such as Canada, the United States, Russia, Denmark, and Norway all lay claim to territory in the Arctic Circle—territory that includes the sea bed, a potentially rich source of oil and natural gas.

What should be considered? There are international laws: the United Nations Convention on the Law of the Sea allows countries to control resources in waters up to 370 km from their coast. It also grants countries control of territory extending 111 km off their continental shelf. Canada has until 2013 to submit its claim to seabed territory to the UN.

Who should decide? In a matter of international concern, the UN will probably take a lead role in deciding what each country may claim. Each country will bring its concerns and claims to the world. Will the voices of those who live in the region—the Inuit, for example—also be heard? That remains to be seen.

UNITED STATES

ARCTIC OCEAN

RUSSIA

CANADA

0   350   700
kilometres

North Pole

DENMARK

NORWAY

GREENLAND (DENMARK)

NORWAY
FINLAND
SWEDEN

 Disputed area   Lomonosov Ridge   —— Current borders

▶ **How have people shaped the land?**

As you read earlier in the chapter, **cultural landscapes** are a part of the geographical study of place. How might **culture** and attitudes influence how people view and use the land? The Cree of the Interior Plains did not view the land and its resources in the same way as European fur traders and settlers. Today, as you have learned, the Mikisew First Nation is concerned about the effects the oil sands have on their way of life, while others see economic benefit. Opposing attitudes often result in crisis. You will read more about these conflicts in later chapters.

cultural landscapes landscapes that have been changed by human societies

culture the behaviour, arts, beliefs, and institutions of a particular community or population

FIGURE 1–38 The diversity of Canada's population can often be seen in its buildings. Some are a combination of the many cultural backgrounds of Canadians.

Settlement and Population

At the beginning of the 20th century, only eastern Canada had seen the effects of large-scale settlement. Before the building of a railway to the West, great distances and the rugged landscape of the Shield restricted settlement to the St. Lawrence Lowlands. Only in the north and the west, apart from some small communities, did the landscape remain mostly in its natural state. The prosperity of the Laurier era, which will be described in Chapter 7, brought large-scale settlement to western Canada and changed the physical and cultural landscapes.

The cultural background of newcomers generally determined where they settled. English and Chinese immigrants tended to move to cities to work in industries. People coming from farming communities in Europe were attracted to the grasslands of the Prairies. Immigrants from regions of Eastern Europe with similar extremes of climate were better able to survive the first hard years as homesteaders on the Prairies.

Even dividing the land was based on cultural background. Métis farmers in Manitoba followed the French practice of setting up farms in long narrow

FIGURE 1–39 All settlements have functions, or activities responsible for economic and social development. Places with a large population are able to support many functions. For example, Victoria has more functions than Nanaimo but not as many as Vancouver. However, with the growth of the Internet, people in smaller centres now have access to many services formerly restricted to those living in larger cities.

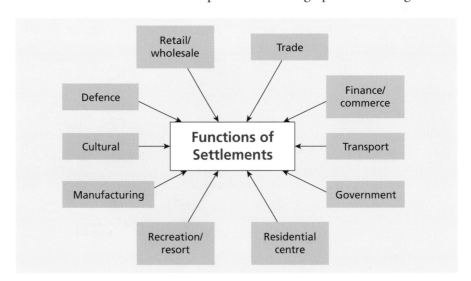

strips along rivers. However, the Canadian government followed the English grid system when it surveyed the west. These differences, as you will see, brought English and French ways into conflict in Manitoba's Red River area.

Aboriginal peoples view the land without artificial boundaries. Aboriginal concepts of the land as a place owned by the community and coexisting with the environment were shattered by the European idea of surveyed areas owned and sold by individuals.

Where people decide to settle depends on several factors, but the most important are the physical environment, the climate, and economic possibilities. Landforms and climate play a key role in determining how many people will permanently settle in an area. A combination of flat land, mild winters, adequate rain, and good soil are some of the factors that draw people to an area. These advantages can also lead to **urbanization**. Agricultural communities on the Prairies and in British Columbia follow this pattern.

Places that lack the benefits of good land and fair weather can still experience population growth in brief spurts. This is because people almost always live where they can find work, and many are willing to move to work in harsh environments far from home. For example, many people from Newfoundland and Labrador have moved to Fort McMurray in Alberta to work in the oil sands.

Many resource towns in Canada still go through cycles of **boom and bust** as a resource is developed and then depleted. Communities such as Barkerville, British Columbia, were built around a single resource such as gold and were dependent on that resource for survival. Today the trend is to build temporary settlements in remote areas to extract a resource with a short life. The northern diamond mines in the Northwest Territories and Nunavut are examples of this new trend.

FIGURE 1–40 On the Prairies, cities such as Edmonton grew rapidly in areas with water and flat land.

urbanization the process of becoming an area with a large, concentrated population

boom and bust words used to describe a healthy (booming) economy and/or one that is failing (bust)

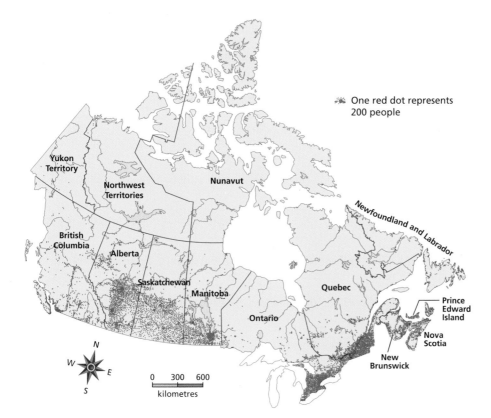

One red dot represents 200 people

FIGURE 1–41 Canada's resource towns do not employ as many people as do the industries centred in larger cities. That is one reason why two-thirds of Canada's population is concentrated in major cities. Compare this map to the maps of physical and natural regions seen earlier in this chapter. What other reasons account for the patterns evident on this map?

Aboriginal peoples regard the land in a way that is different from Western attitudes. Their relationship to the land is spiritual, rather than economic. Life is shaped by a traditional knowledge of the environment, shared through songs, stories, rituals, places that have special meaning, and an understanding of the ecosystem. Such knowledge is passed on by oral tradition.

This tradition forms a "mental map" of a cultural landscape. These maps contain a great wealth of experience and culture—they are more like "pictures of experience." When colonization created new boundaries and divisions, oral tradition preserved the Aboriginal cultural landscape.

Even by the late 1700s, the interior of North America was known to only a few Europeans. Early European explorers relied on traditional knowledge when they asked for guidance from Aboriginal peoples. While there were seldom permanent maps, a picture could be sketched in the snow or sand. Even maps on birchbark were only meant to guide those who followed or give directions and then be discarded.

Some of these maps were copied by explorers or traders. They provide evidence of the great knowledge contained in these cultural landscapes.

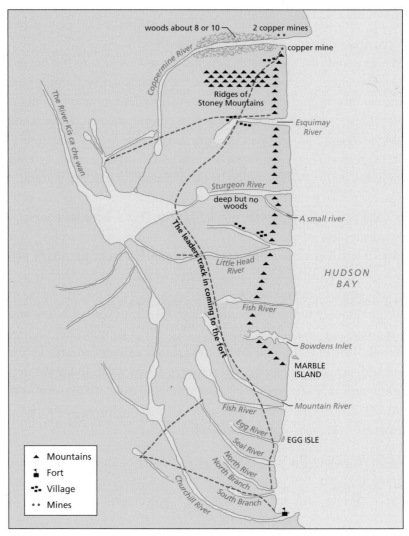

FIGURE 1–42 Europeans relied on men like Matonabbee, a Dene Suliné who led Samuel Hearne across most of the territory shown here. This map is a copy of a map drawn by Matonabbee at the request of the Hudson's Bay Company in 1767. The centre is Great Slave Lake. Rivers, lakes, and paths were part of the cultural landscape, since they were crossed by hunting parties every year.

WHAT DO YOU THINK?

1. Why is it important to include Aboriginal maps and cultural landscapes in textbooks and atlases?

2. How do Aboriginal maps differ from other maps? How do these differences show what people value, and what they believe in?

3. Using only memory, make a map of a place that has a special meaning to you. Explain what this map says about you.

Boundaries: The Lines on a Map

As people settle in a place for any length of time, they come to identify with the area, calling themselves New Brunswickers or British Columbians. The physical and natural landscape, together with climate, can shape people's lives and affect their identity. People in Saskatchewan identify with the big sky and open prairie, while those living in the Atlantic Provinces are affected by the ocean. In British Columbia, the mild climate, the mountains, and the ocean have an impact on people's lifestyles.

These provincial and territorial boundaries are familiar to us, and it is easy to forget that they are artificial. Before European settlement, the First Nations, Métis, Inuit, early explorers, and traders divided the land according to its natural boundaries—physical features of the Shield, lowlands, plains, mountains, rivers, and forests. While some political boundaries follow natural features, most do not.

Eventually, frontier zones were replaced by political boundaries. Geographic knowledge of some remote areas was limited, which led to strange decisions and sometimes conflict. An example is the 49th parallel of latitude, which set the boundary between British and American territory in the West. People who had been accustomed to crossing a natural area were now hemmed in by lines on a map. Also, due to climate change and the loss of pack ice, Canadians now face a new problem in establishing political boundaries in the Arctic.

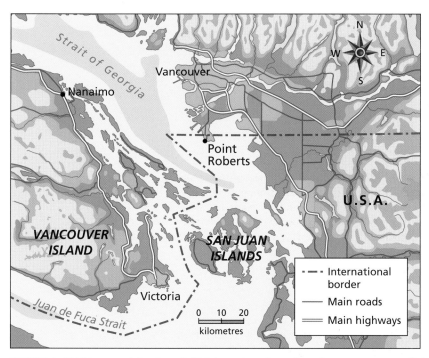

FIGURE 1–43 This map of the Canada/U.S. boundary shows how lines on a map pay little attention to natural features, as in the case of Point Roberts, or the route through the Gulf Islands.

FIGURE 1–44 How might future treaties change boundary lines in Canada?

Aboriginal Peoples and Boundaries

In the past, Aboriginal peoples did not have an influence on the drawing of political boundaries. In the last decades of the 20th century, this began to shift. The Inuit and First Nations have become more successful in reclaiming control of their traditional territories. In British Columbia, because the right of Aboriginal land title was recognized in the Constitution Act of 1982 and in later court decisions, new lines marking First Nations land claims have appeared on maps of British Columbia. The Nisga'a First Nation, for example, signed a treaty with British Columbia and Canada in 1998.

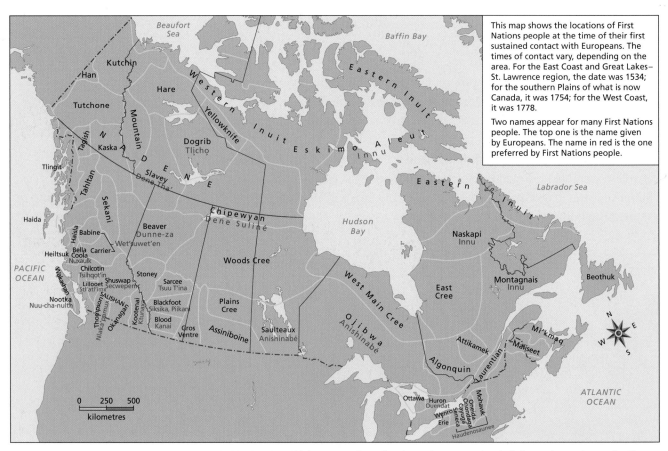

This map shows the locations of First Nations people at the time of their first sustained contact with Europeans. The times of contact vary, depending on the area. For the East Coast and Great Lakes–St. Lawrence region, the date was 1534; for the southern Plains of what is now Canada, it was 1754; for the West Coast, it was 1778.

Two names appear for many First Nations people. The top one is the name given by Europeans. The name in red is the one preferred by First Nations people.

FIGURE 1–45 Which present Canadian boundary most closely follows the territory of a First Nations language group?

ACTIVITIES

1. Do some research to determine the most and least urbanized provinces in Canada. Use a Venn diagram to compare and contrast the two provinces as a way of discovering the reasons for their differences.

2. Report on the cultural landscape in your community. What does it look like? How was it formed? Use text, images, or a recording to make your report.

3. Examine Figure 1–41 and refer to information in this chapter including the five themes of geography to explain

   a) the small number of people living above 55 degrees north latitude

   b) the distribution of population in the southern Prairie region

   c) the concentration of population in the Great Lakes–St. Lawrence region

Explore the Big Ideas

Many say Canada's geography has influenced the way Canadians see themselves. People from different regions and provinces identify with where they live. People in the Yukon often think of themselves as hardier than Canadians living in the south. Maritimers feel that the Atlantic Ocean and fishing shape the way they see themselves. In British Columbia, the climate fosters an outdoor lifestyle that often determines how people think about leisure and work.

1. How has the land shaped us? How have we shaped the land?

   a) Using an organizer like the one below, demonstrate your understanding of how each element of Canada's geography might shape the way Canadians think about themselves and Canada. Add your own ideas for elements as necessary.

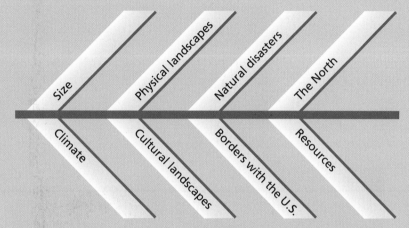

   b) Now approach the organizer from a different direction—explain how people have affected each element.

2. Choose a country with geography that is very different from Canada. Using the five themes of geography as a framework, compare and contrast that country with Canada. How has geography shaped the people and culture of your chosen country?

3. In a small group, discuss which of the elements shown in the organizer above have the greatest impact on people in your community.

   a) Use the results of your discussion to imagine how your community would react to a proposed economic development that would have a significant impact on either the physical landscape, the cultural landscape, or both. Be sure to list pros and cons for the development.

   b) Organize your findings and summarize them in a letter, a blog entry, or an interview with the local media.

4. You are a time traveller visiting Canada 100 years ago. Would Canada seem like a foreign country to you? Describe physical features and the cultural landscape. What features have remained the same? What has changed? Ask the same questions for 50 and 100 years in the future. Present your ideas in a travelogue, including maps or other images.

5. Canada is experiencing some of the early impacts of climate change. Compile a list of the ways global warming may change Canada by the year 2050, or 2099. Predict the biggest effect on the environment and human lifestyles as a result of changes in climate.

6. Find a map of the Nisga'a land claim. How do the boundaries of the land claim relate to natural and artificial boundaries? How might this add to the challenge of resolving Aboriginal land claims?

2

Our Developing Nation

This unit helps you investigate these questions.

- Why might people have immigrated to Canada between 1815 and 1867?

- What was the impact of interactions between Aboriginal peoples and European settlers?

- How did responsible government evolve in Canada?

- How and why did Canada become a nation?

First Nations. European settlers disrupted First Nations communities by taking their land. First Nations leaders, such as this Anishinabé man, often signed treaties in order to save some land for future generations. What are the effects of these treaties today?

Colonial life. Daily life for the colonists was challenging by today's standards. People worked long days clearing land, planting and harvesting crops, caring for livestock, and raising their children. How would the hardships of colonial life affect the growth of communities?

Rebellions. In 1837, dissatisfaction with colonial government led to rebellions in Upper and Lower Canada. The British government sent Lord Durham to the colonies to bring about reform. What would be the consequences?

The Charlottetown Conference. In 1864, delegates from the colonies met in Charlottetown to discuss uniting as a dominion. The pro-Confederation party convinced enough delegates that Confederation could work. What might have happened if they had been unsuccessful?

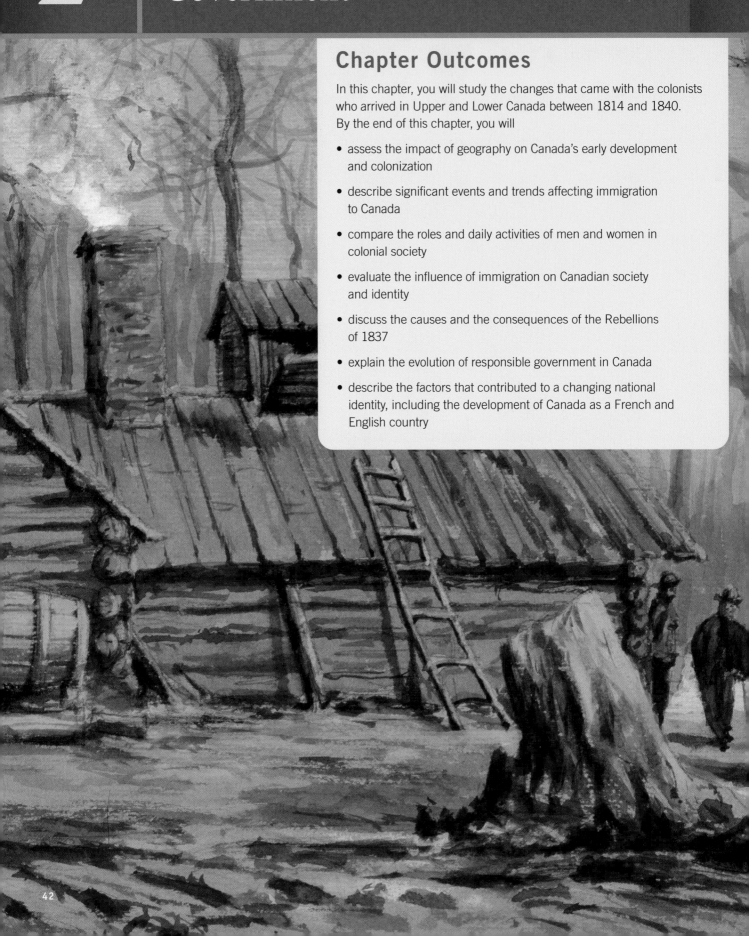

2

The Colonists: Land and Government

Chapter Outcomes

In this chapter, you will study the changes that came with the colonists who arrived in Upper and Lower Canada between 1814 and 1840. By the end of this chapter, you will

- assess the impact of geography on Canada's early development and colonization

- describe significant events and trends affecting immigration to Canada

- compare the roles and daily activities of men and women in colonial society

- evaluate the influence of immigration on Canadian society and identity

- discuss the causes and the consequences of the Rebellions of 1837

- explain the evolution of responsible government in Canada

- describe the factors that contributed to a changing national identity, including the development of Canada as a French and English country

The 1845 portrait, shown above, depicts three sisters, all born in York, the capital of Upper Canada. The painting to the left shows settlers with a typical rural cabin. Do you think the people shown in these images would agree with the quotation below? What do you think they might say about using the term "waste land" to describe Upper Canada?

What factors shaped Canada at this time? Land, people, or politics?

Imagine what it would be like to arrive as a colonist in Upper or Lower Canada in the early 1800s. Would you think you were building the foundation of an emerging nation? Would you see the land as a "wilderness" available for the taking? Or would you think that the long-standing presence of First Nations should be acknowledged?

Key Terms

colony	Francophone
Upper Canada	representative government
Lower Canada	
class system	responsible government
Family Compact	oligarchy
Château Clique	nationalism
land speculators	insurrection

A highly civilized and densely populated state possesses extensive waste lands in the colonies. In a state possessing those waste lands (now Canada), all citizens have equal rights—all have a share in the collective right to these waste lands.

—an editorial in the British newspaper, *The Spectator*, September 18, 1847

The Land of Yesterday

TIMELINE

1791 ● Constitutional Act creates Upper and Lower Canada

1814 ● Louis-Joseph Papineau is elected to the Legislative Assembly of Lower Canada

1817 ● Robert Gourlay is arrested for criticizing land policies in Upper Canada

1824 ● William Lyon Mackenzie establishes the *Colonial Advocate*

1826 ● Papineau becomes leader of the Patriotes

1828 ● Mackenzie is elected to the Legislative Assembly

1837 ● November: Battle of St. Charles
● December: Battle of Montgomery's Tavern

1838 ● Lord Durham arrives in Quebec

1840 ● Act of Union is passed

colony the overseas possession of another country that governs and uses it for its own purposes

Upper Canada British colony "up" the St. Lawrence, mostly English speaking

Lower Canada British colony "down" the St. Lawrence, mostly French speaking

▶ **What was British North America like in the early 19th century?**

Imagine what your community might have looked like when it was first settled. Were there thick forests or rocky areas? To the early European colonists, British North America was very challenging compared to their homelands. To many, the environment in which Aboriginal peoples already lived may have seemed like a vast wilderness that had to be conquered.

The eastern part of the country was growing and developing. The War of 1812, in which the United States declared war on Britain and its colonies over trade and other issues, had ended. Newcomers now poured into the **colony** of **Upper Canada** (now southern and eastern Ontario). Forests were cleared to build farms, small communities, and roads.

At the same time, **Lower Canada** (Quebec and along the St. Lawrence River) was building its economy. Its busy trading capital, Montreal, attracted Scottish and American entrepreneurs.

The Maritime colonies (now New Brunswick, Prince Edward Island, Nova Scotia, and Newfoundland and Labrador), long settled and stable, specialized in fishing, forestry, and shipbuilding. Trade with Britain and the United States kept these industries booming.

In the north and west, the Hudson's Bay Company held sway. It claimed all lands drained by rivers flowing into Hudson Bay, bringing a huge part of the continent of North America under its control. As a result, the fur trade expanded west. In competition with the HBC, the North West Company, based in Montreal, built its own trading relationships with Aboriginal leaders and explored the west.

FIGURE 2–1 This painting shows the living conditions of some of Canada's early newcomers. Using this image as a primary source, discuss what living and farming in this area at that point in time might have been like.

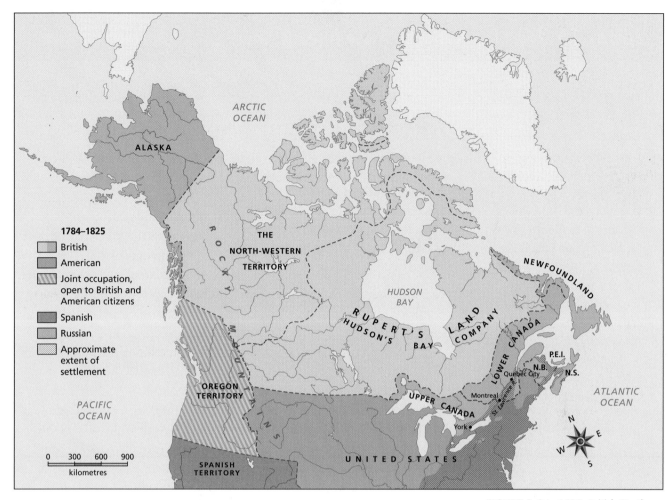

However, the growth of the colonies came at the expense of Aboriginal peoples, although they had once been military allies of the British and were still a vital part of the prosperous fur trade. Many died from diseases brought by Europeans, or they starved after losing land and access to traditional food sources. First Nations were often forced to give up their land to make way for European immigrants. Those who grew crops lost their farmlands, while others lost access to traditional fishing and hunting areas. Most newcomers paid little attention to such hardship and injustice, which continued throughout Canada's history, as you will learn in later chapters.

FIGURE 2–2 In 1825, British North America consisted of six colonies. In the colonies, community building, farming, and forestry began to radically change the land. In the northwest, the Hudson's Bay Company and the North West Company encouraged the trade of furs. Which activity might have had more of an impact on Aboriginal societies? Why?

FIGURE 2–3 Anishinabé fishers at Sault Ste. Marie. The Anishinabé traditionally used this area to meet and fish every year. By 1887, Sault Ste. Marie had become a town. How do you think the growth of a town might have changed their way of life?

The Colonists: Land and Government **45**

First Nations ways of life were heavily affected—and in some cases destroyed—by European colonization. Disease, for example, took a heavy toll, sometimes decimating entire First Nations communities.

Loss of land was another factor. European attitudes toward land were alien to the First Nations, who did not "own" land in the European sense, believing rather that they belonged to the land and not the other way around.

Colonial governments and land developers were quick to take advantage of this difference in attitude. To Europeans, land that had not been surveyed and did not legally belong to anyone was considered free land, waiting to be taken. Although the **Royal Proclamation of 1763** provided some protection for First Nations, the British government expected to gain control of First Nations land through treaties. However, most land set aside for the use of First Nations had, over time, been taken away again. Usually, First Nations were left with a fraction of their former traditional territories. Loss of land led not only to a loss of freedom of movement and access to resources necessary for survival, but also to a loss of a way of life. Newcomers to Canada made their homes on land that was once the territory of the First Nations.

- Discuss the immediate consequences of loss of land to Aboriginal peoples in North America. What land rights issues still exist today for Aboriginal peoples in Canada?

Royal Proclamation of 1763 a British declaration confirming Aboriginal title to lands west of the Mississippi River

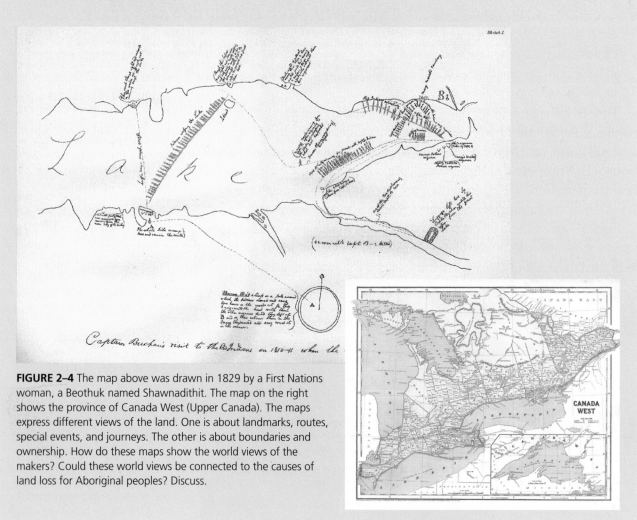

FIGURE 2–4 The map above was drawn in 1829 by a First Nations woman, a Beothuk named Shawnadithit. The map on the right shows the province of Canada West (Upper Canada). The maps express different views of the land. One is about landmarks, routes, special events, and journeys. The other is about boundaries and ownership. How do these maps show the world views of the makers? Could these world views be connected to the causes of land loss for Aboriginal peoples? Discuss.

Many words have **implicit** meanings that can affect how people think, although they might be unaware of it. You may be familiar with insulting names for different groups that are based on religion, ethnicity, or gender, but you could be surprised how subtle some words can be. A look at some words used to describe Aboriginal issues reveals the hidden influence of ordinary words.

For instance, the term "settlement" is commonly used to describe the colonization of North America. This word implies that the land was wild or unoccupied, and it becomes easy to forget that Aboriginal peoples had "settled" the land long before Europeans arrived. From the perspective of the Aboriginal peoples, their land was invaded, not discovered, and they did not think their land needed to be "settled." It is also worthwhile noting that the word "handout," often used to describe payments from the government to Aboriginal peoples, is inaccurate. These payments were the result of complex treaty negotiations based on the sale of land, and they were never charity.

Word use can also change through time. An example of this concerns the Métis, who you will study in later chapters of *Horizons*. Recently, the events during which the Métis defended their lands have been called a "resistance" rather than a "rebellion." Why the change? Resistance implies a struggle against unfair treatment, while rebellion implies an illegal act against legitimate authority. Changing perspectives on the history of the Métis has led historians and writers to acknowledge that the Métis were more likely to resist unfair treatment rather than rebel against a government that did not recognize them as citizens.

The power of words to shape our perspectives should not be underestimated.

- Using the example of the Métis, discuss other examples of changing word use through time. Why might these words change? What impact do the changes have?

implicit something that is implied, and not openly expressed

FIGURE 2–5 This 1550 engraving of Secota, an Algonquin village, is based on a drawing by John White, an English colonist who lived on the east coast of North America. What does this representation of village life tell you about what he saw? How might it contrast to a typical idea of how First Nations people lived in the past?

Land for the Fur Trade, or for the Colonies?

As European settlement of the British colonies continued, colonists generally accepted that the lands west and north of the Great Lakes were reserved for the fur trade. Most Aboriginal peoples living in that region were involved in the fur trade in some way. By 1820, however, any European immigrants living in the northwest and not involved in the fur trade numbered less than a dozen.

Even if European or American immigrants wanted to farm the northwest, those involved in the fur trade were determined to prevent this. Colonists wanted fixed boundaries, surveys, roads, and most importantly, land they could own. These goals conflicted with the culture, lifestyle, and economy of the fur traders. Fur traders eventually became the natural allies of Aboriginal peoples, particularly the **Métis**. As you will learn in Chapter 4, both fur traders and Aboriginal communities had everything to lose and very little to gain from colonization.

Métis a person of both Aboriginal and European descent

FIGURE 2–6 This painting shows First Nations hunters and fur traders in their camp. Examine the image and theorize what travel, hunting, and daily life must have been like for this group. What might happen if settlements were built in their lands?

ACTIVITIES

1. Summarize your understanding of life in 19th century British North America in one or two sentences. What stands out for you? The land? Exploration? The potential for conflict?

2. Think about the needs of fur traders, Aboriginal hunters, and farmers (for example, land, water, and food). Create an organizer that shows how these and three other needs might come into conflict.

3. Examine the portrait of the three sisters on page 43. What do you think the women want others to see? What are they trying to say about life in Canada?

4. With a partner, discuss how the lives of Aboriginal inhabitants of the northwest might have been affected by the Hudson's Bay Company. For example, how would hunters have reacted to a company that traded in furs?

Upper Canada

▶ **What was life like in Upper Canada?**

In the early 19th century, Upper Canada was the newest of the colonies of British North America. There were few roads. Places 30 or 40 km away from the village of York (which later became Toronto) took more than a day to get to on horseback. Most people had to walk. The forest was very dense, and the hardwood trees had massive trunks and root systems. Clearing the land was usually a newcomer's first task, but it was not possible to clear more than a hectare in a year—an area a little larger than a city block.

The War of 1812 ended in 1815. Invasion attempts by the Americans during this war, and again during the American Revolution, served to reinforce Upper Canada colonists' ties with the British Empire. Colony and community leaders were often members of **Loyalist** families, pensioned British army officers, or members of the British **gentry**. This leadership tended to unite the colony under British rule, and with British laws.

FIGURE 2–7 The corner of Yonge and Dundas streets in Toronto today. These streets were once tracks in the bush.

Loyalist Americans who did not support the American Revolution, many of whom moved to the British colonies

gentry the upper class in Britain

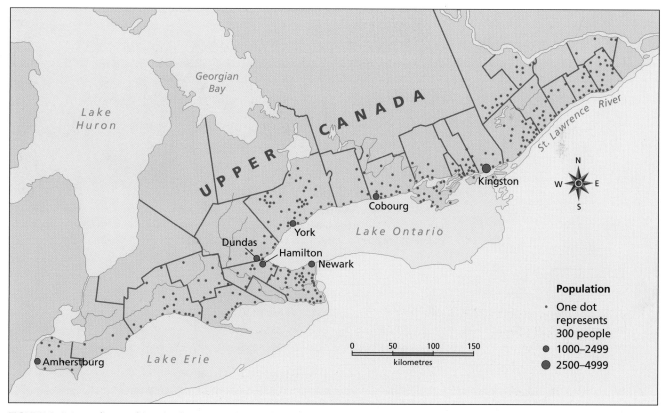

FIGURE 2–8 According to this map showing settlement patterns in 1825, where did most colonists choose to live? Examine a physical map of southern Ontario. What geographic features helped determine settlement patterns?

Daily Life for the Colonists

What was it like to live in Upper Canada in the 1820s? If you could travel back in time, you might notice the quiet and the darkness. Those of us who live in modern cities and towns are used to constant noise and light. Colonists heard only the noises of the weather, the barnyard, and work. To colonists, a watermill or a smithy might seem loud. Of course, there was always the sound of music at social gatherings. At night, light came from candles, oil lamps, or the moon; there was no constant glow from streetlights or signs.

People depended on each other and formed close communities. They looked forward to going to church or being visited by a travelling member of the **clergy**. Sometimes communities came together to build a small school and hire a teacher, often paying for the service with food and lodging.

Making a living in farming was hard, as it is for many people today. It took years to raise a crop that could be sold. Almost everybody was in debt at one time or another, and many had to **mortgage** next year's crop to buy supplies. Colonists also depended on a **barter economy**. For example, a farmer might pay the local blacksmith with wheat instead of money. Some colonists built a relationship with First Nations people in the area, learning from their knowledge of the land and the seasons.

clergy people ordained for religious service

mortgage to use something as security for a loan

barter economy an economy based on trading services and products instead of using money

FIGURE 2–9 Most newcomers in Upper Canada lived in small log cabins that they built themselves. The buildings shown here are part of Upper Canada Village, a recreated colonial village in Ontario. Do you think the village accurately portrays past life in the colonies?

When Europeans first came to North and South America, they did not find Asia's treasures as they had hoped, but they did find enormous wealth. Not only did they profit from fur, gold, and silver, but they also found that plants farmed by Aboriginal peoples were extremely useful. Some of these plants changed the world forever.

Aboriginal farmers in the Americas cultivated more than 300 varieties of plants, which today equal more than half of the crops grown around the world. The potato, introduced to Europe in 1536, proved to be such an easily grown food that it quickly nourished a population boom. The potato also provided a lesson in the importance of crop diversity. Aboriginal peoples in the Andes had developed more than 3000 varieties of potato, but Europeans took back a limited number, leaving the plants open to disease. In Ireland, a combination of a dependency on potatoes as food and the potato **blight** led to devastating famine.

Corn, or maize, was also an unexpected treasure. First cultivated about 9000 years ago in what is now Mexico, it was eventually grown throughout North America. Today, corn is one of the most common crops in the world, and is used in thousands of different products, from plastics to fuel.

The most influential crop to leave the Americas was cotton. The soft fibre of the cotton plant can be spun into thread, which can then be woven into cloth. Aboriginal peoples in South America had been harvesting cotton to make clothing for centuries. They grew long-fibre cotton, suitable for European mass production. Soon millions of bales of cotton were spurring the invention of the Spinning Jenny, the Water Frame, and other machines made to spin and weave cotton quickly and efficiently. By 1850, cloth would make up half of England's exports. The machinery of this booming industry needed a workforce, and soon thousands of people were working in factories. The industrial revolution had begun.

- What other crops grown in Canada today have been imported from other areas of the world? Why might this still happen?

blight a disease caused by mold, fungus, or bacteria that can kill plants

FIGURE 2–10 Aboriginal peoples grew corn with two other plants—beans and squash. Known as the Three Sisters, the plants provided nutrients and shade for each other, and they were always grown together. This painting of the Three Sisters is by Carson Waterman of the Seneca Nation. What other Aboriginal products and technologies would be adopted by Europeans?

FIGURE 2–11 Colonists from neighbouring farms often worked together. Clearing land was hard, time-consuming work. How are land clearing and construction different today? Explain both the advantages and disadvantages of this work during colonial times and today.

estate a tract of land often covering thousands of hectares, owned by one person

tenant farmer someone who farms land owned by someone else, keeping part of the produce as payment

class system a society in which those born into privileged groups have rights and advantages that others do not

The Importance of Social Class

Most people today tend not to judge others based on who their parents are. This was not the case in Upper Canada, where family background meant a great deal—especially to the upper class. Upper-class people wanted to keep the privileges they enjoyed in Britain when they came to Canada, but life in the colonies had ways of removing some of the barriers between social classes. Many children of British aristocrats, as well as retired British army officers, came to settle in the colony only to discover that they had to do the back-breaking labour of clearing and maintaining a farm. Cheap labour and servants were simply not as readily available as they had been in Britain.

Most colonists, no matter what their background was, needed the cooperation of their neighbours. Some people adapted easily to this new fact of life, but others did not. Many continued to think of Britain, not Upper Canada, as their real home. Educated newcomers were often so interested in what happened in Britain that they even sent their children to England to be educated. They did not see themselves as Canadians, but rather as British people transforming a raw land into part of the British Empire.

The efforts of the ruling classes in both Upper and Lower Canada to become richer and more powerful eventually brought them into conflict with poorer colonists who were attracted to American-style democracy, something that the upper classes feared. To counter this, Britain tried to copy its own society in its Canadian colonies, complete with gentry, large **estates**, and **tenant farmers**. These plans angered immigrants who had hoped to escape the **class system** of their homelands. Unfair land policies and bad government based on privilege would set the stage for violent confrontation between the classes in the colonies.

The **Family Compact** was a small group of upper-class officials who made up the Executive Council of Upper Canada after 1812. They had control over the government, over who got government jobs, and over the spending of tax money.

On a social level, they were snobs. Others were simply not welcome into their clique—you may have seen this kind of behaviour happen in your school. Even aristocrats newly arrived from Britain had a hard time breaking into the Family Compact. All members knew each other, and they were often related. They even dressed alike.

- Why do you think the Family Compact operated as a clique? How does a clique maintain control? Discuss these questions with a classmate.

- Examine the quotation and the image shown here. What do they tell about how the upper class was seen in the past?

- Are there modern-day equivalents to the upper class? Do they still have political power? Explain.

Family Compact the small group of wealthy elite who controlled government in Upper Canada

Château Clique the wealthy elite who controlled Lower Canada, mostly made up of English-speaking merchants

> *They dress well and expensively, and are very particular to have their clothes cut in the newest fashion. Men and women adopt the reigning mode so universally that they look all dressed alike... if green was the prevailing colour, evey lady would adopt it, whether it suited her complexion or not...*
>
> —Susanna Moodie, colonist and author

FIGURE 2–12 Members of the ruling class were known as the Family Compact in Upper Canada and the **Château Clique** in Lower Canada. In this painting, some of the Château Clique watch the launching of the steamship *Royal William*. Compact and Clique members invested in ships and canals with government money. Why do you think they would do so?

The Problem of Land

Almost everybody who came to Upper Canada wanted to own and farm land. Those who chose not to farm worked in industries that supported agriculture, such as selling seed, blacksmithing, and making wagons. But many colonists arrived to find that much of the good land was already owned by **absentee landlords** and **land speculators**. This was not what immigrants had expected. Advertising campaigns led people to believe that they could get good, cheap farmland close to towns and markets.

absentee landlord a person who owns and rents out a property, but does not live in the region

land speculators those who buy property at a low price and sell it at a higher price, usually without spending much of their own money

Those who held the best land in Upper Canada were members of the Family Compact. Other colonists resented the money the Compact members made at the expense of others. Speculators took ownership of large areas of prime land in Upper Canada and kept much of it off the market. The land they did sell went for high prices. Many colonists had no option but to go to remote areas that had inferior land, which was all they could afford. They often suffered great hardship as they struggled to raise crops on poor soil.

Even members of the gentry were duped by land speculators. The problem of land was at the root of the anger people felt toward the Family Compact and the colonial government of Upper Canada. This issue would become one of the major causes of the Rebellions of 1837.

Crown and Clergy Reserves

Crown and clergy reserves were blocks of land set aside to provide income (through sale or rent) for the government and for the Anglican Church—in total, two-sevenths of all the land in Upper Canada. For the most part, these lands stayed uncleared and unoccupied. Since colonists had to build their own roads, no roads existed within the reserves. When travelling, farmers had to journey around these blocks of land—a waste of time and a source of irritation. Moreover, the reserves often tied up prime farmland, causing the value of available land to rise even higher. Remember—to a colonist, land was everything.

FIGURE 2–13 Colonel Thomas Talbot controlled a huge tract of land in Upper Canada. More than 30 000 people lived on his lands, and Talbot interviewed all of them. Those he did not like were refused. Why might he have had that kind of power?

The Role of the British Government

Upper Canada's land problems were mainly the result of attitudes in the British government and the desire to duplicate the English model of land ownership in Canada. England was divided into large estates controlled by aristocrats, so the British government believed that aristocrats would be the best rulers for the colonies. Privileged owners of large blocks of land were also more likely, in the government's view, to maintain strong ties with Britain and its institutions.

This view was contrary to the views of many immigrants, especially those from the United States. They thought that people should succeed on their own merits and efforts, and that many principles of British policy were discriminatory and anti-democratic.

The last thing Britain wanted was to allow colonists to adopt American attitudes and values, which had previously led to the American Revolution and the loss of the Thirteen American Colonies. One upper-class British colonist wrote the following excerpt:

These immigrants, having generally been of the lowest class of society in their respective countries... as soon as they arrive in Canada, begin to assume an appearance of importance... they are [tireless] in acquiring a knowledge of the Rights of Man, The Just Principles of Equality, and The True Nature of Independence and, in a word, of everything which characterizes an American; and they quickly become divested of common manners and common civility... indeed this latter virtuous quality is rather uncommon on this side of the Western Ocean.

Britain's plans for Upper Canada were first implemented in the late 1700s, continuing even after the War of 1812. It was difficult to attract important aristocrats to Upper Canada, but many junior members of such families were interested. Usually, younger sons could not hope to inherit land in Britain, so the promise of their own estate in the colonies was very tempting.

In Upper and Lower Canada the government allowed speculators such as the Canada Land Company to buy huge tracts of land at low prices in order to sell it to the British gentry. By 1815, almost half of the good farmland in Upper Canada was owned by speculators, who were also part of the Family Compact.

At the same time, some First Nations leaders, such as leaders of the Mohawks in Upper Canada, worried that their lands would be sold off by Britain. Other First Nations signed treaties in attempts to secure land for their people. These attempts were not completely successful.

FIGURE 2–14 York (left) was the capital of Upper Canada. It grew rapidly in the 1830s, with new buildings designed by English architects. The same area today is downtown Toronto (right). Use these images to assess continuity and change in downtown Toronto. How are things the same? How are they different?

Land, Colonists, and Aboriginal Peoples

CRITICAL INQUIRY — Cause and Consequence / Significance

British colonies also existed in Asia, Africa, Australia, and New Zealand, where colonists displaced Aboriginal peoples and disrupted or destroyed their cultures. In New Zealand, the Maori resisted British colonizers in the New Zealand Wars, a series of conflicts fought between 1843 and 1872.

In 1840, when New Zealand was made a British colony by royal proclamation, the new governor negotiated a treaty between the Maori and the British government. Called the Treaty of Waitangi, it promised to protect Maori land rights if the Maori became British citizens. Not all Maori liked the treaty, and neither did many colonists, who felt that they had a right to own the land. Conflicts arose when the government began to break the treaty, gradually selling Maori land to colonists.

The Maori, who had settled in New Zealand after travelling from Polynesia centuries before, were numerous, well organized, and used to fighting. However, internal conflict among the Maori ensured that the fighting would last for years. By the end of the wars, the Maori lost huge tracts of land—more than 16 000 km^2

were confiscated by the government as punishment for the "rebellion." Although about half was eventually paid for, the loss of the land deeply affected Maori society. To this day, struggle for land rights and compensation continues in the courts.

DID YOU KNOW...

The Maori see land as being important not only to their survival, but to their identity. This feeling of belonging is called *turangawaewae*, "a place to stand."

FIGURE 2–15 In 2008, demonstrators in New Zealand commemorate the signing of the 1840 Treaty of Waitangi. Give reasons why the government was able to ignore and break this treaty.

WHAT DO YOU THINK?

1. How is the experience of the Maori in New Zealand similar to that of Aboriginal peoples in Canada? How is it different? What were the consequences in both countries?

2. Research the New Zealand Wars or the treatment by colonists of Australia's Aboriginal peoples. Create an organizer on colonialism that shows its goals and its effects on Aboriginal societies.

ACTIVITIES

1. Colonists hoped to find land in Upper Canada. Identify three barriers they faced, ranking them in importance.

2. Identify one or two early signs of conflict in the colonies. Who was involved, and why was there unrest?

The Immigrant Experience

▶ **Why did so many people immigrate to British North America?**

No one who lived in the colonies could have been prepared for the waves of immigrants that arrived after the War of 1812. They settled in both Upper and Lower Canada. Many English-speaking immigrants settled in the Eastern Townships. Elsewhere in Lower Canada, French culture prevailed and life based on the **seigneurial system** continued as it had for generations. Soon, however, the lack of farmland would become a problem.

Most immigrants came from Britain, the United States, and Europe. Attracted by promises, immigrants soon learned the realities involved in leaving home. For many the first rude awakening was the journey across the Atlantic Ocean, which was expensive and dangerous.

Leaving home was highly emotional. Immigrants knew that they would likely never again see those they left behind. Such separation is difficult to imagine today, when it takes only hours to travel by plane between Canada and Europe. At that time, it took more than a month to travel by ship to the colonies—a journey some immigrants did not survive, especially the poorest people, who had to endure passage in the infamous **coffin ships**.

seigneurial system the system of landholding in New France; seigneurs were given estates and responsibilities to settle the land and oversee its administration

coffin ship a death ship; disease and death were common on cargo vessels used to carry passengers at this time

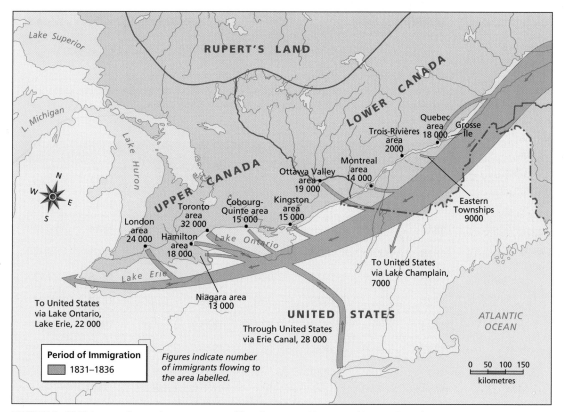

FIGURE 2–16 This map shows the movement of immigrants to Upper and Lower Canada between 1831 and 1836. By 1831, Quebec City was 45 percent English speaking. How do you think the French-speaking population perceived this trend?

Deadly Journeys

Britain's overpopulated cities and countryside provided Canada with many new immigrants. Poor farmers from Ireland and Scotland were motivated by the chance to own land, but few could afford to travel in above-deck cabins on good ships. Instead they travelled in **steerage** in filthy, overcrowded cargo vessels.

The owners of cargo ships realized that they could make money if they converted their ships to carry passengers when they were sailing without cargo. Steerage holds were equipped with bunks, but there were no bathrooms. Poor food, bad hygiene, and crowded conditions made disease inevitable. Cholera, smallpox, and other diseases killed thousands of immigrants. Entire ships would be quarantined when they reached North America. In 1832, half of all immigrants who made it to the colonies were seriously ill.

steerage the area below decks on a ship, used to store cargo

WEB LINK ●
Learn more about the immigrant journey to Upper and Lower Canada on the Pearson Web site.

FIGURE 2–17 Those hopeful for a new life in British North America pay for their passage at a busy emigration agent's office in London. Why might an artist choose to depict this scene? What else might illustrate the immigrant experience of that time?

DID YOU KNOW...
Immigrants were expected to feed themselves during the voyage, which could take weeks. They would starve if they did not bring enough food for the journey.

Immigration into Canada from Great Britain 1815–1850							
1815	680	**1824**	8774	**1833**	28 808	**1842**	54 123
1816	370	**1825**	8741	**1834**	40 060	**1843**	23 518
1817	797	**1826**	12 818	**1835**	15 573	**1844**	22 924
1818	5136	**1827**	12 648	**1836**	34 226	**1845**	31 803
1819	23 534	**1828**	12 084	**1837**	29 844	**1846**	43 439
1820	17 921	**1829**	13 307	**1838**	4577	**1847**	109 680
1821	12 955	**1830**	30 574	**1839**	12 658	**1848**	31 065
1822	16 013	**1831**	58 067	**1840**	32 293	**1849**	41 367
1823	11 355	**1832**	66 339	**1841**	38 164	**1850**	32 961

Cultural Diversity in Colonial Canada

How is history written, and who tells it? The most popular journals and accounts of life in the colonies of British North America were written by relatively well-to-do English-speaking people. However, many colonists in Upper Canada did not consider themselves to be English—they were American, Irish, or Scottish. They brought their language, culture, music, values, and traditions with them.

In Lower Canada, which had previously been the French colony of New France, the population was mostly **Francophone**, with a distinct culture and history. Their desire to remain distinct from English-speaking groups often led to conflict, as you will read in this chapter and later in *Horizons*.

In the past, historians often ignored the achievements and histories of Aboriginal peoples and non-English immigrants. The contributions of women were not discussed, which tells us a great deal about how history is recorded. If the contributions of some groups are highlighted and others are ignored, how accurate can our knowledge of the past be? By detecting this kind of discrimination, we learn to pay more attention to those who have been ignored. We also learn about peoples' values and attitudes in colonial times, especially their belief that Europeans had a duty to "civilize" the world. Ideas like these were taught in schools and churches for many years, even well into the 1950s. The contributions of other cultural groups and of women were neglected, and few history books even acknowledged them.

Francophone a French-speaking person

DID YOU KNOW...

Celtic music, mostly from Scotland and Ireland, is one of the roots of today's popular music, particularly rock and roll and country music.

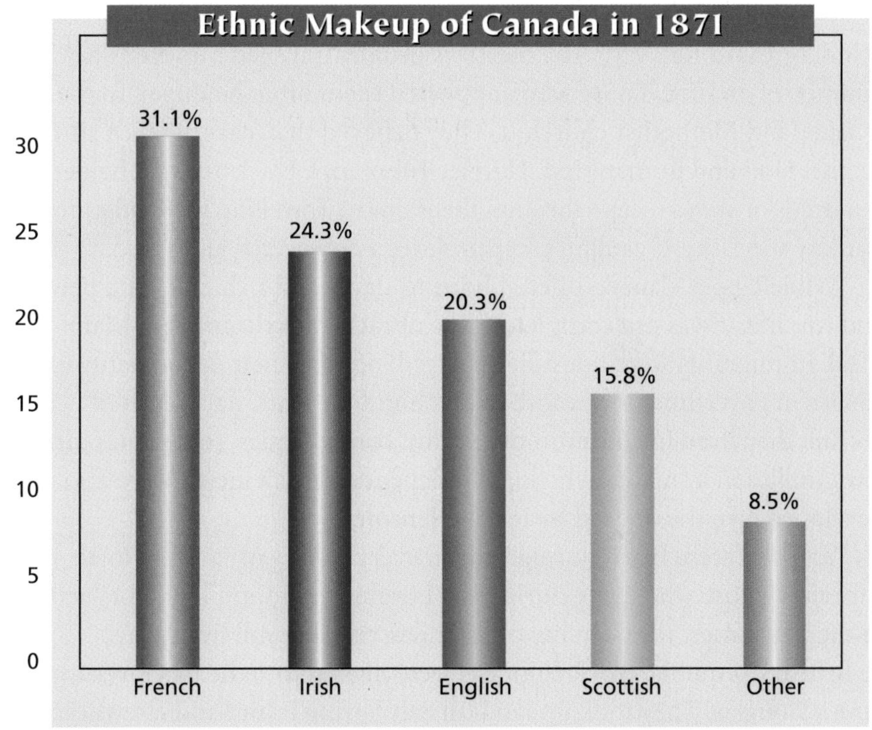

FIGURE 2–18 In this graph, "Other" refers to Black people, Aboriginal peoples, other Europeans, and Asians. What is the majority group shown here? What challenges did minorities face in colonial Canada?

Black Canadians

The deep wound that slavery inflicted on North American society would not be easily healed. Slavery existed in New France from the mid-1600s to the 1700s, and many loyalists brought slaves with them into Canada during the American Revolution. Although slavery was abolished everywhere in the British Empire in 1833, courts in Upper and Lower Canada refused to support slavery well before that date. In fact, slavery came to an end in Upper and Lower Canada long before it did anywhere else in North America. In 1793, Chloe Cooley, an enslaved Black woman, was forcibly taken from Upper Canada to the United States to be sold. Governor John Simcoe added this incident to his arguments against slavery in Upper Canada. By July of that year, an Act was passed to prevent the slave trade in Upper Canada.

One major factor in the abolishment of slavery in Upper and Lower Canada was that most Black Canadians living there were free. In fact, many were refugees from the slave states in America. Also, during the Loyalist wave of immigration, many free Black Americans came to the British colonies as Loyalists and were promised land in return. The Black Militia fought against rebels led by William Lyon Mackenzie in the Rebellions of 1837, when most Black colonists believed that a victory for the rebels would result in American domination of Canada and a return to slavery.

The Underground Railway

Upper Canada became a refuge for Black Americans escaping slavery. They used a network of secret routes and safe houses called the "Underground Railway." The fugitives usually travelled hundreds of kilometres on foot. Those who supported them often belonged to the Quaker and Methodist churches. They believed that slavery was a sin against God and humankind. Harriet Tubman, a Black activist, helped hundreds of slaves escape through the Railway. Travelling the Underground Railway was risky. If caught, escaped slaves were severely punished.

While Upper Canada offered hope to slaves and a chance for a new and free life, it was not completely free of racial discrimination. Many Black immigrants were not fully accepted, nor did their descendants find a place in government for more than a hundred years. As a result of racism, they lived in communities within communities, sometimes just a few families in a small town. Some independent settlements were also developed, like the one led by Josiah Henson.

Yet there were Black immigrants in every colony of British North America. Those who came during the Loyalist migration tended to settle in the Maritimes, where many of their descendants still live today. In British Columbia, Black colonists were invited to settle by Governor James Douglas. They took up land on Salt Spring Island and elsewhere.

TIMELINE
A Partial History of Black Canadians

1606 ● Mathieu Da Costa, Champlain's interpreter, aids in exploration of the east coast

1776– ● Black Loyalists
1783 immigrate to Canada

1793 ● Chloe Cooley is forcibly taken to America to be sold
● Governor Simcoe passes an Act to limit and then abolish slavery in Upper Canada

1812 ● Black Militia fight in the War of 1812

1837 ● Black Militia units fight against rebels

1851 ● The North American Convention of Coloured Freemen is held in Toronto

1853 ● *Provincial Freeman* newspaper is founded in Windsor, Ontario
● Mary Ann Shadd becomes the first woman editor in Canada

FIGURE 2–19 Find out more about Josiah Henson and the Dawn Settlement. What were the contributions of Henson and other Black immigrants to the development of Upper Canada?

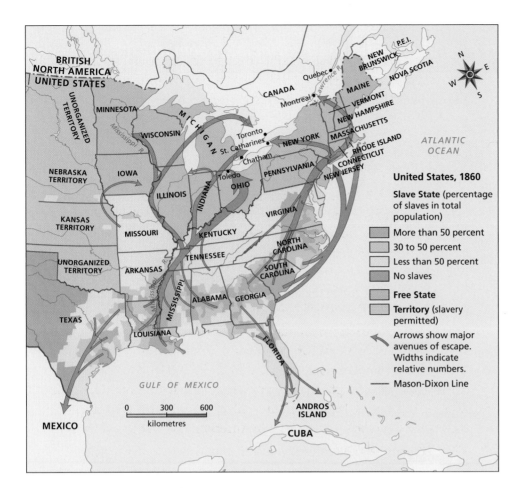

FIGURE 2–20 The Underground Railway was a network of "safe houses" along travel routes that led from the slave-holding American states to the free northern states and to Canada. How do you think slaves might have heard about the Railway?

In the early years, some Black immigrants remembered their lives before slavery and wanted to see their homelands again. Richard Pierpoint, a Loyalist who settled near present-day St. Catharines, Ontario, wrote the following letter. His request was denied, but Pierpoint was granted land. The community he founded would become part of the Underground Railway.

WEB LINK ● · · · · · · · · · · · · · ·

Find out more about the Black Canadian experience on the Pearson Web site.

> *Most humbly showeth,*
>
> *That your Excellency's Petitioner is a native of Bondu in Africa: that at the age of Sixteen Years he was made a Prisoner and sold as a Slave: that he was conveyed to America about the year 1760, and sold to a British officer; that he served his Majesty during the American Revolutionary War in the Corps called Butler's Rangers... That your Excellency's Petitioner is now old and without property; that he finds it difficult to obtain a livelihood by his labour; that he is above all things desirous to return to his native Country; that his Majesty's Government be graciously pleased to grant him any relief; he wishes it might be affording him the means to proceed to England and from thence to a Settlement near the Gambia or Senegal Rivers, from whence he could return to Bondu...*
>
> —York, Upper Canada, July 21, 1821

By the mid-19th century, the interests of Black Canadians were represented by the *Provincial Freeman*, a newspaper founded in Windsor, Ontario, by Samuel Ringgold Ward in 1853. Mary Ann Shadd was its first editor, and the first woman editor of any Canadian newspaper. Like other newspapers then and now, the *Freeman* was supported by advertisements. It often published poetry and featured helpful hints, along with local and international news and opinion.

Mary Ann Shadd was well educated. She had escaped from the United States after a law was passed that could have returned her to slave status.

An advocate of Black education, women's rights, and the **abolition** of slavery, she founded a school before becoming editor of the *Freeman*. Widowed when her children were still small, Shadd also attended law school in the United States, but was denied graduation because she was a woman. She was finally able to practise law at age 60.

- Research Mary Ann Shadd to learn more about her life and accomplishments. Using this evidence, theorize about her historical significance. What "big story" would you say she is a part of? Why?

abolition putting a legal end to slavery

FIGURE 2–21 Mary Ann Shadd's strength of character is evident in this photograph.

> *You have a right to your freedom and to every other privilege connected with it and if you cannot secure these in Virginia or Alabama, by all means make your escape without delay to some other locality in God's wide universe.*
>
> —**Mary Ann Shadd**

Immigrant Women in Upper Canada

> *I had just finished the first stage of my cooking and was about to shift my character from cook to gentlewoman...*
>
> —**Mary O'Brien, a colonist in York, Upper Canada**

WEB LINK • • • • • • • • • • • • • • •
Read about women in Upper Canada and see their diaries on the Pearson Web site.

Women colonists in Upper Canada defined themselves in large part according to their social class, which determined their expectations, values, lifestyle, and beliefs. They tended to think of their own success in terms of the success or failure of their fathers and husbands.

In colonial society, almost all women were married. Because they usually did not own property or work outside the home, widows and unmarried women had to rely on relatives for support and a place to live.

FIGURE 2–22 In colonial society, work came first. This woman is baking bread in an outdoor oven. How might her life compare to yours today?

Divorce did not exist, so choosing the right partner was very important. A good marriage gave a woman status in ways that are difficult to understand today. Even resourceful, educated colonial women such as Susanna Moodie, Catherine Parr Traill, Anna Jameson, and Mary O'Brien seemed preoccupied with the activities of their husbands.

Finding a good marriage prospect for a young woman was so important to families that many social events included matchmaking. Romantic love was deemed less important than friendship and duty, although it was an ideal that many hoped for. Among the upper classes, the match had to be arranged with an "equal" or better. A man might "marry down," but a woman could never do so because a wife took on the status of her husband.

In colonial Canada, too much work had to be done for anyone to be idle. Even upper-class women had much to do. Mary O'Brien had many friends in government and spent time visiting them, but she also took part in running the farm, as she recorded in her diary:

> *It was very busy again until twelve o'clock, first in directing my old Yorkshire man how to cut up a fat pig which was slaughtered last night and then in assisting the old Irishwoman to salt and pack away the same. I value myself on being able to put more in a barrel than anyone else except Southby, though this part of the business is usually the province of a man.*

WEB LINK • • • • • • • • • • • • • • • • • •
Learn more about Mary O'Brien and the society she lived in on the Pearson Web site.

FIGURE 2–23 British immigrant Anne Langton maintained a comfortable lifestyle in Upper Canada. Her letters and journals, *A Gentlewoman in Upper Canada*, were published in 1950. How do you think her way of life compared to that of the woman in Figure 2–22? How are the lives of these women similar to the lives of women today?

Clearing farmland in the forest was hard work, and completion often depended on help from others. This cooperation tended to break down social barriers, which many appreciated. For immigrant women, hard work and long hours were the norm. Division of labour was one sided; men were not expected to look after household tasks, such as cooking, washing, or sewing, but women helped with planting, harvesting, and other farm jobs. All colonial women learned how to preserve food and to make candles and soap.

Colonial women were expected to have large families, especially in farming communities where children were needed to help with chores. For women, childbirth was an additional risk in a society where life expectancy was not high. Medical care was expensive and often hard to obtain. Overcrowding and poor sanitation in small colonial cabins added to the risks.

ACTIVITIES

1. Create a map to show how and why colonists came to Upper Canada in the early 19th century. Consider country of origin, reasons for leaving the "old country," and means of transport.

2. The table on page 58 shows British immigration to Canada from 1815 to 1850. Is there a pattern evident in the data? In which years did the numbers change dramatically? Develop a working theory to explain the changes, making connections between events and their causes. At the end of this chapter, reconsider your theory in light of what you have learned.

3. Imagine that you are a Black immigrant to Upper Canada in 1830. Write a short letter to a family member you left behind. Explain how you feel and describe your experiences during your journey on the Underground Railway. You can use the Web link provided to learn more about the experiences of Black immigrants to Upper Canada.

4. How did increasing immigration affect the lives of Upper Canada's Aboriginal inhabitants? Consider British attitudes about race and class. Create an agenda for a meeting of Aboriginal nations in Upper Canada. What economic, social, and political issues might be discussed?

5. Describe how the roles of men and women were governed by their place in colonial society. Propose what alternatives there might have been for the social structure at that time.

Significance

6. Develop a five-point editorial policy for a colonial newspaper representing the interests of one of the social groups that made up colonial society. Focus your policy on changes your newspaper would want to bring. Explain their significance to colonial society.

Colonial Government and the Need for Reform

▶ **What created the need for government reform in Upper and Lower Canada?**

Government in the colonies of British North America was neither representative nor responsible. A **representative government** is made up of people who are elected by voters to make laws on their behalf. **Responsible governments** can be voted out if elected representatives fail to please a majority of the people who elected them. Democratic governments are both representative and responsible.

Colonial governments, on the other hand, were indirectly run from Britain. This policy placed power in the hands of a small group of wealthy and influential men—the Family Compact, as you read earlier in this chapter. Rule by a small select group is called an **oligarchy**. Although Britain appointed a governor, he ruled according to the wishes of the oligarchy. As an aristocrat and an outsider, the governor had much more in common with the upper class than with most colonists.

The government of Upper Canada had been established in 1791 by the Constitutional Act. This Act divided Upper Canada from Lower Canada and gave it an elected law-making Legislative Assembly, a governor, and two councils. Since all male citizens who owned property could elect Assembly members, the government appeared to be democratic. However, actual power was in the hands of the governor and the two councils he appointed. They could **veto** any laws passed by the Assembly. Since the councils, whose members came from the Family Compact, had different priorities from those of ordinary colonists, they used their veto power often. They could shut down projects, such as building roads. They ignored problems created by land speculation and crown and clergy reserves. Conflict was bound to occur, and it did.

representative government
a government made up of officials elected to office by the people

responsible government
a government subject to the votes of the people

oligarchy rule by a small, select group of people

veto to stop with authority

FIGURE 2–24 This painting shows the first meeting of the Legislative Assembly of Upper Canada. Who is present in this room? Who is not present? How do you think attendance by some groups and not others influenced the actions of the Assembly?

FIGURE 2–25 This diagram shows the structure of Upper Canada's colonial government in 1791 and in 1849, after it had been reformed. What are the similarities and differences between the government in 1849 and Canada's government today?

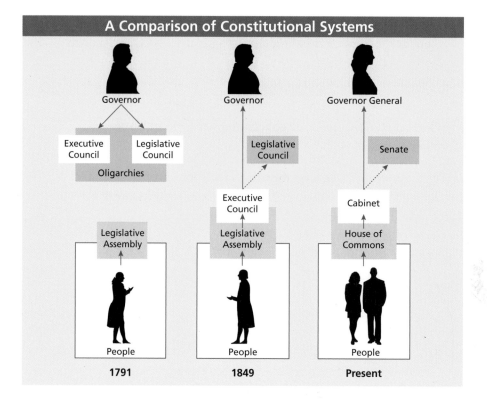

A Comparison of Constitutional Systems

Governor — Executive Council / Legislative Council — Oligarchies — Legislative Assembly — People — **1791**

Governor — Legislative Council — Executive Council — Legislative Assembly — People — **1849**

Governor General — Senate — Cabinet — House of Commons — People — **Present**

WEB LINK

Learn more about the evolution of Canada's federal government on the Pearson Web site.

A List of Grievances in Upper Canada

> *The most extraordinary collection of sturdy beggars, parsons, priests, pensioners, army people, navy people, place-men, bank directors, and stock and land jobbers ever established to operate as a paltry screen to a rotten government...*
>
> —**William Lyon Mackenzie, writing about the Family Compact**

FIGURE 2–26 What aspects of character can you see in this portrait of William Lyon Mackenzie? What message is this image sending to the viewer?

Colonists complained loudly about land and roads. As you have seen, land speculators and absentee landowners overpriced or tied up prime land, while crown and clergy reserves blocked the building of roads that would have connected communities and farmers with their markets.

Most knew that the Family Compact was to blame and did not disguise their anger. When Robert Gourlay, a land agent, surveyed farmers about life in Upper Canada, he was shocked to discover the extent of their discontent with the government and its policies. Gourlay drew up a list of grievances and, with the colonists, a petition demanding change. He was arrested and then sent out of the colony. The government was not interested in listening to complaints, and it was not about to change its policies, no matter what the average farmer thought.

Gourlay's arrest hardened opposition to the Family Compact. Eventually, Gourlay's place as a leader of radical reformers would be taken by another Scot, William Lyon Mackenzie.

Mackenzie had strong political convictions. An argumentative man, he often disagreed with more moderate reformers, such as Egerton Ryerson and Robert Baldwin, who hoped to bring about change through negotiation. Mackenzie took a more aggressive approach. He started a newspaper called the *Colonial Advocate* and published articles that strongly criticized the government and the Family Compact. When angry members of the Compact ransacked his offices and smashed his printing press, he did not back down—he sued. Soon, he was at the centre of a group of people who wanted radical change. He was elected to the Legislative Assembly in 1828 and became one of the most important leaders of the reform movement.

Cross Currents

Political Action and Protest

Canadian elections have changed considerably since the 1830s. You might be shocked by what went on at the polls in Upper Canada. There was no secret ballot, as there is now. Voters—men only—had to openly declare whom they would vote for. Votes could be bought, and sometimes voters were intimidated by the supporters of one candidate or another.

Election reform eliminated most of these problems and made elections more honest and fair. Today Canadian elections are more efficient. Canada even sends representatives to other countries to help monitor elections. However, this does not mean that political protest is a thing of the past. Today Canadians have a legal right—some would say a responsibility—to protest. But how far does that right go?

WHAT DO YOU THINK?

1. "One way to take political action is to exercise your right to vote." Do you agree with this statement? Why or why not? What is the record for voter turnout in Canada today? How does that affect democracy in Canada?

FIGURE 2–27 When voters still had to declare the candidate of their choice, election days often turned into brawls.

FIGURE 2–28 Today, the Charter of Rights and Freedoms guarantees our right to protest and to vote.

One of the most important tasks that historians and geographers do is to ask questions about their subjects. As a student, you are probably more used to answering questions than asking them. However, asking questions is a way to focus your inquiry and to apply critical thinking skills.

As you read this text, continue to ask questions. You can also write them down as you work through the text. The practice of writing your questions can help you understand the material. It can also uncover new perspectives, inspire fresh ideas, and lead you to new and interesting information.

The 5W + H Model

There are many different types of questions. Most questions follow the 5W + H model. Think of approaching a historical event as if you were a reporter. For example, if you were approaching the problem of land in Upper Canada, you might look for answers to these questions:

1. **Who** was affected by land division in Upper Canada?
2. **Where** did it happen most often?
3. **When** did it happen?
4. **Why** did it happen where it did?
5. **How** did it affect Aboriginal peoples?
6. **What** could have been done to address the issue fairly?

Factual and Opinion Questions

Factual questions usually require simple, straightforward answers. Other questions are not so straightforward—they can have more than one answer. They may ask someone to provide expert judgement and can bring out different perspectives on a topic.

In the examples of the 5W + H questions shown here, questions 1 to 3 are factual. Question 4 could have a factual answer, or it could require expert opinions to analyze complicated causes. Questions 5 and 6 could require expert judgement and will also draw out different perspectives.

Research Questions

As you work with this text, you will be asked to research different topics as part of your study. Research questions will help you focus your inquiry and find answers more quickly. (Refer to the Skills Tool Kit, page 368, for more information on the research process.)

There are three types of research questions: causal, comparative, and speculative. To find out more about each type of question, examine the table below.

Question Type	History Examples	Geography Examples
Causal (look for causes of events)	What caused the increase of immigration to Upper and Lower Canada?	What geographic features encouraged newcomers to settle in certain areas?
Comparative (make comparisons)	How does life today compare to life for the colonists and Aboriginal peoples of that time?	What differences can be seen between communities of that time and communities today?
Speculative (infer the answer)	How might life have been different for Aboriginal peoples if immigrants had not come to the colonies?	What type of industry would be best suited for the conditions in the colonies at that time?

Critical Thinking Questions

Asking critical thinking questions can help you see beyond what you are reading on the page. These types of questions will also help you understand different perspectives. You will begin to form your own point of view and defend that position, while discovering what you think and why.

For example, as you study immigration to Upper and Lower Canada after 1814, you may want to ask questions such as these:

1. What is the issue?
2. What are possible solutions?
3. What are the consequences?
4. Whose point of view is expressed? Is there an opposing point of view?
5. What is the significance of this person or event?

APPLY IT

1. Choose a person or topic you have recently studied in this book. Write six questions for which you would like to know the answers.

   a) What types of questions would you find most useful?

   b) Which question do you consider the most important? Explain.

2. Look at the map shown below. Explain how the types of questions discussed above can be used to better understand and analyze the map. Give four examples of questions that can be asked about the map.

3. Use the questions you created in question 1 to do some additional research on the person or topic. Keep a short journal to explain how the questions helped guide your research. Did the questions change as you went along? Why or why not?

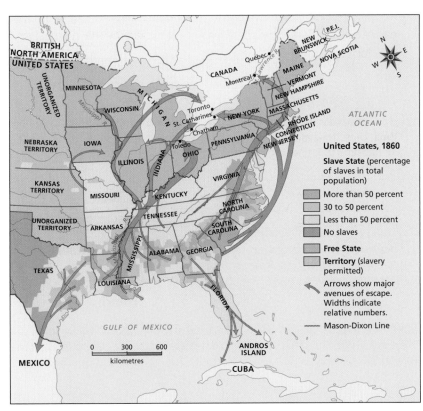

United States, 1860

Slave State (percentage of slaves in total population)
- More than 50 percent
- 30 to 50 percent
- Less than 50 percent
- No slaves

Free State

Territory (slavery permitted)

Arrows show major avenues of escape. Widths indicate relative numbers.

— Mason-Dixon Line

The Situation in Lower Canada

Lower Canada also had serious political problems, which were worsened because the ruling class in Lower Canada was English, and the majority of the population was French. With language and cultural roots dating back to Champlain, French Canadians had never completely adjusted to British rule.

Exposed to the democratic ideals of the French and American Revolutions, and to the democracy of the United States, many French Canadians found British rule without democracy intolerable. Lower Canada's equivalent to the Family Compact, the Château Clique, controlled government and business. It included merchants, such as English brewer and banker John Molson, and former British army officers. The Château Clique was supported by church hierarchy and wealthy French-Canadian landowners. Both had considerable influence in Lower Canada. Even those who were destined to become leaders of the Rebellions of 1837, such as Louis-Joseph Papineau, came from seigneurial families.

The English-speaking minority in Lower Canada still had most of the wealth and power, even though they formed less than one quarter of the population. Many French people believed that the seigneurs and the Church had "sold out" to the English. An attempt to unite Upper and Lower Canada in 1822—and to make English the official language— seemed like an attack on French culture and society.

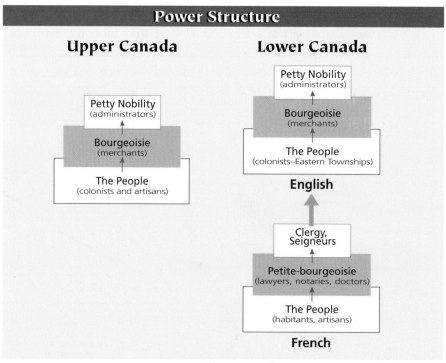

FIGURE 2–29 This chart shows how the population of Lower Canada saw the power structure of their society. Why would the clergy and the seigneurs still have a place in this structure, even after British rule began?

Economic Woes

Lower Canada did not experience the same kinds of land problems that were at the root of discontent in Upper Canada. However, as the population increased, the amount of arable land available was limited, and soil was becoming less fertile. Wheat crops began to fail, and the only alternative was to import wheat from Upper Canada. Unfortunately, this created a huge economic **deficit**. Farmers could only grow enough to feed their families, and the agricultural economy failed.

deficit a situation where there is more spending than income

Many turned to forestry. However, while forestry employed many French Canadians, not everyone had a share in the profits. Also, the new limit on farmland (seigneurs now wanted forests, not farms), created more dissatisfaction among the rural population.

Nationalism

French Canadians mistrusted the English, and feelings of **nationalism** were strengthened by opposition to British rule. These feelings were supported by a need to protect their language and religion. They also feared that Britain might be trying to solve its "French problem" by bringing more English-speaking immigrants into the colony. This trend made the French a minority, weakening them politically and socially.

nationalism devotion to the support of one's culture and nation, sometimes resulting in the promotion of independence

This situation led to powerful feelings of mistrust. In 1832, when immigrant ships brought a cholera epidemic to Lower Canada, many thought that Britain was trying to kill off the French population with disease.

French Canadians were also frustrated by the undemocratic nature of their government. Most citizens were struggling to pay taxes, some of which paid government salaries, and yet received no voice in return. As in Upper Canada, reformers fought to bring change.

FIGURE 2–30 Louis-Joseph Papineau, shown here giving a speech, got many of his ideas about rebellion and political change from revolutions that were happening in Europe. Why would these ideas alarm the British colonial government?

Three Issues for Reform

WEB LINK

For more information about Louis-Joseph Papineau, visit the Pearson Web site.

Three issues—discrimination against the French, lack of representation in government, and taxes—became the focus of reform in Lower Canada. Louis-Joseph Papineau, leader of the radical reformers, was a powerful public speaker. A seigneur and a lawyer, he had originally supported British rule. Like other French Canadians, he had been optimistic that British rule would bring change for the better. When it did not, he joined in the cause for reform. In 1815, he became Speaker for the Legislative Assembly for Lower Canada. He also became leader of the Parti Canadien, which lobbied for reform.

Not all reform leaders were French—Wolfred Nelson, an English doctor, was mayor of Montreal and later became a leader of the rebel Patriotes. Edmund O'Callaghan, the Irish publisher of the radical newspaper, *The Vindicator*, also joined the Patriotes. They all believed that the Assembly should have control of the government's budget, and they wanted a democratic system.

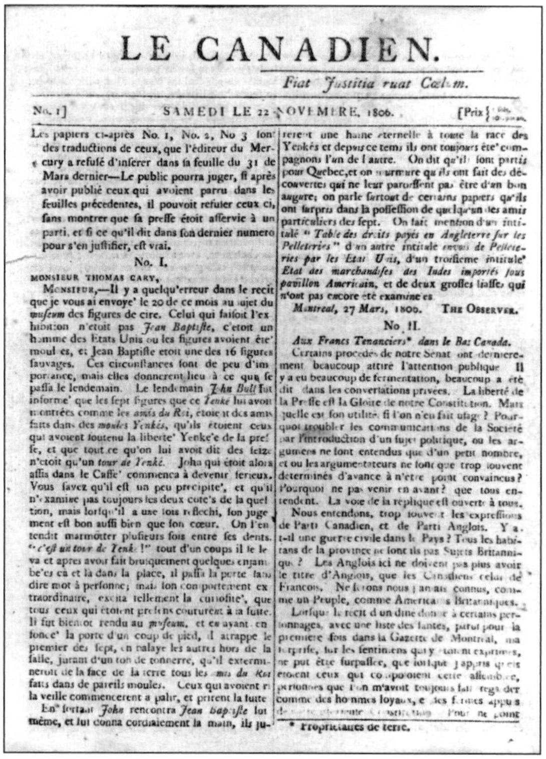
LE CANADIEN.

Fiat Justitia ruat Cœlum.

No. 1] SAMEDI LE 22 NOVEMBRE, 1806. [Prix [illegible]

Les papiers ci-après No. 1, No. 2, No 3 sont des traductions de ceux, que l'éditeur du Mercury a refusé d'inserer dans sa feuille du 31 de Mars dernier—Le public pourra juger, si après avoir publié ceux qui avoient parru dans les feuilles précedentes, il pouvoit refuser ceux ci, sans montrer que sa presse étoit asservie à un parti, et si ce qu'il dit dans son dernier numero pour s'en justifier, est vrai.

No. I.

MONSIEUR THOMAS CARY,

MONSIEUR,—Il y a quelqu'erreur dans le recit que je vous ai envoye' le 20 de ce mois au sujet du *museum* des figures de cire. Celui qui faisoit l'exhibition n'etoit pas *Jean Baptiste*, c'etoit un homme des Etats Unis ou les figures avoient ete' moulees, et Jean Baptiste etoit une des 16 figures sauvages. Ces circonstances sont de peu d'importance, mais elles donnerent lieu à ce qui se passa le lendemain. Le lendemain *John Bull* fut informe' que les sept figures que ce *Yenke* lui avoit montrées comme les *amis du Roi*, étoient des amis faits dans des *moules Yenkés*, qu'ils etoient ceux qui avoient soutenu la liberte' Yenke'e de la presse, et que tout ce qu'on lui avoit dit des seize n'etoit qu'un *tour de Yenké*. John qui étoit alors assis dans le Caffe' commenca à devenir serieux. Vous savez qu'il est un peu precipite', et qu'il n'examine pas toujours les deux cote's de la question, mais lorsqu'il a une fois reflechi, son jugement est bon aussi bien que son cœur. On l'entendit marmotter plusieurs fois entre ses dents. "*c'est un tour de Yenke!*" tout d'un coups il se leva et apres avoir fait brusquement quelques enjambe'es çà et là dans la place, il passa la porte sans dire mot à personne; mais son comportement extraordinaire, excita tellement la curiosite', que tous ceux qui etoient presens coururent à sa suite. Il fut bientot rendu au *museum*, et en ayant enfonce' la porte d'un coup de pied, il attrappe le premier des sept, en balaye les autres hors de la salle, jurant d'un ton de tonnerre, qu'il extermineroit de la face de la terre tous les [illegible] *du Roi* faits dans de pareils moules. Ceux qui avoient r[illegible] la veille commencerent a palir, et prirent la fuite.

En sortant *John* rencontra *Jean Baptiste* lui même, et lui donna cordialement la main, ils jurerent une haine eternelle à toute la race des Yenkés et depuis ce tems ils ont toujours été compagnons l'un de l'autre. On dit qu'ils sont partis pour Quebec, et on murmure qu'ils ont fait des découvertes qui ne leur paroissent pas être d'un bon augure; on parle surtout de certains papiers qu'ils ont surpris dans la possession de quelqu'un des amis particuliers des sept. On fait mention d'un intitulé "*Table des droits payés en Angleterre sur les Pelleteries*" d'un autre intitulé *envois de Pelleteries par les Etats Unis*, d'un troisieme intitule' *Etat des marchandises des Indes importés sous pavillon Americain*, et de deux grosses liasses qui n'ont pas encore été examine'es.

Montreal, 27 Mars, 1806. THE OBSERVER.

No. II.

Aux Francs Tenanciers dans le Bas Canada.*

Certains procedés de notre Sénat ont dernierement beaucoup attiré l'attention publique. Il y a eu beaucoup de fermentation, beaucoup a été dit dans les conversations privées. La liberté de la Presse est la Gloire de notre Constitution. Mais quelle est son utilité, si l'on n'en fait usage? Pourquoi troubler les communications de la Société par l'introduction d'un sujet politique, ou les argumens ne sont entendus que d'un petit nombre, et ou les argumentateurs ne sont que trop souvent determinés d'avance à n'etre point convaincus? Pourquoi ne pas venir en avant? que tous entendent. La voie de la replique est ouverte à tous.

Nous entendons, trop souvent les expressions de Parti Canadien, et de Parti Anglois. Y a-t-il une guerre civile dans le Pays? Tous les habitans de la province ne sont ils pas Sujets Britanniques? Les Anglois ici ne doivent pas plus avoir le titre d'Anglois, que les Canadiens celui de François. Ne serons nous jamais connus, comme un Peuple, comme Americains Britanniques.

Lorsque le recit d'un diné donné à certains personnages, avec une liste des santes, parut pour la premiere fois dans la Gazette de Montreal, ma surprise, sur les sentimens qui y etoient exprimés, ne put être surpassée, que lorsque j'appris quels etoient ceux qui composoient cette assemblée, personnes que l'on m'avoit toujours fait regarder comme des hommes loyaux, et des fermes appuis de [illegible] constitution. Pour ne point

* Proprietaires de terre.

FIGURE 2–31 The reformers openly criticized the government in their newspapers. What could be the advantages and disadvantages of this?

In rival newspapers, and in the Assembly, the Château Clique and the reformers squared off against each other. Britain did little to ease the tension. In 1807, the Colonial Office appointed James Craig as governor of Lower Canada. Craig, who was openly anti-French, immediately arrested those who criticized the government. He also closed *Le Canadien*, a reformer newspaper.

Although French protest brought an end to the Union Proposal of 1822, feelings toward the government grew more hostile. After British soldiers shot protestors in Montreal, Papineau and other reformers submitted "Ninety-Two Resolutions" to the governor. These resolutions were demands for major changes in the colonial government. Lord John Russell, in charge of the Colonial Office in Britain, replied three years later with "Ten Resolutions" that denied the rights of the Assembly. After 30 frustrating years of attempting political reform, Papineau and his Patriotes openly rebelled against the government.

ACTIVITIES

1. In a table or a Venn diagram, summarize the main ideas that eventually led to rebellion in Upper and Lower Canada.
2. List at least three examples that show how the governments of Upper and Lower Canada were not democratic. Rank them according to importance.
3. How did language and cultural differences emphasize discontent in Lower Canada? What could have been done differently? Are there any examples of this divide today?
4. Write an editorial that either supports or defies government reform in Upper or Lower Canada. Suggest an effective solution to the problems being faced.

The Rebellions of 1837

▶ **What were the events and consequences of the Rebellions of 1837?**

Reformers in the colonies of British North America were in constant contact with each other, sharing their views on government, and exchanging possible solutions to problems, even though their goals were sometimes different. For example, language was not an issue in Upper Canada as it was in Lower Canada. Reform leaders realized that change in one colony would set a pattern for change in the other. When it became clear that the government could not be reformed from within, Mackenzie and Papineau prepared for armed rebellion.

Rebellion in Lower Canada

Since Britain did not have enough troops to fight rebels in both colonies, leaders planned to coordinate their revolts. However, while Papineau was busy organizing protests and assemblies, armed rebellion suddenly broke out when a group of Patriotes chose to resist arrest. A branch group of the Patriotes, the more militant *Fils de la Liberté* (Sons of Liberty) soon joined in. This group had been openly parading with their weapons in the streets of Montreal, and were ready for a fight.

Full rebellion began with the attempted arrest of Papineau, who quickly fled to the United States. The battle moved to the countryside. Led by Wolfred Nelson, the Patriotes took Saint-Denis, a village in the Richelieu valley. However, the Patriotes soon lost battles in Saint-Charles and Saint-Eustache. By December of 1837, not even a month after it began, the rebellion was over in Lower Canada.

FIGURE 2–32 During the Battle of Saint-Eustache, 1500 British troops surrounded the Patriotes' stronghold, set fire to it, and shot them as they escaped. This drawing is called *Defeat of the Insurgents*. What point of view do you think the drawing illustrates?

DID YOU KNOW...

National Patriotes Day is now an official holiday in Quebec, replacing Victoria Day.

If the Catholic Church had supported the rebels in Lower Canada, they might have been successful. Instead, church leaders advised their parishioners to remain loyal to Britain. Also, many people were intimidated by the British army, which had been looting and burning villages.

Encouraged by American supporters, some Patriotes prepared for a second rebellion, which broke out in 1838. Although hoping to cut off communication between Montreal and the countryside and create a full rebellion involving French farmers, the rebels were disorganized and poorly supplied. Unfortunately, many of them also took part in looting the countryside, which did not gain them much support. After one small victory, the rebels quickly scattered when approached by a large British division. There were rumours of further uprisings, but Papineau eventually left for exile in France and the United States, and nothing happened.

Although rebellion in Lower Canada had ended, resentment lingered. To this day, feelings about that period remain a factor in Quebec and Canadian politics.

Rebellion in Upper Canada

In Upper Canada, Mackenzie and other radical leaders decided that they wanted American-style democracy as well as closer ties to the United States. This decision distanced them from those colonists who saw the United States as an enemy. Nevertheless, many people, including those of Mary O'Brien's social class, wanted better government.

FIGURE 2–33 Rebels prepare to march on York. Mackenzie spent a great deal of time training farmers to be fighters. Do you think these men would make an effective army? Why or why not?

Moderate reformers found their hopes dashed by Lord Russell's Ten Resolutions, which were direct rejections of their requests for government reform, and by the appointment of Sir Francis Bond Head as lieutenant-governor in 1835. Head allied himself with the Family Compact and misused his power. When the Assembly reprimanded him, he dissolved it, and then went on to win a disputed election by advocating loyalty to Britain. Mackenzie took this defeat of the reform movement as a call to arms.

Mackenzie decided to strike after hearing that Head had sent soldiers to Lower Canada, leaving York relatively defenceless. Mackenzie planned to seize weapons and ammunition, take the governor prisoner, and set up a new government. Although he had little support, he chose to attack. Read what happened in Window on Canada.

The Rebels have lost. In disguise, Mackenzie flees to the United States.

U.S. BORDER
30 MILES

John A. Macdonald fought against the rebels in Upper Canada.

Another Father of Confederation—George-Étienne Cartier—fought with the rebels in Lower Canada.

A First Nations response to the rebellions.

...let the people who like powder & ball fight their own battles...

Meanwhile in Lower Canada...

The time has come to melt our spoons to make bullets.

At Saint-Eustache, *Patriotes* are shot fleeing the burning church.

Without the support of the Church and the people, we can no longer fight.

Wolfred Nelson

Louis-Joseph Papineau

Mackenzie uses an island in the Niagara River as his base and declares himself "President of the Republic of Canada" The British burn his supply ship.

Hundreds of rebels were arrested. Some were transported to penal colonies in Australia.

SAMUEL LOUNT
PETER MATTHEWS

Lount and Matthews were executed, although thousands protested the sentence.

1838: Lord Durham arrives to report on the Rebellions.

He's too radical!

He is too easy on the rebels.

He doesn't like the French.

1871: Susanna Moodie looks back on the Rebellions.

...the blow struck by that injured man, weak as it was, without money, arms, or the necessary munitions of war... gave freedom to Canada and laid the foundation of the excellent constitution that we now enjoy.

Do you think she was right?

Punishing the Rebels

With the rebellions in Upper and Lower Canada now over, captured rebels remained imprisoned. The rebels probably expected little mercy from the government. The British legal code prevailed in the colonies, and it gave the death penalty for **insurrection** against the government. British justice focused on punishment rather than rehabilitation; judges hoped that severe penalties would deter others from committing similar acts. Rebellion against the government was considered a serious crime.

While many were pardoned—including, eventually, Mackenzie and Papineau—some rebel leaders, such as Samuel Lount, were quickly tried and publicly executed by hanging. Others were transported to Tasmania, an island off the coast of Australia. Transportation was a severe punishment in those times. During the long sea voyage to the penal colonies, prisoners were kept in the cramped spaces between decks, chained to the walls. Many died during the journey. Once they arrived, prisoners were used as slave labour, working on plantations, farms, and government projects. Many of Australia's early colonists were transported convicts.

insurrection taking up arms against the government

FIGURE 2–34 Today, a monument in Tasmania honours the exiled rebels from Upper Canada. Why might the exiles be remembered in this way?

FIGURE 2–35 This image shows convicts who have just arrived in Tasmania—they will soon start work as labourers. The Upper Canada rebels would have had the same experience. Do you think their punishment was just and fair?

The Aftermath

The Rebellion in Lower Canada ended French-Canadian hopes for justice and democracy under the British Empire. The Act of Union, which followed in 1840, joined the colony with English-speaking Upper Canada. Radical ideas were purged, and English became the language of government. While union may have resulted in a larger, stronger colony headed in the direction of a more responsible government, it also brought a sense of loss to many of the residents of Lower Canada. Feelings of loss and betrayal meant that political strife in the Canadas was not at an end, as you will read in the next chapter.

Lord Durham's Report

FIGURE 2–36 Lord Durham was a young British aristocrat who made a fortune from coal mines. How do you think the social class of the reformers might have influenced what they proposed? Try linking your answers to the quotes shown on this page.

> *I found two nations warring within a bosom of a single state.*
>
> —Lord Durham, 1838

> *The language, the laws and the character of the North American continent are English, and every other race than the English race is in a state of inferiority. It is in order to release them from this inferiority that I wish to give the Canadians our English character.*
>
> —Lord Durham, 1838

After the Rebellions of 1837, Britain realized that the old ways of governing the colonies had to change and appointed Lord Durham, a reformer in England, as governor-in-chief of the Canadas. Lord Durham remains a controversial figure. Hailed in English Canada as one of the founders of Canadian democratic government, he has the reputation in French Canada of a racist who wanted to erase French culture.

Durham arrived in the spring of 1838 and immediately upset the powerful Family Compact and Château Clique when he let it be known that things would have to change. Though an aristocrat and a very wealthy man, Durham had progressive ideas. He appointed experts in colonial reform—Charles Buller, Thomas Turton, and Edward Gibbon Wakefield—to his staff. He treated captured rebels as leniently as possible and pardoned most of them. Still, without the Councils and the Assembly, Durham was really a **dictator**. He also ignored many British laws.

dictator a ruler with unrestricted power, without any democratic restrictions

Even though the results of Durham's actions were generally beneficial, he made enemies, particularly among those who had lost property during the rebellions. Many complained about him to Britain. Durham realized he had little support—even his pardons were overturned—so he resigned and went home to England to complete his report.

The Durham Report is an important document in Canada's history. It recommended that Upper and Lower Canada be joined together and given responsible government. It also recommended that all the colonies of British North America be brought together.

However, the Durham Report was not well received in Lower Canada. It proposed the same union that had been rejected in 1822. Durham's opinions about the French were well known, and his solution was to force the French to assimilate into English Canada.

Union and Beyond

Durham had correctly reasoned that peace could never be achieved in Canada without some form of democracy. His recommendations for responsible government came as a result of his own liberal ideas, those of his advisors, and those of moderate reformers such as Robert Baldwin and Louis LaFontaine. This responsible government would not represent an independent country, however. Canada would still be a colony of Britain, which would control external affairs and the military.

Durham proposed changes to the structure of the colonial government, including removing the power of the Legislative Council to make laws. Although Durham's proposal became the basis for our present system of government, governors who followed him were either unwilling or unable to make the change. Nevertheless, reform leaders in both colonies continued to press for responsible government.

A United Canada

Durham's union proposal was accepted by the British government and by his successor as governor, Lord Sydenham. Sydenham was instructed by the British government to bring about unity and, in spite of protests in Lower Canada, used the Act of Union of 1840 to make it happen. In 1841, Lower Canada and Upper Canada ceased to exist. They became the Province of Canada, with Montreal as its capital. Union was accomplished without the support or participation of the French. In fact, the Act of Union even declared that all government documents were to be in English. These actions created problems that even today have not been fully resolved.

DID YOU KNOW...

Lord Durham concluded that the real problem in the Canadas was the cultural conflict between the English and the French. As a result, he recommended the assimilation of French culture through union and the immigration of English-speaking people.

Lord Sydenham was business-like and efficient. His job, as he saw it, was to unite the colonies of Upper and Lower Canada and introduce limited self-government, and to do it in ways that did not overly upset reformers or French Canadians.

However, the Act of Union, which Sydenham engineered, was seen as tremendously unfair to French Canada. It made English the language of government, and took seats away from Lower Canada. (Even though the population of Lower Canada was much greater than that of Upper Canada, the two provinces had the same number of representatives in the Legislature.) As well, citizens of Lower Canada were expected to help pay off the debts of Upper Canada.

• Read this extract from Sydenham's Act of Union speech. As you read, imagine that you are a French Canadian in the 1840s. What would you feel as you read or heard the speech? Would anything make you doubt Sydenham's word?

In obedience to the commands of the Queen, I have this day assumed the government of the province of Canada. Upper and Lower Canada, separated for 50 years, are once more re-united and henceforward will form but one province under one administration. Efforts have been… made to deceive the unwary, and especially some of our fellow subjects of French origin, upon this point: to represent these provisions as [harmful]… and to excite opposition which can only prove as mischievous as it must be useless. I rely, however, on these efforts proving unavailing, and I appeal with confidence to the loyalty and good sense of the inhabitants of Lower Canada, of whatever origin, so to use the power which is now again committed to their hands as to justify the trust which our Sovereign and the Imperial Parliament have reposed in them and cordially to join in an endeavour to promote the common interest of the united province…

—Lord Sydenham, 1841

ACTIVITIES

1. Who do you think was responsible for the rebellions? In your opinion, did the rebellions fail? Keep your answer in mind as you continue reading the following chapter.

2. Create a timeline for each of the rebellions in Upper and Lower Canada. Identify key events, and briefly describe the significance of each event you include.

3. Develop a "position paper" for the colonial government regarding the rebellions. Represent the wishes of either the Family Compact or the Château Clique.

4. Explain why Aboriginal peoples tended to avoid involvement with the Rebellions of 1837.

5. Examine Lord Durham's words on page 78. Explain why it would have been difficult for French Canadians to see Durham in a positive light. Do you think Durham's ideas were unusual in his day? Why would Durham not have been more guarded about what he said, as modern politicians often are?

Significance

6. Discuss the significance of the following for both English and French Canadians: a) the Rebellions of 1837, and b) the Act of Union.

Explore the Big Ideas

You have read about life in Canada between 1815 and 1840, and have a better understanding of the impact of immigration on the economy, society, politics, and people of Upper and Lower Canada. You have learned about the interaction between Aboriginal peoples, immigrants, and the government. You have also learned about the Rebellions of 1837, ultimately leading to union and responsible government.

1. What factors shaped Canada at this time? Use an organizer like the one below to show your thoughts on this question. Consider main ideas such as geography, immigration, Aboriginal peoples, social class, the actions of individuals, and changes in government. Decide if certain factors can be grouped together, include supporting details, and explain your organization of the information.

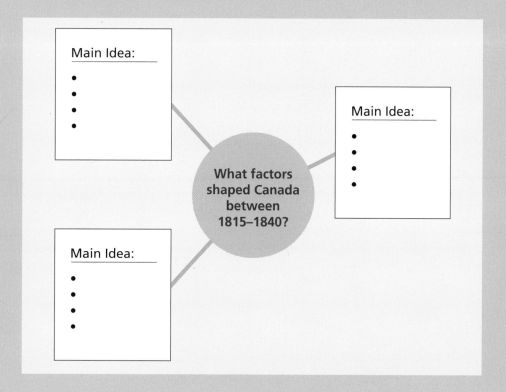

Main Idea: _____
-
-
-
-

What factors shaped Canada between 1815–1840?

Main Idea: _____
-
-
-

Main Idea: _____
-
-
-
-

2. What was life like for people living in colonial Canada? Research at least two primary sources to find information about life for men or women in Upper or Lower Canada. Create a journal entry describing a day in that person's life.

3. Why would anyone decide to go against the British government, the most powerful empire of that time? Create a chart to show the events and players of the rebellions in both Upper and Lower Canada. How were the rebellions similar? What were the differences? Indicate what you think was the most important factor that led to the rebellions and explain your thinking.

4. Debate the following statement: "Based on its origins, Canada does not deserve a reputation as a 'peaceful country.'"

The debate should be properly organized with speakers for and against the proposal, rebuttals, and all other elements of formal debate.

5. Choose an event listed in one of the timelines in this chapter. Explain in a few short sentences both the causes and the consequences of the event.

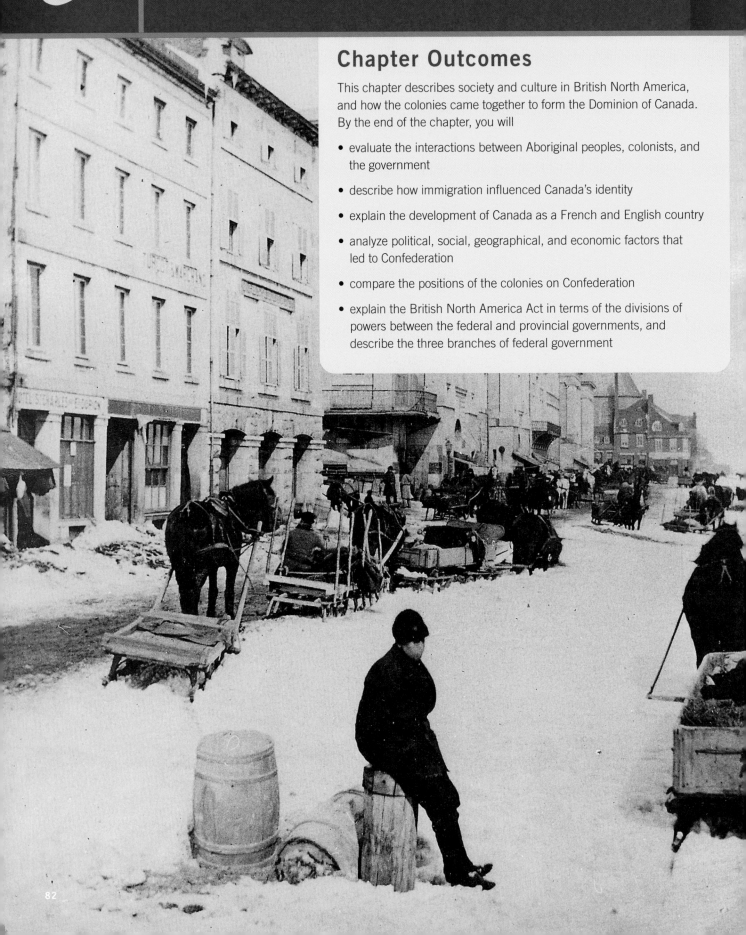

3 Building a Nation

Chapter Outcomes

This chapter describes society and culture in British North America, and how the colonies came together to form the Dominion of Canada. By the end of the chapter, you will

- evaluate the interactions between Aboriginal peoples, colonists, and the government

- describe how immigration influenced Canada's identity

- explain the development of Canada as a French and English country

- analyze political, social, geographical, and economic factors that led to Confederation

- compare the positions of the colonies on Confederation

- explain the British North America Act in terms of the divisions of powers between the federal and provincial governments, and describe the three branches of federal government

Significance
Patterns and Change
Judgements
CRITICAL INQUIRY
Evidence
Cause and Consequence
Perspectives

What were the social, economic, and geographical factors behind the struggle to unify the colonies in Confederation?

Many people in the colonies of British North America were deeply divided on the issue of union. National unity and the gains that could come with it conflicted with fears of loss—loss of language, culture, identity, and freedom. These issues were especially important to those who were not members of the British ruling class.

Key Terms

Victorian	Rebellion Losses Bill
reserves	federation
assimilate	Manifest Destiny
enfranchisement	coalition
infrastructure	representation by
mercantilism	population
	constitution

The image of Montreal's Bonsecours Market shown on the opposite page was taken in 1875, less than ten years after Confederation. Imagine being one of the people in the marketplace. How might you interpret the Confederation ball, depicted above? Now look at both images in light of the quotation below. What can you learn about some of the difficulties in creating national unity in Canada?

[Those who support Confederation] are a few ambitious individuals, who feel our legislature too small for their capacity, and its rewards too [small] for their acceptance...

—*Halifax Citizen*, November 1864

The Colonies in the Reign of Queen Victoria

Victorian of or pertaining to the reign of Queen Victoria; also someone who shares the values of that period

TIMELINE

1837 • Rebellions in Upper and Lower Canada

1838 • Lord Durham's report is issued

1841 • United Province of Canada is formed

1849 • Lord Elgin signs the Rebellion Losses Bill
• Crown Colony of Vancouver Island is created

1854 • Reciprocity Treaty is signed with the U.S.

1857 • Gradual Civilization Act is passed

1858 • Colony of British Columbia is created

1864 • Great Coalition is formed
• Charlottetown Conference takes place
• Quebec Conference is held

1865 • American Civil War ends

1866 • The London Conference is held

1867 • Canada becomes a Dominion

▶ **What effects would an increase in British immigration have on society, culture, and the people of the Canadian colonies?**

After the Rebellions of 1837 ended, there was a new rush of immigrants to Upper and Lower Canada. Most were from the British Isles, and the population of English-speakers soon outnumbered the French. When the colonies of Upper and Lower Canada were joined together as the Province of Canada in 1841, this imbalance became even more pronounced and alarming for the French. English colonists of all classes still considered themselves to be British and happily followed the views, styles, activities, and prejudices of the **Victorians** in England.

Queen Victoria reigned over the British Empire for more than 60 years, from 1837 to 1901. Britain was the world's superpower, and its empire was vast. The Victorians grew increasingly proud of their empire, to which the British North American colonies belonged. No one suggested that the colonies should be a multicultural society—quite the contrary, in fact.

FIGURE 3–1 In the mid-1800s, Toronto became a city with businesses, banks, and busy streets. Large buildings were constructed, such as Toronto's Crystal Palace (1858), which was used as an exhibition space. This expensive building copied London's Crystal Palace, which was built in 1851. How would feelings for the "mother country" influence those governing the colonies?

Victorians Rich and Poor

In the mid-1800s, quality of life often depended on the social class to which a person belonged. With money, education, and social standing, life was comfortable and secure. With no income tax, it was possible to make a lot of money and keep it. The very rich, who lived in splendid houses with many servants, grew even richer after 1840. Most wealthy people were considered **middle class**—not aristocrats, but still very wealthy. Thousands of others, however, lived in poverty in tiny one- or two-room houses or apartments.

middle class at the time, a social class that had very wealthy members without aristocratic heritage

In general, workers were not paid well and worked long hours. Work weeks were usually six days long, and there were no vacations. At that time, society had no employment insurance, no welfare, and no universal health care. In fact, there was no government assistance as we know it today, although churches and relatives provided help when they could. Everyone in a family was expected to work.

Into this social structure came many new immigrants to Canada. Coming from Ireland and Scotland, many had been forced to leave their homelands. Most were desperately poor and had little education. Some went to Toronto or to other growing towns, where they looked for work as manual labourers; others rented farmland in return for part of the harvest. Some immigrants could only afford to homestead cheap land, usually where the soil was thin and rocky. While many immigrants had opportunities in British North America that they did not have in Britain or Europe, life was still hard and often disappointing.

Religion was an important part of life. Christianity was the official religion, encompassing different faiths. Irish immigrants were often Catholic, while most Scots were Presbyterians. Upper- and middle-class people were usually members of the Anglican church, which was the official church of Upper Canada. Towns usually had at least one Anglican,

FIGURE 3–2 This illustration from December 1875 shows wealthy people visiting the poor. Winter was the hardest time of year for those who could not afford heating. What obstacles did these residents face in trying to make a better life?

FIGURE 3–3 St. James Cathedral was built in Toronto between 1850 and 1874. How does this church reflect the social standing of its members?

Presbyterian, Methodist, and Catholic church. The first Jewish synagogue in Canada was founded in 1768 in Montreal, but the Jewish population of British North America remained small until after Confederation.

Almost everybody went to church. Churches and their congregations were communities within communities, putting on social events, running charities, and sponsoring missionaries. Church leaders made decisions about education and schools, as well as community matters—even telling people whom to vote for. People felt that giving money to their church was a responsibility, but being active in the church also provided prosperous people with opportunities to show off their wealth.

Victorian Attitudes and Values

During her reign, Queen Victoria's tastes, values, and behaviour set the standard in the British Empire. Victorians stressed morals, hard work, and personal success. They were sure of themselves and had few doubts about their values and beliefs.

Victorians placed a high value on modesty, seriousness, and duty. Nevertheless, the Victorian age was an optimistic one. The British Empire grew larger and stronger, and Britain's navy was almost beyond challenge. Discoveries in science, technology, and medicine were made almost daily.

Canadian newspapers were often filled with accounts of British triumphs. Many Canadians enjoyed reading these stories because they still thought of themselves as British.

Victorians were conscious of social class and status, even in the colonies. Occupation and social standing were determined by a person's family background, particularly by what one's father did for a living. Although many Europeans had immigrated to North America to escape the class system, they found no shortage of snobbery when they arrived.

sentimentalize to appeal to emotion rather than reason

FIGURE 3–4 After 1840, the styles of homes in Canada West usually copied English and American fashions. What made it possible for the rich to build such large, lavish homes, such as this one on Jarvis Street in Toronto, built in 1867? What purpose would such a mansion serve?

FIGURE 3–5 It is easy to **sentimentalize** life in Victorian Canada, but for many it was very hard. Scan this picture and make note of your observations about working conditions. How does it compare to the image to the left?

In fact, many immigrants would not have been invited to the Victorian homes of upper- and middle-class Canadians.

Victorians believed that people could be easily tempted to stray from "proper" behaviour, and they worried a lot about sin. However, they were also **materialistic** and enjoyed spending money on clothes and accessories, homes, and furniture. The Victorian preoccupation with status extended to the style of church buildings, which were often the largest and most important buildings in town, and even to elaborate funerals and gravestones.

materialistic valuing material possessions and physical comfort above all else

Get to the Source • An Age of Contradiction

This illustration shows Queen Victoria near the end of her reign. Look carefully at the picture. Note the following: desperate people reach out for Victoria's attention. The Queen pauses. What will she do?

- What do you see? Is this picture critical or supportive of Queen Victoria? How might a Victorian audience interpret the image?

- Look at the left side of the image.

  1. What are the British troops doing?

  2. Who might the poor people be? Why might they be trying to get the Queen's attention? What does the illustrator imply about their request?

- Look at the right side of the image.

  1. What is the social class of the people shown here?

  2. How do the colours of this side of the image compare with the colours of the other side?

  3. What do you think the illustrator is suggesting about the Queen's opinion of her people?

FIGURE 3–6 An illustration of Queen Victoria at one of her jubilees, which was an official celebration of her reign.

A New Age of Science and Medicine

British North America benefited from the growth of science and technology during the Victorian era. After 1850, life changed dramatically, particularly in the cities, as scientists and inventors made breakthrough after breakthrough. Exciting discoveries were reported in newspapers, which sometimes mixed fact and fiction. While science excited people, it also frightened them—usually people did not have reliable information or up-to-date news reports on what was happening.

Discoveries came so fast, and many ideas were so new that lack of understanding was common. For example, many people died after receiving medical treatment simply because nobody knew anything about bacteria and infection. When bacteria were first studied under microscopes in the 1870s, some scientists thought they were insect eggs. Although pioneering work on vaccinations had been done at the end of the 18th century, it wasn't until the mid-1800s that ordinary people could get vaccinations against terrible diseases such as smallpox.

Nevertheless, people hoped that scientific discoveries would be made to prevent and treat serious diseases. Smallpox was common, as was cholera, typhoid fever, scarlet fever, influenza, and tuberculosis. These diseases and others continued to kill millions of people into the 19th and 20th centuries, particularly children and poor people. Since doctors knew almost nothing about hygiene, they did not think that sterilizing operating theatres or medical instruments was necessary. They sometimes even smoked during surgery. So much bacteria could be introduced into a patient's body during surgery that it is astonishing that some people survived it.

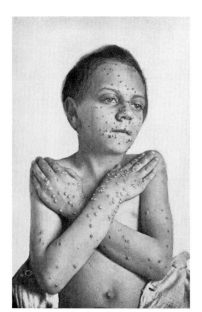

FIGURE 3–7 Smallpox, once one of the most devastating human diseases, was eradicated worldwide by 1980. Why do you think samples of the virus are still kept in two laboratories today?

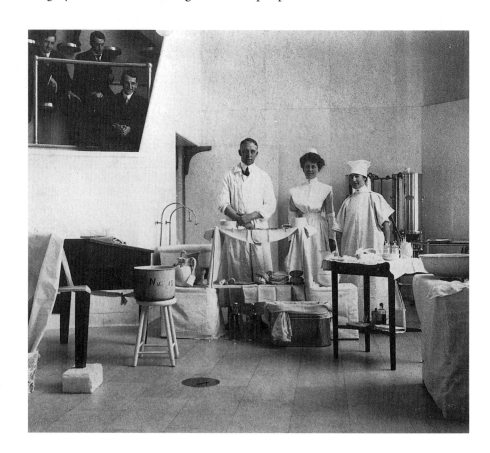

FIGURE 3–8 This early Canadian operating room—complete with a viewing gallery—was modern in its time, but it shows why many people thought that going into a hospital was risky. Make a list of things shown here that you would not expect to see in a modern operating room.

A breakthrough came in 1857 when a French scientist, Louis Pasteur, theorized that bacteria caused many illnesses, including anthrax, cholera, and rabies. He used carbolic acid as an **antiseptic** and vaccinated people and animals. Incidentally, Louis Pasteur did not become wealthy because of his discoveries, as some medical researchers do today. He chose instead to live a simple, generous life, and found satisfaction in his work. The process of pasteurization—heating a food or liquid, such as milk, to kill bacteria—is named after him.

antiseptic something that kills and prevents the spread of bacteria

Zoom In ⊘ Breaking Barriers: Emily Stowe

 **Patterns and Change**

Emily Stowe, a Canadian woman, was one of the first female doctors in the British Empire. This was a remarkable achievement for the time because many Victorians believed that women should not have legal rights. Until 1884, married women could not own property or have bank accounts. In line with that thinking, education and job training for women were considered useless.

Emily Stowe was born in 1831. Her Quaker parents gave her a good education and, at age 16, she became a schoolteacher—one of the few jobs open to women—and Canada's first female principal at 23. When her husband became ill with tuberculosis, she decided to become a doctor. In Canada, medical schools did not accept women, so Stowe went to New

York Medical College for Women and graduated in 1867. Even then, she could not legally practise in Canada because Canadian doctors had to have Canadian training. Stowe practised medicine illegally until she was granted a licence in 1880. She also worked hard for women rights, including the right to vote. She founded the Toronto Women's Literary Club and helped establish the Toronto Women's Medical College. She died in 1903.

• Given what you know about the time period and Emily Stowe's accomplishments, how would you describe her character?

• Do women still face challenges in modern Canadian society? What are they?

• Are there any modern examples equivalent to Stowe's struggle to become a doctor?

FIGURE 3–9 Emily Stowe became a physician in 1867 after studying in the United States. Many Victorians believed that women should not enter the professions and that upper-class women should not even work outside the home.

Leisure and Technology

Victorian Canadians liked to be entertained, so they attended concerts, fairs, circuses, and shows. In the country, people went to barn raisings, quilting bees, and dances. Books and magazines were also very popular. Blood sports, such as bear baiting, always had an audience. Other sports soon became popular—swimming for fun caught on in Canada after first

FIGURE 3–10 Bare-knuckle boxing was popular in the Victorian period. The best fighters were celebrities like mixed martial arts fighters and boxers today. Why do you think such sports are still popular? What does this pattern tell us about society?

huckster a person who usually uses aggressive selling tactics to make a profit

whist a card game for four players divided into two teams

leisure travel travelling just for the fun of it, to get away for a holiday

infrastructure the roads, canals, sewers, public services, and transportation networks that allow a community to function

becoming fashionable in France. Bare-knuckle boxing matches were also well attended; sometimes boxers fought in bouts that lasted more than a hundred rounds.

Canadians also attended medicine shows. In these shows, **hucksters** sold mixtures that were supposed to cure almost anything. Most brews were harmless, but sometimes they were made from poisonous ingredients. At that time, the government did not regulate medicine.

With no television, radio, movies, CDs, or downloads, people relied on more personal ways to entertain themselves, particularly on dark winter evenings. They played music, held dances, did crafts, and played parlour games. Card games like **whist** were very popular, as well as checkers and chess. Some games crossed cultural boundaries. For example, lacrosse, a sport of Algonquin origin, was adopted by organized clubs in Lower and Upper Canada as early as 1856.

Leisure travel became more widespread after the mid-1800s, made possible by better roads and technology. Even transatlantic travel was easier, as steam engines shortened travel time to only a week or two. Wealthy travellers often went on tours to Europe.

Changing Technology

The steam locomotive was one of the most important new technologies of the Victorian age. Imagine how thrilling it would have been to suddenly make trips that earlier would have seemed impossible. Train tickets were also relatively cheap, and soon people of all classes could travel by train.

Railways and steamships became part of Canada's **infrastructure**—the network of transportation routes and services that supports the life and economy of a country. Canada's first railway, the Champlain and Saint Lawrence Railroad, was 40 km long and connected Montreal to Saint Jean. The train travelled at almost 48 km per hour, an amazing speed in an age of horse-drawn wagons.

Like all successful technologies, trains improved rapidly. New lines were built, train cars were more comfortable, and speeds increased to 80 km an hour. By 1865, rail lines ran from Windsor to Halifax, with branch lines to other cities. They even connected with American railways to become part of a greater North American system. Expansion meant access to new markets and ice-free ports, and a boost to the Canadian economy. Railways also became a vital part of the plan for Confederation, as you will see later in this chapter.

Railways kept strict timetables to keep goods and people moving, and to prevent trains from colliding on the same length of track. For this reason, even today, a train can be late but rarely early.

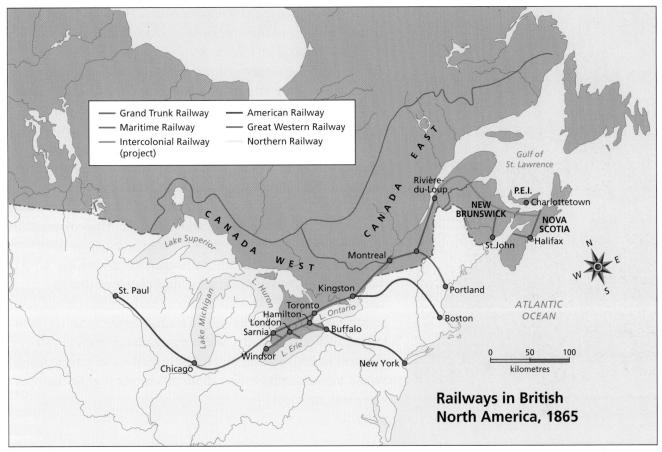

FIGURE 3–11 Canada entered the railway age after 1837. By the end of the 19th century, rail lines linked major cities and connected with railway systems in the United States. Today, many rail lines have been abandoned. Compare this map with a modern road map of Canada. What took the place of trains? Can you make an argument for bringing back rail transportation?

Victorian Media: The Newspaper

Canada's first newspaper, *The Halifax Gazette*, started in 1752. By the mid-1800s, every town in Canada had at least one newspaper—sometimes several. Some newspapers were published every day of the week, either in the morning or evening. Others were published weekly, especially in small towns. The newspaper was the media in Victorian Canada. Politicians used them to promote their ideas, as you saw with Mackenzie and his calls for reform. Businesses used them to sell products, and advertising quickly became a way for newspapers to make money. Canadians loved their newspapers, which became their principal source of news and information.

Victorian Canadian newspapers were much like today's papers, but with important differences. They had no sports section, for example, because professional sports, other than boxing and horse racing, did not really exist. Aside from political cartoons, Victorian newspapers had no comics. There were no horoscopes, advice columns, or technology sections. There were few non-news or special interest features, except for "helpful hints." By today's standards, newspapers had limited sources of information. So how did they attract readers?

FIGURE 3–12 The *Canadian Illustrated News* was a weekly magazine published in Montreal from 1869 to 1883. This illustration shows a woman, who represents Canada, welcoming new immigrants. Why were illustrations an important part of newspapers at this time?

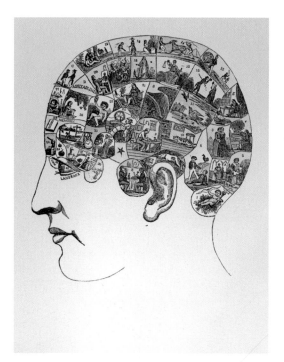

FIGURE 3–13 Can the bumps on a person's head hold the secrets to the personality within? This Victorian drawing demonstrates a fad science of the day— phrenology. What does this notion tell us about Victorian beliefs and ideas?

Victorian newspapers sensationalized the news. They were usually biased and sometimes not very truthful.

They also focused on local news, which people liked. Court reports with the names, crimes, sentences, and fines of the offender made for interesting reading. In one paper, for example, Mary Morrison was fined 25 cents for using "abusive language."

Self-help articles, recipes, and helpful hints were regular features aimed at women. Cures and medicines were also promoted, along with strange sciences. Phrenology, for example, was very popular. Phrenologists claimed to be able to tell a person's personality and future based on a study of bumps on the head.

Today, Victorian Canadian newspapers may seem quaint; however, they help us understand how people of the era thought and lived and what people considered important, just as our present-day media will do for future generations. Newspapers also played a role in the campaign for Confederation, offering support or criticism and giving people in the colonies information about the decisions politicians were making.

ACTIVITIES

1. Write a conversation or a short one-scene play that involves people from different social classes in Victorian Canada. Show what social class means and how it affects what people do and think. How did Victorian views of social class influence the identity of Canadians?

2. Research medical discoveries of the Victorian age, and rank the discoveries in terms of importance. Compare them with present discoveries.

3. Describe how Canada's infrastructure developed after 1830. What aspects of life were affected by this development?

4. Can you think of any fad sciences that are popular today? How are they made popular?

Patterns and Change

5. Create a PMI Chart (Plus/Minus/Interesting) of Victorian values and sensibilities. As you complete your chart, consider the positive aspects of your chosen values and the negative aspects. Then, include other considerations that you find neither positive nor negative. Explain why you find them interesting.

6. a) Are there Victorian values still evident today? Explain with examples.

   b) If Queen Victoria was the main influence of Victorian values, who or what do you think influences our values today?

   c) In this chapter, you saw some contradictions in Victorian values.
   Are there similar contradictions in values today? Explain.

Victorian Times and Aboriginal Peoples

▶ **How would immigration and government policies at this time affect the Aboriginal peoples of British North America?**

Immigration had an enormous impact on Aboriginal peoples. Pushed aside to make room for colonial settlement, First Nations in **the Canadas** were forced to live on **reserves**, land that was only a fraction of their former traditional territories. They suffered greatly from disease, poverty, and other social problems. Aboriginal culture, which was based on a close relationship with the land, was hard to preserve under such conditions. Adapting to European ways often became a matter of survival.

For some Aboriginal communities, traditional ways of life were based on hunting and fishing instead of agriculture, and they lived in small family groups. The government usually tried to force them to settle and farm, a severe change in lifestyle that many resisted. Others, such as the Mohawks along the Grand River, were more successful in dealing with the government. They lived in larger communities, had farmed for centuries, and had a long-standing, internal government. They also had a long history of negotiating with colonial officials, merchants, and land speculators. However, this relationship changed as time and the pressures of colonial development continued.

Many Aboriginal leaders came to realize they were no longer being treated as allies by the colonial governments. A leader of the Anishinabé wrote this letter to the governor:

FIGURE 3–14 This studio portrait from about 1850 shows Maungua-daus, also known as George Henry, a leader of the Anishinabé. He is posing in a costume he wore during public appearances. What did Henry or the photographer hope to project by showing him in traditional dress, which was no longer worn in everyday life?

> *...you have become a great people, whilst we have melted away like snow beneath an April sun; our strength is wasted, our countless warriors dead, our forests laid low; you have hounded us from every place as with a wand, you have swept away all our pleasant land, and like some giant foe you tell us "willing or unwilling, you must now go from amid these rocks and wastes..."*
>
> —Little Pine, 1849

the Canadas Canada East and Canada West, within the Province of Canada

reserves land set aside by governments for the use of First Nations

WEB LINK • • • • • • • • • • • • • •
For more information about Victorian times and Aboriginal peoples, visit the Pearson Web site.

As colonial settlement moved into Aboriginal territories, land buyers pressured the government to sell them the best land. Sometimes, immigrants and local governments challenged the terms of established treaties, forcing Aboriginal leaders to defend what had already been agreed to.

FIGURE 3–15 These two maps show settlement patterns. The first shows Anishinabé reserves in the mid-1800s, where the Anishinabé were sent to live by the government. The second map shows the location of towns and cities at that time. What conclusions can you draw by comparing these two maps?

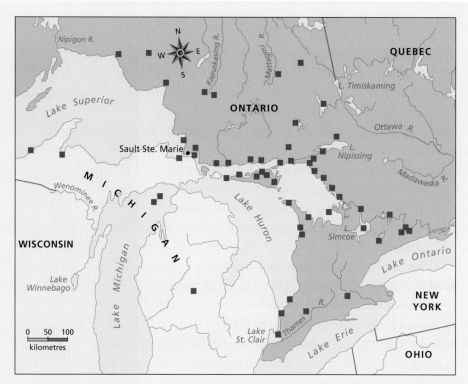

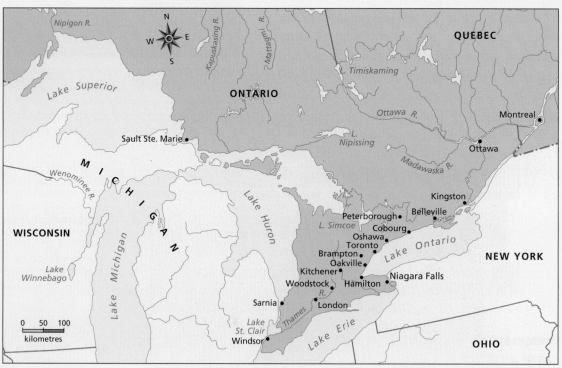

The government often persuaded **bands** to rent out good farmland on reserves, and then would sell the rights to immigrants. Since some bands were struggling financially, taking the money seemed to be one of the few options available to them. As a result, large sections of territory guaranteed by treaty were lost, often permanently.

In 1857, the government of the Province of Canada passed the Gradual Civilization Act, which was meant to **assimilate** Aboriginal peoples by making them citizens of Britain. If they were citizens of Britain, they would have none of the treaty rights or protected status of First Nations, and the government would be able to ignore agreements made in the past. **Enfranchisement** within the British Empire was presented by the government as a privilege, but for Aboriginal peoples this was just another way to make them more like Europeans. This legislation was the beginning of what would become the Indian Act, which was passed in 1876.

Interactions between the government of the time and Aboriginal peoples were coloured by the general feeling among the Victorians that Aboriginal peoples were uncivilized and childlike—so-called noble savages. Today, this attitude is considered condescending and insulting, but to the British Empire, Aboriginal peoples were "wild children." This attitude influenced both popular culture and government legislation, as you will read in the following pages and in later chapters of *Horizons*.

In spite of tremendous pressure to change and assimilate into European society, Aboriginal culture was not entirely lost. **Elders** kept alive many traditions and oral histories that continue to this day.

band an Aboriginal community recognized by the government as an administrative unit

assimilate to join another culture and to give up one's own language and traditions

enfranchisement granting someone the rights and protection of a citizen of a particular country

Elders people respected for their wisdom and understanding of traditional knowledge

FIGURE 3–16 In 2001, outside the Supreme Court of Canada, a protestor listens to speeches at a protest rally for Aboriginal land rights. The process of assimilation of Aboriginal peoples included taking their lands. Are there other examples of assimilation in Canadian history? What is being done about it today?

In the 1930s, a man who called himself "Grey Owl" became one of the most popular celebrities in Canadian history. His books, films, and lectures were influential in early efforts to preserve the Canadian wilderness. The world knew him as an Apache, yet his identity as Grey Owl was a fraud. In fact, he was only pretending to be Aboriginal, and he became famous by taking advantage of a stereotype.

The growing interest about Aboriginal peoples and their ways of life had led to the stereotype of the "noble savage." Aboriginal peoples were considered "noble" for their spirituality, non-materialism, and closeness to nature. They were considered "savage" for their hunter-gatherer lifestyle and their lack of modern technology or Christianity.

Interest in Aboriginal lifestyles became a fad, and for some people it was an obsession. Grey Owl's real name was Archibald Belaney, and he was born in England in 1888. As a boy, he developed a rich fantasy life based on North American Aboriginal culture. At 17, he left England for Canada, where he befriended an Anishinabé family, learning their language and how to trap and live in the wild.

In 1925, he married an Iroquois woman named Anahareo. She convinced him to give up trapping and to protect wild animals instead. Grey Owl became a bestselling author. He also made films. Once he became a public figure, Grey Owl's fraud was complete. He told everyone he was the son of an Apache, and appeared dressed in Aboriginal clothing.

Grey Owl became one of the most famous Canadians of his day. Although his relatives, and almost all of the Aboriginal people he met, knew the truth, he was not exposed until after his death in 1938. Today, he is still considered a powerful early voice for conservation—his love of nature was genuine.

When Grey Owl was famous, he was a larger-than-life example of the romantic stereotype of Aboriginal peoples. This stereotype has appeared in countless Hollywood films and TV shows. In real life, Grey Owl was a bigamist who drank too much and someone who dyed his hair and skin. However, if he had not become famous, would his calls for conservation have been heard? Was Grey Owl a hero or a villain?

FIGURE 3–17 Archie Belaney as a boy in England. Compare this image with how he presented himself as "Grey Owl" below.

WEB LINK

Learn more about Grey Owl on the Pearson Web site.

WHAT DO YOU THINK?

1. Grey Owl is usually seen as a hero, and has even been the subject of a Hollywood movie starring Pierce Brosnan. Does his positive image regarding his support for conservation excuse him, even though he committed a huge hoax? Did the end justify the means? Write your opinion in a letter to the editor.

Many people believe that the act of settling First Nations on reserves and forcing them to adopt European ways was **cultural genocide**. Colonial government policy was to assimilate Aboriginal peoples, often by relocating them away from their original homes, as Lieutenant-Governor Colborne's policy shows (right).

cultural genocide the act of completely destroying the culture of a people

1st. To collect the Indians in considerable numbers, and settle them in villages with a due portion of land for their cultivation and support.

2nd. To make such provision for their religious improvement, education and instruction in husbandry [farming]…

3rd. To afford them such assistance in building houses; rations; and… such seed and their agricultural implements as may be necessary…

—Sir John Colborne, Lieutenant–Governor, 1828

• Many Aboriginal cultures were based on small groups who travelled across extensive areas. How did this lifestyle fit with Colborne's policy?

• What happened to Aboriginal societies when people were "settled" in villages that were not their homes?

• How are Aboriginal peoples working to regain their culture today? Research an Aboriginal organization and explain the purpose of their work.

WEB LINK • • • • • • • • • •
Read the United Nations convention on the Prevention and Punishment of the Crime of Genocide on the Pearson Web site.

FIGURE 3–18 After 1920, First Nations and Inuit children were forced to attend residential schools far from home. They were punished if they spoke their own language. How did residential schools contribute to the destruction of Aboriginal language and culture? What does the photo above tell us about this school?

ACTIVITIES

1. Aboriginal culture is based on oral tradition. Speeches and stories were used to address important issues. Create a speech to protest the policy of assimilation of Aboriginal peoples.

2. Today, the Canadian government does not try to force people to give up their culture. Why was assimilation the government's goal in the past?

3. Do you see examples of "the noble savage" in today's popular culture? Present your findings in a visual format that demonstrates the presence or absence of such stereotypes today.

SKILLBUILDER • Bias in the News

In this book, you will study a variety of primary sources. These sources will include first-person accounts, speeches, newspaper editorials, illustrations, cartoons, and paintings.

Newspapers are good primary sources from the past. They often expressed popular opinion, which gives us an impression of society at the time. However, editorials were also used to sway opinion. They generally held a biased point of view, like the ones shown on the opposite page.

Bias was common in newspapers in Victorian Canada. Papers usually had connections with different political parties. As you saw in Chapter 2, newspapers promoted political reform—or rebellion, in the case of William Lyon Mackenzie. Fortunately, there were lots of newspapers, and most people knew who ran them and what views were being promoted.

How can we detect bias when reading newspapers from the past? Is bias still common today?

There are three checkpoints to remember when detecting bias in primary sources:

1. Recognize fact versus opinion, and remember that fact and opinion can be combined within the same document.

- A fact can be verified with evidence.

- An opinion is based on a belief or point of view, not on evidence.

2. Recognize the language of bias. Assertive or extreme language tends to show bias.

3. Identify the author's purpose. Who wrote the article? Why was it written?

Following these checkpoints will help you become a critical reader of primary sources. Remember that while a source may be biased, that fact may lend insight to the events and people you are studying, showing what people thought about a particular subject. Look for evidence from many different sources in order to create a balanced view of the past.

Keep this exercise in mind as you continue with this chapter and explore the issues surrounding Confederation.

bias strongly favouring a point of view to the point of misrepresenting other views

FIGURE 3–19 Political cartoons were commonly used in newspapers to promote opinion. Here, artist Jean-Baptiste Côté depicts Confederation as a monster controlled by politicians. What can you tell about *La Scie*'s view of Confederation from this image?

WEB LINK ● · · · · · · · · · · · · · · · ·

Are you interested in learning more about reading political cartoons, such as the one on page 98? Check the Pearson Web site.

But it is said that the Canadians have outgrown their Constitution... If they are in trouble let them get out of it; but don't let them involve us... Are not the Canadians always in trouble? Did not Papineau keep Lower Canada in trouble for twenty years, and McKenzie [sic] disturb the Upper Province for about the same period? Then did not both Provinces break out into open rebellion, which it cost the British Government three or four millions sterling to suppress? What would have been the situation of the Maritime Provinces then, had they been controlled by the Canadians? But they were not... They maintained their loyalty unsullied.

—*Morning Chronicle,* Halifax, January 11, 1865: "The Botheration Scheme"

So far as the people of Upper Canada are concerned, the inauguration of the new Constitution may well be heartily rejoiced over as the brightest day in their calendar. The Constitution of 1867 will be famous in the historical annals of Upper Canada, not only because it brought two flourishing Maritime States into alliance with the Canadas, and opened up new markets for our products, and a direct railway route to the Atlantic through British territory, but because it relieved the inhabitants of Western Canada from a system of injustice and demoralization under which they had suffered for a long series of years. The unanimity and cordiality with which all sections of the people of Canada accept the new Constitution, gives the happiest omen of its successful operation. We firmly believe, that from this day, Canada enters on a new and happier career, and that a time of great prosperity and advancement is before us.

—*The Globe,* Monday, July 1, 1867: "Confederation Day"

APPLY IT

1. What important issue do the accounts address? Why might this have been an issue at that time?

2. How is each source biased? Provide examples to illustrate your answer. Think about what the account leaves out, what it leaves in, and the choice of words.

3. How do these accounts corroborate, or support, each other? How do they contradict each other?

4. Give examples of modern television shows or newspapers where people use the host's or writer's bias as entertainment.

5. Can bias be justified? Give examples of circumstances where media bias is justified and where it is not.

Toward Confederation

▶ **What economic and political situations led to the idea of Confederation?**

As you saw in Chapter 2, Lord Durham had recommended joining together Lower Canada and Upper Canada. Although Lower Canada, which would become Canada East, was opposed to the idea, the British government favoured the plan and acted upon it immediately. Lord Sydenham declared the Act of Union in 1840.

However, Durham had also recommended responsible government for the colonies, an idea that was not well received in Britain—or by the Château Clique and the Family Compact. The idea that the colonies should govern themselves—democratically—was entirely new. Nobody knew if, or how, self-government would work. Many thought that it would seriously weaken the British Empire and perhaps even strengthen Britain's political enemies (such as France and the United States). Some feared that government by amateurs—inexperienced elected politicians—would be economic suicide. The old idea of **mercantilism**, which had always been good for colonial Canada, was still strong. The economic relationship between the colonies and Britain gave the colonies a significant advantage, so most people wanted to remain under British rule.

mercantilism an economic system based on colonialism, in which the home country uses raw goods imported from the colonies to manufacture goods

Corn Laws laws which protected agriculture in the British Empire by limiting the import of grain from other countries

tariff a duty, or charge, that must be paid on an imported item

economic depression a period of low economic activity marked by high unemployment

Economic Pressures

Britain's economic relationship with the colonies, however, was already changing. In 1846, the British government repealed the **Corn Laws**, which were part of the Navigation Acts and gave preferential treatment to British colonies. Canadian grain came into Britain with lower **tariffs** than grain from other countries. This helped Canadian producers by increasing profits, but limiting the import of grain from other countries made bread in Britain expensive. This contributed to the starvation the Irish suffered during the Potato Famine. By repealing the laws and not restricting itself to Canadian grain, Britain could buy wheat, flour, and other products at the lowest price—from any country.

The end of the Corn Laws drove the colonies into an **economic depression**. Although Canadians exported timber and agricultural products, they manufactured very little. With the old economic relationship now in tatters, and with few factories or industries, Canadians began to look at the union of all of the colonies as a way of helping their economy. Joining together would mean larger markets, more industry, and better transportation systems. A more independent Canadian government could develop its own economic policies—policies that would serve Canada rather than Britain.

To achieve this, self-government was needed. Still the colonial governors who came after Durham did not like the idea. Even though Governor Charles Bagot had brought reformers such as Robert Baldwin and Louis-Hippolyte LaFontaine into the councils, Bagot did not think that he had to do what other people wanted. In other words, the governor still governed, not the elected Assembly. This was not responsible, democratic government. It would take direction from Britain for any change to be made.

Lord Elgin and Responsible Government

In 1846, the British government appointed James Bruce, Lord Elgin, as governor general of Canada. As Lord Durham's son-in-law, Elgin shared some of Durham's ideas for reform. Elgin's job was to make responsible government a reality. This policy would help relieve Britain of economic responsibility for the colonies while still keeping them in the British Empire. (It was becoming too expensive for Britain to continue to govern, defend, and economically support the colonies.) Elgin set out to make Canada a semi-independent nation and to introduce enough democracy that the citizens of the new nation would not be drawn into a revolution—as the Americans had in 1775.

DID YOU KNOW...

In 1848, Nova Scotia became the first British colony in the world to achieve responsible government. Journalist and politician Joseph Howe (see page 112) had led the call for reform.

WEB LINK

Read more about the modern-day structure and functions of the Canadian federal government on the Pearson Web site.

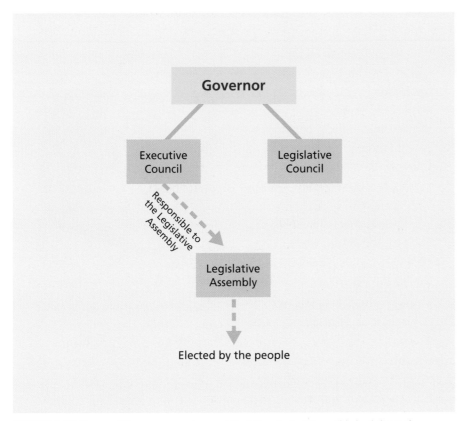

FIGURE 3–20 Responsible government meant that the elected Assembly had the real authority to make laws. In time, the Executive Council would become today's Cabinet, and the Legislative Council would become today's Senate. What is the modern equivalent to the Legislative Assembly?

Rebellion Losses Bill a bill promising compensation to people of Canada East who suffered property damage during the Rebellions of 1837

During the Rebellions of 1837, many people suffered property damage. In 1849, the newly elected and reformist government presented the **Rebellion Losses Bill**. The bill proposed to use tax money to compensate anyone in Canada East who lost property in the Rebellions—even some of the rebels, unless they had been convicted of treason. The bill was modelled on compensation that had already been offered to those in Canada West. However, as you saw in Chapter 2, the rebellions in Canada East were more violent and lasted longer than the rebellions in Canada West. There were still deep feelings of resentment and anger at those who had taken part in the fighting.

After Elgin signed the bill, some English-speaking citizens in Montreal were furious. A mob attacked Elgin's carriage as he left Parliament, pelting him with stones and rotten eggs. English newspaper headlines stated that "the end has begun." After two days of violence, the mob set fire to the Parliament Buildings, which burned to the ground. Following the riot, some angry English merchants and citizens published the Annexation Manifesto—a plan to allow the United States to take over Canada.

DID YOU KNOW...

After the riots in Montreal, Elgin moved the location of Parliament to Ottawa, which later became the capital of Canada.

Zoom In ⊘ Lord Elgin's Dilemma

Ironically, although the Rebellion Losses Bill had been written to help heal divisions in Canada East, the bill outraged many people. Some politicians were violently opposed to the bill. They still saw the rebels as traitors to Britain and thought it was a crime to give tax money to people who may have participated in the rebellion. Fearing the loss of political power, they also saw the bill as a move by the French to gain political sway in the colonies. Despite their protests, the bill was passed by the reform-minded legislature. They then turned to Lord Elgin to stop the bill.

Personally, Elgin had his doubts. He, too, saw the bill as a reward to possible traitors. At the same time, he was determined to follow the principle of responsible government. He felt that the governor had no right to veto a bill that had been passed by the elected Assembly.

Threats, arguments, and anti-French speeches and headlines did not stop Elgin from signing the bill into law in 1849.

• If you had been in Elgin's position, what would you have done?

FIGURE 3–21 This cartoon of Elgin appeared in a Canadian newspaper at the time of the riots. Why would a cartoonist portray Elgin in this fashion? What statement is he making?

Annexation never happened. However, by signing a bill he did not agree with because he believed in responsible government, Elgin had laid the foundation for Canadian democracy. Responsible government had passed its first test, and the colonies were now heading toward the complicated process of Confederation.

Building a Nation

> ...the scheme [Confederation] as a whole has met with almost universal approval.
>
> —John A. Macdonald, 1864

John A. Macdonald, one of the architects of Canadian Confederation, said the words above when giving a speech in 1864. His speech was brilliant and engaging but untruthful in parts: he ignored the fact that almost as many people were against the union of the colonies as were for it.

First, the colonies felt that if they were joined together in a **federation**, they would lose their independence. There would be a central government, and it would most likely control defence, foreign affairs, money, postage, and taxation. Although Britain already controlled some of these areas of responsibility, many colonists preferred dealing with London, which was far away, rather than a new government located in Canada West or Canada East.

federation a union of provinces, each of which keeps certain powers but gives up other powers to a central, national government

FIGURE 3–22 This painting shows the Parliament Buildings burning after Elgin signed the Rebellion Losses Bill. The riots lasted for two days and involved thousands of people—mostly English-speakers. Strongly anti-French speeches and headlines appeared just before the riots. Why did the mob choose to attack the Parliament Buildings?

FIGURE 3–23 John A. Macdonald was well known for his skills as a public speaker. How did this talent help him promote his plans for Confederation?

Second, most people did not feel any great attachment to the people of the other colonies. French Canadians felt they had little in common with English-speaking Canadians. They had no desire to become even more of a minority in a larger, mostly English-speaking country. Nor did the people in the Maritime colonies feel that they should be part of a greater "Dominion of Canada." Their economies had closer links to Britain and eastern United States than to the Canadas.

Third, the idea of Confederation started "at the top." The population at large had to be convinced, which was not easy. In addition, Confederation could cost a lot of money, which would have to be paid for with more taxes. Victorian Canadians were as skeptical of what politicians promised as people are today. Those who wanted union had to convince people that their proposal had merit, which involved a lot of time and effort.

With these varying factors and conflicting concerns, the process of Confederation took a great deal of debate from all sides. In fact, the Maritime colonies remained more interested in a Maritime union than Confederation for quite some time. However, even though these political decisions affected them as well, minority groups, such as Aboriginal peoples and French-speaking Acadians were not consulted.

Even so, the idea of creating a new country was exciting. The new nation envisioned by Macdonald would one day extend from the Atlantic to the Pacific and to the Arctic Oceans, becoming one of the largest countries on earth. Still, while the idea might be exciting, those who wanted union needed something more to make it happen.

ACTIVITIES

1. What happened to Canada's economic relationship with Britain in the 1840s? What brought on the change? Write a letter to the editor explaining why you think Canada should be more independent.

2. Be a witness to the Montreal riots. Write a one-minute news item for television, describing the scene and giving background information.

3. Explain the reasons for anti-French sentiments before and during the Montreal riots. How were these sentiments connected to the Rebellion Losses Bill?

Cause and Consequence

4. Why was signing the Rebellion Losses Bill a difficult decision for Lord Elgin? Why was it important that he sign the bill?

Political Factors

▶ **How might Confederation solve political problems for the colonies?**

Until 1867, with the exception of the Province of Canada, the colonies of British North America were separate and independent of each other. The people living in the colonies were British subjects, and the British colonial office was responsible for their well-being. The colonies were often on good terms economically and socially, but they had separate legislatures and operated like small, independent countries.

After Union and the repeal of the Corn Laws, Confederation became a hot topic. Some argued that the comfortable days of the past were over, and that adaptation was the key to survival. Trading between the colonies, for example, would replace the trade lost with Britain. Joining together politically would make this easier, and would benefit all of the colonies.

The West and the American Threat

Confederation opened up another possibility—that of expansion to the West. The vast western territories, which were held by the Hudson's Bay Company, could be **annexed** to Canada, and therefore denied to the United States. Canadians were suspicious of American intentions in the West. After all, American politicians made speeches about **Manifest Destiny**, which claimed that the destiny of the United States was to own all of North America. Americans had already invaded Canada twice— during the American Revolution and during the War of 1812. The small, scattered colonies of British North America had almost no defences against American aggression, but the United States would be less likely to invade a united, sovereign country.

The **American Civil War**, which began in 1861, heightened the threat. When the war ended in 1865, the army of the victorious northern states could have easily invaded Canada because it had more soldiers than the total population in all the Canadian colonies. Britain had also angered the North by supporting the South during the war, providing warships and money. Confederates (southerners) had been able to attack the northern states by travelling through Canada. Many wondered if the North would retaliate against Britain by sending the army into Canada.

annex to take over a territory and add it to the territory of another country

Manifest Destiny an American idea that it was the fate of the United States to control all of North America

American Civil War also called the War Between the States, it began in 1861 and ended in 1865. The industrialized North fought the agricultural South. A divisive issue was slavery, which the South supported.

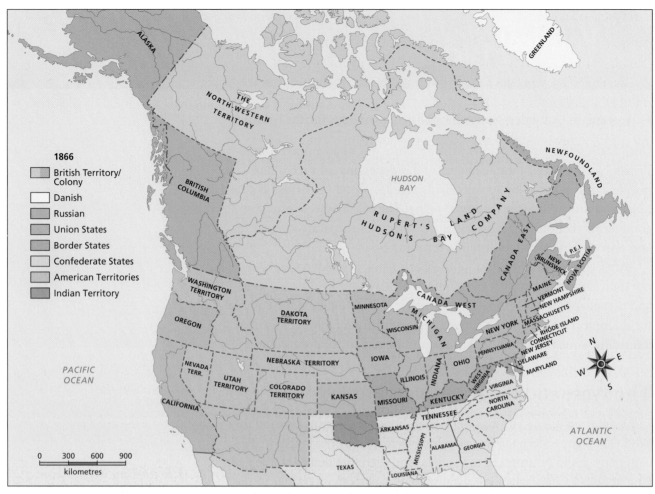

FIGURE 3–24 The colonies of British North America covered vast territories but had a much smaller population than the United States. Why were Canadians afraid of American expansion?

The Promise of Better Government

Confederationists promised to replace an inefficient system with better government, especially in Canada East and Canada West, which together were called the Province of Canada. Today, modern political parties keep members of the party in line—and working with the leader—so that everyone in the party speaks with one voice. The person responsible for party discipline is called the **whip**. The whip ensures that members of the party vote together on bills. While this practice reduces the independence of members, it also makes the party stronger and more efficient.

By contrast, the government of the Province of Canada was filled with independent politicians who answered to no one. These members could topple a government by voting against one of its bills, a situation that created crisis after crisis as governments tried to survive. The government of Canada was always made up of a number of parties—a **coalition**. If even one party left the coalition, the government would fall. Governments survived by doing nothing. People hoped that Confederation would bring change.

whip the person who is responsible for ensuring discipline and solidarity within a political party

coalition in politics, when one or more political parties or interest groups work together to achieve a common goal

Party Politics

Political parties were a relatively new concept in pre-Confederation Canada. A political party attracts people who have similar ideas and goals. In Canada, political parties formed to represent the interests of the French and the English. Other groups, including Aboriginal peoples, had no representation and no party. Parties developed a platform, which described the changes they wanted to make and how they would achieve their goals.

In Canada East, Louis-Joseph Papineau, former radical and rebel, led the *Parti Rouge*. It represented French-speaking farmers and business people, wanted American-style government, and despised the Act of Union. The *Parti Bleu*, led by George-Étienne Cartier, had similar support but focused more on economic development and the protection of French-Canadian culture and rights. It was not as radical as the Parti Rouge, and it had the support of the Catholic Church. The Parti Bleu was prepared to work with politicians in Canada West to achieve its goals, as long as English Canada did not threaten French interests.

In Canada West, the Clear Grits, a more radical party, was led by George Brown. Brown was the publisher of the Toronto newspaper, *The Globe*. The Grits attacked **corruption** in government, wanted more democracy, and defended English-Canadian interests. Brown was an abrasive man who disliked both Catholics and the French, and he made enemies easily, so an alliance between the Grits and a French party was unlikely.

corruption in politics, taking bribes or using one's influence to gain an unfair advantage

FIGURE 3–25 George-Étienne Cartier was a wealthy Francophone who invested in railways. As a young man, he was part of the Lower Canada rebellion. Later, Cartier was a driving force behind Confederation. Why do you think Cartier would have changed his mind about Canada?

FIGURE 3–26 George Brown used his newspaper, which is today's *The Globe and Mail*, to spread his views. Why would owning a newspaper, or any media outlet, be an advantage to a politician? Do you think individual politicians should be allowed to own media?

representation by population
a form of proportional representation
in government; areas with higher
populations have more elected officials
in government

The Grits pushed for **representation by population**: the number of members in the Legislative Assembly representing an electing area, or riding, should be determined by the population of the riding. This is an important feature of democratic government, but it was not popular in Canada East, where "rep by pop" meant fewer seats for French Canadians.

The middle ground in Canada West belonged to the Tories, led by Macdonald. His views were less democratic than Brown's, but he was a more astute politician. Macdonald made a deal with the Parti Bleu that enabled the combined party—the Liberal-Conservatives—to form a government. This important step toward Confederation also helped with the problems of double majority, which was another barrier to good government.

Double majority meant that a bill became law only if a majority in both Canada East and Canada West voted for it in the Legislative Assembly. Imagine how hard this would be. It would be like passing identical laws in British Columbia and Quebec—what works for one is not necessarily good for the other. Bills concerning taxation, trade, language, or education did not usually pass, which severely limited the government's work.

The problems arising from French–English and Catholic–Protestant divisions were serious barriers to the government of the united Canadas. Without having their own provincial governments to legislate matters of provincial interest, both groups were forced to work in a single government. As a result, there was little progress.

FIGURE 3–27 Issues of proportional representation in government continue in Canada today. These voters are acting as "Doctors of Democracy," encouraging reform of Ontario's electoral system in 2007.

ACTIVITIES

1. List in order of importance three ways the United States was a factor in Confederation. Defend your choices with examples.

2. Explain the concept of Manifest Destiny. How much of a threat to British North America was the United States?

3. In what ways did politicians expect Confederation to solve economic problems in the colonies? Assess their expectations.

4. Chart the major political parties in Canada East and Canada West, listing two or three characteristics of each.

5. Explain the "double majority" principle of government. Why would it make effective government difficult?

Confederation Achieved

▶ **What brought the colonies together to form Confederation?**

In addition to political pressures, the colonies were under tremendous pressure economically. Supporters of Confederation argued that Canada and the other colonies would prosper because trade barriers and tariffs between the colonies would end. Trade would also be improved by a new national railway. Individual colonies could never finance a railway on such a large scale, but they could do it together.

In addition, linking the central colonies with the Maritimes would mean that goods travelling to Europe in winter could use the ice-free port at Halifax. Access to Halifax would certainly benefit central Canada, since the large port of Montreal was closed in the winter months. As well, a railway could go all the way to the Pacific—to the new colonies of British Columbia and Vancouver Island. Suffering from economic depression, fear of the United States, and struggling to organize politically, the colonies were suddenly willing to make a deal.

FIGURE 3–28 The Maritime colonies had close economic ties to Britain and the New England states. Why might changes in these trading relationships make the Maritime colonies more interested in Confederation? Why might some in the Maritime colonies want to preserve these trade links?

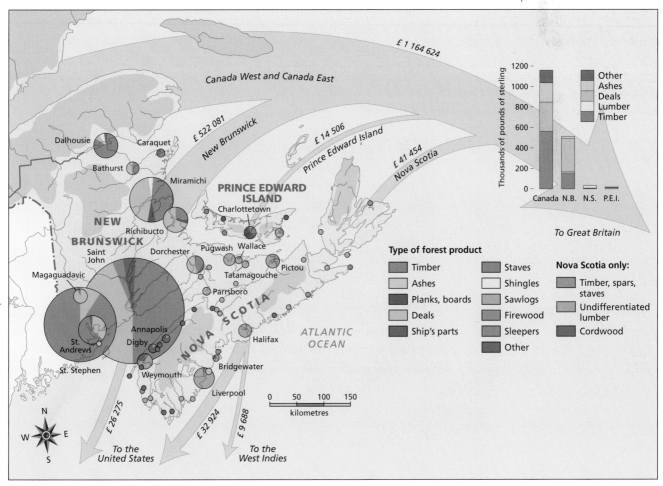

Negotiating the terms of Confederation, however, would be difficult. Macdonald wanted a strong central government and not much power for the provinces. Contrary to this view, the idea that they would be ruled by central Canada did not sit well with Maritimers. They had a sense of shared identity and history. They also traded far more with the United States than with the Province of Canada. Why should the Maritime colonies give up anything?

New Brunswick and Nova Scotia: A Maritime View

WEB LINK ● ·················
Read more about how the different colonies responded to Confederation on the Pearson Web site.

In the 1860s, New Brunswick and Nova Scotia were small, prosperous colonies. Their populations were mainly made up of the English, French-speaking Acadians, Scots, Irish, and Mi'kmaq and Maliseet Nations. Many New Brunswickers and Nova Scotians could trace their lineage to British and Black Loyalists who had escaped the American Revolution by moving north. Saint John and Halifax were large and busy port cities, comparable to Montreal and Toronto at that time.

Both colonies had already achieved responsible government—Nova Scotia in 1848 and New Brunswick in 1854. This fostered a feeling of independence and self-sufficiency—a sentiment that was not favourable to Confederation. Many felt that in joining Confederation they would become a smaller part of a whole, rather than an equal partner in the Dominion of Canada. Minority groups, such as the Acadians and the Irish Catholics, were particularly fearful.

However, there were also vocal supporters of union. They believed that Confederation would offer security and that the railway would provide larger markets for their products. Loyalty to England was also a factor, as this editorial shows:

> *Ask a true man, who loves his country for itself why he is in favor of Union, and he will tell you: I am in favor of Union, because I wish to remain a loyal subject of Queen Victoria; because it will cement more closely these Colonies and the Mother Country; because England desired it in order to consolidate our strength; because it will ensure us against aggression...*
>
> —From *The Pictou Colonial Standard*, Nova Scotia

Protection was a particular concern for New Brunswickers, who shared a border with the United States. This fear would come to a head with the Fenian attack on Campobello Island in 1866.

Then came news that the United States would end **reciprocity**, a free-trade agreement that had helped the colonies after Britain repealed the Corn Laws. Also, new ships were now being made of steel instead of wood, which did not help the Maritimes, where building wooden ships was a vital industry. Macdonald tried to convince Maritimers that Confederation would help their economies but Newfoundland and Prince Edward Island were not convinced. In their view, a new railway would be a drain on their resources, with no benefit.

In spite of opposition, planning for Confederation went ahead. The province of Canada had the most to gain—it was almost bankrupt, and its government hardly worked at all. In fact, 12 different governments came and went between 1849 and 1864. Finally, George Brown joined John A. Macdonald and George-Étienne Cartier in the Great Coalition to promote Confederation.

reciprocity an agreement that provided for free trade between the United States and the British colonies

Zoom In ⊳ The Fenian Raids

CRITICAL INQUIRY Cause and Consequence

When the American Civil War ended in 1865, an Irish organization known as the Fenians planned to attack the British Empire in revenge for the injustices inflicted on Ireland by the English. One strategy involved former Civil War soldiers attacking Britain's colonies, including the Canadas and the Maritimes.

In 1866, the Fenians captured Fort Erie in Canada West, but they were turned back to Buffalo. In the same year, Fenians crossed into Canada East, where they remained for two days. They also launched an unsuccessful raid into New Brunswick, attacking Campobello Island.

The Fenian attacks convinced many colonists, including those in New Brunswick and Nova Scotia, that the American threat was real. At the same time, Irish people in the colonies were caught between sympathy to the Irish cause and the desire to appear loyal to

their own governments. In the end, many Irish, such as those in New Brunswick, threw their support behind Confederation in order to show their loyalty. John A. Macdonald was able to use the raids to gain support for Confederation and to counter

opposition from Joseph Howe and others.

- Did the Fenians succeed in punishing the British? Explain the consequences of the Fenian raids in this context.

FIGURE 3–29 This romanticized painting shows the Fenians fighting British troops in Canada West. In reality, the Fenians were a ragtag group dressed in old Civil War uniforms. Without the support of the American government, the Fenians were doomed to fail. Why were they successful in inspiring fear among the colonists?

Confederation stirred emotions for many reasons, perhaps because it raised questions of identity—in particular, the question of a Canadian identity. Read the following excerpts from speeches by John A. Macdonald and Joseph Howe. Notice how the speakers cleverly link identity to other issues. What are some of these issues? Howe, a long-time Nova Scotia politician who had guided the colony to responsible government, strongly opposed Confederation and was a vocal critic of Macdonald.

Why should anything be done? Nova Scotia, secure of self-government, can even bear with serenity an Administration that certainly tries her patience at times. She has been blessed with a good crop, an abundant fishery, her mining interests are extending; her shipyards have been busy all the year; her railroads are beginning to pay, and her treasury is overflowing... We have not a question to create angry discussion with the mother country, with our neighbours in the United States, or with the Governments of the surrounding colonies. We have entirely reorganized our militia, and drilled every man liable to be called out under the law, within the year. Who says, then, that something should be done? Those who desire to daub this peaceful picture, with the hues of their distempered imaginations.

—Joseph Howe

We find ourselves with a population approaching four million souls... With the increased security we can offer to immigrants who would naturally seek a new home in what is known to them as a great country... our future progress will be vastly greater... Instead of looking at us as merely a dependent colony, England will have in us a friendly nation—a subordinate but still a powerful people—to stand by her in North America in peace or war. I implore you not to let this opportunity pass. If we do not take advantage of the time it may never return, and we shall regret having failed to found a great nation under the fostering care of Great Britain and our Sovereign Lady, Queen Victoria.

—John A. Macdonald

FIGURE 3–30 Joseph Howe was a famous journalist and newspaper publisher in Nova Scotia. Later he became a politician. He considered Confederation to be bad for Nova Scotia.

WHAT DO YOU THINK?

1. In an organizer, list Howe's points against Confederation (and any others you think he might have made) in one column and Macdonald's points in favour of Confederation in the other.

2. Compared to Canada today, what circumstances were different for Howe and Macdonald? (Consider factors such as cultural differences or communications technologies.) How do you think these factors influenced their thoughts and actions?

A major force behind Confederation was the need for ecomomic union between the colonies, which were much like the small countries of Europe. What might have happened if the architects of Confederation had chosen an entirely different model of union, such as the one that has evolved into today's European Union?

After the Second World War, Europe looked for ways to recover from the war and improve trade. In 1946, British Prime Minister Winston Churchill called for a "United States of Europe."

The first to try this were Belgium, the Netherlands, and Luxembourg, who eliminated trade barriers between them in 1948. In 1951, France, West Germany, and Italy joined. By 1993, the group had 12 members, and was now called the European Union (EU).

In the EU, trade can move freely across the borders of member countries. Each member nation maintains its sovereignty, but labour and environmental laws, quality control, and agricultural policies are harmonized. If an outside nation, such as Canada, wishes to export goods to a member of the EU, then it must meet EU standards. As a result, other countries find it difficult to trade with the EU. Some observers call it "Fortress Europe."

The Fathers of Confederation probably never saw the possibilities of a system like the European Union, where individual member states would retain a high level of independence and national identity even though they were connected by economic and environmental laws and practices.

WHAT DO YOU THINK?

1. How would Canada look today if Confederation had been similar to the European Union? Would the "Canadian Union" be better off economically than the current nation of Canada? Why or why not?

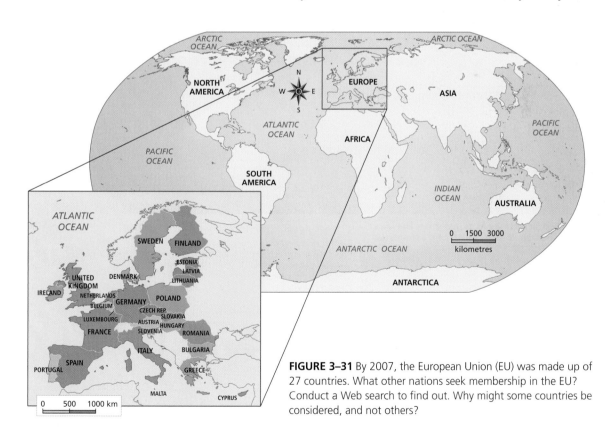

FIGURE 3–31 By 2007, the European Union (EU) was made up of 27 countries. What other nations seek membership in the EU? Conduct a Web search to find out. Why might some countries be considered, and not others?

In 1820, five-year-old John A. Macdonald emigrated to Canada from Glasgow, Scotland. The family settled in Kingston, Ontario.

TRAGEDY STRIKES

John experienced many personal tragedies in his life. When he was seven, he witnessed the traumatic killing of his younger brother.

James!

By the age of 15, John was apprenticing with a Kingston lawyer. Intelligent and driven, by age 21, he had his own law practice. As a teenager, John drank heavily. This was the beginning of a lifelong abuse of alcohol.

In 1837, John served in the volunteer militia and helped to put down William Lyon Mackenzie's rebels at the Battle of Montgomery's Tavern [also known as the Bar Fight on Yonge Street] during the Upper Canada Rebellion.

In 1843, the year John entered politics, he married Isabella Clark. They had two sons, but their first born, Alexander, died at 13 months. Sick most of their married life, Isabella became addicted to opium and died in 1857.

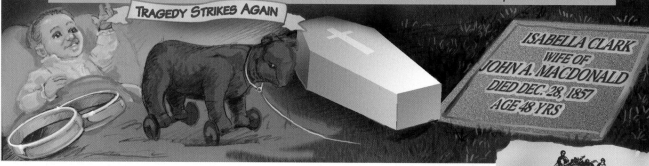

TRAGEDY STRIKES AGAIN

ISABELLA CLARK
WIFE OF
JOHN A. MACDONALD
DIED DEC. 28, 1857
AGE 48 YRS

John worked hard to build support for the idea of Confederation. In 1867, his dream came true.

CONFEDERATION!

John was knighted on July 1, 1867.

In the year of Confederation, John married Susan Agnes Bernard. Their daughter, Mary, was born with physical and mental disabilities. John doted on his daughter, reading to her every night before dinner, and even taking her to Parliament to listen to his speeches.

Baboo, shall we read this one again?

PROCLAMATION!

WHEREAS, THE
Honorable Thomas D'Arcy McGee

REWARD
OF
$2000

On April 7, 1868, John came home with blood on his clothes from carrying the body of his good friend D'Arcy McGee, murdered for his support of Confederation.

The Conferences

Confederation was only possible if an agreement could be hammered out among the leaders of the colonies. To accomplish this, conferences were held. The first was in Charlottetown, Prince Edward Island, in September of 1864. In fact, this meeting was intended to be a conference for the premiers of Nova Scotia, New Brunswick, and Prince Edward Island about a union of their colonies. Seizing their chance, Macdonald, Brown, and Cartier, the three members of the Great Coalition, accompanied by land speculator and railway builder Alexander Tilloch Galt, asked to join the discussion to present their plans for Confederation. They convinced New Brunswick's Samuel Tilley, Nova Scotia's Charles Tupper, and Prince Edward Island's Edward Whelan that Confederation could work. All agreed to attend another conference in Quebec to work out the details. Newfoundland also agreed to send representatives, even though there was little support for Confederation in that colony.

The delegates to the Quebec Conference, which was held in October of 1864, were planning a new nation, a difficult and time-consuming task. There was much to decide, such as the operation and powers of the new federal government, the powers of the new provinces, and the issue of protecting French language and culture. However, it is likely that no one gave any thought to Aboriginal peoples.

After much discussion, the delegates decided that provincial governments should retain many powers. Macdonald had wanted a strong national government, but he had to compromise. In the end, the Quebec Conference produced 72 Resolutions and a blueprint for Canada.

FIGURE 3–32 The "Fathers of Confederation" met in Charlottetown, P.E.I., in September of 1864. John A. Macdonald and George-Étienne Cartier are in the middle in this photograph. How would the composition of such a group be different today? Who was left out in 1864?

The conference delegates had made decisions about Confederation, but they still needed their legislatures to approve the proposal. Whether the issue was railway building or the powers of Ottawa, there was a lot of opposition. Powerful speakers such as A.A. Dorion of Quebec and Joseph Howe spoke against Confederation. Others, such as Thomas D'Arcy McGee, who was later assassinated, were for it.

Although all the delegates to the conference were men, they were accompanied by their families. Unofficial activities included banquets and balls (see page 83). Only recently have historians discussed the influence of the women present at these events. Although they were relegated to the background, they certainly played a role. As one historian wrote, they helped build a "sense of communal solidarity" among participants who were otherwise divided by language and politics.

New Brunswick, Nova Scotia, and Canada agreed to Confederation, but needed the agreement of the British government. In 1867, the British Parliament passed the British North America Act, which created the new Dominion of Canada.

On July 1, 1867, Canadians celebrated their new Dominion in style. Communities all across the new provinces had parties, concerts, and fireworks. Plans were already being made to bring the Northwest and British Columbia into Confederation, and it was hoped that Newfoundland and Prince Edward Island would join too.

DID YOU KNOW...

While Newfoundland and Labrador was the last colony of that time to join Confederation in 1949, the creation of Nunavut in 1999 made that territory the last region of Canada to officially join the country.

FIGURE 3–33 Canada at Confederation, 1867

FIGURE 3–34 Amor De Cosmos pushed for union of the colonies. Why would the promise of a railway link to central Canada be attractive to some people in British Columbia?

The new nation still had some old problems. Aboriginal peoples, particularly the Métis, strongly opposed plans that deprived them of their rights and land. Transcontinental railways were extremely expensive. Long-standing disputes between the French and the English did not suddenly go away— many remain unresolved to this day. And yet, Canadians had embarked on a new and exciting enterprise based on compromise. Most believed that all the new country's problems could be solved, a belief in keeping with Victorian optimism.

British Columbia and Union

While British Columbia was not an official participant in the Charlottetown and Quebec Conferences, people in that colony were very interested in what was going on. Western supporters of Confederation, such as Amor de Cosmos, publisher of the *British Colonist*, attended the events. He and others believed that a railway link to central Canada would foster growth and development of the West.

The first step in extending Canada took place in the West, when Canada bought Rupert's Land from the Hudson's Bay Company. The history, rights, and interests of the First Nations and the Métis, who lived in the Northwest, were not considered. You will learn more about the consequences in later chapters of *Horizons*.

ACTIVITIES

1. Construct three-point arguments for and against Confederation from the point of view of the Canadas, New Brunswick, and Nova Scotia. Consider political, economic, social, and identity issues.

2. Was Confederation something to celebrate, or something to mourn? Explore the question from different perspectives, including the French, the British, Aboriginal peoples, and others. Present your learning in an essay, a dramatization, or an illustration.

3. In what ways did the conferences reflect Victorian values and beliefs? Describe what a constitutional conference would look like today, and who would be included.

Perspectives

4. Aboriginal leaders were not invited to Confederation conferences. How might they have viewed Confederation?

   a) Outline major points you think Aboriginal leaders would have wanted discussed at the conferences.

   b) Prepare a protest petition demanding Aboriginal representation.

Cause and Consequence

5. What compromises did Macdonald make at the conferences? How do you think Canada would have been different if Macdonald had succeeded in forming the strong national government he desired instead of a federation with strong provincial governments?

The British North America Act

▶ **What was the foundation of Canada's constitution?**

The British North America (BNA) Act, which was passed by the Parliament of Britain, created the country of Canada. Canada's birth as a nation was different from that of the United States, which had independently declared itself a nation, fought a revolution, and formulated its own rules for government. Although the BNA Act—which has evolved over time into Canada's **constitution**—was written mainly by Canadians and was based on the Quebec Act, it still recognized the supreme authority of the monarch.

Because Canada came about as a result of negotiations between equal partners, the BNA Act is full of compromise. You can almost imagine the delegates sitting around the table until dawn, thrashing out details such as who was responsible for ferry services, or who looked after education and schools. These responsibilities were then divided or shared between the provincial governments and the national, or federal, government.

Canada's Federal Government

The structure of Canada's federal government is set out in the constitution. It has been divided into three branches: executive, legislative, and judicial.

Executive branch	**Prime Minister**: the leader of the political party with the majority of elected seats
	Cabinet: a council of ministers chosen and led by the Prime Minister
	Civil service: civilian employees of the government
	Governor General: the head of state in Canada, appointed by the monarch as his or her representative
Legislative branch	**Senate**: called the "Upper House," its members are chosen by the Prime Minister
	House of Commons: called the "Lower House," its members are elected by the people of Canada
	Political parties: organizations based on common views, with specific goals; these parties make up the majority of elected officials (some are independent of any party)
Judicial branch	**Supreme Court**: the highest court in Canada
	Federal court: a trial court that hears cases under Federal law

As you read the following selections from the BNA Act, discuss how each section might be served by a branch or branches of the federal government. Why would other responsibilities be given to the provincial governments?

The Powers of the Federal Government (Section 91)

Clause	Item	Excerpt from the Act
3	Taxation	*The raising of money on the public credit.*
7	National defence	*Militia, military and Naval Service.*
14–21	Regulation of banks, currency, and other economic necessities	*Currency and Coinage; Banking, Incorporation of Banks, and the Issue of Paper Money; Savings Banks; Weights and Measures; Bills of Exchange and Promissory Notes; Interest; Legal Tender; Bankruptcy and Insolvency.*
24	Aboriginal affairs	*Indians, and Land reserved for the Indians.*
27, 28	Criminal law and jails	*The criminal Law, except the Constitution of Courts of Criminal Jurisdiction, but including the Procedure in Criminal Matters.* *The Establishment, Maintenance, and Management of Penitentiaries.*

The Powers of the Provincial Government (Section 92)

Clause	Item	Excerpt from the Act
2	Limited powers of taxation	*Direct Taxation within the Province in order to the raising of a Revenue for Provincial Purposes.*
5	Lands	*The Management and Sale of the Public Lands belonging to the Province and of the Timber and Wood thereon.*
7	Health care	*The Establishment, Maintenance, and Management of Hospitals, Asylums, Charities and Eleemosynary Institutions in and for the Province, other than Marine Hospitals.*
8	Local government	*Municipal Institutions in the Province.*
10	Roads and bridges	*Lines of Steam or other Ships, Railways, Canals, telegraphs, and other Works and Undertakings connecting the Province with any other or others of the Provinces, or extending beyond the limits of the Province.*
14	Provincial courts	*The Administration of Justice in the Province, including the Constitution, Maintenance, and Organization of Provincial Courts, both of Civil and Criminal Jurisdiction, and including procedure in Civil Matters in those Courts.*

Note: Education is exclusively given to the provincial legislatures in Section 93.

ACTIVITIES

1. Prepare a PMI (Plus/Minus/Interesting) chart on the sections of the British North America Act featured in this chapter.

2. If the BNA Act was drawn up today, would it be different? Would there be similarities? Explain.

Explore the Big Ideas

In this chapter, you learned about society in the British colonies of North America during the years before Confederation. People's beliefs and values and their concerns about the future played a part in the process of building a nation. Geography and feelings of regional differences were also factors.

1. Who or what is responsible for the creation of Canada? What social, economic, and geographical factors led to Confederation? Could Confederation have happened without Macdonald? What were the roles of Cartier, Brown, the Fenians, and the railway? Create a timeline like the one below to outline the participants, events, and major factors leading to Confederation. Add notes or images to illustrate the influences of values, concerns, geography, and economics on the events of that time. Explain the historical significance of each item you include.

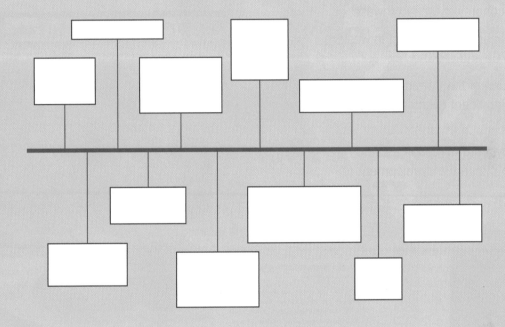

2. Continue your research on Canadian history from 1837 to 1867. Based on what you discover, build a portrait gallery of selected people from the period, with captions explaining their importance. In your gallery, include blank portraits to acknowledge those left out of the process, and explain the significance of these people's contributions to the nation.

3. For Aboriginal peoples, what were the consequences of the growth of Canada and the development of Confederation?

4. Debate the pros and cons of Confederation from the perspectives of the different colonies.

5. In a small group, develop an advertising campaign to influence the delegates to the Charlottetown Conference. Present either a pro or con campaign with posters, slogans, a song, or other materials. Explain why you think Canada retained its ties to the British Empire.

6. Describe the structure of the Canadian federal government today. How does the modern government deal with the same issues present during Confederation—politics, identity, culture, and economic differences?

4 | The Northwest

Chapter Outcomes

In this chapter, you will study the effects of contact between fur traders, immigrants, and Aboriginal peoples in the Northwest. By the end of the chapter, you will

- describe contributions made by Aboriginal peoples to the development of Canada

- analyze the impact of the fur trade on the First Nations and the Métis

- assess the role of First Nations and Métis women in the fur trade

- discuss the creation of the Red River Settlement

- evaluate the interactions between Aboriginal peoples and stakeholders in the fur trade (Hudson's Bay Company, North West Company, voyageurs)

- assess factors that led to the expansion of Canada, including the purchase of Rupert's Land

- analyze key events and consequences of the Red River Resistance

How did conflict and cooperation change the Northwest?

In the 18th and 19th centuries, the fur trade was a thriving economic activity in North America. Competition between fur-trading companies led to further exploration and exploitation of the land. The effect of this activity on the Aboriginal peoples of the Northwest would have consequences for years to come.

Key Terms

Hudson's Bay Company (HBC)
Rupert's Land
North West Company (NWC)
hivernants
voyageur
bison
pemmican
Selkirk Settlement
free trade
Red River Resistance
provisional government

Although the Métis were part of the Red River Settlement—and built watermills, like the one shown here—the arrival of immigrants had a profound effect on their lives. Louis Riel, whose statue (above) now stands at the Manitoba Legislature, led the Métis in their fight for recognition. How might you characterize Louis Riel? Do you think he was an inspiring leader?

The Métis are a creation of the country, and our history...

—Mark McCallum, a Métis from Alberta

The Fur Trade

▶ **What were the consequences of the fur trade for the people and the land of the Northwest?**

The driving force behind trade and European settlement in the Northwest was the fur trade. Trade opened up contact between First Nations and Europeans and caused exploration of the vast region. Two companies, the Hudson's Bay Company and the North West Company, were major players in the fur trade.

The Hudson's Bay Company

The **Hudson's Bay Company (HBC)** was founded in 1670. Explorers Pierre-Esprit Radisson and Médard Des Groseilliers had convinced Charles II of England that with his support they could help England become competitive in the fur trade. Claiming the land surrounding Hudson Bay for England, Charles II also gave the HBC a royal charter, granting exclusive trading rights in all lands drained by rivers flowing into Hudson Bay. This territory, called **Rupert's Land**, was the size of almost one-third of modern Canada. It would be owned by the HBC for 200 years.

The HBC built trading posts at the mouths of rivers, on the shore of Hudson Bay. First Nations trappers and traders travelled long distances to bring their furs to the trading posts and exchanged them for trade goods. The company followed this "stay by the bay" policy for decades.

The HBC was primarily after beaver, the most valuable type of fur in the fur trade. The value of all other furs and trade goods was calculated by comparing them to the value of a beaver pelt. The HBC was strict when it came to trade, and rarely bargained.

TIMELINE

1670	Founding of the HBC
1783	Founding of the NWC
1810	Métis settle in the Red River Valley
1812	Founding of the Selkirk Settlement
1814	Pemmican Proclamation
1816	Battle of Seven Oaks
1821	HBC and NWC merge
1869	Canada buys Rupert's Land • Red River Resistance • Métis List of Rights is created
1870	Execution of Thomas Scott • Manitoba enters Confederation

Hudson's Bay Company (HBC) the oldest commercial corporation in North America; once a major player in the fur trade, it is still in business today as a department store retailer

Rupert's Land a territory consisting of the drainage basin of Hudson Bay

FIGURE 4–1 York Factory, an HBC post on Hudson Bay. Find York Factory on a map. What were the advantages and disadvantages of its location?

Each summer, a ship from England delivered supplies, trade goods, and new employees to York Factory on Hudson Bay. The vessel then loaded furs for transport back to England. At first, the HBC had no direct competition, but this situation soon changed.

The North West Company

By the mid-1700s, fur traders from New France (which later became Lower Canada) had established trading posts along rivers in the Northwest. French traders could now go deeper inland and make new contacts. First Nations traders often preferred dealing with the French, since trading with them meant not having to travel to Hudson Bay.

When the British took control of New France in 1763, the French fur trade was taken over by English merchants living in Montreal. These men continued to employ French traders. By 1783, several of the merchants had formed the **North West Company (NWC)**. This partnership put the inland trading posts under the control of one company, centred in Montreal.

In order to direct the flow of goods and furs more efficiently, the NWC built Fort William on Lake Superior. Each spring, trade goods were shipped from England to Fort William, via Montreal. From Fort William, the goods were transported by river to inland posts. In late summer, furs were transported to Montreal. Timing was critical—a round trip voyage from Fort William to the most distant NWC post could take as long as 120 days.

Company Differences

The HBC and the NWC, rivals in the same business, were different in structure and company policy. The HBC's "stay by the bay" policy, for example, can be compared with the NWC's choice to use forts farther inland, along the rivers.) Each company's success hinged on these decisions. Compare the policies outlined in the table shown on the following page.

DID YOU KNOW...
Beaver was especially valuable in the fur trade because it was used to make expensive and trendy beaver hats.

North West Company (NWC) the HBC's main rival in the fur trade; based in Montreal

FIGURE 4–2 The logo of the North West Company. Why do you think their motto would be *Perseverance*?

Differences Between the Hudson's Bay Company and the North West Company		
Hudson's Bay Company	**North West Company**	**Effect**
Managed from London	Managed from Montreal	New employees and instructions took longer to arrive from London
Only London directors could share in company profits	Hivernants, partners who worked in the Northwest year-round, could share in company profits	The NWC had employees in the Northwest with an added incentive to expand business
Would not bargain; would not trade alcohol	Open to bargaining; would trade alcohol	NWC was often seen as the more popular company to deal with
Held to a "stay by the bay" policy	Explored deeply into the Northwest, setting up forts along major rivers	It was easier for First Nations trappers to reach NWC trading forts
Discouraged partnerships with First Nations women; only factors were allowed to marry	Encouraged partnerships with First Nations women; all ranks were allowed to marry	Although the HBC later changed this policy, NWC traders had a social and economic advantage due to their links to First Nations

Identify what you think made each company successful.

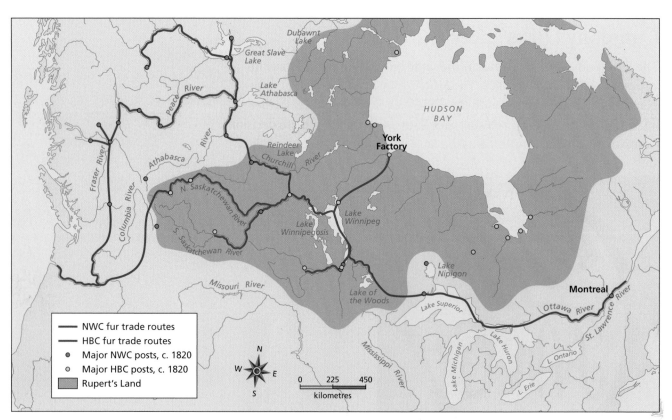

FIGURE 4–3 Major trading posts and routes of the HBC and NWC around 1820. Describe the geographic advantages and disadvantages each company might have had. Revisit Chapter 1 for more information on Canada's physical regions if necessary.

During the 18th and early 19th centuries, explorers and surveyors employed by the HBC and the NWC travelled throughout the Northwest. Hired to find new areas for trapping, they also kept journals and made maps.

The greatest of these explorers was David Thompson, who travelled more than 120 000 km across the Northwest during his career. At first, Thompson worked for the HBC, surveying what is now Saskatchewan. In 1797, the NWC lured him away with a hefty pay raise and the promise that he could explore and map where he chose.

In 1799, Thompson married Charlotte Small, the Métis daughter of NWC partner Peter Small. They were married for 57 years. They had 13 children, and travelled as a family on most of Thompson's expeditions.

Thompson spent the next 15 years exploring what is now British Columbia, Washington, and Oregon. He mapped the relationship of the Pacific coast to the Northwest and found a route for NWC traders through the Rocky Mountains.

Thompson was a careful surveyor, using time-consuming methods to fix the location of thousands of features across the West. He used a sextant, which measures the distance between a star and the horizon, to calculate his position. All of the readings he took would be drawn on future maps. The Blackfoot First Nation called him Koo-koo-sint, which means "he who looks at the stars."

Between 1812 and 1814, Thompson transformed 25 years of observations into an enormous map of the Northwest, shown here.

Thompson resigned from the NWC in 1815. When the American border was formalized in 1818, he was chosen to survey it. However, when Thompson died in 1857, he was almost penniless and unknown.

Thompson's map of the Northwest was so accurate that it formed the basis of future maps of the region. In the 1880s, Canadian geologist Joseph Burr Tyrrell rediscovered Thompson when he found him to be the source of accurate maps of the Rockies. Tyrrell was greatly impressed and later published Thompson's journals. Today, Thompson is recognized as the best map-maker in Canadian history.

- How is a study of Thompson, his maps, and his journals useful to us today?

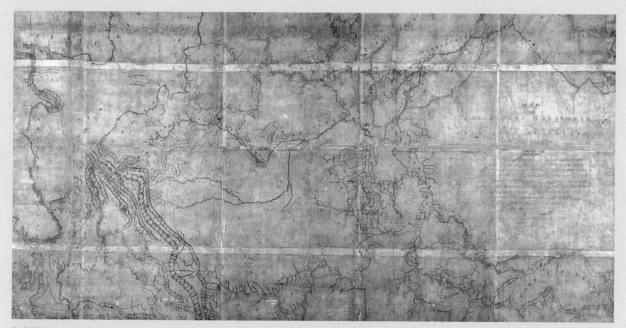

FIGURE 4–4 David Thompson's original map of the Northwest is kept at the Archives of Ontario. Why is it important to maintain this type of artifact?

Getting Around the Northwest

Exploration and trade in the Northwest meant travelling on the region's extensive system of rivers and lakes. Unfortunately, rivers do not always run in the same direction you are travelling, nor do they easily connect. Rapids and waterfalls forced **voyageurs** to **portage**, or carry, both boat and cargo on land to the next part of the river.

The North West Company used canoes adapted from those traditionally used by the First Nations. To travel from Fort William to Montreal, the NWC used the large *canot du maître*; for journeys within the Northwest, they used the slightly smaller *canot du nord*. The Hudson's Bay Company used York boats, which were based on small fishing boats developed by Orkney islanders in Scotland. They came in two sizes, and the larger boat was used on main routes.

The York boat had a number of advantages over canoes. They were sturdier than canoes and could withstand collisions with rocks or other hazards. They could also be used later in the year because they were ice-worthy. With its greater **beam** and high bow, a York boat was also steadier than a canoe. York boats could withstand sudden lake storms, which might swamp loaded canoes. The York boat also had a large sail, which increased speed and helped the crew save their energy for portages.

voyageur someone hired to transport goods by canoe from one trading post to another

portage to carry boats and goods around dangerous parts of a river

beam the most extreme width of a vessel, usually at the mid-point

FIGURE 4–5 York boats photographed in the late 1880s. Why were the fur traders so reliant on water travel?

The strength of the average person who crewed either canoes or York boats was phenomenal. When portaging, an individual was expected to carry two 45-kg pieces of cargo—at a jog—over rugged ground.

> The novice who could undergo the run of the Robinson [1.5-km portage on the Hayes River] without a stop until he had conveyed 1200 pounds [545 kg] from end to end, rose to the status of a first-class tripping man.
>
> —John Peter Turner, "The La Loche Brigade," *The Beaver*, December, 1943

After the merger of the HBC and NWC in 1821, canoes were generally abandoned in favour of York boats, which were used by the HBC throughout the 19th century.

Canoes and York Boats					
Vessel	Length (m)	Beam (m)	Weight (kg)	Cargo (kg)	Crew
Canot du maître	11	1.8	275	2950	11
Canot du nord	8	1.4	136	1250	5–7
Large York boat	13	3.2	1360	4500	9
Small York boat	10	2.4	900	2730	7

Which vessel would you prefer to use if you were a trader in the Northwest? Explain.

The First Nations of the Northwest

The geography of the Northwest is predominantly defined by the Canadian Shield, which is covered by boreal forest, swift-running rivers, lakes, and muskeg. Around Hudson Bay, the forest gives way to small trees and lichen-covered rocks. In the southwest, the forest slowly changes to parkland, and then to grassy plains. This vast region is home to four major First Nations: the Cree (Nehiyaw), the Anishinabé (Ojibway), the Nakoda (Stoney), and the Dene (Chipewyan). By 1800, First Nations of the Northwest had long been involved in the fur trade as trappers, traders, and guides.

The Impact of the Fur Trade

The fur trade had a significant impact on First Nations in North America. Most First Nations became so deeply involved in the fur trade that it disrupted their way of life. As competition between the North West Company and the Hudson's Bay Company intensified, First Nations trappers responded to the increased demand for furs by spending more time and resources on trapping. They chose to set aside parts of their yearly cycle of fishing, hunting, and preserving food, knowing that they could use the furs to buy supplies of flour, sugar, and bacon from the trading posts.

However, this practice would no longer work when local populations of fur-bearing animals were hunted to near extinction. Without furs, the money to buy supplies was also gone. Many First Nations families, facing starvation, were forced to move to new areas.

Contact with Europeans also exposed the First Nations to illnesses against which they had no immunity. The two deadliest epidemics were smallpox and measles. As you will discover in later chapters of *Horizons*, First Nations populations were frequently destroyed by epidemics. In the Northwest, the Dene and the Cree around Hudson Bay were seriously affected by disease between 1780 and 1782. One European trader noted that a First Nations community of 29 had been reduced to just three people during a single winter. Such outbreaks were devastating to cultures that survived on **oral tradition**.

oral tradition a way of remembering the past through stories and spoken explanation, rather than in writing, although objects to aid memory were also used

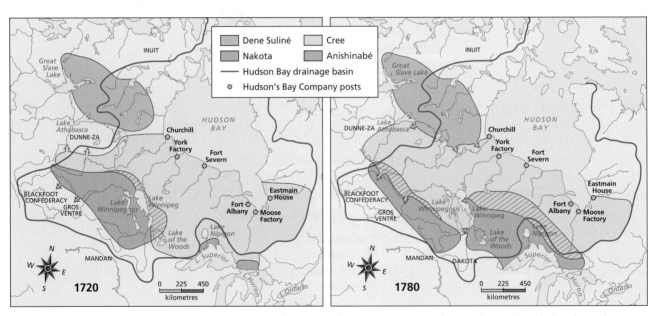

FIGURE 4–6 These maps show the movement of some First Nations during the 18th century. As fur-bearing animals became scarce in one area, people moved elsewhere. How did such movement affect relations between different nations?

Canadians are well known for saying "eh," and for many it has become part of their identity. What many people do not know is that the use of "eh" may be a direct result of the fur trade, which led to decades of close interaction between Aboriginal peoples and Europeans. "Eh" is a short version of *Eha*, which means "yes," or "I agree," in a prominent language of the fur trade—Cree.

Aboriginal peoples once formed the majority of the population in Canada, so it is not surprising that Europeans adopted some of their behaviours. In many cases, the colonists' survival may have depended on what they learned.

Canadians are often considered to be patient and polite. Patient, reflective behaviour makes sense when you consider that people had to be patient while hunting and polite while living in close quarters over long winter months. Aboriginal children also learned to sit quietly, observe, and listen, especially when Elders were present.

Canadians are also known for their commitment to peace. While battles and conflicts occurred, the history of Canada is generally one of peaceful coexistence and compromise— especially when compared with the history of Europe or the United States. Among Aboriginal peoples, the Great Law of Peace Wampum, which is considered the first constitution drafted in the Americas, is a document meant to establish peace. Also, vast spaces and abundant resources generally meant less competition and conflict. Significant interest in trade resulted in rules of courtesy and hospitality that can still be seen today.

The Canadian reputation for humility and generosity may have also been influenced by contact with Aboriginal cultures. Aboriginal cultures were largely non-material, with status more often determined by what was given away rather than what one owned. While leaders emerged when they were needed, the idea of a boss was European. In fact, "chief" is not an Aboriginal word—it comes from feudal Europe.

As you have seen, many cultures have contributed to shaping Canadian identity. You have also studied the impact newcomers had on Aboriginal cultures— much of it destructive. Still, the history of interaction between Aboriginal peoples and newcomers can be seen as part of shaping Canadian identity.

FIGURE 4–7 Canada has less than 1 percent of the world's population, yet we have provided 10 percent of the world's peacekeeping forces. Why do you think this is so?

WHAT DO YOU THINK?

1. As a class, debate the following statement: "Canadians continue to draw on many cultures to create a unique society." Use evidence to support your arguments.

FIGURE 4–8 This First Nations woman is drying Saskatoon berries. Why were women's contributions to food production and transportation so vital to the fur trade?

First Nations Women: Vital to the Fur Trade

First Nations women played important roles in the fur trade. They assisted in the collection, processing, and transportation of furs. First Nations women also provided food, medicine, clothing, and shelter, making them valuable contributors to the community's labour force.

As First Nations entered the fur trade, the work of women became very important. For example, without women to gather pine gum to make and repair canoes, the fur trade could have come to a grinding halt.

When Europeans travelled farther into the Northwest, isolation led them to rely on First Nations' knowledge, especially in gathering and preparing local food, making and mending clothing and shelter, and curing hides and furs. This knowledge came from First Nations women and benefited both the Hudson's Bay Company and the North West Company.

First Nations women also worked as guides, interpreters, and negotiators, travelling with explorers to smooth over any encounters with other First Nations. A Dene woman named Thanadelthur is remembered for her work in negotiating peace between her people and the Cree. This peaceful settlement allowed the Dene and the Cree to trade with the HBC at York Factory, an arrangement that benefited all three groups. James Knight, the factor at York Factory, wrote these words at Thanadelthur's death:

> *She was one of a very high spirit and of the firmest resolution...
> I am sure the death of her was a very considerable loss to the
> Company.*
>
> —James Knight, York Factory, 1717

As European men began wintering in the Northwest, more and more began to marry First Nations women. Their union not only solidified trade relations between Europeans and First Nations, but it also created an entirely new people: the Métis. As time went on, First Nations women gradually found themselves replaced by the Métis women who adopted the economic and social roles they had filled with such skill.

Get to the Source • Your Honours' Employees

The skills that First Nations women brought to the fur trade were not lost on the European fur traders. This defence of the work of First Nations women appeared in a letter sent to the London Committee of the HBC, which resisted paying for the clothing of their employees' wives.

- Why were the traditional roles of First Nations women so important to the fur trade?

> *...the women are deserving of some encouragement from your Honors. They clean and put into a state of preservation all beaver and otter skins brought [in] undried and in bad condition. They prepare line for snowshoes and knit them also without which your [employees] could not give efficient opposition to the Canadian [NWC] traders. They make leather shoes for the men who are obliged to travel... and are useful in a variety of other instances; in short they are virtually your Honors' [employees].*
>
> —York Factory Council, 1802

ACTIVITIES

1. Discuss the differences between the Hudson's Bay Company and the North West Company. Use a T-chart to contrast and compare the companies. Which one do you think was the better organization? Why?

2. The fur trade could not have existed without the contributions of the First Nations and the Métis. Evaluate this statement, giving reasons for your answer.

3. Identify the positive and negative impacts of the fur trade on the First Nations and the Métis. Select what you believe to be the greatest impact (either positive or negative) and explain your thinking.

4. Discuss how the activities of the fur trade might have brought an increased level of conflict between various First Nations.

The traditional view of the first European explorers who travelled to a previously unvisited part of North America is that they were "boldly going where no one had gone before." This view, of course, is not accurate, as Aboriginal peoples had already been living in these areas for thousands of years. In fact, explorers relied heavily on Aboriginal peoples as guides and translators throughout North America. In the Northwest, First Nations' knowledge about the land was extensive and valuable. Not only did First Nations have detailed knowledge of the region's topography, they also knew where valuable resources, such as food and water, could be found.

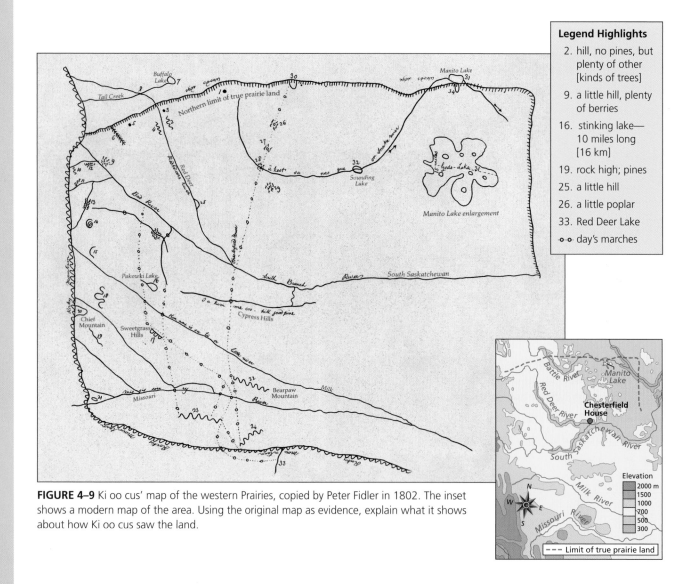

Legend Highlights

2. hill, no pines, but plenty of other [kinds of trees]

9. a little hill, plenty of berries

16. stinking lake— 10 miles long [16 km]

19. rock high; pines

25. a little hill

26. a little poplar

33. Red Deer Lake

o-o day's marches

FIGURE 4–9 Ki oo cus' map of the western Prairies, copied by Peter Fidler in 1802. The inset shows a modern map of the area. Using the original map as evidence, explain what it shows about how Ki oo cus saw the land.

The map shown here was drawn by Peter Fidler, an HBC trader and explorer in 1802, but it was based on a sketch by Ki oo cus (Little Bear), a Siksika chief. It shows the topographic features of the central region of what is now Alberta, Saskatchewan, and the northern United States. This is what geographers call a "mind map." It shares information about a cultural landscape, as described in Chapter 1.

The purpose of a mind map is to recall important places, their relative distance, why a location may be important, and any significant features of the terrain (a swift-flowing river or particularly rugged landscape, for instance). For example, Ki oo cus notes the location of important berry bushes (an excellent source of "trail food"). This map is one of several adapted by Fidler, who used them as the basis of his own maps of the area.

The region shown on this map was not formally mapped until 1865, when explorers from the Palliser Expedition published their map of Canada from Lake Superior to the Okanagan Valley. Their map confirmed that most of Ki oo cus' information—although collected without any mapping technology—was accurate.

APPLY IT

1. What physical features does Ki oo cus include on the map? Why are these features important? Why include berry patches on the map?

2. Provide three reasons fur traders would find Ki oo cus' map useful.

3. Use your memory to create your own mind map of the area near your home and school. Include these key locations:

   • your house

   • your school

   • main roads

   • bus stops (if you use public transportation)

   • places where you shop, and stores where you buy food

   • where you work (if you have a part-time job)

   Now add other locations that are important to you. For example, the houses of friends and relatives, a park you like to visit, or landmarks you feel are special. Anything else that is important to you and your life can be considered part of this cultural landscape.

The Northwest from 1800 to 1860

▶ **How did life in the Northwest change between 1800 and 1860?**

In the early 1800s, competition between the NWC and the HBC became intense. Fur resources were becoming dangerously depleted, and fur traders were spreading out across the Rocky Mountains and into the North. Both companies set aside their standards of trade in an effort to undercut one another. By 1820, both the HBC and the NWC were nearly bankrupt.

The Métis

French-Canadian fur traders had been spending winters in the Northwest from as early as the mid-1700s. They commonly spent the season with local First Nations, and eventually traders began marrying the daughters of local First Nations families. This practice was encouraged and accepted, as First Nations women generally had free choice in whom they were to marry. As well as creating social connections, the marriages also firmed loyalty and economic ties between the traders and the First Nations with whom they worked. Also, as you have seen, First Nations women brought valuable skills and knowledge that proved vital to the European traders and to the fur trade itself.

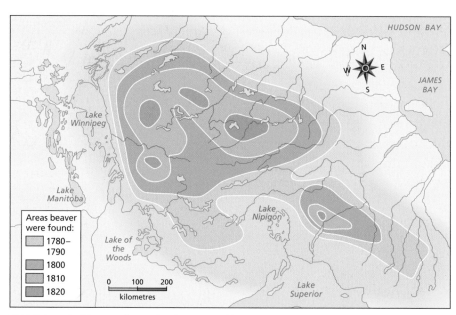

FIGURE 4–10 This map shows the depletion of beaver in part of the Northwest. How do you think the depletion of beaver affected the First Nations in the area?

Marriage to a trader was not a simple choice for First Nations women, however. While the wives of fur traders might have enjoyed an improved standard of living, they had to leave their families and live in the fur-trading posts. They could be separated from family for years at a time.

The NWC did not oppose the marriages. In fact, the weddings were important social events, carried out *à la façon du pays*—in the custom of the country. In contrast, the HBC did not approve of such marriages. The company felt that too many dependants would be a drain on its finances. In fact, the HBC initially tried to impose a policy of **celibacy** on its employees, but the remote location of the Northwest meant that this policy could never really be enforced. By the end of the 18th century, most HBC employees had also taken First Nations wives.

Children of the Fur Trade

A growing number of people in the Northwest were children of European fur traders and First Nations women. Belonging completely to neither parent's culture, they were, in effect, the children of the fur trade. A new culture soon evolved—something entirely unique to Canada.

celibacy refraining from sexual relations

By about 1810, those of French-Canadian and First Nations descent were calling themselves Métis (from the French word for "mixed"). They spoke a distinct language called Michif, made up of French nouns and Cree verbs. Some Nakoda, Saulteaux, and Anishinabé words are also found in Michif. This language is still spoken by some Métis today, and efforts are being made to keep the language alive.

Other Métis had either Scottish or English and First Nations ancestry. They spoke a now extinct language called Bungee. Similar to Michif, Bungee combined English and Gaelic with Cree and other First Nations languages.

Those with British and First Nations ancestry initially preferred the term "country born," but gradually they became known as English- or Anglo-Métis. Today, any person of European and First Nations ancestry is considered to be Métis.

Settling at Red River

By 1810, a large number of Métis had settled in the Red River Valley, near the junction of the Red and Assiniboine Rivers, in what is now southern Manitoba. Here they developed a way of life that was a unique combination of First Nations and European traditions.

FIGURE 4–11 A Métis family in southern Alberta, 1890. Look closely at this photo, especially at what this family is wearing. What evidence does this photo provide about the merging of two cultures?

WEB LINK ● • • • • • • • • • • • • • •

For more information about the Métis in Canada, visit the Pearson Web site.

bison also called buffalo; large grazing animals that travel in herds

pemmican dried meat pounded to a paste and mixed with melted fat and berries

Red River carts two-wheeled carts used on the Prairies

buffalo runners small horses specially trained to be used during the buffalo hunt

The Red River Valley consists of some of the best farming land on the Prairies, and the Métis established farms along the banks of both rivers. Their farms were laid out in the French-Canadian style, in long narrow lots starting at the riverbank. Behind the river lots was an area called the "hay privilege," where a farmer could grow hay. The Métis also hunted **bison**, and by 1820, the bison hunt had become a central part of Métis life.

The Bison Hunt

The bison hunt usually took place in the summer and early autumn. Bison provided meat and hides. Most of the meat was dried to make **pemmican**, while the hides were tanned and made into buffalo robes. Robes and pemmican were sold to the North West Company. Pemmican was high in calories and protein, and could be stored in leather bags for years at a time. It was also portable, much like protein bars available today. The pemmican trade was vital to both the Métis and the NWC, as it provided income for the Métis and an important source of food for the long voyages of the NWC traders.

The bison hunt was an important event that involved the entire community. Métis women, men, and children set off across the Prairie in search of bison. Women and children drove the **Red River carts**, pulled by horses and oxen and used to transport the meat. Hunters rode **buffalo runners**—horses with speed and agility specially trained for the hunts.

FIGURE 4–12 This watercolour sketch of a Métis bison hunt is by artist Paul Kane, who travelled and lived with the Métis in 1846. Was it common for artists at that time to live and work among the subjects of their paintings? What advantage would this bring?

The Red River cart was a means of transportation unique to the Northwest. It was built with simple hand tools and was made entirely of wood. It had just one axle, two large wheels, and a wooden box for carrying both people and goods. It was sturdy and could carry up to 500 kg.

Red River carts were pulled by either oxen or horses. Oxen were usually preferred because although they were slower, they could pull more weight. Because of the dusty prairie summer, the axles were never greased, which resulted in an incredible amount of noise as the wheels turned. According to one European immigrant, the noise was both distinctive and uncomfortable:

Combine all the discordant sounds ever heard in Ontario and they cannot produce anything so horrid as a train of Red River carts. At each turn of the wheel, they run up and down all the notes of the scale without sounding distinctly any note or giving one harmonious sound.

If the Métis were moving in a large group, the carts would travel side by side in order to avoid the dust created by the movement of the carts. A group of carts could stretch across 10 km. With thoroughfares so wide, imagine the effect on the cultural landscape of prairie towns. The widest street in Canada is Main Street in Winnipeg, which was built to accommodate 10 Red River carts travelling side by side.

- If the carts were so noisy and the journey so uncomfortable, why do you think people continued to use them? What do you think eventually made them obsolete?

WEB LINK

On the Pearson Web site, watch a video of a modern Métis journey using Red River carts.

FIGURE 4–13 This painting by Paul Kane shows a Métis cart brigade travelling across the prairie. Discuss how the formation of farms, towns, and cities might affect Métis travel.

FIGURE 4–14 A photo of Main Street, Winnipeg, in 1879. Why would such a wide street be unusual in a town or city?

muzzle loaders any firearm loaded through the muzzle (open end of a firearm)

The Métis hunters and their buffalo runners were so well practised that they acted together. Hunters directed the horses using their knees, which kept their hands free to use their rifles. The rifles were **muzzle loaders**, and the bravery and skill of the Métis hunters were admired by many 19th-century observers of the bison hunt. The hunt itself was extremely dangerous—guns could misfire, horses could trip and fall, and the bison could be aggressive. Death and serious injury were common. Once enough bison had been killed, everyone helped butcher the meat. The entire hunting party then returned to the Red River Valley and held a well-earned celebration.

During the hunt, the Métis sometimes came into conflict with the First Nations who also hunted bison, such as the Blackfoot and the Lakota. In 1851, 64 Métis bison hunters were overtaken by a group of about 2000 Lakota. The Métis circled their carts in a defensive formation, dug rifle pits, and held off charge after charge in a three-day battle. In the end, the Lakota retreated, vowing never to attack "the wagonmen" again.

The bison hunt did more for the Métis than supply meat and clothing; it fostered a strong sense of community, pride, and discipline.

Get to the Source • The Laws of the Bison Hunt

CRITICAL INQUIRY Evidence

The Métis developed rules for the bison hunt. These rules were so strictly enforced that a hunt could be seen as a military expedition. The Captain of the Hunt, who was elected by the hunters before the party left Red River, had absolute authority during the hunt.

The Laws of the Hunt

1. No buffalo to be run on the Sabbath Day [Sunday].

2. No party to fork off, lag behind, or go before, without permission [from the Captain of the Hunt].

3. No person or party to run buffalo before the general order.

4. Every captain with his men, in turn, to patrol the camp and keep order.

5. For the first trespass [violation] against these laws, the offender to have his saddle and bridle cut up.

6. For the second offence, the coat to be taken off the offender's back, and be cut up.

7. For the third offence, the offender to be flogged.

8. Any person convicted of theft, even to the value of a sinew, to be brought to the middle of the camp, and the crier to call out his or her name three times, adding the word "Thief" each time.

- What do these rules tell us about the bison hunt? What do they show about the Métis?

- What information is missing? What other questions could be asked to gain more information?

ACTIVITIES

1. Summarize the main reasons why the Métis established a farming community in the Red River Valley.

2. Identify and examine several reasons that explain why the bison hunt was so important to the Métis.

The Selkirk Settlement

▶ **How did European colonists come to live in the Red River Valley, and what changes did they bring?**

In 1812, European colonists arrived where the Red and Assiniboine Rivers meet, where Winnipeg, Manitoba, is today. This event would have profound implications for the Hudson's Bay Company, the North West Company, and the Métis.

The Earl of Selkirk

Thomas Douglas, the fifth Earl of Selkirk, was a man of vision. A **liberal democrat**, Selkirk was troubled by the plight of poor tenant farmers in his native Scotland. He was determined to help them, and because he was very wealthy, he had the means to do so.

Near the end of the 1700s, many landowners in Scotland began evicting their tenant farmers. They wanted to convert the land occupied by tenants to pasture for sheep, since wool brought in more money than the rent paid by the tenants. The displaced tenant farmers had two choices: they could migrate to cities like Glasgow and become factory workers, or they could emigrate to British North America and become farmers.

Most tenant farmers were far too poor to make the journey across the Atlantic. It was these people Lord Selkirk wanted to help by creating agricultural colonies in British North America. By 1810, Selkirk had established colonies in Prince Edward Island and Upper Canada. Since Selkirk was also one of the directors of the HBC, he then decided to use his influence to launch a far more ambitious project in the Northwest.

liberal democrat in the 19th century, someone who fought for the rights of the poor and underprivileged

> ### DID YOU KNOW...
> Selkirk campaigned vigorously before the British government to sell his idea of establishing colonies in British North America. He also wanted to help Irish farmers. In 1805 he wrote and published a book to promote his theories.

FIGURE 4–15 A family of tenant farmers is driven from their home in Scotland. What parallels can be drawn between this family's experience and that of the First Nations pushed aside by European settlement in Upper and Lower Canada? What impact do you think a European colony in the Northwest might have on the Métis?

Choosing the Red River Valley

Selkirk Settlement also called the Red River Colony; a settlement organized by the Earl of Selkirk in what is now southern Manitoba

Selkirk had learned that the soil of the Red River Valley was especially fertile. He also knew that it was expensive for the HBC to ship food and other supplies from England to its employees in the Northwest. Selkirk felt he could help both the tenant farmers and the HBC by creating a farming colony, the **Selkirk Settlement**, in the Red River Valley. The farmers would be able to maintain their way of life in a new land, and the HBC would have a source of farm products to supply its operations.

In 1811, Selkirk convinced the HBC to grant him 300 000 square kilometres in what is now southern Manitoba and North Dakota. Selkirk and the HBC felt they had a legal right to this territory because it was part of Rupert's Land. Neither gave much thought to the people already living in the region, and how they might react to the arrival of colonists.

In 1811, 36 Scottish and Irish labourers left Britain under the command of an ex-militia officer named Miles Macdonell. Their job was to travel to the Selkirk Grant to find a suitable spot for the colonists. However, they arrived at York Factory in late summer and were forced to spend the winter there. They did not arrive at Red River until the end of August 1812. Only two months later, more than 100 men, women, and children arrived. They were forced to seek shelter at Fort Pembina, surviving on local supplies of pemmican.

> ### Did You Know...
> Selkirk conducted extensive research for his newest settlement, but he failed to consider the difficult climate of the Northwest, which was far harsher than that of Scotland.

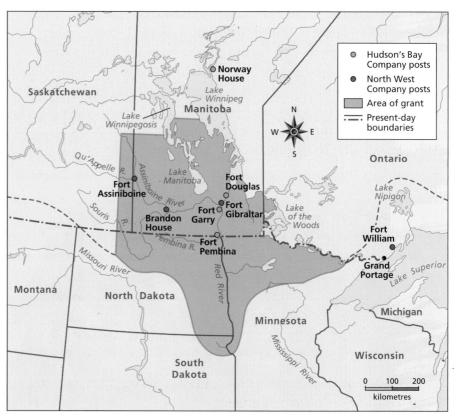

FIGURE 4–16 The Selkirk Grant. Use an atlas to find out what this area is like today and what it is used for. Why did Selkirk choose this area for his settlement?

In the spring, Macdonell led the group back to the Red River Valley. They cleared the land and planted crops, but the harvest failed, and the colonists were forced to spend a second winter at Fort Pembina. In the meantime, a second group of 83 colonists had landed at Fort Churchill. They marched in winter to York Factory, a journey that brought them to the brink of death. This group did not reach the colony until the spring of 1814.

The Pemmican Proclamation

Miles Macdonell, fearing that crops might fail for a second year, issued the **Pemmican Proclamation** in January 1814. It effectively banned the sale and export of pemmican from the Red River Valley for one year. This ban was meant to protect the colonists from starvation, but it was a blow to the Métis of the area, who made a living from the pemmican trade. The Métis were infuriated. The NWC, which already saw the Selkirk Settlement as part of an HBC plot to drive its employees from the area, relied on pemmican to supply its fur traders. The company was equally outraged.

The Pemmican Proclamation actually ran contrary to Selkirk's instructions not to interfere with the operations of the NWC. Macdonell, already disobedient, then attempted to force NWC employees out of the Red River Valley.

Pemmican Proclamation issued in 1814 to prevent the export of pemmican from the Red River Valley

The North West Company Strikes Back

In the summer of 1814, the NWC ordered two of its employees, Alexander Macdonell and Duncan Cameron, to drive the British colonists away. Cameron enlisted the Métis to carry out the NWC directive and appointed Cuthbert Grant as Captain of the Métis. The NWC and the Métis harassed the colonists, burning buildings, destroying crops, and firing rifles at night. By early 1815, more than 100 colonists had left, and Miles Macdonell was arrested. They were taken to Fort William on Lake Superior. Soon after, the remaining colonists left for Norway House at the north end of Lake Winnipeg.

Alexander Macdonell saw that in acting against the Red River colonists, the Métis were inspired to recognize their rights and fight for their land. He wrote:

> *The new nation under their leaders are coming forward to clear their native soil of intruders and assassins.*
>
> —Alexander Macdonell, NWC employee

This new sense of identity had a profound effect on the Métis and later changed the course of history for the Northwest.

FIGURE 4–17 Cuthbert Grant was an important leader of the Métis. He later became a sheriff and magistrate in the region. Why did the North West Company turn to him for help in the Red River Valley?

The Battle of Seven Oaks

Colin Robertson, an HBC factor, led the British colonists back to the Red River Valley within the year. Robertson set out to make peace with the NWC and the Métis until Robert Semple, a new governor for the colony, could arrive. When Semple came with 84 new colonists, Robertson warned him to cooperate with the NWC and the Métis. Unfortunately, Semple ignored Robertson, and he ordered the burning of Fort Gibraltar, an empty NWC post. The Métis saw this as a sign that the colonists intended to make war.

In May 1816, a party of Métis led by Cuthbert Grant raided several HBC York boats on the Assiniboine River. A large supply of pemmican was taken. Grant decided to move the pemmican to Lake Winnipeg, where they could supply the NWC fur traders. Grant meant to avoid the Red River colony, but on June 19 they were seen by a lookout at Fort Douglas.

Robert Semple and 28 men rode out to confront the Métis. The Métis quickly split into two groups and surrounded Semple and his men, a move that Semple failed to notice. An attempt at a **parley** by Grant failed when angry words were exchanged and a colonist fired at the Métis. A gunfight began, and within 15 minutes it was over. Semple and 20 of his men were killed; one Métis died. This skirmish became known as the Battle of Seven Oaks, but the Métis refer to it as the Victory at Frog Plain. It is considered by some Métis historians as a defining moment in Métis history.

parley a discussion under truce, sometimes to discuss peaceful alternatives to battle

FIGURE 4–18 This depiction of the Battle of Seven Oaks was painted by Canadian artist C.W. Jefferys in 1914. It shows Semple (the white-haired man) and his men confronting the Métis. In what ways do you think this painting is accurate? How might it be inaccurate?

Cuthbert Grant ordered that the remaining colonists be allowed to leave Red River without harm, and they again retreated to Norway House. At the same time, Lord Selkirk was travelling west to visit the colony. He brought 100 Swiss mercenaries with him as a protective force. On the way, he was told about the Battle of Seven Oaks. Selkirk quickly moved west and seized the NWC post of Fort William. He then descended on the Red River Valley and took control of the area. Promised protection by the Swiss soldiers, the colonists once again returned to the settlement.

The following spring, in 1817, Selkirk negotiated a treaty with the local Anishinabé and Cree Nations to lease the land along both the Assiniboine and Red Rivers. He distributed the land among the colonists, and promised that a church and school would soon be built. By the time Selkirk left the Red River Valley, he believed he had left the colony at peace.

Selkirk also thought he had settled matters with the NWC. He was wrong. When he returned to England, he was confronted by lawsuits filed against him and his employees, and for the next three years, he waged a costly court battle. Selkirk died in the spring of 1820, just short of his 49th birthday.

WEB LINK •.........
Read more about the life and legacy of Cuthbert Grant on the Pearson Web site.

Zoom In > Cuthbert Grant

 **CRITICAL INQUIRY** Significance

The first acknowledged leader of the Métis was Cuthbert Grant, who became instrumental in giving the Métis a sense of identity. Grant was born in 1793 at Fort Tremblant, a NWC trading post. His mother was Métis, and his father was a Scottish trader. As a boy, Grant was sent to school in Montreal. He returned to the Northwest in 1812 and worked as a clerk for the NWC. Fluent in both English and French, he was later made Captain of the Métis.

Grant was polite, soft-spoken, and very persuasive. By the time George Simpson arrived at Red River in 1821, Grant was the settlement's most prominent citizen. As the new head of the HBC, Simpson appointed Grant Warden of the Plains, a post that carried an annual salary of £200 and a sizeable land grant. In this position, Grant was expected to enforce the HBC's rules among the Métis, a job he tactfully carried out for 20 years.

When he realized that the new boundary with the United States would cut off a group of Métis from the rest of the settlement, Grant convinced more than 100 Métis families to resettle in the northern part of the valley. Where they settled would eventually be called Grantown.

Grant used his medical knowledge to help people, allowed his home to be used as a school, and was both magistrate and sheriff for the area.

When American settlers were moving into the territory south of the 49th parallel in the 1840s, HBC rules prevented the Métis from trading with them. Grant's continued enforcement of these rules weakened his position with younger Métis. In 1849, he retired to his farm. He died in 1854.

- Why is Grant historically significant? What can we learn from his experiences and his decisions that will help us understand this period?

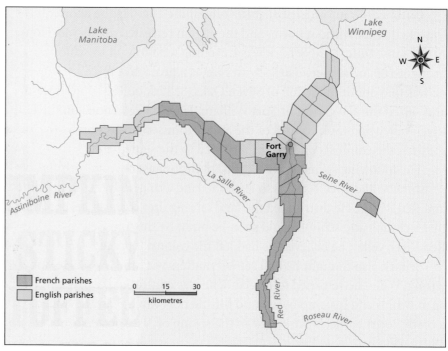

FIGURE 4–19 By 1870, the Red River Settlement had been divided into sections called parishes, based on language. Why do you think the settlement developed in this pattern?

The Merger of the HBC and NWC

The conflict in the Red River Valley was part of a larger struggle between the HBC and the NWC for control of the fur trade. By 1820, this struggle had brought both companies to the verge of bankruptcy. There were simply not enough furs in the Northwest to justify full-scale operations by two rival companies. In 1821, the British government, which feared loss of control of the Northwest if both companies failed, forced the HBC and the NWC to agree to a merger of their two companies.

A new company was formed, under the name of the Hudson's Bay Company, with 100 shares. The NWC partners received 55 shares, and the HBC directors received 45 shares. The British Parliament gave the new company control over Rupert's Land and upheld the trading monopoly enjoyed by the old HBC. In fact, new legislation extended both the land grant and trading monopoly west of the Rocky Mountains and north to the Arctic Ocean. The new HBC now controlled more than 7 million square kilometres—over half of what is now Canada.

FIGURE 4–20 After the merger, the new HBC began expanding into the area west of the Rocky Mountains. Fort St. John, shown here, was renamed by the HBC in 1821 and operated for another two years. What challenges were faced by traders working west of the Rockies?

Changes in Organization

Because the direct route from York Factory to England via Hudson Bay was cheaper, the Fort William to Montreal route was abandoned, and York boats were adopted as the main means of transportation. The new HBC also drastically reduced the number of trading posts and employees.

The company now increasingly relied on First Nations and Métis to support its operations. The Métis became the primary suppliers of pemmican and labour to the HBC, while First Nations were employed as trappers, translators, guides, and map-makers.

The HBC also appointed a new head of operations for North America. The man they selected was George Simpson, a Scottish sugar broker. Simpson did not know much about furs and knew less about the Northwest, but he did know how to run a company. In 1820, in his early thirties, he was named Governor-in-Chief of the HBC. He ran the company for the next 40 years.

Simpson was a dynamic man and a hands-on manager. He refused to run the HBC from behind a desk in Montreal. Between 1821 and 1829, Simpson criss-crossed Rupert's Land from Hudson Bay to the Pacific Coast. Typically, he set off by canoe in the spring and spent the summer and autumn visiting as many trading posts as he could. Simpson preferred to arrive without warning and spent hours grilling traders and factors.

FIGURE 4–21 George Simpson in 1857. When visiting trading posts, Simpson dressed formally and entered the post to the music of a bagpiper. Why do you think he might have chosen to present himself this way?

ACTIVITIES

1. Describe how European settlement had an impact on the Métis. Identify two or three main ideas with supporting details that explain and support your response.

2. Lord Selkirk has been called an "unrealistic idealist." Find evidence to support or refute this claim and discuss your views with a partner.

3. Was the conflict over Selkirk's Red River Settlement inevitable? Provide reasons for your answer.

Patterns and Change

4. How could the Battle of Seven Oaks be seen as a turning point in Métis history?

5. How could the merger of the HBC and the NWC be seen as a turning point in the history of the Northwest?

March 15

I am keeping these stories to show to my children when I am old. My nohkom tells us stories from her childhood so we can learn about her people. I would like my children and their children to read my stories. I am Marie Garneau, and I am 17 years old. I live on a farm with my mother and father. We are Métis. Both of my grandfathers were French traders for the North West Company. My father's mother, my nohkom, is Saulteaux, and my mother's mother was Cree. I have two younger brothers. My uncle has taught all of us to read and write, and the paper that I write on is a special gift from him!

March 26

I should tell you about where we live. Our farm is long and narrow, and stretches back from the Red River. We have neighbours on either side—the Levines and the Cardinals. We grow vegetables and keep chickens and cows. We all work hard on the farm. I milk the cows, even in the winter, when my hands get as cold as ice. Sometimes my parents also find work with the North West Company. We hunt bison twice every year, in the spring and the fall. The bison hunt is the biggest event of the year and involves our whole village—even women and children. We load up the carts with enough supplies for three weeks. The carts are so noisy that sometimes I think the bison will hear us coming!

May 20

Today I was riding with the men, away from the camp to look for bison. Suddenly I heard a noise like thunder. Bison! I rode quickly up to the crest of a hill so I could see them. There were so many—a herd that stretched as far as I could see, right up to where the sky met the earth. I turned around and went straight to Mr. Grant to tell him what I had seen. Later, I watched the hunt from the ridge. If only my parents would let me ride in the hunt! They say it is too dangerous. Today three men fell from their horses and had to be carried back to the camp.

October 3

Two years ago, people from Scotland came to live here. Their leader is a man called Macdonell. Papa has told me that Macdonell claims the whole valley and the rivers for his people, because his king said so. I think that since we have lived here for so long, we have a right to stay here and farm. Papa says that if you live on the land and farm it, you own it. This is our land for all time.

January 20

Papa came home today with bad news. Macdonell has just ruled that we are no longer allowed to trade pemmican. We are all shocked. When Macdonell and his people came here, it was our pemmican that helped keep them from starving. My mama even gave some of the sick ones medicine. Now Macdonell says that our pemmican must only go to him. But if we can't sell or trade our pemmican with the Northwest Company, our lives will be much harder. My parents are worried that this is how Macdonell will force the Métis off our land and our farms. Some of the younger men are trying to scare Macdonell and his people away by shooting their rifles and setting fires. I don't think that violence is the answer to our problem, but I am proud that my people are standing up for our rights.

The Red River Valley: 1821–1860

▶ **Did the settlement in the Red River Valley develop and thrive, or did it return to conflict?**

By 1821, peace had come to the Red River Valley. For the next 40 years, the settlement developed into a stable, close-knit community. The settlement now consisted of the Métis, the Scottish colonists, the Swiss mercenaries, and employees of the new Hudson's Bay Company. It was an isolated and self-sufficient community, with little direct contact with the outside world until the late 1840s.

In 1821, the population was evenly divided between the Métis and the European colonists. However, by 1860, more than 80 percent of the population was Métis.

The economy of the Red River Valley revolved around the needs of the HBC. The Scottish settlers grew crops and sold the produce to the HBC. The Métis also farmed, but they contributed to the economy in other ways. The Métis bison hunt continued to provide both pemmican and hides, and many Métis worked as labourers, as crew on York boats, or as HBC clerks.

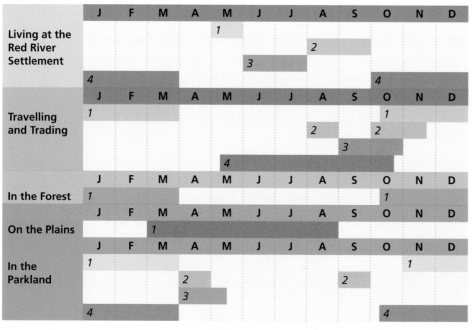

Living at the Red River Settlement
1. Planting vegetable and grain crops
2. Harvesting and haying
3. Cultivating crops and looking after animals
4. Making items for the household, including carts

Travelling and Trading
1. Fur trading
2. Trading pemmican to HBC and Red River settlers
3. Trading farm produce to HBC
4. Travelling to York Factory and other destinations

In the Forest
1. Hunting and trapping

On the Plains
1. Organizing and conducting the annual bison hunt

In the Parkland
1. Fishing at the lake
2. Hunting geese
3. Sugaring
4. Trapping; occasionally bison hunting

FIGURE 4–22 Seasonal activities of the Métis in Red River. In what ways was the Métis way of life European? In what ways was it similar to that of the First Nations?

Race and Social Class in Red River

In 1829, George Simpson took a leave from his duties as Governor-in-Chief of the HBC and travelled to England. Like most traders, Simpson had a Métis wife and several children. However, Simpson was to **turn off** his Métis wife and children. In fact, he predicted that the "fashion" of marrying Métis women would come to an end once European women began arriving in the Northwest. When Simpson left for England, his plan was to find an English bride.

Simpson's choice was his 18-year-old cousin, Frances. In 1830, he brought her to Red River. Simpson was determined to "improve" the society in the Red River Settlement, which meant introducing well-born European women who would become the settlement's new social elite.

Frances Simpson soon announced that she would not socialize with any of the Métis wives or relatives of HBC employees. In a small community, this was a foolish move. The Simpsons soon found themselves isolated, since there were actually few European women of Frances Simpson's social class in Red River.

The biased and elitist attitude expressed by the Simpsons was very common outside the Northwest in the 19th century. In general, fur-trade society was exceptional in terms of its tolerance of racial and cultural differences, so it is little wonder that the Simpsons did not find their attempt at "improving" Red River society successful.

In the spring of 1832, the Simpsons' infant son died. They both left the Red River Valley the following year, eventually settling in Montreal. While Simpson continued to travel during his work for the HBC, he never again lived in the Northwest.

turn off to leave behind a Métis wife and children or to replace a Métis wife with a European wife

FIGURE 4–23 Frances Simpson was a teenager when she arrived in the Northwest, a land she called "romantic." How do you think she might have felt when beginning her new role in Red River?

FIGURE 4–24 In an isolated community such as the Red River Settlement, how would social structure affect people's everyday lives? How do you think newcomers would have been treated?

A Self-Sufficient Community

Isolation from other colonies of British North America fostered a sense of self-reliance among the inhabitants of the Red River Settlement. Crop failures meant real hardship, and what we consider ordinary foods were often scarce. In 1834, one colonist recalled seeing a ripe tomato for the first time in 15 years. There was little variation in diet, especially in winter, when pemmican was the staple.

Life was physically demanding, primarily because most tasks had to be done by hand. For instance, both men and women used scythes to harvest the grain, and women performed the time-consuming task of cleaning, carding, and spinning wool for clothing. Women also did the cooking for their families, making **bannock** and other foods. Many Métis women, skilled in traditional medicine, acted as both midwives and health care specialists.

"Le commerce est libre! Vive la liberté!"

As the 1840s progressed, Red River colonists began expanding into what is now North Dakota, Wisconsin, and Minnesota. The Métis looked on these homesteaders as a market for many of their products, especially pemmican and buffalo robes, but they were forbidden to trade independently because of the HBC trade monopoly. Throughout the 1840s, an increasing number of Métis, believing they had a right to trade freely, began to deal with colonists regardless of HBC rules. In 1849, the matter came to a head when four Métis were charged with illegal trading, and one, Pierre Guillaume Sayer, was brought to trial.

When the trial began, the courtroom was packed, and more than 200 Métis surrounded the courthouse. The presiding judge was known to be hostile to French-speaking Métis and actually told the jury that they had no option but to find the defendant guilty—which they did—to the dismay of the angry crowd. The jury foreman quickly recommended mercy, and Sayer was freed, without penalty. Outside, the Métis proclaimed, *"Le commerce est libre! Vive la liberté!"* ("Business is open! Long live freedom!") The HBC could no longer enforce its monopoly, and **free trade** became a fact of life in the Red River Valley.

FIGURE 4–25 A traditional wooden scythe. Heavy and awkward, it required a great deal of strength to use. Considering the location of the colony, how might new technology reach the people of Red River?

bannock a simple bread, fried or baked, consisting of flour, baking powder, and salt

free trade a system of trade that is not fully regulated by government control

ACTIVITIES

1. Describe the attitudes of George and Frances Simpson toward the people of the Red River Settlement. What impact do you think these views had on the Simpsons and on the settlement as a whole?

2. What roles did women play in the daily life of the Red River Settlement? How did their lives compare with life for women colonists in Upper Canada?

3. How was the Sayer trial of 1849 a victory for the Métis?

4. Despite some significant conflict, the Red River Settlement was largely peaceful from 1821–1860. Give some reasons why this may have been so.

Changes: The Red River Settlement from 1860–1870

▷ **How would the arrival of newcomers be a turning point for the Red River Settlement?**

The 1860s brought significant changes to the Red River Settlement. The fur trade and the influence of the HBC had declined, and more and more people began to move into the area, changing the balance of the population and bringing new cultures to the region.

It was the arrival of new colonists—especially those from the Canadas—that had the greatest impact. The quickly growing population of Canada West meant that most of the good farmland had been taken. By 1860, many Canadians were looking for new areas to farm. The Red River Valley, with its fertile soil and established community, was an appealing prospect.

DID YOU KNOW...

According to an 1870 census of the Métis and Canadian populations of Manitoba, the Red River Settlement consisted of

- 5720 French Métis
- 4080 English Métis
- 2428 Canadians

Rising Tensions

Most of the new arrivals in Red River were Protestant and members of the Orange Order, an anti-French, anti-Catholic movement. Not surprisingly, their arrival led to increasing racial tension in the Red River Settlement. The French Métis were discriminated against because of their language and Catholic religion, but the English-speaking Métis, many of whom were Protestant, were also discriminated against because of their First Nations heritage.

One of the first immigrants to arrive in 1861 was "Doctor" John Christian Schultz. Schultz had never completed his medical degree and had no intention of practising medicine. Instead, he opened a general store and took over the only newspaper in the settlement, the *Nor'Wester*. By the late 1860s, he had organized a small group of supporters into the "Canadian Party," which he hoped would eventually gain political control of the colony. Schultz used the *Nor'Wester* as a platform for his anti-Métis views. Statements such as these only increased tension within the community:

FIGURE 4–26 John Christian Schultz. How might his writings be viewed today?

> [The Métis], the indolent and the careless, like the native tribes of the country, will fall back before the march of superior intelligence.
>
> —John Christian Schultz

Economic problems during the 1860s also contributed to rising tensions at Red River. There were several crop failures, and the bison hunts were less successful than in earlier years. The HBC was also losing interest in the area.

Canada Purchases Rupert's Land

Politicians such as John A. Macdonald were interested in creating a Dominion of Canada, one that stretched from coast to coast. At the same time, the HBC realized that running Rupert's Land was becoming too expensive. The company decided to give up control of Rupert's Land.

Soon after Confederation, in 1867, the Canadian government and the HBC began negotiations to transfer control of Rupert's Land. The HBC did not consult those living in the Red River Settlement. Rumours regarding the deal soon began to circulate, and everyone was worried, especially the Métis.

In 1868, government surveyors arrived in the Red River Valley to survey the area. The surveyors assumed that the riverside farms of the Métis were not legally owned.

An agreement on the transfer of Rupert's Land was signed in November 1869. The Canadian government then joined Rupert's Land with the North-Western Territory, renaming the entire region the North-West Territories in 1870.

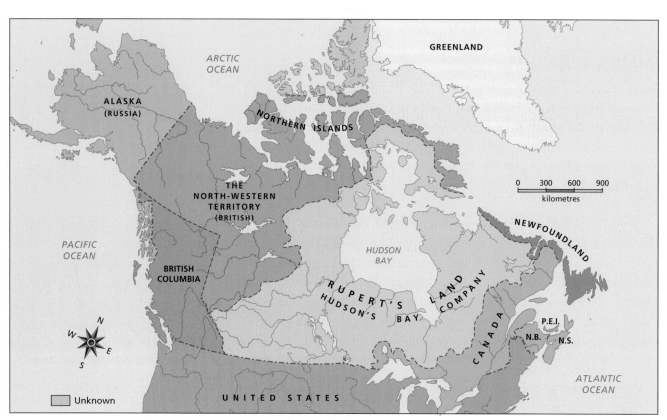

FIGURE 4–27 Rupert's Land and the North-Western Territory were joined together to become the North-West Territories in 1870. What would be the consequence of this change in the political landscape?

ACTIVITIES

1. How did immigrants from Canada drastically change the composition of the population of the Red River Settlement between 1860 and 1870?

2. Discuss why both the Canadian government and the HBC might have ignored the interests of those living in the Red River Valley.

The Red River Resistance

▶ **After so many years of peace and cooperation, why did the Red River Settlement return to open conflict?**

In 1868, a Métis named Louis Riel returned to Red River from Montreal, where he had been sent to be educated. He was now a lawyer, fluent in both French and English, and an excellent **orator**. Although just 24, he would soon take the role of a leader in what would become known as the **Red River Resistance**.

Tensions had been rising in Red River since the arrival of the surveyors. People were angry that the Hudson's Bay Company was selling Rupert's Land without consulting them and that the surveyors were ignoring their rights. Most felt that the Canadian government planned to take their land. Riel soon organized groups of Métis to observe the surveyors.

In October 1869, surveyors were seen on a Métis hay privilege. Riel was quickly sent for, and he arrived with a party of horsemen. They told the surveyors that they were trespassing, and one Métis stood on the surveyors' chain, stopping their work. The following week, Riel formed the **National Métis Committee** in order to fight for Métis rights, including the right to their land.

orator an eloquent public speaker, able to inspire an audience

Red River Resistance events leading up to the Métis' attempt to achieve recognition of their rights and self-government; also known as the Red River Rebellion

National Métis Committee an organization formed to support Métis rights in the Red River Valley

provisional government a temporary government

The Provisional Government

John A. Macdonald had already appointed William McDougall as lieutenant governor of the North-West Territories, and the National Métis Committee's first act was to inform McDougall that he was not welcome. McDougall ignored them, and the next day, the National Métis Committee occupied Upper Fort Garry, seizing weapons and ammunition. Riel and the Métis were determined to fight, if necessary, for their rights.

Still, Riel and his supporters had no intention of rebelling against the government. In fact, they were not opposed to entering Confederation, as long as the rights of the people of Red River were protected. To ensure that the Métis would have a voice, Riel decided to set up a **provisional government**. This government would help maintain order and would give the people of Red River the power to negotiate an agreement to enter Confederation. Riel feared that if Lieutenant Governor McDougall, who was known to be strongly anti-French, had

FIGURE 4–28 Louis Riel and members of the provisional government. Why was the formation of this government such an important event for the Red River Settlement?

complete control of the area, he would give all power to the Orange Order's Canadian Party.

John A. Macdonald decided to postpone the transfer of Rupert's Land until matters could be resolved. He sent a letter to McDougall, telling him to take no action. Before the letter arrived, however, McDougall crossed the border and proclaimed himself governor of the North-West Territories. He then quickly recrossed the border into the United States. Copies of McDougall's proclamation were soon circulated in the Red River Settlement.

Ironically, with the release of the proclamation, the authority of the HBC ceased, but because McDougall was in the United States, authority did not officially transfer to Canada. The letter he failed to receive held a warning from Macdonald:

> *An assumption of the Government by you, of course, puts an end to that of the Hudson's Bay Company's authorities... There would then be, if you were not admitted into the Country, no legal government existing... it is quite open by the Law of Nations for the inhabitants to form a Government... for the protection of life & property, and such a Government has certain sovereign rights...*
>
> —Sir John A. Macdonald to William McDougall, November 27, 1869

sovereign rights the right to form a government or country

Because of McDougall's mistake, Riel's provisional government was now, in fact, the legal government of the area, with "**sovereign rights**" and the right to negotiate with the Canadian government. Also, any actions that might be taken by the Canadian Party against Riel's government would be considered against the law.

Riel Takes Action

Riel feared that the Canadian Party was already armed and prepared to take control of the Red River Settlement. In early December of 1869, he decided to act first. A party of armed Métis arrested John Schultz and 48 of his supporters, confining them in Upper Fort Garry.

Once the news reached Ottawa, John A. Macdonald sent Donald Smith, a senior official in the Hudson's Bay Company, to negotiate with Riel. However, Macdonald was considering other options:

> *Smith goes to carry the olive branch. We must not think of military force until peaceable means have been exhausted. Should these miserable half-breeds not disband, they must be put down.*
>
> —Sir John A. Macdonald

Smith arrived in Red River in January 1870. Eventually he and Riel agreed that the provisional government should send negotiators to Ottawa. In the meantime, Schultz and some of his men had escaped from Upper Fort Garry and had tried to free the remaining prisoners. The Métis stopped them, capturing several members of the raiding party, including a man named Thomas Scott, who was later executed by Riel.

While many people regretted what happened with Thomas Scott, this event marked the end of the threat of war between the Métis and the Canadian Party. By the end of the month, a delegation including both Métis and members of the Canadian Party left for Ottawa in a more optimistic mood. They were on their way to negotiate the creation of the province of Manitoba.

Zoom In The Trial and Execution of Thomas Scott

Thomas Scott was born in northern Ireland and settled in Red River in late 1869. Scott was known to be a difficult person, hot headed and prone to violence. He aggressively voiced his anti-Métis views, believing that white people were superior.

Scott had a deep, personal dislike for Louis Riel. Recaptured with other members of the raiding party, Scott became impossible to handle. Accounts show that he spent most of his time hurling insults at his guards, and he threatened to kill Riel once he was released. The abuse was so distasteful that even his fellow prisoners asked that Scott be put in a separate cell.

By early March, the guards' patience was exhausted. After a physical assault by Scott, they demanded that Riel take action.

On March 3, 1870, Scott went on trial for treason. After calling a number of witnesses, the board concluded that Scott was guilty and, by a majority vote, passed the sentence of death by firing squad. On March 4, Scott was executed. This action would have profound implications for the Métis and Louis Riel, even though many agreed that Scott's behaviour was his downfall.

- If you had been part of the board that determined Scott's fate, what questions would you have asked to help determine his innocence or guilt?

FIGURE 4–29 The trial and execution of Thomas Scott was big news in Canada. What feelings might the picture evoke in an audience? Why would a newspaper choose to show this image?

There is no doubt that he [Scott] would have been spared and let out when we were, had he behaved himself.

—George Sanderson, member of the Canadian Party

Manitoba Is Created

Unfortunately, John Schultz reached Ontario before the official Métis delegation. He had quickly whipped up a wave of violent anti-French, anti-Catholic, and anti-Métis hysteria. Thomas Scott was depicted as a Protestant martyr, cruelly murdered at the hands of the "evil" Louis Riel.

By the time the Red River delegation arrived in Ottawa, Ontario was in an uproar, and John A. Macdonald, who had already expressed anti-Métis sentiments, proved a difficult negotiator. He refused to allow provincial control of public lands, but he did offer a compromise: a grant of 200 000 hectares to the "children of the Métis." On May 12, 1870, legislation creating the province of Manitoba was passed by the House of Commons.

Still, Macdonald had to show his support of the calls for justice from Ontario. He dispatched a force of 1200 militia (many of them members of the Orange Order) to Red River, under the command of Colonel Wolseley. He instructed Wolseley to keep the peace until the transfer of power to the provincial government was complete. He also made it clear that the force was not to treat Riel or his followers as a legitimate government.

Ironically, Riel *was* the leader of a legitimate government—even in the words of Macdonald himself, in his letter to McDougall quoted on page 158. When Wolseley's force finally reached the Red River in late August, Riel had fled the area. He feared, with justification, that his life was in danger. Eventually, all members of the provisional government were granted an amnesty by the Canadian government—all except Louis Riel, who remained in exile in the United States.

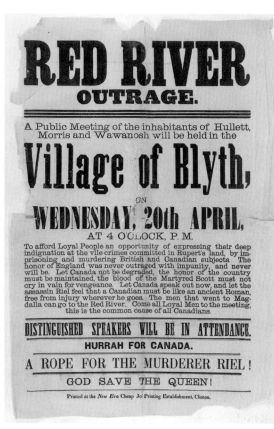

FIGURE 4–30 An anti-Riel poster, 1870. What sort of sentiments are expressed here? How does this compare to the image of the execution of Thomas Scott?

ACTIVITIES

1. John A. Macdonald was in the Orange Order, yet he worked and was friends with French-speaking Catholics—people the Orange Order considered inferior. How do you explain Macdonald's position? How might the Orange Order have influenced his decisions about Riel and the Métis?

2. Evaluate key incidents in the Red River Resistance. What might have happened if Scott had not been executed? With a partner, discuss this question and share your findings with the class.

3. Summarize the main events that led Macdonald to dispatch 1200 militia to Red River.

Rights and Freedoms

The Métis List of Rights, agreed to by the Convention of the Red River Settlement on March 22, 1870, is an important Canadian document. It later became the base of the Manitoba Act, and reflected the concerns of those living in the Red River.

- As you read through the document, consider how it is similar to excerpts from the Canadian Charter of Rights and Freedoms on the following page. Classify your findings according to the five themes in the Charter (Fundamental Freedoms, Democratic Rights, etc.).

1. That the people have the right to elect their own Legislature.

2. That the Legislature have the power to pass all laws local to the Territory over the veto of the Executive by a two-thirds vote.

3. That no act of the Dominion Parliament (local to the territory) be binding on the people until sanctioned [approved] by the Legislature of the Territory.

4. That all Sheriffs, Magistrates, Constables, School Commissioners, and so on, be elected by the people.

5. A free Homestead and preemption Land Law.

6. That a portion of the public lands be appropriated for the benefit of Schools, the building of Bridges, Roads and Public Buildings.

7. That it be guaranteed to connect Winnipeg by Rail with the nearest line of Railroad, within a term of five years; the land grant to be subject to the Local Legislature.

8. That for the term of four years all Military, Civil and Municipal expenses be paid out of Dominion funds.

9. That the Military be composed of inhabitants now existing in the Territory.

10. That the English and French languages be common in the Legislature and Courts, and that all Public Documents and Acts of the Legislature be published in both languages.

11. That the Judge of the Supreme Court speak the English and French languages.

12. That Treaties be concluded and ratified between the Dominion Government and the several tribes of Indians in the Territory to ensure peace on the frontier.

13. That we have a fair and full representation in the Canadian Parliament.

14. That all privileges, customs and usages existing at the time of transfer be respected.

Cross Currents

Rights and Freedoms

The Canadian Charter of Rights and Freedoms was entrenched as part of the Canadian Constitution under the terms of the Constitution Act, 1982. Here are some excerpts.

habeas corpus requiring that the lawfulness of a person's arrest or detention be investigated by a judge or court

Fundamental Freedoms

2. Everyone has the following fundamental freedoms: (a) freedom of conscience and religion; (b) freedom of thought, belief, opinion and expression, including freedom of the press and other media of communication; (c) freedom of peaceful assembly; and (d) freedom of association.

Democratic Rights

3. Every citizen of Canada has the right to vote in an election of members of the House of Commons or of a legislative assembly and the right to be qualified for membership therein.

Legal Rights

7. Everyone has the right to life, liberty and security of the person and the right not to be deprived thereof except in accordance with the principles of fundamental justice.

8. Everyone has the right to be secure against unreasonable search or seizure.

9. Everyone has the right not to be arbitrarily detained or imprisoned.

10. Everyone has the right on arrest or detention (a) to be informed promptly for the reasons therefore; (b) to retain and instruct counsel without delay and to be informed of that right; and (c) to have the validity of the detention determined by way of **habeas corpus** and to be released if the detention is not lawful.

12. Everyone has the right not to be subjected to any cruel and unusual treatment or punishment.

Equality Rights

(1) Every individual is equal before and under the law and has the right to equal protection and equal benefit of the law without discrimination and, in particular, without discrimination based on race, national or ethnic origin, colour, religion, sex, age or mental or physical disability.

Official Languages of Canada

16. (1) English and French are the official languages of Canada and have equality of status and equal rights and privileges as to their use in all institutions of the Parliament and government of Canada.

WHAT DO YOU THINK?

1. How are the two documents similar and dissimilar? Consider the reasons for the creation of each document.

2. What can the Métis List of Rights tell us about the Métis resistance?

Explore the Big Ideas

The fur trade, and the people who were part of it, played a significant role in the development of the Northwest. Fur-trading companies, such as the HBC and the NWC, were big players in an industry that affected both the land and the people of the region. One of the most important results of the fur trade was the contact between First Nations and European fur traders. This contact led to the emergence of the Métis, who played a role in the creation of Manitoba.

1. How did conflict and cooperation change the Northwest? Use an organizer like the one below to explore the changing relationships between the fur traders, the First Nations, and the Métis.

Time Period	Groups Involved	Examples of Interaction/Turning Points
Fur trade before 1812		
Selkirk Settlement, 1812–1821		
Red River Settlement, 1821–1860		
Immigration into Red River, 1860–1869		
Red River Resistance, 1869–1870		
Aftermath		

2. Examine the impact of the fur trade on the First Nations and Métis of the Northwest.

   a) In a class debate, discuss this question: Was the fur trade harmful to the First Nations of the Northwest?

   b) As a class, discuss and record the contributions of Aboriginal peoples to the fur trade. How did these contributions influence the development of Canada? Create a cause/event/consequence chart to explore this issue further.

3. Was the violent conflict that erupted over the Red River Valley avoidable? Suggest how the conflict could have been avoided during the creation of the Selkirk Settlement.

4. You are a resident of the Red River Settlement in 1870. Thomas Scott was executed yesterday. In a poem, letter, cartoon, or picture, describe your feelings about this key event. You could take the viewpoint of a Métis, a colonist, or a member of the Orange Order.

5. Create a compare and contrast chart to show the similarities and differences between the life of a Métis teenager in the mid-1800s to that of a teenager today. Use the Window on Canada (pages 150–151) and other information in this chapter to complete your chart.

6. What was the most significant event in terms of First Nations, Métis, and European Canadian relations? Justify your thinking with specific details from the text and your own research.

7. Choose one of the conflicts explored in this chapter. Was the conflict inevitable? Was the outcome just? Explain.

5 Changes Come to the Prairies

Chapter Outcomes

In this chapter, you will study the development of the Prairies and the impact of these changes on the Aboriginal peoples of the Northwest. By the end of the chapter, you will

- describe contributions made by Aboriginal peoples to the development of Canada

- evaluate the rationale for the numbered treaties and their impact on First Nations and the Métis

- identify causes and key events of the Northwest Uprising

- assess the impact of Macdonald's National Policy on Canada

- describe the events surrounding the construction of the Canadian Pacific Railway and analyze its importance to the development of the Canadian West

- assess factors that led to the expansion of Canada, including the national railway and sea-to-sea unification

1885 ~ SIXTY YEARS OF PROGRESS ~ 1945

A DREAM COME TRUE

When on November 7, 1885, the last spike was driven linking the rails of the Canadian Pacific Railway, developments only dreamed of that day were to follow.

Soon Canadian Pacific ships were plying the Pacific . . . then the Atlantic. There followed a chain of hotels and resorts . . . steamships . . . express and telegraph services—forming an all-Canadian system stretching more than half way round the world.

In 1939, this vast system was dedicated to the winning of the war. That has been achieved. Now the Canadian Pacific faces the future, ready to do its part in providing modern, efficient transportation by land and sea.

Canadian Pacific

What is the first image that comes to mind when you think of the Prairies? You might think of open spaces or fields of wheat. For those who built the transcontinental railway, the prairies may have been something to cross or to own. For them, the CPR was "progress." How might this perspective contrast with that of First Nations leaders, shown here with Canadian troops sent to the West, or Chief Grande Oreilles, quoted below?

> *What are these Landworkers? What brought them here?...it would appear that these Strangers, these makers of gardens, look upon them-selves as the real possessors of these lands.*
>
> —Grandes Oreilles, a chief of the Anishinabé, in a speech to NWC partners

How did the actions of the Canadian government affect people living in the West?

After Confederation, great changes were in store for the Northwest, including the creation of new territorial boundaries, the building of the railway, and the arrival of immigrants. Would everyone already living on the Prairies benefit from these changes?

Key Terms

scrip
North West Mounted Police (NWMP)
Indian Act
Métis Bill of Rights
Canadian Pacific Railway (CPR)
Northwest Uprising
National Policy

The Métis in the 1870s

▶ **What were the hopes and dreams of the Métis after 1870? What was the reality?**

TIMELINE

1870 ● North-West Territories is created
● Manitoba becomes a province

1871 ● Treaty process with the First Nations of the Northwest begins
● Canadian Pacific Railway Company is formed

1872 ● Canadian Pacific Railway (CPR) survey begins

1873 ● "Pacific Scandal"
● Laws of St. Laurent are formalized
● Cypress Hills Massacre
● North West Mounted Police is formed

1877 ● Treaty process ends

1879 ● National Policy is enacted

1881 ● Canadian Pacific Railway is incorporated; building begins

1885 ● CPR is completed
● Northwest Uprising
● Louis Riel is executed

militia civilians with military training who are called to service in times of war or unrest

The Manitoba Act

The passage of the Manitoba Act in 1870, which made the lands surrounding the Red River the new province of Manitoba, was welcomed by many Métis. It was a remarkable achievement for Louis Riel and his provisional government, as it showed their influence on Canadian legislation. After all, much of the Manitoba Act was based on the Métis List of Rights.

The new legislation seemed to protect Métis rights, as well as those of future generations of Métis. The Act made French and English the official languages of the province, and it provided for two education systems— one Protestant and one Roman Catholic. In addition, 566 580 hectares were put aside for the "children of the Métis" as farmland, and the rights of the Métis to their existing lands were protected.

Unfortunately, any optimism proved to be unfounded. Now a province, Manitoba was firmly under the control of Ottawa and the provisional government was at an end. Following the Red River Resistance, John A. Macdonald sent Canadian troops, led by Colonel Wolseley, to Manitoba to "keep the peace." Most of these troops were **militia** from Ontario and members of the Orange Order, the same Protestant group that had caused so much trouble for the Métis in the Red River Valley (see Chapter 4).

The militia was less concerned with keeping the peace than avenging the execution of Thomas Scott. Members committed acts of violence against the Métis, including arson, assault, rape, and murder. Although the acts were not officially permitted, the men who committed these crimes were never punished. Macdonald's opinion was clear:

> *These impulsive Métis have got spoilt by the émeute [uprising] and must be kept down by a strong hand until they are swamped by the influx of settlers.*
>
> —Sir John A. Macdonald

The Issue of Land

Up to this time, land ownership in the Northwest had not been straight-forward or conducted in any official way. Still, the Métis had assumed that with the Canadian government now in charge, they would be confirmed as owners of land they already occupied. They also believed that they would be able to select land for their children once the new province was surveyed.

However, in order to gain title to the land that was reserved for them, all Métis in Manitoba were required to have **scrip**, a piece of paper similar to money. Two kinds of scrip were issued to the Métis—money scrip or land scrip. Money scrip had a value of $160 or $240, an amount based on the value of farmland. Money scrip could be converted to cash. Land scrip could be exchanged for a homesteader's land grant—160 acres. Land scrip could also be sold for cash.

The survey of land in Manitoba progressed slowly, and it was not until late 1875 that land was finally made available and scrip issued. Adult Métis were entitled to scrip valued at $160 each; their children received $240. However, the children's land grant was not what the Métis had expected. The land was open prairie up to 6 km away from the rivers. It was distributed by lottery, and recipients had no control over where their land grant was located.

scrip a piece of paper that could be used to certify possession of land or be exchanged for money

DID YOU KNOW...

To claim land they were already living on, Métis had to prove occupation. This meant that they had to have "adequate" housing and at least two hectares under cultivation. Many claims were rejected when these conditions were not met.

FIGURE 5–1 Métis scrip issued to Jean Baptiste Forcier. Think about what the Métis wanted to use the land for. Was all land equal in value? Why was it a problem to base scrip on the value of land?

Land Speculation in Manitoba

Land speculation, the practice of buying and selling land for a profit, had existed in Manitoba before the Red River Resistance. Many people in Red River had taken part in land speculation, including Louis Riel. However, combined with the new scrip system and environmental factors, it became a serious problem.

With the militia's intimidating presence, many Métis found life in Red River very uncomfortable. Also, by the early 1870s, the number of bison decreased significantly in the eastern Prairies. With the bison went a large part of the Métis economy, and the slow process of land distribution led many frustrated Métis to sell their land entitlements to the nearest speculator and leave. In many cases, these entitlements were sold for far less than what the scrip was worth—sometimes for as little as $30 or $40. Speculators who purchased these entitlements could then convert them to scrip, making a profit.

By the mid-1870s, many Métis had left Manitoba. They moved west and north, wanting to recreate the way of life they had enjoyed in Red River. Some settled in established Métis communities near Fort Edmonton, on the North Saskatchewan River. More took up land near the junction of the North and South Saskatchewan Rivers near Prince Albert.

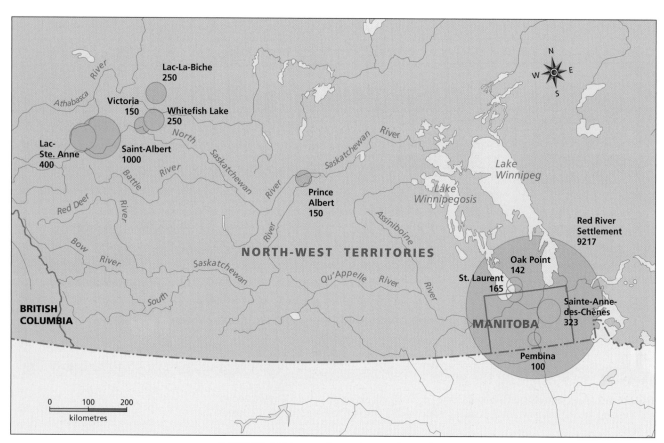

FIGURE 5–2 This map shows the population distribution of the Métis by 1870. Research some of the communities shown here. Are any still in existence? What are they like today?

The Métis Move North and West

In the North-West Territories, the Métis from Manitoba found established Métis communities organized in familiar ways. Farms were laid out in the traditional pattern: long lots about 200 metres across and over 3 km deep, stretching back from a river. The economy was based on subsistence farming, hunting bison, and hauling freight for the Hudson's Bay Company. (Although it had given up official administration of the region with the sale of Rupert's Land, the company was still in operation.)

However, the Métis and First Nations, such as the Blackfoot, had already noticed an alarming trend. The bison herds, which had once numbered in the thousands, were rapidly declining. Since bison was still the main source of food for Aboriginal peoples of the plains, and because the Métis continued to trade hides and pemmican, some Métis chose to take action.

In 1873, the Métis of St. Laurent, a community on the shore of Lake Manitoba, wrote down and formalized the Laws of St. Laurent. These laws, based on the informal "laws of the Prairies," governed all aspects of life in the community, including the regulation of the bison hunt.

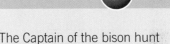

Get to the Source • The Laws of St. Laurent

CRITICAL INQUIRY Evidence

Why did the Métis take the step of making their own laws? The Laws of St. Laurent were formalized by the Métis council of the village. The laws were a natural result of the Métis practice of organizing bison hunts by appointing Captains and councils. Governance was a practical solution for a group that depended on carefully organized hunts involving large numbers of people, animals, and equipment. Usually, councils came and went with the bison hunts, but in St. Laurent a permanent elected council developed.

The formal Laws of St. Laurent also extended beyond the bison hunt, covering many other aspects of life. Still, the Métis were careful to state that they had no wish to be independent of the Canadian government, even though they were taking steps to govern themselves, as can be seen in the extract shown here.

Among other items, the Laws of St. Laurent ruled that

1. The community was to elect a council, which would have the authority to rule on any disputes in the community.

2. The Captain of the bison hunt was to regulate the hunt and all provisions.

- In the extract shown here, why were the Métis so clear in their intentions? What does this tell us about the Métis?

- Why did the Métis strictly regulate the bison hunt?

It is well understood that in making these laws and regulations the inhabitants of St. Laurent in no wise pretend to constitute for themselves an independent state, but the actual situation of the country in which they live obliges them to take measures to maintain peace and union amongst them... But in forming these laws, they acknowledge themselves as loyal and faithful subjects of Canada, and are ready to abandon their own organization and to submit to the laws of the Dominion, as soon as Canada shall have established amongst them regular magistrates with a force sufficient to uphold in the country the authority of the laws.

—From the Laws of St. Laurent

Lawrence Clarke and the Laws of St. Laurent

Lawrence Clarke, the Hudson's Bay Company factor at Fort Carlton in what is now Saskatchewan, believed that the Métis were inferior to Europeans. Deliberately using his power against them, he paid Métis carriers as little as he could and made their lives as difficult as possible.

When the North-West Territories was created, Clarke requested that the Canadian government provide a **magistrate** to enforce Canadian law in his area. The government appointed Clarke, and he quickly began to use his increased authority for the benefit of the HBC. For example, any Métis who objected to low pay could be imprisoned.

The winter of 1874–1875 was very difficult for the Métis and the First Nations on the Prairies, mainly due to the loss of the bison. Tensions began to rise. That spring, a group of Métis started hunting bison before the officially sanctioned hunt had begun. Gabriel Dumont, the hunt captain, arrested and fined the participants in this illegal hunt in accordance with the Laws of St. Laurent.

The Métis charged in the incident appealed to Magistrate Lawrence Clarke, who issued warrants for the arrest of Dumont and his men. Clarke imposed only minor fines, but his ruling still made the Laws of St. Laurent invalid. This was seen as a direct attack against the authority of the Métis, and some bison hunters now felt free to ignore the Métis laws.

> *Everyone took their freedom and ran on the buffalo without any other guide than their insatiable keenness, passion for killing, greed, and avarice. Anarchy and self-interest reigned on the prairie. They exterminated the poor buffalo with more frenzy than ever.*
>
> —an Oblate priest of St. Laurent

magistrate an officer with limited authority to administer and enforce the law

FIGURE 5–3 By the age of 12, Gabriel Dumont was an expert hunter and could speak more than six languages. He later proved to be a competent military leader. Why did these skills give him standing in the Métis community?

FIGURE 5–4 A camp of Métis hunters on the Prairie. Considering the migratory behaviour of the bison and the geography of the Prairie, why do you think it might have been difficult to enforce the Laws of St. Laurent?

Were the Métis of St. Laurent unreasonable in setting out such strict rules for the bison hunt? The accounts shown here take very different sides.

The hunters left as usual under the leadership of brave Gabriel Dumont… they began to sight buffalo which gave them courage and hope. [Then they learned] that many Métis [of another parish] without respect for the laws and rules and without concern for their brothers went on ahead. Immediately it was decided in a general meeting that it was necessary… and in the interest of everyone, to observe the laws. [Dumont], with his captains and soldiers, carried out the decision of the meeting, brought to the camp all the delinquents with the exception of two who preferred to pay [a fine] which was granted to them on the condition they immediately go to Carlton. Hardly had they arrived at Fort Carlton when they complained of having been maltreated, robbed, almost assassinated. They knew whom to make these complaints to; it was to people who had looked [with suspicion] at the creation of the laws of the Colonies. If one were to believe the celebrated **knave** *and his agents, the Métis of Carlton… were in full revolution against the Dominion of Canada.*

—**a priest in St. Laurent**

Two-thirds of this population (150 families constituting the settlement of St. Laurent) are connected by marriage and other degrees of kinship, and have assumed to themselves the right to enact laws… which the minority of settlers are perforce bound to obey or be treated with criminal severity. From this body, a court has been constituted numbering fourteen persons presided over by a man named Gabriel Dumond [sic] who is designated president before whom all delinquents are made to appear, or suffer violence in person or property… The past spring a party of "freemen" made their way to Carlton… and having disposed of the products of their hunts, purchased fresh supplies of necessaries and started prairie wards to hunt… joining a party of other hunters and Indians who were leaving for the same purpose. Dumond dispatched a courier with a letter ordering the party to retrace their steps and join the St. Laurent camp. To this the Indians and Métis [objected]; when Dumond with 40 of his bodyguards fully armed… followed in pursuit, and having come up with the party seized all the horses and carts together with provisions and effects they had secured leaving the **plundered** *people on the plains naked of transport. Dumond… then returned the stolen property and, after using violent threats to individuals, levied by force a heavy fine upon the party and returned to their camp.*

—**Lawrence Clarke**

knave an untrustworthy person

plunder to rob someone of goods or valuables by force

WHAT DO YOU THINK?

1. How is each account biased? Provide examples to support your answer. Start by looking for extreme language, such as "assassinated" or "plundered." Refer to the Skill Builder in Chapter 3, pages 98–99, for a review on recognizing bias.

2. How do these accounts support each other? How do they contradict each other?

What Happened to the Bison?

In the 1600s, an estimated 70 million bison roamed the grasslands. Well before the 1870s, however, First Nations of the plains had begun to express concerns about the shrinking numbers of bison. The Blackfoot, Nakoda, and Sioux, and later the Métis, depended on the bison for food and shelter. Losing such a vital part of their livelihood threatened their existence.

The slaughter of bison was part of the American government's campaign to force First Nations onto reservations so that the American West could be made available to European settlers. Bison hunting by Europeans was encouraged. American General Phillip Sheridan knew that the loss of the bison would weaken the First Nations of the plains:

> *Let them kill, skin and sell until the buffalo are exterminated. Then your prairies can be covered with speckled cattle and the festive cowboy.*
>
> —General Phillip Sheridan, 1875

The trade of hides and pemmican also reduced the population of bison, and in the 1800s, the building of transcontinental railways in Canada and the United States both divided the great herds and brought in more hunters. Thousands were killed by the day, and in only decades, bison herds so large that they darkened the Prairie were becoming only a memory. First Nations and Métis struggled to maintain their ways of life after such swift devastation. A doctor for the NWMP observed:

> *The disappearance of the buffalo has left them not only without food, but also without robes, moccasins, and adequate [shelter]...*
>
> —Augustus Jukes, NWMP doctor

Facing starvation, many First Nations were eventually forced to ask the government for assistance.

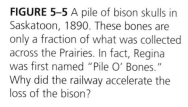

FIGURE 5–5 A pile of bison skulls in Saskatoon, 1890. These bones are only a fraction of what was collected across the Prairies. In fact, Regina was first named "Pile O' Bones." Why did the railway accelerate the loss of the bison?

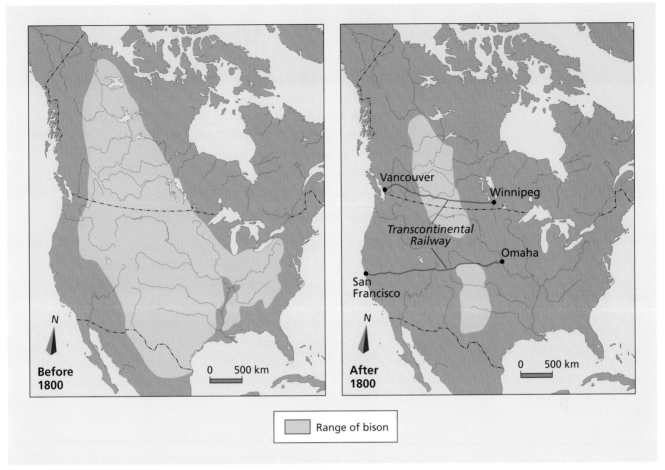

FIGURE 5–6 These maps show changes in the range of the bison herds before and after 1800. Compare these maps to a modern map of North America. Would the range of the bison herds be any different today if their numbers had survived? Explain.

ACTIVITIES

1. Who would have found the Manitoba land assignments unfair? Why?

2. Given what you have learned so far, suggest some reasons why the Métis were growing dissatisfied with the Canadian government.

3. With a partner, discuss what contributed the most to the Métis' loss of land and political power in Manitoba and the North-West Territories. Was it the militia, the Canadian government, the Orange Order, or the Métis themselves? Use written and visual evidence in this section to support your argument.

4. As you read further in this chapter, note the consequences of the destruction of the bison. How would these consequences affect interactions between the Canadian government and Aboriginal peoples?

The First Nations of the Northwest

▶ How were the First Nations affected by the Canadian government's policies in the Northwest? Do you think people at that time would have seen the government as dishonest?

The North West Mounted Police

Even though Manitoba and the North-West Territories had come under Canadian control in 1869, it took time before Ottawa's authority could be fully enforced throughout such a vast region. One of the first problems facing the government was the arrival of American fur traders. The American fur trade consisted of a number of small companies that traded strong, cheap liquor called "firewater" to First Nations trappers in exchange for furs. Although this trade was outlawed, it was very successful. The centre of the whisky trade was Fort Whoop-Up, near what is now Lethbridge, Alberta. The whisky trade devastated local Blackfoot communities, leading to widespread alcoholism, malnutrition, disease, and death.

The Canadian government was worried that the presence of the American whisky traders might lead to the loss of territory to the Americans. In 1873, the government created the **North West Mounted Police (NWMP)**. This group acted as a police force and a **paramilitary** organization for the Northwest, enforcing the law and establishing a Canadian presence in the region. Later that same year, an incident in Cypress Hills accelerated the arrival of the NWMP in the region.

North West Mounted Police (NWMP) Canada's national police force, now called the Royal Canadian Mounted Police (RCMP)

paramilitary a force that operates like the army but is not part of it

FIGURE 5–7 Fort Whoop-Up, 1874. This fort was one of many where whisky was traded for furs. How were traders in this area able to engage in illegal trade for so long?

The Cypress Hills Massacre

In June of 1873, a group of Nakoda camping in Cypress Hills was attacked by a party of American "wolfers," trappers who put out poisoned bison meat to kill wolves and coyotes. More than 20 Nakoda were killed, and the incident came to be known as the Cypress Hills Massacre. Outrage erupted in eastern Canada, where people saw the attack as a threat to Canadian sovereignty in the West. In response, the government sent a force of 275 NWMP to the Prairies to take control.

By the time the NWMP reached Fort Whoop-Up, they discovered that the whisky traders had fled. Hoping for stability and peace, many First Nations people thought that the presence of the NWMP would put an end to the lawlessness that had plagued the region.

> *If the police had not come to the country, where would we all be now? Bad men and whisky were killing us so fast that very few of us would have been left today.*
>
> —Crowfoot, a chief of the Blackfoot

The Treaty Process

The Canadian government was determined to open the Prairies to European and Canadian settlers. However, this was not possible until the question of First Nations title to the land had been settled. In 1870, all land in Manitoba and the North-West Territories was still held by First Nations. The exception was land in the Selkirk Settlement, leased by Selkirk in an 1817 treaty with the Saulteaux and Cree.

The government was determined to gain control of land as quickly and as cheaply as possible. First Nations leaders, recognizing that they would have to share some land, wanted to make the best possible deal to secure the future of their people.

FIGURE 5–8 RCMP officers re-enact the NWMP march west in 1999. The NWMP resembled a British military cavalry unit, complete with red uniforms. What impression do you think these uniforms would have made?

FIGURE 5–9 This painting is called *The Treaty Line*. It was not intended to be a realistic depiction of an actual event, but it is symbolic. What does the painting symbolize? What does it show about the point of view of the artist?

First Nations had a long-standing tradition of negotiating agreements. They were accustomed to give and take, which formed a key element in successful negotiation. First Nations also tended to bargain in good faith; people stood by their word and meant what they said. When negotiating treaties with the Canadian government, they believed they were making an exchange—sharing their land for the protection and support of their people.

In 1871, the Canadian government began the treaty process with the First Nations of the Prairies. Indian Commisioner Wemyss Simpson was sent to Manitoba to begin talks with the Cree and Anishinabé. Read the two quotations below. What points of view do they express? Do you think these views would have led to successful negotiations?

> *God intends this land to raise great crops for all his children, and the time is come when it is to be used for that purpose. White people will come here to cultivate it under any circumstances. No power on Earth can prevent it.*
>
> —Wemyss Simpson, 1871

> *I have turned this matter of a treaty over in my mind and I cannot see anything in it to benefit my children. This is what frightens me. After I showed you what I meant to keep for a reserve, you continued to make it smaller and smaller… Let the Queen's subjects go on my land if they choose. I give them liberty. Let them rob me. I will go home…*
>
> —Ay-ee-ta-pe-pe-tung, 1871

Henry Prince, chief of the Anishinabé, asked how the government intended to assist the First Nations if they agreed to end their traditional way of life and settle on reserves.

The Cree and Anishinabé did not want to give up all of their land. They wanted to retain control of about 60 percent of the province of Manitoba. However, Simpson had instructions to offer only 160 acres (64.7 hectares), the standard homesteader's quarter-section, for every family of five. While this offer was not acceptable to the Cree and Anishinabé, they knew that no other offer would be made. Still, they managed to include some conditions: the government eventually agreed to supply farm equipment, supplies, and instruction in farming techniques. By the end of August 1871, Treaties 1 and 2, covering the southern part of Manitoba, had been signed.

FIGURE 5–10 Mistawasis (front row, right) and Ahtahkakoop (front row, left), negotiators for Treaty No. 6. Why did these leaders insist on receiving start-up assistance for their people?

Zoom In Treaty No. 6

Treaty No. 6 was a historic agreement between the Cree and the government. As you read, consider what each side gained and lost as a result of the agreement.

In the summer of 1876, Alexander Morris, the Lieutenant-Governor of the North-West Territories, travelled to Fort Carlton to settle a treaty with the Cree who lived in the area. The Cree insisted on using their own interpreter, Métis Peter Erasmus, when they discovered that the interpreters provided by the government did not speak their language. Initial negotiations lasted almost 10 days, longer than had been anticipated. Cree leaders discussed at length the proposed treaty terms and drew up amendments that they felt had to be accepted.

Mistawasis and Ahtahkakoop, two senior Cree leaders, both knew that eventually they would have to agree to a treaty. They felt they had little choice in the matter, since the destruction of the bison meant that many Cree were already starving, and the government promised food if the treaties were signed. Nevertheless, they wanted guarantees that assistance would be provided if their people began the task of farming on their reserves.

Younger leaders, like Poundmaker, argued against the

treaty. Mistawasis could only ask, "Have you anything better to offer our people?"

In the end, the senior leaders had a clause added to the treaty, which they felt provided the guarantees they were seeking: direct assistance for three years in the form of farming tools, supplies, and instruction. Morris seemed to think that the Cree wanted ongoing assistance, but Mistawasis and Ahtahkakoop were emphatic that their desire was to eventually become self-sufficient.

Can we stop the power of the white man from spreading over the land like the grasshoppers that cloud the sky and then fall to consume every blade of grass and every leaf on the trees in their path? I think not. Before this happens let us ponder carefully our choice of roads.

—Plains Cree Chief Ahtahkakoop

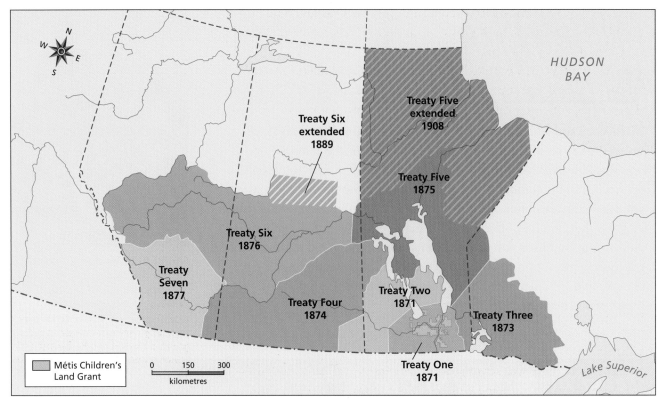

FIGURE 5–11 Treaties signed in the 1870s (including later extensions). Reserves were created throughout the treaty areas, while the Métis children's land grants were the only lands officially allotted to the Métis. Why was the Canadian government not yet concerned about territory farther north?

Treaty Rights

Under the terms of the numbered treaties, and those that followed in other regions of Canada, Aboriginal peoples agreed to share their land in exchange for specific rights. These rights included access to resources, health care, and education. Many Aboriginal rights—such as the right to hunt or fish, or to self-government—can be seen as rights Aboriginal peoples have had for time immemorial. Other rights guaranteed under the treaties are part of official, negotiated agreements with the government.

Aboriginal rights in Canada are protected under the Canadian Constitution. However, there have been challenges to these rights, and many Aboriginal groups have had to fight for recognition of their treaty rights. You will learn more about some of these challenges in later chapters of *Horizons*.

First Nations Farming

By the end of the 1870s, seven treaties were in place across the southern Prairies. Many First Nations had already been escorted by the NWMP onto the reserves, and they soon began to farm the land.

As you read in Chapter 2, First Nations such as the Ouendat and the Haudenosaunee were successful farmers on the fertile lands around the Great Lakes. They supplemented their hunting and fishing with crops such

Did You Know...

Treaties continue to be signed in Canada today. Most reinforce or clarify the rights of Aboriginal peoples in a province or territory. In later chapters, you will read more about modern treaties such as the Nisga'a Treaty.

WEB LINK ●

Read a copy of Treaty No. 6 on the Pearson Web site.

as squash, corn, and beans. However, farming on the Prairies could be a challenge. Many farmers, both European and First Nations, struggled with poor crops, insects, and drought.

Even though he had objected to Treaty No. 6, Poundmaker also tried farming. One year, his crops died in a drought. Another year, he harvested a bumper crop, only to find that the Canadian government would not provide the mill needed to grind the wheat into flour. Poundmaker and other leaders soon realized that their people were no further from the brink of starvation than they had been before.

Was Failure Unavoidable?

The main problem for the First Nations farmers of the Prairies was that the tools, supplies, animals, and instruction guaranteed by the treaties proved inadequate, when they appeared at all. The plows were poorly made and were useless for prairie soils. Furthermore, the oxen that were provided could not pull plows. The seed was sent too late in the year, and First Nations farmers were forbidden to use steam-powered **threshing** machines after the harvest.

It seemed as if the Canadian government and its officials wanted the farms to fail, even while telling First Nations that they should become farmers. The attitude of Indian Commissioner Hayter Reed in the 1880s can be seen as an illustration of the government's view. Reed believed that it was "unnatural" for First Nations to use machinery—although it is impossible to grow and harvest sustainable amounts of wheat without it. Nor did Reed want First Nations farmers to sell surplus wheat. According to Reed, if they grew more than what was necessary for their own needs, they were planting too much. In the face of such attitudes, and in spite of their best efforts, by 1900 almost all First Nations living on prairie reserves had abandoned farming.

threshing the process of separating grain from stalks or husks; the steam-powered threshing machine saved time and labour

FIGURE 5–12 Blackfoot men sow by hand on their farm south of Calgary. What does this image tell you about the needs of First Nations farmers? How did the policies of the Canadian government lead to the failure of First Nations farms?

The Indian Act

WEB LINK ● ● ● ● ● ● ● ● ● ● ● ● ● ● ●
For more information about the Indian Act, visit the Pearson Web site.

DID YOU KNOW...

The potlatch, an important giving ceremony for First Nations of the west coast, was illegal in Canada until 1951.

The Canadian government introduced the **Indian Act** in 1876. This act formalized the assimilation of First Nations, providing government administration of reserves and treaty rights across the Dominion. The Act changed through time, with new regulations being applied as Canada developed. The Indian Act had an enormous impact on the Aboriginal peoples of Canada.

The **paternalistic** attitude of the government, which you explored in Chapter 3, continued. In this case, the government made decisions on behalf of Aboriginal peoples. Most decisions, as seen in the case of Hayter Reed, were influenced either by prejudice or misunderstanding. The Indian Act ruled that

- First Nations were wards of the government, living only on reserves.

- First Nations were required to register with the government; if they did not, they were considered "non-status" and would lose their rights.

- Special passes were required to come and go from reserves. For some time, Europeans were not allowed on the reserves, which created a feeling of distrust between First Nations and their neighbours.

- First Nations children had to attend residential schools. As you have seen, the aim of residential schools was to assimilate First Nations people.

- Traditional ways of self-governance, such as choosing leaders, were also denied, as were important ceremonies, such as the sun dance.

Many First Nations felt that the government had failed them. Poverty, isolation, and the loss of their rights and freedoms caused profound discontent. Was the outcome of this discontent unavoidable? Find out more as you read this chapter.

ACTIVITIES

1. How did the creation of the NWMP impact Canada? Identify and support two or three possible consequences.

2. Why did the Canadian government want treaties to be signed? Explain how the government's attitude had an impact on the agreements.

3. Some people believe the Canadian government demonstrated bad faith in terms of treaty agreements. Others believe their actions were necessary in building a nation. What do you think? Use specific examples to support your answer.

4. Discuss the Indian Act with your class.

   a) Did the government have the right to make decisions for Aboriginal peoples?

   b) What effect would the Indian Act have on the identity of First Nations in Canada?

   c) In what ways would the Act have been different if First Nations had been consulted?

The Northwest Uprising

What were the causes and consequences of the Northwest Uprising?

By 1884, the Métis in the North-West Territories were losing patience with the Canadian government. They had not been part of the treaty process, and their status under the Indian Act was unclear. They were beginning to fear that their rights would again be ignored.

After their experiences in Red River, and with the coming of the new transcontinental railway—which brought more European and Canadian newcomers to the Northwest—the Métis felt they needed to act. They sent petitions to the government, asking that their rights be recognized.

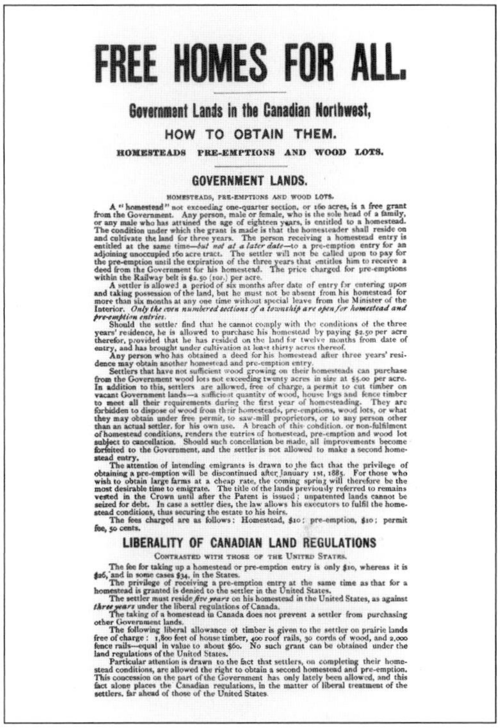

FREE HOMES FOR ALL.

Government Lands in the Canadian Northwest,

HOW TO OBTAIN THEM.

HOMESTEADS PRE-EMPTIONS AND WOOD LOTS.

GOVERNMENT LANDS.

HOMESTEADS, PRE-EMPTIONS AND WOOD LOTS.

A "homestead" not exceeding one-quarter section, or 160 acres, is a free grant from the Government. Any person, male or female, who is the sole head of a family, or any male who has attained the age of eighteen years, is entitled to a homestead. The condition under which the grant is made is that the homesteader shall reside on and cultivate the land for three years. The person receiving a homestead entry is entitled at the same time—*but not at a later date*—to a pre-emption entry for an adjoining unoccupied 160 acre tract. The settler will not be called upon to pay for the pre-emption until the expiration of the three years that entitles him to receive a deed from the Government for his homestead. The price charged for pre-emptions within the Railway belt is $2.50 (10s.) per acre.

A settler is allowed a period of six months after date of entry for entering upon and taking possession of the land, but he must not be absent from his homestead for more than six months at any one time without special leave from the Minister of the Interior. *Only the even numbered sections of a township are open for homestead and pre-emption entries.*

Should the settler find that he cannot comply with the conditions of the three years' residence, he is allowed to purchase his homestead by paying $2.50 per acre therefor, provided that he has resided on the land for twelve months from date of entry, and has brought under cultivation at least thirty acres thereof.

Any person who has obtained a deed for his homestead after three years' residence may obtain another homestead and pre-emption entry.

Settlers that have not sufficient wood growing on their homesteads can purchase from the Government wood lots not exceeding twenty acres in size at $5.00 per acre. In addition to this, settlers are allowed, free of charge, a permit to cut timber on vacant Government lands—a sufficient quantity of wood, house logs and fence timber to meet all their requirements during the first year of homesteading. They are forbidden to dispose of wood from their homesteads, pre-emptions, wood lots, or what they may obtain under free permit, to saw-mill proprietors, or to any person other than an actual settler, for his own use. A breach of this condition, or non-fulfilment of homestead conditions, renders the entries of homestead, pre-emption and wood lot subject to cancellation. Should such concellation be made, all improvements become forfeited to the Government, and the settler is not allowed to make a second homestead entry.

The attention of intending emigrants is drawn to the fact that the privilege of obtaining a pre-emption will be discontinued after January 1st, 1885. For those who wish to obtain large farms at a cheap rate, the coming spring will therefore be the most desirable time to emigrate. The title of the lands previously referred to remains vested in the Crown until after the Patent is issued; unpatented lands cannot be seized for debt. In case a settler dies, the law allows his executors to fulfil the homestead conditions, thus securing the estate to his heirs.

The fees charged are as follows: Homestead, $10; pre-emption, $10; permit fee, 50 cents.

LIBERALITY OF CANADIAN LAND REGULATIONS

CONTRASTED WITH THOSE OF THE UNITED STATES.

The fee for taking up a homestead or pre-emption entry is only $10, whereas it is $26, and in some cases $34, in the States.

The privilege of receiving a pre-emption entry at the same time as that for a homestead is granted is denied to the settler in the United States.

The settler must reside *five years* on his homestead in the United States, as against *three years* under the liberal regulations of Canada.

The taking of a homestead in Canada does not prevent a settler from purchasing other Government lands.

The following liberal allowance of timber is given to the settler on prairie lands free of charge: 1,800 feet of house timber, 400 roof rails, 30 cords of wood, and 2,000 fence rails—equal in value to about $60. No such grant can be obtained under the land regulations of the United States.

Particular attention is drawn to the fact that settlers, on completing their homestead conditions, are allowed the right to obtain a second homestead and pre-emption. This concession on the part of the Government has only lately been allowed, and this fact alone places the Canadian regulations, in the matter of liberal treatment of the settlers, far ahead of those of the United States.

FIGURE 5–13 By 1882 the Canadian Pacific Railway was advertising that land was available for newcomers in the North-West Territores. Why might immigration put added pressure on the Métis?

The Métis Petitions

The Métis wanted legal title to the land they occupied, and they wanted the land to be surveyed respecting to their long river lots. The government proved to be inconsistent in this regard. In 1881, a surveyor listened to local farmers and laid out half the land in St. Laurent in long lots. The next year, another surveyor arrived to finish the job. He did not consult anyone and laid out the rest of the land using a township system.

In their petitions to the government, the Métis expressed their concerns about their land. They also asked for assistance in becoming successful farmers. Like the First Nations, they were losing their livelihood and had to adjust to farming due to the loss of the bison.

Others shared the Métis' concerns. During the late 1870s, European homesteaders had arrived in the area near St. Laurent. European farmers also found that their concerns about land title and financial assistance were not being addressed by the Canadian government.

The Government's Agenda

The government had its own plans for the land in the North-West Territories, including land already occupied by the Métis and the European farmers. Surveys of the Prairies told the government that there were about 6.4 million hectares of farmland still available. Much of this land was already held by land speculators, but the rest could be sold by the government. The potential for profit was huge—John A. Macdonald calculated that if this land were sold, the government could collect about $71 million. There was no way the government would risk losing this potential revenue by listening to petitions from the Métis or the homesteaders about "their" land.

Did You Know...

Sensing trouble, the government amended the Indian Act to forbid the sale or trade of ammunition to Aboriginal peoples in the Northwest in 1884. This amendment contradicted the treaty agreements and later contributed to the future uprising.

FIGURE 5–14 William Henry Jackson

asylum a hospital that treats people with mental illnesses

Métis Bill of Rights a document that outlined grievances of the Métis and others in the North-West Territories

The building of the railway, which you will read about later in this chapter, also influenced the way the government treated the First Nations. As the cost of railway construction rose, the government slashed the budget of the Indian Affairs department. First Nations were now reduced to relying on the government just to survive. The government also kept control of communities by refusing assistance to those who were "difficult." Many people were on the verge of starvation.

These actions could only lead to trouble. In 1884, a NWC clerk quoted Gabriel Dumont:

> The Government should not be surprised if we side with the Indians. They are our relatives, and when they come to us when they are starving, we have to feed them. The Government is not doing right by them… I have heard the speeches and explanations given of the Treaty [No. 6], not only they would live as well as they had before, but better… Is that taking place now? Now they are allowed to go about starving and the burden of feeding them falls on us.
>
> —Gabriel Dumont, 1884

Louis Riel Returns

In the spring of 1884, the Métis decided that they needed a leader who could get the government to pay attention to their petitions. They felt there was only one possible choice—Louis Riel.

After the events of the Red River Resistance, Riel was forced into exile in order to escape being charged with the murder of Thomas Scott. During his time in exile, he turned to religion and became convinced that he was chosen by God to be the leader of the Métis. He had even spent time in an **asylum**. By 1884, Riel had recovered and had settled in Montana. He was married, had two small children, and was working as a teacher. When a delegation led by Gabriel Dumont approached him, Riel agreed to return to Canada to fight on behalf of the Métis.

That fall, Riel and William Henry Jackson, a representative of the local European farmers, collaborated on the **Métis Bill of Rights**. They hoped this document would address the Métis' grievances. Like the 1870 Métis List of Rights, which Riel had also written, it included the concerns of non-Métis people living in the North-West Territories.

The new document was far more detailed, reflecting the Métis' frustrations. It was sent to Ottawa in December 1884. The government acknowledged that it had received the document. After years of other petitions being ignored, the Métis considered this a victory. However, the celebration was premature.

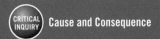
The Métis Bill of Rights (different from the List of Rights set out in 1870) had a number of similarities with the Declaration of Independence, written by American colonists in 1776. Both documents laid out reasons for dissatisfaction with the government. However, the Métis Bill of Rights was not a call for revolution, but a request for equality and negotiations. Here are some key clauses:

1. That the [First Nations] are so reduced that settlers are compelled to furnish them with food... partly to preserve the peace in the Territory.

2. That the Métis of the Territory have not received 240 acres of land, as did the Manitoba [Métis].

3. That the Métis who are in possession of land have not received [title].

4. That no effective measures have yet been taken to put the people of the Northwest in direct communication with the European markets, via Hudson Bay.

- The Métis Bill of Rights also detailed a number of other grievances against the government. How do these clauses inform our understanding of the Métis' needs and their desire for change?

FIGURE 5–15 Steve Powley, a Métis from Ontario, spent 10 years fighting for his right to hunt. In 2003, the Supreme Court of Canada ruled in his favour. It was a landmark decision because the rights of the Métis had not been defined in the Canadian Constitution. Why do you think the Métis continue in their struggle for recognition by the government?

Trouble Builds in the Northwest

Riel's return added to tensions already present in the Northwest, and John A. Macdonald's government was facing one crisis after another, most of them involving the railway. Some historians speculate that Macdonald saw a way to solve everything—secure the North-West Territories, deal with the Métis, and finish the railway—by letting Riel "make trouble." If it happened, troops could be sent by rail to deal with it. The public would see the necessity of the **Canadian Pacific Railway (CPR)** for the nation's security, and spending government money to finish it would be acceptable.

One person who initially supported the return of Louis Riel was, surprisingly, Factor and Magistrate Lawrence Clarke. During his time in power, Clarke had become involved in land speculation and party politics. He was now a wealthy man, and he feared he would lose everything if the Métis were granted their land. Were the government to crush a rebellion, Clarke would prosper.

The government already knew that there could be trouble in the Northwest but needed more information. Clarke became the government's informant. He also started false rumours and reported on the reaction of the Métis. As a result of his actions, the level of tension, uncertainty, and distrust rose in the Métis community.

Canadian Pacific Railway (CPR)
Canada's first transcontinental railway

DID YOU KNOW...

Several people thought that Riel might accept a bribe to leave. Riel himself considered leaving, fearing that the government would not negotiate with him. He told Lieutenant-Governor Dewdney's representatives that he would accept a payment of $35 000 to leave. Dewdney told this to the prime minister, but Macdonald rejected the idea.

"Justice Commands Us"

The Métis knew that the Canadian government was in possession of their Bill of Rights, and Riel decided that they should send another petition to Ottawa—one that demanded responsible government for the North-West Territories. Riel and his council picked Lawrence Clarke as their representative, thinking that with his political connections and his apparent sympathy, he was the best choice. Clarke left in February and returned on March 18 with this message: the only answer the Métis would receive for their petition was bullets. He also said that a force of 500 North West Mounted Police was on its way to arrest Riel. The first statement was probably true; the second was a blatant lie.

On March 19, Riel spoke to the Métis at Batoche. He told them that a peaceful solution was impossible and that the Canadian government was determined to make war. He concluded with the declaration, "Justice commands us to take up arms."

Conflict Begins

The only North West Mounted Police force in the area was the detachment at Fort Carlton, and they were too few to withstand a direct attack. Lieutenant-Governor Dewdney had sent reinforcements, but it would take a week for them to arrive. When the Métis moved on Fort Carlton in order to seize supplies, falling just short of attacking the fort itself, Lawrence Clarke did two things. He sent a message to the reinforcements, delaying their arrival by one day. He then publically accused NWMP Superintendent Crozier of cowardice. Crozier responded by riding out to meet the larger force of Métis at Duck Lake on March 26, 1885.

Angry words were exchanged, and two Métis negotiators were shot. Both sides opened fire. Twelve NWMP officers were soon dead, with another 25 wounded. Crozier evacuated Fort Carlton the next day. The **Northwest Uprising** had begun.

DID YOU KNOW...

During the wait to receive news from Ottawa, Riel reportedly began to pray for long periods, perhaps returning to his earlier behaviour. However, he broke with local church leaders on what course of action to take. Riel favoured fighting, while the church did not.

Northwest Uprising a series of battles in 1885 between the Métis and the Canadian forces, brought about by the Métis' attempts to gain recognition of their land rights

FIGURE 5–16 Fort Carlton today. Now restored as a provincial park, Fort Carlton is much like it was in the past. What features in this image show why the fort would have been a good location for the only NWMP force in the region?

Battles at Fish Creek and Batoche

The Canadian government quickly mobilized more than 5000 Canadian soldiers, and the first troops were boarding trains for the West as early as March 30—four days after the incident at Duck Lake. Most were in Manitoba within 10 days. General Middleton was in charge of the Canadian troops. He split his force into several groups, since he was worried about resistance from the First Nations. By the middle of April, General Middleton was approaching Batoche.

On April 24, Gabriel Dumont, who had convinced Riel that the Canadian troops should be attacked before they arrived at Batoche, ambushed Middleton's force at Fish Creek. Fewer than 300 Métis stopped the advance of 1600 militia soldiers.

On May 9, Batoche was attacked by the Canadian troops. Dumont concealed his men in rifle pits, where they could fire from cover. However, Middleton had cannons and a **Gatling gun**. He stationed the artillery around Batoche, firing from a distance.

Gatling gun a large, rapid-fire weapon with multiple rotating barrels, cranked by hand

The Métis were short of bullets. After three days, they were reduced to firing rocks and nails from their guns. Exhausted, with more than half of their number wounded, they were forced to surrender or flee. Riel was distraught over the Métis defeat and the loss of life. Dumont escaped to the United States, and Riel surrendered on May 15. He still hoped to bring the plight of his people to national attention—through a trial if necessary.

The uprising was over. Its death toll included 53 Canadian soldiers and volunteers, and about 35 Métis and First Nations people. The financial cost to the Canadian government was $5 million.

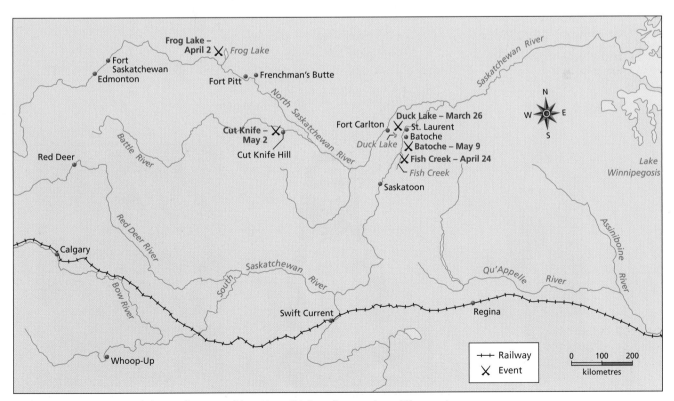

FIGURE 5–17 Key events of the Northwest Uprising. How did the railway make a difference in the outcome?

By the early 1880s, Poundmaker was openly critical of the government's failure to honour its obligations. In response, the government refused food rations for his people. However, when Louis Riel asked for Poundmaker's support, he refused, believing that resistance was futile.

In 1885, as the Northwest Uprising began, Poundmaker led his people to Battleford for supplies.The townspeople panicked, hiding in the nearby fort. The Cree left the next day, but the town was looted and partly burned. Poundmaker was blamed.

Two months later, Poundmaker's people defended themselves when attacked by Canadian troops at Cut Knife Hill. Poundmaker then heard about Riel's defeat, and went to Batoche. He was arrested for treason and sentenced to three years in prison. Released after seven months, Poundmaker died shortly after.

Cree chief Big Bear would not sign Treaty No. 6 until he could consult with his people. His determination gave him the reputation of being "difficult." For six years, Big Bear refused to sign the treaty. Finally, starvation forced him to sign in 1882.

Big Bear also refused to join the Northwest Uprising. In April 1885, his band was refused supplies at Frog Lake. Starving and angry, the Cree's young war leader, Wandering Spirit, took nine townspeople as hostages. Through a misunderstanding, the hostages were killed. Big Bear was blamed. After several weeks, he surrendered, and Wandering Spirit was hanged for murder. Big Bear was convicted of treason and sentenced to three years. He died shortly after his release in 1888.

Siksika chief Crowfoot followed a different path. While he did not like the treaties, he was resigned to them. In 1877, he signed Treaty No. 7.

Six years later, the railway encroached on Crowfoot's reserve. He confronted the rail crews, and work on the line stopped. Father Albert Lacombe, who had lived among the Siksika since 1870, led negotiations between Crowfoot and the CPR. Crowfoot received additional land as compensation. William Van Horne, manager of the CPR, was pleased with the peaceful outcome and awarded both Lacombe and Crowfoot lifetime passes on the railway.

When the Northwest Uprising began, Crowfoot refused to take part. While he did not like the fact that Europeans were settling the Prairies, he recognized the inevitability of change and did his best to protect his people. Crowfoot died of tuberculosis in 1890.

- How did each leader's response have an impact on the development of Canada?

FIGURE 5–18 Poundmaker

FIGURE 5–19 Big Bear

FIGURE 5–20 Crowfoot

The Trial of Louis Riel

After his surrender, Louis Riel was taken to Regina to stand trial for treason. Riel was defended by two lawyers, one from Quebec and one from Ontario. They wanted to demonstrate that he was not guilty by reason of insanity. Riel disagreed; he wanted to show that the Métis had been goaded into their uprising by the actions of a government that wished to destroy them.

In Regina, only a six-man jury was required. Had the trial been held in Manitoba, the judge would have been a superior court justice, and Riel would have faced a twelve-person jury. Historians have suggested that the government feared a Manitoba jury, which would have included both English and French jurors who might have been sympathetic to the Métis.

The trial began on July 28, 1885. Riel was prevented from questioning witnesses and could not make a statement until a verdict was announced. The jury found Riel guilty of treason on August 1, after only an hour of deliberation, but they recommended mercy. Riel then made an impassioned speech:

> *The agitation of the North-West Territories would have been constitutional, and would certainly be constitutional today, if, in my opinion, we had not been attacked. Perhaps the Crown has not been able to find out the particulars, that we were attacked, but as we were on the scene, it was easy to understand. When we sent petitions to the government, they answered us by sending police... So irresponsible is that government... that in the course of several years, besides doing nothing to satisfy the people of this great land, it has even hardly been able to answer once or give a single response. That fact would indicate an absolute lack of responsibility, and therefore, insanity complicated with paralysis.*
>
> —**Louis Riel, 1885**

DID YOU KNOW...

When Riel's lawyers attempted to have all the Métis petitions admitted into evidence, the judge refused.

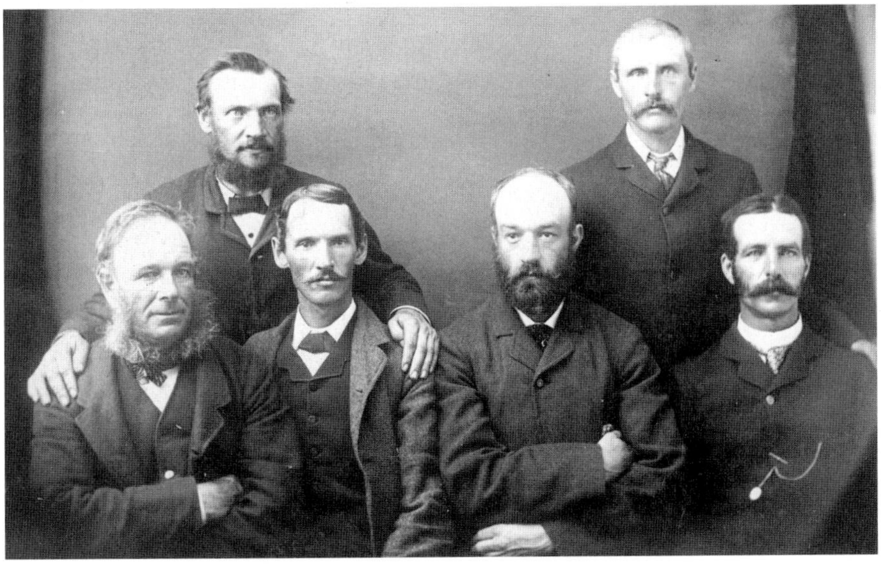

FIGURE 5–21 The jury for Riel's trial. Although over 30 men received summons to be part of the jury, only one spoke French. Riel was tried by a jury of English and Scottish Protestants. How do you think the trial might have turned out if Riel had faced a jury representing all peoples of the Northwest?

FIGURE 5–22 Louis Riel (standing, centre) addresses the judge at his trial. Do you think Riel should have been tried for treason? Why or why not?

WEB LINK ● ● ● ● ● ● ● ● ● ● ● ● ● ● ● ● ● ●

Read a transcript of a speech Macdonald gave in the House of Commons about the Northwest Uprising. Visit the Pearson Web site.

Judge Richardson sentenced Louis Riel to death, as the law required. Riel's lawyers launched appeals all the way to the federal cabinet, but to no avail. Although John A. Macdonald was deluged by petitions and letters from Quebec demanding that Riel be spared, he was unmoved. Riel was hanged in Regina on November 16, 1885.

> *He shall hang, though every dog in Quebec shall bark in his favour.*
>
> —Sir John A. Macdonald, 1885

Aftermath of the Uprising

The consequences of the Northwest Uprising would be severe for the Métis and First Nations of the Northwest. The Métis, having lost the struggle to gain title to their land, moved farther north and west into the hinterland. In order to live, they were forced to **squat** on public land reserved for roads and eventually became known as "the road allowance people."

The Métis also faced decades of discrimination and prejudice. The word "half-breed," which once meant "a person of mixed ancestry," became an insult. Many Métis moved to the cities, where they could hide their First Nations heritage.

Although few First Nations people had actively participated in the fighting (and, in some cases, had only fought when attacked), 81 First Nations men were charged with treason or murder, and 44 were convicted. In court, very little translation was offered, and prisoners were not allowed to make statements in their own defence. Eight First Nations men were hanged for murder; they were executed together in Battleford on November 17. Those who went to jail usually became ill, and many died soon after release.

squat to settle on unoccupied land without legal title and without paying rent

First Nations were confined to their reserves. They found themselves at the mercy of a government that saw them as children who needed a firm hand, rather than as a proud, independent people. The work done by careful leaders such as Big Bear, who tried to gain some independence and self-sufficiency for his people, was undone by the conflict. Rules became harsher, First Nations communities were isolated from each other (and from European communities), and gathering ceremonies were banned. These restrictions lasted well into the 20th century.

It would take decades of struggle and determination for both the Métis and the First Nations to regain a measure of respect from the rest of the Canadian population. This struggle continues to this day.

FIGURE 5–23 After the uprising was over, the government captured and charged more than 200 people, including these Métis and First Nations prisoners. What was the basis of a treason charge against people who had not been treated as citizens by the government?

ACTIVITIES

1. How did the government maintain social control over the First Nations of the Northwest?

2. Summarize the Canadian government's reactions to the petitions from the Métis. What motivated such reactions?

3. Identify the key events of the Northwest Uprising. For each event, summarize the historical significance.

4. For what reasons did Sir John A. Macdonald want an uprising in the Northwest?

5. On the following pages, read the Window on Canada feature about Riel. Why do some people see him as a hero, while others see him as a villain? How do you explain such contradictory perceptions? Why might these perceptions change over time?

Judgements

6. Was Louis Riel's apparent willingness to accept money to go away a contradiction of his principles? Provide reasons for your answer.

Cause and Consequence

7. Macdonald's decision to have Riel executed had far-reaching consequences. Consider the different groups that were affected, and identify how each was affected by the government's actions. Then, with your class, discuss what might have happened if Macdonald had not decided to execute Riel.

No figure in Canadian history has stirred as much controversy as Louis Riel. His fight for the rights of the Red River Métis has become an iconic piece of Canadian history. Passions still run high around this man whose impact on Canada was monumental.

HERO?

MURDERER?

TRAITOR?

MADMAN?

FREEDOM FIGHTER?

FATHER OF CONFEDERATION?

MARTYR?

PROPHET?

Born in Red River in 1844, Riel was a bright and well-educated child. At age 14 he was sent to Montreal and studied for 10 years to become a Catholic priest. Four months shy of his goal, he left his studies when he fell in love. The woman's family would not agree to the marriage because he was Métis, and he returned to Red River. By age 25 he was politically involved in the rights of the peoples of the North-West.

In 1869, the Hudson's Bay Company sold Rupert's Land to the Canadian government. Without consultation, Canada sent surveyors to the Red River Valley—home to the Métis—to claim the land for Protestant and English-speaking settlers. The Métis, fearing the threat to their way of life, named Louis Riel their leader and formed a provisional government.

MÉTIS PROVISIONAL GOVERNMENT 1869

The Métis believed the settlers would fence the land and disrupt the bison hunt on which they depended.

Thomas Scott was part of a group that tried to attack Fort Garry. He was jailed and then executed by order of the provisional government. His death fired up religious, political, and racial tensions.

This land belongs to Canada. They will not dare to shoot me!

IN ONTARIO

...We call upon the government to avenge Scott's death, pledging ourselves to assist in rescuing Red River territory from those who have turned it over to popery, and bring to justice the murderers of our countrymen.

MEANWHILE, IN QUEBEC...

We pass a unanimous resolution asking the governor general to grant amnesty to Riel.

Riel escaped before Canadian troops arrived to arrest him for the murder of Thomas Scott.

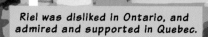

Riel was disliked in Ontario, and admired and supported in Quebec.

The National Dream

> ▶ **Why was a transcontinental railway built in Canada, and what were the consequences?**

DID YOU KNOW...

Threat of annexation by the United States was one reason why Macdonald was eager to connect the West to the rest of Canada. You will read more about this issue in Chapter 6.

incentive something that encourages action or greater effort

In 1871, British Columbia entered Confederation with the promise of a rail link to the rest of Canada within 10 years. No one at the time had any clear idea of the route the railway would take across the West or how much it would cost, but it was part of John A. Macdonald's long-held dream to create a single Dominion from sea to sea.

Who Will Build the Railway?

Macdonald knew that the Canadian government did not have the resources to complete such a massive project. He decided to offer **incentives** to wealthy business and railway owners who might be willing to finance the construction of the railway.

This caught the attention of Jay Cooke, an American who knew the potential of the Canadian West. American railway owners saw Canada as a natural extension of the American rail network, since Canada was a market for American goods and a source of natural resources.

The only Canadian with the means to take on a transcontinental railway project was Sir Hugh Allan, who had made his fortune in shipping, manufacturing, and railways in eastern Canada. Allan believed that it made sense to build a rail link to the West, and he joined forces with Jay Cooke.

In 1871, Allan formed the Canadian Pacific Railway Company, a company that seemed to be Canadian but was actually controlled by Jay Cooke. Also, Allan's railway would not be a truly *transcontinental* railway but a branch line of the American Northern Pacific Railway. Allan concealed these facts from the government. If word leaked out that Americans controlled the Canadian railway, it would kill the entire project.

FIGURE 5–26 Another railway line built to fulfill Confederation promises was the Intercolonial Railway, connecting the eastern provinces with central Canada. Did this railway present the same building challenges as the proposed line to British Columbia? Why or why not?

Political scandals happen when a politician or a government behaves in a way that is either inappropriate or illegal. Sometimes, even the suggestion of some **impropriety** is enough to destroy a career or force a government to resign.

In the summer of 1872, John A. Macdonald called a general election—the first since Confederation. During the election, the Conservatives realized they needed more money for their campaign. In those times, political candidates openly made promises to secure a person's support. Macdonald asked his Minister of Defence, George-Étienne Cartier, to find out if the wealthy Hugh Allan could help with the campaign. In return, Macdonald promised a guaranteed railway contract. Allan was agreeable. Cartier wrote two memos, one promising Allan the railway contract, the other listing the amounts needed by Conservative candidates.

The Conservatives won the 1872 election with a slim majority in the House of Commons. In 1873, the contents of the memos and the American involvement in Allan's Canadian Pacific Railway were made public. Now it looked as though the prime minister was in the employ of both Hugh Allan and his American backers.

Macdonald denied everything, but when more hard evidence was released to the press—including a note he sent—he was forced to resign.

impropriety improper activity or conduct

> The friends of the Government will expect to be assisted in the pending elections and any amount which you or your Company shall advance for that purpose shall be recouped by you. A memorandum of immediate requirements is below:
>
> Sir John A. Macdonald $25 000
>
> Hon. Mr. Langevin $15 000
>
> Sir G.E.C. $20 000
>
> —George-Étienne Cartier to Hugh Allan, 1872

WHAT DO YOU THINK?

1. What do you think of Macdonald's behaviour? How should we judge Macdonald and the Pacific Scandal?

2. Are there still connections between big business and politics in Canada? Has a scandal such as this one happened since 1872? In a group, research a contemporary political scandal, at the provincial or federal level, and create a short presentation about it. Your presentation may include background information, photos or political cartoons, primary sources, consequences, and what kind of damage control was attempted by those involved.

Alexander Mackenzie and the Railway

In 1873, after John A. Macdonald resigned because of the Pacific Scandal, Alexander Mackenzie led the Liberals to power. Mackenzie thought that building a transcontinental railway was a waste of time and money, especially in the current economic climate. The Liberal leader had taken office just as a major economic depression hit North America.

However, Mackenzie was bound by Macdonald's promise of a rail link to British Columbia, and his lack of action was not well received. British Columbian politicians complained to Mackenzie and to the Governor General. They threatened to **secede** from Confederation if the railway was not built as promised. Finally, Mackenzie decided to allow the land survey to continue. This decision gave the impression that he was doing something about the railway that was as costly as building it.

secede to formally withdraw from an alliance or a federal union

The Railway Survey

No one really knew where the railway should go, so all possible routes would have to be explored. While building a railway line through the Canadian Shield would not be easy, the biggest challenge was passing through the Rocky Mountains. Building a railway through mountains would be difficult, and careful planning was essential.

At the time, the only major settlements in British Columbia were the capital city of Victoria and New Westminster (Vancouver did not exist yet). With mountain passes, deep ravines and valleys, lakes and rivers, and a coast cut by inlets, the best way to reach these settlements was anyone's guess.

The task of directing the survey fell to Sandford Fleming, surveyor for the Dominion. Fleming sent dozens of surveyors into British Columbia, and they brought back valuable information. While this data was used to make the first accurate map of the interior of British Columbia, the survey also led to serious disagreements—much like today, when new roads or bridges cause endless debate among those who will be affected. This debate was known as "the Battle of the Routes."

FIGURE 5–27 This map shows the various routes proposed by those involved in the Battle of the Routes. Why would people have wanted the railway to pass through their area? Predict why the CPR chose the route it did.

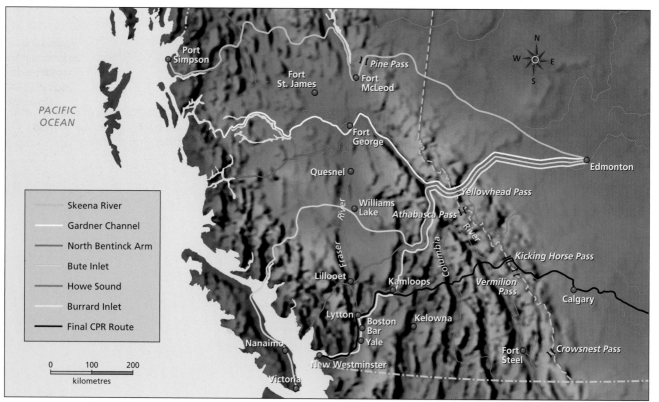

Sandford Fleming favoured a route that ran through the Yellowhead Pass and then south to Burrard Inlet, near New Westminster. This route appealed to mainland politicians in British Columbia. Marcus Smith, Fleming's deputy, proposed a route that ran through the Homathco River Valley to the head of Bute Inlet and then across a bridge to Vancouver Island. Politicans in Victoria were in favour of this route. Other people thought a route to Port Simpson in northern British Columbia made more sense because it was closer to Asia than ports in the south. In the 1870s, in spite of the intense debate, no decision was officially made about this part of the route.

> **DID YOU KNOW...**
>
> One survey party was sent to investigate the Lillooet Icefield and the nearby Ring Pass as a possible route. The party disappeared and was never found.

The National Policy

Sir John A. Macdonald was out of office for five years, from 1873 to 1878. He often thought about the railway. He knew that a transcontinental railway was essential to the survival of Canada, but he needed a political platform to convince all Canadians. In 1876, he developed the **National Policy**, which became the basis of the Conservative election platform in 1878. The voters agreed with Macdonald's vision, and he and his party returned to office with a large majority.

The National Policy was not just an election campaign promise. Macdonald believed that it was a formula for successful nation building, and it remained a central part of Canadian government policy well into the 20th century. The National Policy had three main parts: a system of protective tariffs, increased immigration, and the CPR.

National Policy a mainly economic program introduced by the Macdonald government in 1879

A System of Protective Tariffs

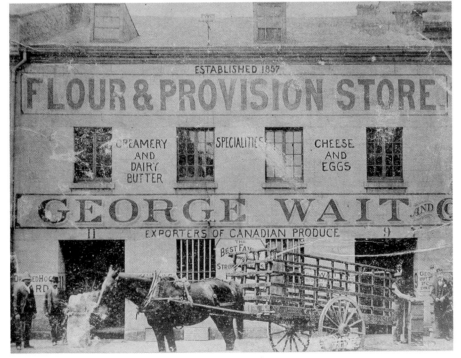

FIGURE 5–28 During the 1870s, the Canadian economy suffered when American companies dumped low-priced goods on the Canadian market. Canadian manufacturers struggled to sell their own goods and still make a profit. Macdonald devised a system of tariffs, or taxes, that would be applied to American goods. Tariffs would protect Canadian manufacturing, mining, and agriculture by making American goods more expensive. What kind of protective system affects the Canadian economy today?

Immigration to the West

FIGURE 5–29 Because the Prairies were suited to agriculture, the Canadian government wanted to bring in immigrants who were farmers. These farmers would produce and export grain, and would buy manufactured goods produced in Ontario and Quebec. Macdonald discouraged the development of manufacturing in the West so that farmers would remain a market for the industrial East. What effect would this policy have on the West? Can the consequences of this policy still be seen today?

The Canadian Pacific Railway

FIGURE 5–30 The West would not develop until goods and people could be transported in and out of the region. Macdonald planned that the CPR would provide the means to ship goods across Canada to and from Asia. Once Macdonald won the 1878 election, building the railway became the government's top priority. How was the railway a cornerstone for the National Policy?

syndicate a group of people who combine their resources to conduct a business together

The CPR Syndicate

Once he was re-elected, it took Macdonald two years to find new investors for the railway. Macdonald found the men he was looking for in George Stephen, president of the Bank of Montreal, Donald Smith of the Hudson's Bay Company, and James J. Hill. Previously, they had purchased the floundering St. Paul and Pacific Railway for just $100 000. Within four years, they had made a profit of $17 million.

In 1880, Macdonald made the group an offer: $25 million in cash, a land grant of 25 million acres, and a monopoly west of Lake Superior for 20 years. In return, the new CPR **Syndicate** was to complete the railway within 10 years.

Planning the Railway

Immediately, the CPR Syndicate changed the planned route of the railway, a route that ran through the fertile land between Saskatoon and Edmonton. Because the northern Prairies was seen as good farmland, many land speculators had moved into the area, buying land they hoped would be near the rail line. However, the Syndicate wanted total control of the project and the land the railway would cross, so they moved the line 300 km south. With no speculators or homesteaders present, the CPR had control over the location of railway stations and towns. The Syndicate also planned branch lines north into the fertile belt, managing all rail traffic on the Prairies.

The change in route made the Canadian Pacific survey useless. The new route would also have to cross the Monashee and Selkirk mountains in British Columbia, and there was no known pass through the Selkirks. Even as the CPR was being built across the southern Prairies, the route through British Columbia was still being studied.

Construction, which began in the spring of 1881, did not go well at first. Work was limited to the line between Winnipeg and Brandon, but by the end of the year, only 230 km had been built. At this rate, the line would not be completed within the promised 10 years. The Syndicate needed a new general manager for the railway—someone with exceptional drive and energy. They chose William Van Horne.

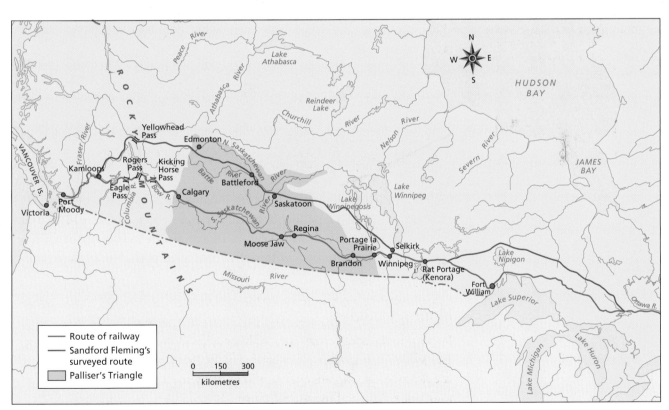

FIGURE 5–31 The change in route demanded by the CPR Syndicate. What advantages did this change give to the CPR?

William Van Horne (1843–1915) was vital to the successful completion of the CPR. Born in Illinois, Van Horne was only 11 when his father died. He left school at 14 after he was punished for drawing cartoons of his school principal. Since his family needed money, he went to work for the local railway. He changed jobs frequently and learned all he could about every aspect of railway work. By the time he turned 21, there was no railway job he could not do.

One of Van Horne's most remarkable accomplishments was his ability to understand Morse code as easily as a second language, unlike most people who had to transcribe the dots and dashes into a readable message.

By the age of 29, Van Horne was general superintendent of the Chicago and Alton Railway. For the next decade, he gained a reputation as a manager who could take a financially troubled railway company and make it profitable. It was this reputation that led the CPR Syndicate to hire him. Van Horne was given almost complete control over the building of the CPR.

A tall and powerful man, Van Horne was forceful, energetic, and dynamic. He slept very little, considering sleep a waste of time. Van Horne also had a photographic memory and an insatiable curiosity.

Van Horne ran the CPR as vice president, president, and chairman of the board from 1885 to 1910. In the early 1900s, while in his 60s, he went to Cuba to help build and organize that country's rail system.

- In what ways was Van Horne historically significant? How was he an agent of change?

FIGURE 5–32 William Van Horne

Building "The Impossible Railway"

Van Horne's arrival quickly energized the CPR. He immediately brought a high level of drive and efficiency into its construction. At a time when all railways were built by hand, he was able to have 800 km laid in 1882 and another 800 km the following year. With Van Horne in charge, the CPR could complete the railway within the contracted period—as long as the money held out.

Money Troubles

One problem for the CPR was that the government paid only when each section of the line was completed, so in the meantime the CPR could not generate any revenue. By the end of 1883, the company was running out of money, and the most costly and difficult sections in British Columbia had yet to be built. George Stephen and Donald Smith each pledged their entire personal fortunes to provide cash for construction, but even that was not enough.

In early 1884, the Canadian government reluctantly passed a bill that provided another $22.5 million for the railway. Macdonald hoped that the extra money would be enough to complete the CPR. Van Horne began cutting expenses. For example, he decided to use temporary wooden trestles and bridges to carry the line over difficult terrain. They could be built quickly, were cheaper than metal bridges, and could be replaced by more permanent structures later. However, even these economies were not enough, and by the end of 1884, the CPR was almost out of money.

The Workforce

Thousands of men were needed to build the railway. Between 1882 and 1885, more than 35 000 workers were employed. Many of these workers came from China, which you will read about in the next chapter.

Living and working conditions were terrible. Dynamite blasts regularly blew dust and broken rock into the air. The workers lived in overcrowded, filthy bunkhouses, with no plumbing. Their diet was dull and unhealthy, with little fresh food, especially during the winter. Most men lived on a diet of porridge, beans, and bacon. There was little medical care; anyone too injured to work was automatically fired, with no compensation. Also, no one was paid when weather conditions put a halt to the work.

FIGURE 5–33 This wooden railway trestle, 33 m high and 270 m long, is in Ontario. Look closely at the landscape and the scale of the bridge. Even though it was the cheaper option, what kind of time and resources would have been spent to build this bridge? How many wooden bridges do you think were built across Canada?

FIGURE 5–34 The official photograph of the Last Spike of the CPR, taken on November 7, 1885. Donald Smith is shown driving the last spike, with William Van Horne and Sandford Fleming standing behind him. From a historical perspective, how does this photo show which individuals were considered more important than others in the building of the railway?

The CPR and the Northwest Uprising

When the Northwest Uprising broke out in 1885, the Canadian government needed to transport troops quickly to the Northwest. The fastest way was by rail, but there were still some gaps in the line, which the troops crossed on foot. At one point, they walked 18 km across the frozen surface of Lake Superior.

Van Horne organized the troop movements with efficiency. The first troops arrived in Winnipeg in just five days, and the entire force was on the Prairies in 10 days. Thanks to the CPR, the government looked as though it could respond to a crisis quickly. Canadians who had been complaining about the high cost of building the CPR now saw why it was necessary. It also meant that the CPR could ask the Canadian government for more money, and in early July, Parliament approved the needed grant. The CPR was completed in November 1885—five years ahead of schedule.

Edward Mallandaine was the boy in the picture—the boy standing next to Sandford Fleming in the image of the Last Spike. Born in Victoria, he was the son of a prominent local businessman. In the spring of 1885, when he was 17, he left Victoria. He told his parents he was planning to work as a carpenter in the interior, but he was really trying to get to the Prairies to take part in the Northwest Uprising.

By the time he reached Revelstoke, the uprising was over, so Mallandaine spent the summer working for the CPR. Realizing it was almost finished, he stayed in the area to witness the driving of the last spike, and he even managed to place himself in this famous photograph.

Once back in Victoria, Mallandaine trained as a civil engineer and worked on several railway projects in British Columbia. In 1897, he helped lay out the town of Creston, where he worked as a CPR land agent for many years. Active in the local militia, he served in the Forestry Corps in France during the First World War. As Colonel Mallandaine, he was a respected local politician, serving as mayor of Creston. He died in 1949.

- How does Edward Mallandaine's story inform our understanding of the past?

FIGURE 5–35 Look for Edward Mallandaine just behind Donald Smith's left arm. Would you want to be part of a famous photograph? Why?

ACTIVITIES

1. What was improper about Macdonald's agreement with Hugh Allan?

2. Examine Figure 5–27. Which route would you choose?

   a) Look at physical maps to examine the terrain of each route. Then measure each route. How would this information influence your decision?

   b) Are there examples of similar battles over roads or bridges in British Columbia today?

3. Consider the three components of the National Policy: protective tariffs, increased immigration, and the CPR. In a chart, summarize the impact each of these had on the development of Canada. Discuss social, political, and economic considerations.

4. Examine the National Policy and determine which aspects favoured specific parts of the country. How do you think people living in various regions of Canada felt about the National Policy?

Significance

5. What kind of narrative is the story of the CPR? Is it a heroic tale, or a scandalous one? Explain your thinking.

6. Explain the historical significance of the CPR. Consider the various elements associated with both its creation (e.g., funding, political scandal, and labour and human rights issues) and its completion (e.g., uniting Canada from sea to sea).

It can be said that the events of 1885 shaped Canada for the next hundred years. For example, the execution of Louis Riel contributed to a level of distrust between English and French Canada, and the nation is still living with the legacy of these events.

The completion of the CPR changed the face of Canada. It allowed for economic expansion and for large-scale European immigration to the West. The CPR became one of Canada's national symbols, recognized all over the world. At great monetary, political, and human expense, Macdonald's National Dream had become a reality.

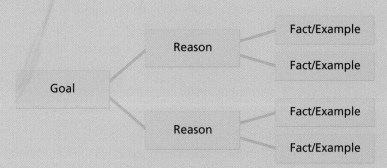

1. In the 1870s, how did the actions of the Canadian government affect those already living in the Northwest? Was there a better way to handle the issue of settlement? Create a chart like the one shown here to indicate the following:

   a) the Canadian government's goal (settlement)

   b) reasons why settlement could have taken place with little or no negative impact on those already living there

   c) facts or examples to support those reasons

   Add to the chart as needed.

2. Research the terms of the numbered treaties. What were the consequences of these agreements? How do they affect First Nations today?

3. Today, when an event has a negative impact on the nation, the government appoints a Royal Commission to investigate. Imagine that a Royal Commission has been called to investigate the events leading up to the Northwest Uprising. You are in charge of the Commission. Determine the causes of the Uprising and recommend changes that could prevent it from happening again. Be sure to provide detailed reasons for your findings.

4. Research the current status of the Métis in Canada. Access Web sites maintained by Métis organizations, or invite a representative of the Métis community to speak to your class.

5. Who built the CPR? Rank the following individuals or groups in terms of importance: Van Horne, the CPR Syndicate, Macdonald, and the workers. Explain your rankings.

6. "The CPR is the reason Canada exists today." Assess this statement in light of what you have learned in this chapter.

7. What makes a good leader? Research the life and leadership decisions of one of the people profiled in this chapter, e.g., Poundmaker, Macdonald, or Riel. Discuss this leader's contributions to Canada. How might this person compare to another world leader?

The Development of British Columbia

Significance

Patterns and Change

Judgements

CRITICAL INQUIRY

Evidence

Cause and Consequence

Perspectives

What led British Columbia to become a Canadian province?

The Pacific Northwest was the last part of North America to be explored and settled by Europeans. What path did British Columbia follow compared with the other colonies in British North America? Who or what had the most influence on its development—individuals, groups, or environmental factors?

Key Terms

Oregon Territory
Aboriginal title
gold rush
annexation

Imagine being in the place of James Douglas, who in 1848 was appointed governor of the colony of Vancouver Island. Read his quote below, and discuss what his job might have included. How might he have related to the different people in his colony—the Chinese, for example, or the Songish, shown above? What challenges would he have faced?

...to create a great social organization, with all its civil, judicial, and military establishments, in a wilderness of forests and mountains, is a Herculean task.

—James Douglas, 1858

The Oregon Territory

▶ **What were the causes and consequences of negotiating the boundary between southern British Columbia and the United States?**

Oregon Territory an area in the Pacific Northwest occupied by both British and American colonists, also called the Columbia District by the British

What was British Columbia like prior to the 1800s? There were no roads, boundary lines, cities, bridges, or ferries, although the territory was inhabited by 80 000 to 100 000 First Nations people. Then, throughout the 19th century, the area was home to an intense and lucrative fur trade. This trade would bring about dramatic changes in the region.

In 1819, the British and American governments agreed that the boundary separating their territories between Lake of the Woods, in what is now western Ontario, and the eastern foothills of the Rocky Mountains would be set at 49° N latitude (also called the 49th parallel). What remained westward was the region between the Rockies and the Pacific Ocean, called the **Oregon Territory**. Because this territory was sparsely populated by Europeans in 1819, the decision as to who should eventually control the area had not been made. As was usual in those times, no one considered the interests of the First Nations inhabitants.

TIMELINE

1792	Captain George Vancouver enters Burrard Inlet
1843	James Douglas begins construction of Fort Victoria
1846	United States takes possession of the Oregon Territory south of the 49th parallel
1858	Colony of British Columbia is formed Fraser Canyon War
1860	Cariboo Gold Rush begins
1862	Construction of Cariboo Road begins Smallpox epidemic
1864	Tsilhqot'in Uprising
1866	Vancouver Island and British Columbia are joined
1868	Victoria is declared the capital of British Columbia
1871	British Columbia joins Confederation
1884	Vancouver is chosen as the CPR terminus
1885	Royal Commission on Chinese Immigration to British Columbia

Different Plans for the Territory

The United States and Britain both wanted to use the Oregon Territory to their advantage. The Hudson's Bay Company, already operating in the region, had no real interest in encouraging settlement, since they preferred to leave the region open for the rich fur trade.

However, at that time, the eastern United States was facing a rapidly increasing population. New areas for expansion became necessary. In 1803, the United States purchased territory west of the Mississippi from France. Most Americans were now convinced that they were fated to control all of North America, an idea they called Manifest Destiny. This belief and the need for more land prompted an aggressive settlement policy in the Oregon Territory. The United States government actively encouraged people from the eastern states to move to the area. Most settled south of the Columbia River near what is now Portland, Oregon, and by the 1830s, the population of this area was growing rapidly.

The Hudson's Bay Company in the Oregon Territory

In 1824, Hudson's Bay Company (HBC) manager George Simpson toured the HBC's Oregon Territory posts. He felt that the company was not making the best use of the region's resources, so he decided to build a new trading post on the north bank of the Columbia River, calling it Fort Vancouver.

Fort Vancouver became the HBC's main trading post in the Oregon Territory. John McLoughlin, a French Canadian, was put in charge. He was directed to expand the fur trade along the Pacific coast to offset the dwindling fur stocks in the Northwest.

McLoughlin was a capable and efficient administrator. He was also a realist. Because he knew that Americans were going to take up homesteads in the region, he decided to take action to limit American competition with the HBC's trade. He encouraged American colonists to settle south of the Columbia River, instead of on the north side. He even offered them supplies and money to get established.

By the end of the 1830s, there was a strong American presence south of the Columbia River. Since the fur trade was still going well, neither the HBC nor the British government paid much attention to this development.

The HBC did have competition from the Russians, who had a number of fur-trading posts along the northern part of the coast. By 1839, the HBC and the Russians had agreed that the Russians would not operate south of 54°40' N latitude (about where Prince Rupert is today). In exchange, the HBC would supply the Russians with food from their farms around Fort Vancouver and on Puget Sound.

In 1841, George Simpson revisited the HBC posts in the Pacific coast region. Disappointed that the coastal fur trade had not expanded as much as he had hoped, he decided to cut costs. All trading posts along the coast were to be closed, with the exception of Fort Simpson. The steamship *Beaver* would be used to trade with coastal First Nations communities.

WEB LINK • • • • • • • • • • • • • • • •

Visit the Pearson Web site to learn more about Fort Vancouver and John McLoughlin.

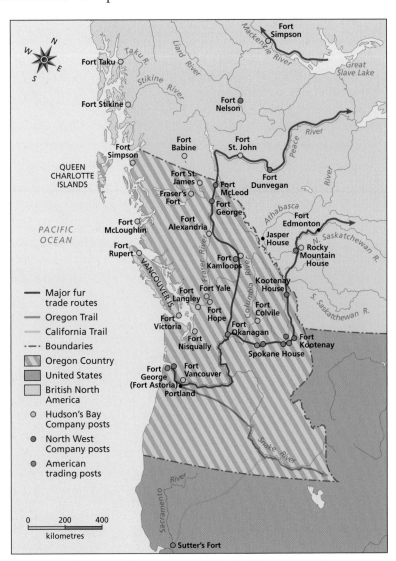

FIGURE 6–1 The Oregon Territory in the 1830s. Find the Columbia River on the map and follow its course to the Pacific. Why did it seem to be a natural boundary between the fur traders and the colonists?

DID YOU KNOW...

John McLoughlin retired from the HBC in 1846 and settled in Oregon City on the Williamette River. He became an American citizen in 1849. Because of his assistance to American settlers, he is known today as "The Father of Oregon."

McLoughlin was furious. Suddenly, 15 years of hard work were undone. He believed that the chain of forts along the coast were an asset to the HBC. Even worse, when McLoughlin's son was killed in a brawl in 1842, Simpson recommended a charge of "justifiable homicide" against his killer. Grief stricken and feeling betrayed, McLoughlin developed an active hatred for both Simpson and the HBC. He continued to promote American settlement south of the Columbia River and discouraged all newcomers from settling north of the river.

Zoom In ⊘ The Pacific Coast's First Steamer

CRITICAL INQUIRY Significance

During the coastal fur trade, one of the problems faced by the Hudson's Bay Company was inaccessibility. Without roads or safe rivers to travel, most places along the coast could be reached only by sea. In order to supply the coastal trading posts, the company decided to build a steamship. The *Beaver*, which arrived in 1836, was the first of its kind to work along the British Columbia coast. For the next 50 years the steamer was a familiar sight.

The *Beaver* supplied HBC trading posts until 1862. From 1863 to 1870, it was chartered by the Royal Navy as a survey vessel. Sold in 1874, the *Beaver* operated as a tugboat until it was wrecked in 1888 on Prospect Point at Vancouver Harbour. The wreck became a popular tourist destination until 1892, when what was left of the *Beaver* sank.

- Why was the *Beaver* essential to the fur trade?

- How would the arrival of the *Beaver* have changed people's lives?

FIGURE 6–2 *The Arrival of the Beaver.* This 1915 painting of the *Beaver* is by Canadian artist John Innes. What questions would you ask to determine if this painting is a reliable source? How reliable do you think it is?

An Official Boundary

The rising population of Americans in the Oregon Territory eventually got the attention of both George Simpson and the British government. Both Britain and the United States now recognized that a permanent boundary was necessary. However, if the 49th parallel was extended from the Rockies to the Pacific, Fort Vancouver would be in American territory.

In 1843, Simpson ordered Fort Vancouver's chief factor, James Douglas, to build a new trading post on Vancouver Island, inside what would likely become British territory. Douglas found a suitable site at the south end of Vancouver Island and named it Fort Victoria.

Simpson's decision was a smart one. In 1844, Democrat James Polk won the United States presidential election, in part because of his campaign slogan: "54 40 or fight." Polk wanted to obtain all of the Oregon Territory up to its northern boundary of 54° 40' N latitude.

However, despite his tough talk, Polk never intended to go to war with the British Empire. Negotiations in 1845 and 1846 simply extended the 49th parallel boundary west, with one exception—all of Vancouver Island remained in British hands. Fort Vancouver and the HBC's farms on Puget Sound were now in American territory, which was a loss for the company. James Douglas spent the next several years transferring the company's operations from Fort Vancouver to Fort Victoria. Fort Vancouver was officially closed in 1849.

FIGURE 6–3 Fort Vancouver. Research to find out what became of the fort after the HBC left. What does it look like today?

ACTIVITIES

1. Think about a piece of information from this section that captured your attention. Explain what you found interesting and why.

2. Use an organizer to compare and contrast the American and British attitudes toward the Oregon Territory.

The Colony of Vancouver Island

▶ **How and why did a colony develop on Vancouver Island?**

In 1848, the British government realized that a more official British presence on the Pacific coast was necessary. To solidify its claim on the region, the government created the Crown colony of Vancouver Island. Britain also gave a trade monopoly to the Hudson's Bay Company, which could sell land to Europeans or Americans who immigrated to the colony.

James Douglas was appointed governor. For 10 years, he was also chief factor of Fort Victoria. Douglas wanted to encourage settlement, so he suggested that free land be offered to colonists. The British government decided to charge for land at a rate of about $5 per acre, with a minimum purchase of 20 acres. However, most of the best land around Fort Victoria had already been purchased by the HBC or its employees, including Douglas himself.

During the 1850s, the economy of the Vancouver Island colony grew rapidly. Coal was discovered, and mines were developed near Nanaimo and Cumberland. Douglas convinced the British to put a naval base near Fort Victoria, with nearby coal as a fuel supply for the ships.

The Royal Navy soon became important to the emerging social life of Fort Victoria, since the aristocratic naval officers were always in demand at social functions, such as balls. Douglas encouraged these activities, but he was not always impressed with the colony's new upper class. Douglas and most of the HBC employees who had settled in the colony had Métis or First Nations wives. They were often shunned by the prejudiced and class-conscious newcomers.

FIGURE 6–4 This map shows the extent of landholdings and population concentrations around Victoria by 1855. What patterns can you find?

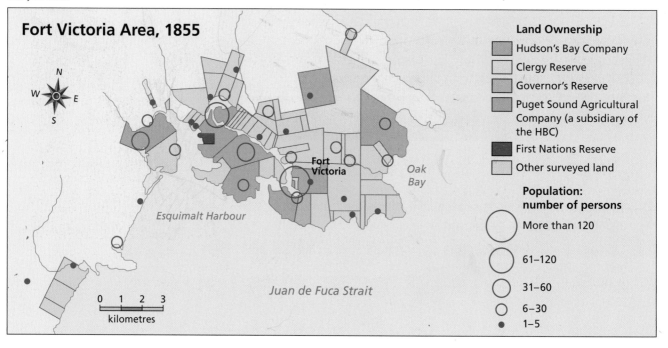

James Douglas was born in 1803 in Guyana, the son of a Scottish merchant and a free Black woman. Educated in Scotland, he began to work for the North West Company when he was 16. He went on to work for the new Hudson's Bay Company after the merger. While on his first visit to Fort Vancouver, he met Amelia Connolly, the Métis daughter of Chief Factor William Connolly. They married in 1828.

Respected for his abilities, Douglas was also known for his quick temper. Nevertheless, he moved up the ranks and was given command of Fort Vancouver, and then Fort Victoria.

In 1851, Douglas became the governor of the newly formed colony of Vancouver Island. His new position soon led to a conflict of interest, possibly because it was difficult to address the needs of both his company and the colony. He was eventually asked to end his connections to the fur trade.

Douglas made decisions that affected the development of not only Vancouver Island but the future colony of British Columbia. His actions to protect British sovereignty, his decisions regarding the First Nations and their lands, and his foresight in the building of the Cariboo Road earned him the title "Father of British Columbia."

Amelia Douglas was the daughter of a North West Company factor and a Cree woman. She married James Douglas when she was 16.

Amelia Douglas was self-reliant. Because her husband was often away on HBC business, she was largely responsible for raising their 13 children.

Well known in fur-trade circles, Amelia Douglas' diplomatic talents often came into play when her husband dealt with First Nations and Métis. In 1828, for example, James Douglas learned that a suspected murderer of two HBC men had taken refuge in a Dakelh First Nation village. Douglas took some men, found the suspect in the chief's house, and had him dragged out and killed.

Unfortunately, Douglas had violated the **sanctity** of the chief's house. The chief was about to kill him in retribution when Amelia Douglas, knowing the customs of the country, offered trade goods to the outraged chief as compensation. The goods were accepted, and James Douglas' life was spared.

Amelia Douglas was the head of one of the most powerful families in the colony. However, although she lived in Victoria for 40 years, she rarely took part in its social scene. This could be a sign that despite her family's position, the society of the time did not accept people of Métis heritage.

sanctity considered sacred

- How might the Douglas' background and experiences prepare them for their role as leaders? Explain.

FIGURE 6–5 Why did the British government choose Douglas, an HBC factor, to be governor of the colony?

FIGURE 6–6 Why was Amelia Douglas essential to James Douglas' success as an employee of the HBC?

When the colony of Vancouver Island was created, the First Nations population of the island far outnumbered the European colonists. There were no reserves, and First Nations freely hunted, fished, and built communities. James Douglas thought that if European immigration to the colony was to succeed, he had to officially gain title to land occupied by the First Nations.

Douglas decided to negotiate treaties in which First Nations would surrender land title to the government. Fourteen treaties were negotiated between 1850 and 1854. Douglas decided that the First Nations could choose where their reserves would be, and he instructed surveyors to make sure to include already established First Nations villages. The size of the reserves was also left up to the First Nations. Range lands for cattle and horses were included, and First Nations were able to keep their traditional hunting and fishing rights.

When Douglas paid for the land surrendered by the First Nations in the treaties, this act acknowledged **Aboriginal title** to the land. This acknowledgement had tremendous significance in the late 20th century during treaty negotiations in British Columbia.

However, once Douglas was out of power, those who took over the government chose to interpret the agreements their own way. Much of the land in the treaties was taken away. Joseph Trutch, Chief Commissioner of Lands and Works for the colony, refused to honour agreements appearing in some of the Douglas Treaties. Trutch openly disliked the First Nations, and he reversed Douglas' policies, even making some of the already established reserves smaller.

After the last Douglas Treaty was signed, there were no other treaties in the rest of the region until 150 years later, when the Nisga'a First Nation signed a treaty with the province of British Columbia.

- Read the following excerpt and discuss what consequences each condition might have in the future.

- Could the colony have developed as it had without the Douglas Treaties? Do we owe a debt to Douglas? Why or why not?

Aboriginal title the claim by Aboriginal peoples that they have ownership of the land because they were the first to occupy it

> *The condition of, or understanding of, this sale is this, that our village sites and enclosed fields are to be kept for our own use and the use of our children, and for those who may follow after us; and the land shall be properly surveyed hereafter. It is understood, however, that the land itself, with these small exceptions, becomes the entire property of the white people forever; it is also understood that we are at liberty to hunt over the unoccupied lands, and to carry on our fisheries as formerly.*
>
> *We have received, in payment…*
>
> —**Common text of the Douglas Treaties, 1850–1854**

ACTIVITIES

1. James Douglas was both chief factor of the HBC and governor of Vancouver Island. Discuss how holding both positions could have been seen as a conflict of interest.

Cause and Consequence

2. Explain how the Douglas Treaties with the First Nations of Vancouver Island were significant. Give evidence that supports your answer.

The Cariboo Gold Rush

▶ **How did the Cariboo Gold Rush have an impact on the development of British Columbia?**

Do you want to "get rich quick?" Many people would like to, and they often take part in schemes that will let them easily obtain the finer things in life. Lottery ticket sales are always higher when the jackpot grows, and although the odds of instant wealth are low, many people want to believe otherwise.

In the 19th century, people were just as influenced by the dream of instant wealth. Thousands had immigrated to Canada or the United States with the hope of finding a better life. Why not also become wealthy? At that time, this optimism was fueled by the **gold rushes** in North America, South America, Australia, and New Zealand. Gold was an exceptionally valuable metal, and when it was found, the rush to claim land and mine its gold led to intense activity. One of these gold rushes was directly responsible for the early development of British Columbia.

The California Gold Rush

In 1848, gold was discovered along the Sacramento River in California. By the following year, thousands of people had travelled to the area. The vast majority of these gold seekers never struck it rich, and many never returned home. Although the gold was real, the gold rush was a fantasy. While many believed that all anyone had to do was walk along a creek picking up gold nuggets, the reality was quite different.

Prospecting for gold was a difficult and often disappointing task. Miners searched for gold deposits by digging up gravel at the side of the creek and swirling it in a wide, shallow pan to expose the gold. A pan of gold valued from 25 cents to a dollar might signal a worthwhile deposit in the area. Miners then **staked a claim** along the creek bank and dug a mine shaft down to the bedrock below. Gold-bearing clay and sand were brought to the surface and washed to reveal the gold. Prospecting and mining gold were time-consuming and back-breaking tasks—not an easy way to strike it rich.

In fact, most of the best claims in California had already been staked by people who were there in 1848. By the time other gold seekers arrived, they often ended up working as labourers to make a living. By the mid-1850s, the gold along the Sacramento River had been mined out, and San Francisco was filled with unemployed former miners who had no way to get home.

> ### DID YOU KNOW...
> The odds of winning the 6/49 lottery jackpot are approximately 14 million to one. The odds of being struck by lightning are only 500 000 to one!

gold rush a period of intense migration of people to an area where gold has been discovered

prospecting searching for gold

stake a claim declare mining rights in a specific area

> ### DID YOU KNOW...
> Gold is a very heavy metal and is usually found in seams far below the surface. In most 19th century gold rushes, the gold was washed downstream from a single deposit called the motherlode. If you could find the motherlode, you would be wealthy beyond your wildest dreams. In most cases, the motherlode was never found.

The Fraser River Gold Rush

In late 1857, an HBC trader arrived in Fort Victoria carrying gold dust and nuggets he had panned along the banks of the Thompson River. He presented what he found to Governor Douglas. Douglas was aware of the social disruption caused by the California Gold Rush. He feared that if news of another gold strike became known, the colony of Vancouver Island might be invaded by thousands of American miners on the way to the mainland to seek their fortune. Also, the mainland, which at that time fell under no political jurisdiction, would be more vulnerable to American **annexation**. Aside from a squadron of Royal Navy warships at Esquimalt, Douglas had no army or militia to call on if serious trouble arose. He communicated his concerns to the Colonial Office in London.

Douglas' fears came true during the winter of 1857–1858. Prospectors in Washington and Oregon began moving north to the banks of the Fraser and Thompson rivers. They discovered gold on the sandbars of both rivers. Word swiftly reached San Francisco, and 450 unemployed miners arrived at Fort Victoria on April 25, 1858. Immediately they went to the mainland using anything that would float, including homemade rafts. More ships arrived as the summer progressed, and by the end of the summer, over 10 000 men, mostly American, were working claims along the Fraser Canyon.

The Fraser Canyon War

While Douglas made an effort to control the number of miners entering the Fraser Canyon, he could never have been completely successful. Determined miners on their way to a gold rush could not be stopped, and eventually, the rush of newcomers into the area led to conflict.

Already living in the Fraser Canyon were the Nlaka'pamux First Nation, also called the Thompson River Salish. Some sources say that trouble began with an attack on a young Nlaka'pamux woman in the fall of 1858. Several gold miners were killed, apparently in retaliation, and the

annexation the act of adding another territory to one's own

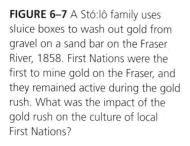

FIGURE 6–7 A Stó:lô family uses sluice boxes to wash out gold from gravel on a sand bar on the Fraser River, 1858. First Nations were the first to mine gold on the Fraser, and they remained active during the gold rush. What was the impact of the gold rush on the culture of local First Nations?

discovery of their bodies started a panic. Informal militias, made up of armed miners, were quickly formed. However, leaders of different militias were soon arguing over how to resolve the situation—one wanted a peaceful solution, while another advocated the complete destruction of the Nlaka'pamux.

As the militias moved up the river, a message of peace was sent to Camchin, a village located where the Thompson and Fraser rivers meet (now called Lytton). Nlaka'pamux leaders, along with representatives of the Secwepemc and Okanagan First Nations, came together in Camchin to discuss what to do. It is said that a leader named Cxpentlum (Spintlum), who trusted James Douglas, argued for peace. When the militias entered Camchin, they were greeted peacefully, and soon the conflict was at an end. Douglas, however, was concerned because the miners had organized themselves and had acted on their own.

FIGURE 6–8 The Lytton Bridge was renamed the Chief Spintlum Bridge in honour of Cxpentlum.

Zoom In 1859: Ned McGowan's War

British control of the mainland would soon be challenged again. Gold miners from San Francisco had come to the Fraser Canyon split into two opposing camps: the Vigilance Committee and the Law and Order Party. Both groups had a long history of conflict with each other.

The leader of the Law and Order Party was Ned McGowan. Battles with the Vigilance Party in San Francisco had ruined him financially, so he travelled to the Fraser Canyon to renew his fortune. He soon found old friends and supporters, and became their leader. They kept a wary eye on the Vigilance Party branch headquartered a few kilometres away.

McGowan became frustrated with a local official named Richard Hicks, who had been appointed by James Douglas. Hicks was corrupt, taking bribes in exchange for permits and claims.

McGowan wanted Hicks gone. Douglas compromised by sending Justice of the Peace Peter Whannell to keep an eye on Hicks. Unfortunately, Whannell was intensely disliked; he was considered corrupt, foolish, and vain.

Events came to a head when a British man was shot by an American in a fight. The American fled to McGowan for protection, and tension erupted as the Vigilance Committee— McGowan's old enemies—suggested it was time for them to take control. When Whannell issued arrest warrants for two of McGowan's men, McGowan persuaded another justice of the peace to arrest Whannell for contempt instead. Although only fined, Whannell was humiliated. He quickly wrote to Douglas, asking that a military force be sent to put down what he called a "rebellion," suggesting that the colony

was in danger. Douglas sent in a group of soldiers, as well as Judge Matthew Begbie and Colonel Richard Moody. McGowan told his own men to ask the American military for help if fighting broke out. If this had happened, American soldiers might have marched into the colony, and the area could have been annexed by the United States.

Luckily, cooler heads prevailed. Moody and Begbie entered the area, calmly settled the dispute without violence, and fired Hicks. The presence of the soldiers calmed all sides, and British rule was kept. The threat of annexation quickly passed.

- Discuss the challenges faced by Douglas in his attempts to control the mainland. Could he have done anything else to prevent this conflict?

WEB LINK • • • • • • • • • • • • • • • •

On the Pearson Web site, read letters sent by the people involved in McGowan's War.

The Colony of British Columbia

In 1858, the colony of British Columbia was created on the mainland, extending from the 49th parallel to 54° 40' N. Douglas was made governor, and the Colonial Office sent a contingent of Royal Engineers. The engineers, who arrived in 1859, were to provide a military presence, survey the region, and assist in laying out new towns and roads. Matthew Begbie was to be chief justice for the new colony. Begbie, known to be tough but fair, was to ensure that the rule of law was upheld.

Gold miners soon began working their way up the Fraser, searching for the motherlode. By 1860, the leading edge of this northward movement had reached the Quesnel River. Several miners discovered large deposits of gold in the creeks flowing into the Quesnel, and the richness of the deposits convinced them that the motherlode was nearby. The Cariboo Gold Rush was underway.

The Cariboo Wagon Road

Getting to the goldfields was extremely difficult in the early 1860s because there were no easy routes inland. Most miners carried their supplies on their backs, or used pack horses over old HBC trails. In 1858, James Douglas hired miners to widen an old HBC trail that bypassed the rapids of the Fraser River. This trail ran from the head of Harrison Lake to Lillooet, and because it was actually a combination of trails and water routes, it was hard to maintain. A better route was needed, both to ease travel and to provide effective government presence.

In 1862, Douglas ordered the construction of the Cariboo Wagon Road. It began at Yale, running northward along the steep walls of the Fraser Canyon to Lytton. There it went directly overland to Quesnel and eventually to Barkerville. Almost 650 km long, the Cariboo Road took three years to build and cost the colonial government $750 000.

Ironically, by the time the Cariboo Road was finished in 1865, the gold rush was already in decline. The hoped-for tax revenues to offset building costs were far lower than anticipated. The colony of British Columbia was left deeply in debt.

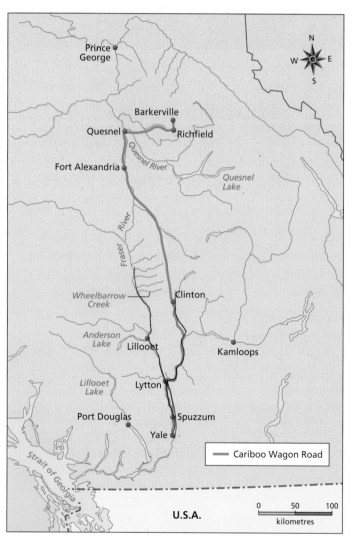

FIGURE 6–9 The route of the Cariboo Wagon Road. Why did such a difficult undertaking seem necessary to the colonial government?

Barkerville

The main town of the Cariboo Gold Rush was Barkerville, the largest of three communities on Williams Creek. It was named after Billy Barker, an Englishman who came north in 1858 after the California Gold Rush. Barker struck gold on Williams Creek in 1862, and other miners quicky followed. By the end of the year, Williams Creek was completely staked, and several small communities had developed around the mines.

Initially, life in the area was hard. Bringing in supplies by pack animals was slow and difficult, and the small loads meant that only the "bare necessities" were affordable. Many everyday items, like fresh eggs, were very expensive.

Barkerville consisted of two streets next to Williams Creek, with wood-frame buildings touching each other. The town was surrounded by miners' shacks and by a network of **flumes**. Water carried by the flumes was used to rinse the gold from the mines.

By the mid-1860s, about 5000 to 10 000 people lived in Barkerville. When the Cariboo Wagon Road opened, business thrived, and the town soon had general stores, boarding houses, a post office, a drugstore, a barbershop, the Theatre Royal, and the Cariboo Literary Society.

FIGURE 6–10 Compare the Cariboo Road, shown here, with modern roads in British Columbia. What environmental impact did the Cariboo Road have?

The People of Barkerville

The gold rush attracted people from all over the world, including Black and Chinese settlers who opened businesses or mined in the area. For example, a Chinese business called the Kwong Lee Company ran a general store. Wellington Moses, part of a group of Black settlers from San Francisco, opened the town's barbershop. One product Moses offered was his "hair invigorator," a tonic that promised to cure baldness. As an observant recorder of events in the town, Moses even managed to solve the murder of a friend.

Barkerville also had a vibrant night life. The Hurdy Gurdy Girls were dancers brought "direct from Germany" by enterprising saloon keepers in 1866. They were employed to dance with miners and got a percentage of every drink they sold.

flume an artificial water channel

WEB LINK ● · · · · · · · · · · · · · · · ·
Visit the Pearson Web site for more information about Barkerville.

FIGURE 6–11 In 1862, freight operator Frank Laumeister imported 23 camels to carry supplies on the Cariboo Road to Barkerville. With the ability to carry huge loads, the camels should have been a success. In fact, they were unsuited to the rocky ground and cold weather. They also terrified horses and mules. Eventually the camels were sold. Some escaped and continued to frighten locals for years. Could a similar situation happen today?

The End of the Gold

On September 16, 1868, most of Barkerville was destroyed by fire. The damage was extensive, and many businesses suffered. However, within three months, the town was rebuilt. Efforts were taken to avoid a second fire, including shipping a fire engine in from San Francisco.

By the early 1870s, most of the easily mined gold had been removed, and only large mining outfits with hydraulic equipment were able to stay in business. By the 1880s, the population was dwindling, and by the 1920s Barkerville was almost a ghost town.

In 1958, on British Columbia's centennial, the provincial government decided to restore the town as a tourist attraction. Today, Barkerville looks a lot like it did at the end of the 1860s, with displays and guides who bring a vanished era to life.

FIGURE 6–12 Barkerville before 1868. Look closely at the image. What was the environmental impact of building the town?

The Tsilhqot'in Uprising

The arrival of thousands of miners and the development of towns, mines, and roads were not a welcome sight to everyone. First Nations in the Cariboo region, already deeply affected by European settlement, famine, and disease, knew that more people in the area would put pressure on food resources, such as game and fish. Roads were cut through traditional lands without permission. What the colonists saw as progress and development, First Nations saw as a radical change to their world and the loss of their lands and lifestyle. Some felt so threatened they took up arms.

In 1862, a businessman from Victoria named Alfred Waddington proposed an alternate route to the Cariboo. His road, which began at Bute Inlet, would cut two weeks' travel time to the gold-fields. Although the Cariboo Road was still being built, he was given permission by the colonial government to build his road.

The route Waddington chose crossed the lands of the Tsilhqot'in (Chilcotin) Nation. Already facing famine, and fearing the threat of smallpox, the Tsilhqot'in decided that the road would only bring more trouble. In April of 1864, a group of Tsilhqot'in attacked the road builders, killing 14 men. Three escaped, bringing news of the attack to the authorities. In the meantime, the group and their leader, Klatsassin, found and killed five more Europeans.

The colonial government responded by sending a search party after Klatsassin and his men. They were not found until Klatsassin surrendered, believing he had been promised immunity.

Klatsassin and his men were charged with murder, despite their claim that they had only fought to defend themselves and their land. Klatsassin and four others were found guilty and executed.

WEB LINK • • • • • • • • • • • •
View resources about the Tsilhqot'in uprising on the Pearson Web site.

WHAT DO YOU THINK?

1. Consider the role of the media (i.e. newspapers) during this time. What coverage of the uprising would you expect? Explain your thinking.

2. Using the Web Link, assess the primary documents provided to develop a historical perspective of the incident. Do the documents change your opinion on what happened?

ACTIVITIES

1. How did the reality of the gold rushes differ from the fantasy?

2. How did the British government act to ensure that mainland British Columbia did not become annexed by the United States?

3. In what ways were the Royal Engineers important to the development of infrastructure in British Columbia?

4. How did the Cariboo Gold Rush impact First Nations people?

Judgements

5. Why was building the Cariboo Wagon Road so essential to the Cariboo Gold Rush and to the development of British Columbia?

The Creation of British Columbia

▶ **What events from 1856–1871 played a role in shaping British Columbia?**

Imagine having almost exclusive control of the new colonies on the Pacific coast. Until 1856, James Douglas was in that position. There was no elected legislative assembly, and the legislative and executive councils were appointed by him. Douglas even made his brother-in-law chief justice. As the population grew, this **autocratic** approach led to protests.

In 1856, Douglas was ordered to create a seven-member legislative assembly for Vancouver Island. Douglas insisted that only those who owned property could vote, which included about 40 of the colony's male citizens. Douglas still retained control; while the legislative assembly could pass resolutions, it had no authority to enforce them. The governor could (and did) ignore resolutions he did not like.

autocrat a person who rules like a dictator

Changes in Population

A census of the population of Vancouver Island was taken in 1855. It showed a non-First Nations population of 774 and a First Nations population of at least 30 000. The total First Nations population along the coast was at least 60 000.

WEB LINK ● ● ● ● ● ● ● ● ● ● ● ● ● ● ● ● ● ● ●

Find out more about the smallpox epidemic in Victoria on the Pearson Web site.

The Smallpox Epidemic

In the spring of 1862, a San Francisco miner brought smallpox to Victoria. The disease spread quickly, especially to First Nations communities nearby, where it caused an epidemic. While colonists were vaccinated, local First Nations villages were quarantined.

FIGURE 6–13 Victoria in 1863. How did the community change as a result of the discovery of gold?

Many First Nations from outside southern Vancouver Island had come to Victoria hoping to find work in the gold rush, but they were now ordered to go home. As they travelled north, the smallpox went with them, and the disease spread. On Haida Gwaii, over 70 percent of the population died in the summer of 1862, and villages that had existed for thousands of years were suddenly empty. It is estimated that by the time the smallpox epidemic had run its course, over half of the coastal First Nations population had died.

Immigration

During the Fraser and Cariboo Gold Rushes, more than 35 000 people arrived from all over the world to seek their fortunes. This increase was only temporary; by the middle of the 1860s, the gold was running out and the miners were leaving. The population of both colonies dwindled to less than 10 000 people.

With fewer people to pay taxes, government revenue dropped. By 1865, the colony of Vancouver Island was $300 000 in debt, and the colony of British Columbia owed more than one million dollars. In 1866, both colonies sought loans from local banks to pay their employees, but the banks refused.

The only solution was to unite the colonies. The British Colonial Office agreed, not wanting to subsidize two colonial governments. On August 6, 1866, the two colonies were officially united as the colony of British Columbia.

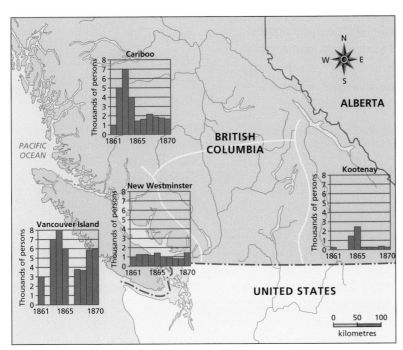

FIGURE 6–14 Great shifts in the population of some areas in British Columbia took place during the 1860s. What caused these changes?

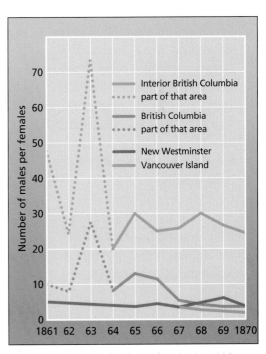

FIGURE 6–15 Ratio of males to females in British Columbia during the 1860s

In 1856, James Douglas was directed to create a legislative assembly to add to Douglas' appointed legislative council. Only those who owned property worth £300 could hold office or vote, which created an **electorate** of just 40 men. They elected seven members to that first assembly.

When the colonies of Vancouver Island and British Columbia joined in 1866, a legislative council of 23 members was created. Only nine were elected (five from the mainland and four from Vancouver Island). Victoria was selected as the capital of the new colony, much to the dismay of the population of New Westminster.

When British Columbia joined Confederation in 1871, a provincial legislative assembly of 25 members was created, with a Lieutenant-Governor appointed by the Crown. Until 1903, there were no political parties in the legislative assembly. As a result, there was little political stability in government—no less than 15 premiers held office during those years.

Today, the legislature of British Columbia is made up of the Lieutenant-Governor and 85 elected Members of the Legislative Assembly (MLAs). Each MLA represents a **constituency**, and Canadian citizens over the age of 18 who have lived in the province for at least six months are able to vote and run for office. Like Members of Parliament (MPs) at the federal level, MLAs are responsible for debating and voting on proposed laws and approving the provincial budget. Since 2001, elections in British Columbia are held every four years.

The Lieutenant-Governor asks the leader of the provincial party with the most seats in the legislature to form a government. Like the Governor General, the Lieutenant-Governor is appointed by the Crown on the advice of the prime minister. The leader of the second-largest party in the legislature becomes the leader of the opposition. The premier chooses elected members to form a cabinet of ministers who are in charge of various ministries, such as education and finance.

electorate the group of persons entitled to vote

constituency a district that is represented by an elected person

FIGURE 6–16 The British Columbia legislative buildings opened in 1898. Francis Rattenbury, the architect, was only 25 years old when his design was chosen. What styles are reflected in these buildings? Why do you think this design was chosen?

DID YOU KNOW...

Women and Chinese Canadians were officially denied the right to vote in 1874; First Nations in 1872. Women gained the right to vote provincially in 1917, Chinese citizens in 1949, and First Nations in 1960.

WHAT DO YOU THINK?

1. Conduct some research to learn about your MLA. Generate a list of questions that will help you better understand who this person is, what he or she believes in, and what actions he or she has taken as a member of the Legislative Assembly. Share your findings with the class.

2. Investigate recent changes in the government of British Columbia. What issues are important to British Columbians, and how have provincial political parties responded to these issues?

WEB LINK
Find out more about the elections process in British Columbia on the Pearson Web site.

On the Northwest coast, where the challenges of a mountainous geography often isolated Aboriginal communities from one another, distinct language groups developed among the Aboriginal peoples. (Check the map on page 38 to see the various language groups in British Columbia.)

Speaking different languages often made communication difficult. As a result, a common language evolved. Called Chinook, or Chinook jargon, Chinook included vocabulary from various groups.

The fur trade solidified Chinook as the common language of the coast. When Europeans arrived, French and English words were added. Some European traders also learned Chinook, so by the early 19th century, Chinook became the common trade language on the coast, spoken from northern California to Alaska.

Simple and easy to learn, Chinook dealt with daily activities. Even during the gold rush, Chinook survived and prospered. By the 1880s, more than one third of the total population of the area could speak Chinook.

However, with the arrival of the CPR and rapid population growth, Chinook soon declined. By 1962, fewer than 100 people in British Columbia could still speak it. However, Chinook words have survived in place names and in common expressions.

Some Chinook words

cheechako: newcomer

chuck: water

saltchuck: ocean

muckamuck: food

potlatch: give

• What does the emergence and decline of Chinook reveal to us about British Columbia's past?

FIGURE 6–17 Siwash Rock in Stanley Park. *Siwash* is a Chinook word meaning "a person of Aboriginal heritage." Research place names in British Columbia. How many come from Chinook?

ACTIVITIES

1. Explain the significance of the smallpox epidemic for First Nations populations in British Columbia.

2. Describe how the emergence of the Chinook language was essential to the develoment of British Columbia. Provide an explanation for the decline of this language.

3. Is loss of language linked to loss of culture? Relate this question to your own experience. Consider your family's roots, language, and culture.

Evidence

4. Examine Figures 6–14 and 6–15.

   a) Which areas had the most significant population decline between 1864 and 1870? Which had the least? With a partner, discuss possible explanations.

   b) What does Figure 6–14 tell you about the population of Cariboo compared with the rest of British Columbia?

• # Judging Geographic Importance

Part of critical thinking in geography is understanding that we do not always get all of the information we need.

For example, is it possible for a map to contain all of the information about a certain area? How does a map's purpose reflect geographic importance?

Ask Questions

Look at these two maps of Victoria.

- What do the maps show?

- How are they similar or different?

- What purpose is implied in each map?

- What does the map-maker think is important to show?

- Who is the audience for each map, and why is that information important to them?

- Does each map help explain something significant about the past or the present?

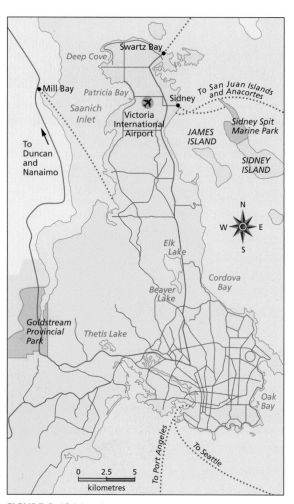

FIGURE 6–18 Map 1

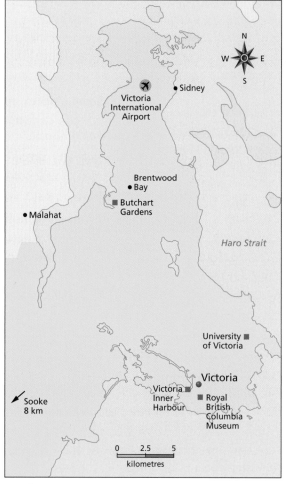

FIGURE 6–19 Map 2

APPLY IT

1. You have been asked for a report on how geography influenced the development of British Columbia. The report must include a map. Plan your map by deciding what features you wish to discuss, and use a chart to organize your ideas. Consider what should be included and what should be left out. Rank the features by importance, and explain your decisions.

The Confederation Debate

▶ **What advantages would joining Confederation bring to British Columbia?**

The populations of the colonies of Vancouver Island and British Columbia were in decline, and financial losses had prompted the colonies to unite. However, union did little to solve their economic woes—the colony still needed more people, more money, and better access to markets. Joining Confederation might help solve those problems. But did everyone agree?

Colonies in other areas of Canada had their doubts about Confederation, and British Columbia was no exception. Debate was frequent and often bitter. Elected representatives on the mainland were strongly in favour of Confederation, and members from Vancouver Island were equally opposed. A third group, mostly Victoria merchants, favoured annexation by the United States.

Arguments For and Against

In 1868, the mainland representatives, called **confederationists**, adopted resolutions that described how and why British Columbia should join Canada. They wanted the Dominion government to become responsible for British Columbia's debt. They also wanted a wagon road to be built from Lake Superior to New Westminster, providing a crucial trade link to the rest of Canada. In addition, they demanded responsible government. Although their resolutions were defeated in the legislative assembly, they continued to promote their ideas in the press.

Those in favour of joining the United States felt it was a better economic deal for British Columbia. Canada was far away, but nearby Washington and Oregon were prospering, and annexation would ensure permanent links to this market. The **anti-confederationists** wanted to maintain ties to Britain, and generally mistrusted Canadians. The First Nations in the region were not asked their opinion.

In late 1868, a new election created a balance of anti- and pro-confederationists in the assembly. Then, in 1869, Governor Seymour died suddenly. The British Colonial Office appointed Anthony Musgrave as his replacement. Musgrave was a personal friend of John A. Macdonald. The British government, tired of supporting the colony, was in favour of Confederation. Musgrave's instructions were simple—get British Columbia to join Confederation as quickly as possible.

confederationist someone in favour of joining Confederation

anti-confederationist someone opposed to joining Confederation

FIGURE 6–20 Governor Seymour with his wife. Seymour was not in favour of joining Confederation, and his sudden death upset the balance in the Confederation debate.

The **annexationists** quickly circulated a petition in favour of joining the U.S. However, in Victoria, a town of 3000 people, they collected only 125 signatures. Turning his attention to the anti-confederationists, Musgrave subtly **co-opted** their support by asking them to work with him on a policy of union. They agreed by writing out a "wish list" of terms, adding a few clauses they were sure would be rejected.

However, when the delegation arrived in Ottawa, the Canadian government agreed with virtually all of the terms—even promising a railway to British Columbia within 10 years. When the delegation returned, the Canadian proposal was unanimously accepted. On July 20, 1871, British Columbia officially joined Canada.

Zoom In Amor De Cosmos    Significance

Born William Smith in Nova Scotia, Amor De Cosmos was a photographer during the California Gold Rush. In 1854, proclaiming his "love of order, beauty, the world, the universe," he changed his name to Amor De Cosmos.

In 1858, De Cosmos moved to Victoria for the Fraser River Gold Rush. There, he started a newspaper—the *British Colonist*.

A supporter of responsible government, De Cosmos started attacking James Douglas. He considered Douglas a tyrant; Douglas responded by trying

WEB LINK •••••••••••••
Listen to a biography of Amor De Cosmos on the Pearson Web site.

to shut down the *Colonist*. De Cosmos supported Confederation, which made him somewhat unpopular. In 1868, De Cosmos helped organize the Confederation League, a group that actively campaigned in favour of Confederation and responsible government. Members of the league organized speeches and assemblies to promote their ideas and perfect their demands.

Elected as one of British Columbia's first Members of Parliament, De Cosmos also served in the provincial legislature, and later became British Columbia's second premier.

De Cosmos believed that First Nations and Chinese people were inferior. He disagreed with

Aboriginal land title, calling the land "unoccupied," and he recommended severe punishment if First Nations trespassed on colonial property. Still, it was an even more openly prejudiced opponent, Noah Shakespeare, who eventually defeated De Cosmos at the polls.

After retiring, De Cosmos became a paranoid recluse, afraid of anything run by electricity. He died in 1897.

• What significance did Amor De Cosmos have for the development of British Columbia?

• How did he influence the formation of the province?

ACTIVITIES

1. Identify the main reason for the union of Vancouver Island and British Columbia. Did the union solve the region's problems? Explain.

2. Create a poster to advertise the cause of the annexationists, the confederationists, or the anti-confederationists. Focus on the advantages each group thought their cause would bring to British Columbia.

The Emergence of Vancouver

▶ **What factors contributed to the development of Vancouver?**

Vancouver is the youngest major community in British Columbia. Almost all other major centres in the province can trace their beginnings to either the fur trade or the gold rush. However, Burrard Inlet is not fed by a main river, and the peninsula was originally covered by thick forests. During the fur trade and the Cariboo Gold Rush, these factors discouraged people from settling there.

When Colonel Moody arrived in New Westminster, he was impressed by the potential of Burrard Inlet, both as an ice-free port and as a harbour with naval advantages. He had the Royal Engineers cut trails through the forest to join the inlet to New Westminster.

Industry Brings Development

In 1860, the future site of Vancouver appeared much as it had for thousands of years. But by 1865, the area had changed. Captain Edward Stamp built Hastings Mill on the south side of the inlet. On the north side of the inlet, American entrepreneur Sewell Moody also built a sawmill. The mill and its surrounding community were known as Moodyville. Both mills specialized in selectively logging "B.C. toothpicks"— timber from trees so large that logs measured 18 metres long and 1 metre in diameter. They were prized as masts for sailing ships and were exported around the world.

Both Hastings Mill and Moodyville were officially **dry** until John "Gassy Jack" Deighton appeared in Burrard Inlet in 1867, with his family and a barrel of whisky. Gassy Jack's saloon became a popular meeting place, especially after payday. Soon, other saloons and stores opened, and buildings appeared along the shores of Burrard Inlet. Officially known as Granville, the village was better known as Gastown, after Gassy Jack.

dry forbidding the selling or drinking of alcohol

FIGURE 6–21 Hastings Mill in the 1880s. Considering raw resources, workers, and the export of products, why might a lumber mill be successful in this area?

The Railway Arrives

For the next decade, life in Burrard Inlet continued as before. Then, in 1881, Port Moody was named the terminus, or end, of the Canadian Pacific Railway line. The focus of activity shifted to the eastern end of the inlet, with speculators buying up land, eager to cash in on what could only be a great future metropolis.

In 1884, William Van Horne arrived at Port Moody to establish the exact location of the CPR terminus. He found the site utterly unsuitable. The harbour was shallow, and there was not enough flat land in Port Moody to accommodate the rail yards the CPR would need. Travelling farther down the inlet, he found what he was looking for—deep-water anchorages close to shore, and wide expanses of flat land perfect for rail yards. Delighted, he named the site Vancouver, announcing it would be the CPR terminus. The speculators of Port Moody were outraged, but there was nothing they could do.

By the spring of 1886, the CPR had been completed and the new city of Vancouver incorporated. By 1890, the city had a population of over 5000; within 10 years, it was more than 20 000.

FIGURE 6–22 Deighton was known as "Gassy Jack" because of his talkative nature. What is Gastown like today?

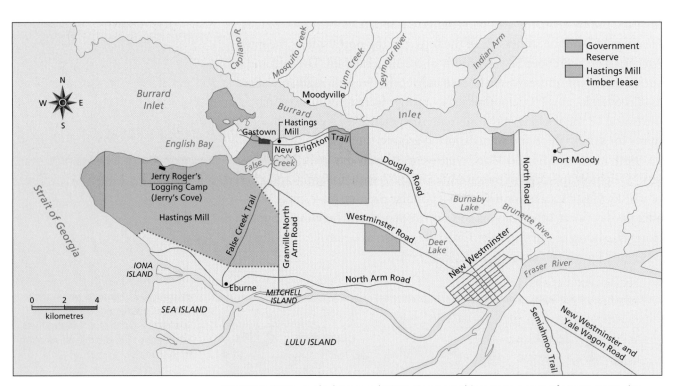

FIGURE 6–23 Burrard Inlet around 1880. Compare this map to a map of Vancouver today. How many modern features began as part of the original layout of the city?

Throughout its history, the Port of Vancouver has dominated the west coast of the Americas as the primary port for exports and imports. It has been the busiest port in Canada for much of its existence, playing a big role in the development of Vancouver as a global city. Since the arrival of the CPR, Vancouver has been Canada's "Gateway to the Pacific."

In 1887, the Port of Vancouver quickly gained world prominence with the arrival of the *SS Abyssinia* and its cargo of tea, silk, and mail bound for London, England. The *Abyssinia* was part of a record-setting, 29-day around-the-world delivery. It took the ship 13 days to take the cargo from Japan to Vancouver. The cargo then travelled by rail across Canada in 8 days, and it took another 8 days to go across the Atlantic to London. This route beat the previous record by 16 days! It was the beginning of a modern trade route that made Vancouver a major shipment point.

When the Panama Canal opened in 1914, Vancouver's port became even busier. Grain and forest products were shipped not only to Asia and Canada, but also to the eastern United States and Europe via the Panama Canal. An influx of imports led to the construction of piers, large rail yards, and warehouses. Facilities for passengers were also improved.

After the Second World War, the Port of Vancouver became more specialized. Besides grain and forest products, the port now handled coal, potash, sulphur, copper, and raw sugar. In the 1970s and 1980s, Vancouver's port expanded with the construction of its first container terminals and facilities for Alaskan cruise ships.

In 2006, the federal government created the Asia Pacific Gateway and Corridor Initiative (APGCI). Billions of dollars were targeted for building infrastructure to improve economic connections to the Asia Pacific and the rest of North America. With these vast improvements, ties to Asia were strengthened.

The Port of Vancouver will continue to develop throughout the 21st century.

FIGURE 6–24 The infrastructure of Vancouver's port is continually being developed. Why might these upgrades be important?

WHAT DO YOU THINK?

1. Do you agree or disagree that the Port of Vancouver is still primarily an export-oriented port facility? Explain with examples.

2. How does the Port of Vancouver affect the economy of the Lower Mainland region of British Columbia? Explain why specific businesses choose to locate near major ports like Vancouver.

3. Complete a Web search of the Port Authorities of Vancouver and Prince Rupert, and check current statistics and updates about the port facilities. Did the APGCI succeed in its plan to upgrade the facilities and encourage more trade with the Asia Pacific?

New Economic Opportunities for British Columbia

With Confederation and the coming of the railway, British Columbia was no longer isolated from the rest of Canada. While earlier trade had focused on north–south trade with the United States, it was now clear that other provinces in Canada were vast potential markets, and this immediately drew the attention of producers and business owners eastward.

Exports of natural resources, in particular, saw an increase following the completion of the railway. For example, the immigration boom in the Prairies created a high demand for lumber to build new homes. The population of British Columbia also began to grow, as the railway made travel through the mountains easier. A greater population meant a larger workforce, and the economy soon prospered. Travel for leisure was also now an option, and the CPR also became a mode of transportation for Canadian tourists drawn to the majestic beauty of the Rocky Mountains.

Goods could now flow easily through the province, both to and from the rest of Canada and to Asian markets. As you have read, Vancouver would develop into an international port, vital to the import and export of goods to and from Canada, as a result of its location and the railway link to the rest of the continent.

ₒACTIVITIES∘

1. Explain why Vancouver developed later than other areas of British Columbia?

2. Describe how geography and the coming of the railway influenced changes in the flow of goods in and out of British Columbia.

3. "Historical figures like Gassy Jack are colourful, but not significant." Do you agree or disagree with this statement? Share your opinion with a partner.

4. Examine Van Horne's decision regarding the relocation of the CPR terminus.

   a) Why did Van Horne relocate the terminus?

   b) Imagine you are a land speculator in Port Moody in 1884. Write a letter to William Van Horne explaining why you think his decision is wrong.

5. Did Vancouver earn the title "Gateway to the Pacific"? Explain.

A Province of Diversity

▶ **How did British Columbia develop as a multi-ethnic province?**

While society in 19th century British Columbia was dominated by Europeans, especially the British, newcomers from other countries came to work, raise families, and contribute to the province's development.

The Kanakas

The first non-European immigrants to British Columbia were the **Kanakas**, who travelled to the west coast of North America from the Hawaiian Islands in the early 19th century. The first Europeans to visit the Hawaiian Islands were Captain James Cook and his crew. Despite the fact that Cook was killed there in 1779, British and American vessels continued to visit the Hawaiian Islands, which were conveniently located halfway between North America and Asia. Ships were often short of crewmen, so Hawaiians were hired to fill the gaps. The new sailors quickly impressed their shipmates with their hard work and their excellent sailing and swimming skills.

By the 1820s, the Hudson's Bay Company was regularly hiring Kanakas to work at HBC posts in the Oregon Territory, especially around Fort Vancouver. By the 1840s, there were more than 200 Kanakas working near Fort Vancouver, mostly as farmers. Many more lived and worked at Fort Nisqually and Fort Langley. They married First Nations women and started families.

Kanaka a person of Hawaiian descent who immigrated to British Columbia to work; many were contracted to work with the HBC

DID YOU KNOW...

Unlike other non-European immigrants, Kanakas were regarded as British subjects and retained the right to vote and hold public office.

FIGURE 6–25 William Nahanee (holding a bag), a Kanaka, is seen in this 1889 photo with a group of longshoremen at the dock of the Moodyville sawmill. Describe this photo in your own words. What can be learned about this group of workers from the photo?

After the border between the United States and Canada was established, the HBC wound up its affairs south of the border and moved its people north. Many HBC employees, including some Kanakas, were encouraged to leave the company and start lives on their own in British Columbia.

Some Kanakas settled in Burrard Inlet, where they established a community in Coal Harbour near what is now Stanley Park and found employment at the Hastings Mill. The "Kanaka Ranch" survived until the 1890s. The descendants of this community still live in the area, mainly in North Vancouver.

The largest Kanaka community was centred on Salt Spring Island in the Gulf Islands, where the Kanaka community continued into the 20th century. In 1994, over 300 Kanaka descendants gathered on Salt Spring Island to hold a family reunion luau.

Black Immigrants

In the spring of 1858, news of the Fraser River Gold Rush reached California. Some Black citizens of San Francisco, who knew that slavery was illegal in the British Empire, travelled north to Victoria to petition James Douglas for permission to settle on Vancouver Island. Douglas agreed, and by the end of the summer, several hundred Black Americans had left California for the relative freedom of Vancouver Island.

Douglas encouraged and assisted the newcomers, even finding some members of the Black community employment. The colony of Vancouver Island had no military force to speak of at the time, so when members of the Black community expressed an interest in forming a militia unit to help defend their new home, Douglas authorized the creation of the Victoria Pioneer Rifle Corps.

FIGURE 6–27 The Victoria Pioneer Rifle Corps, around 1858. Why do you think these men found it necessary to form a militia unit of their own?

Although slavery was illegal in the British Empire, Black immigrants in Victoria faced discrimination. The gold rush had caused property values in Victoria to rise, and as a result, many Black immigrants moved north to farm on Salt Spring Island.

Zoom In Joe Fortes

 Significance

The most noted Black immigrant to British Columbia in the 19th century was not part of a group; he arrived by himself, almost by accident.

Seraphim Fortes was a crewman on a freighter that docked at Hastings Mill in late 1884. When his ship sailed, Fortes decided to stay behind, working as a bartender at a local saloon.

Fortes quickly became known among locals and customers as Joe. A man of strong morals, he disapproved of public drunkenness and often cut off patrons when they had too much to drink.

In the early 1890s, Fortes discovered English Bay and its beaches. Enthralled, he quit his steady job, built a small house on the shore, and established

himself as the unofficial guardian of the beach.

For the next 30 years, Joe Fortes was Vancouver's most popular citizen. He taught virtually every child in town to swim. Joe also saved many lives. At night, he patrolled English Bay, keeping it safe for everyone.

As the city grew, the need for a paid lifeguard became apparent, and the city council hired Fortes, making him a special constable.

In 1922, Joe Fortes died of pneumonia. Thousands of Vancouverites attended his funeral. A memorial to Joe Fortes stands today at English Bay.

- Why are people like Fortes important to the history of our communities?

FIGURE 6–28 Joe Fortes. Discuss the contributions Fortes made to Vancouver and its people.

Jewish Immigrants

The first Jewish immigrants arrived in British Columbia in 1858. They came primarily from England and Europe, and many had already participated in the California Gold Rush. Rather than seeking gold themselves, many went into business, selling supplies to gold miners on both Vancouver Island and on the mainland. By 1863, the Jewish community in Victoria was well established. A synagogue was built, and members became active in community affairs.

DID YOU KNOW...

The synagogue built in Victoria, Congregation Emanu-El, is the oldest synagogue in continuous operation in Canada.

Zoom In > The Oppenheimers

The five Oppenheimer brothers, Charles, Meyer, Isaac, Godfrey, and David, had emigrated with their family from Germany in 1848. In California, they opened several supply stores. Ten years later, the family moved to Vancouver Island, starting a trading company with outlets in Victoria, Yale, and Barkerville.

In the early 1860s, David Oppenheimer led the campaign to persuade James Douglas that the Cariboo Road should go all the way to Barkerville. Oppenheimer also believed that one day Burrard Inlet would become a seaport, especially after the completion of the CPR, which he was sure would end there. He bought a lot of land, and opened a store just west of Gastown.

When William Van Horne arrived in 1884, Oppenheimer knew that the CPR would need a great deal of space, but most of the land in the area was already owned. He offered half of his land in Burrard Inlet, and half of the property of other landowners, to the CPR free of charge. Van Horne readily agreed. It was a shrewd deal. Oppenheimer knew his remaining land would increase in value once the railway was completed.

In 1888, Oppenheimer was chosen as Vancouver's second mayor. In his four terms as mayor, he established most of the city's infrastructure. Pipes were laid under Burrard Inlet to bring a clean supply of water from the North Shore. Oppenheimer bankrolled the new electric streetcar system (the third in North America), built a sewage system, donated land for schools and parks, and established Stanley Park. Fittingly, he is known as the "Father of Vancouver."

- It can be said that the Oppenheimers were responsible opportunists. Do you agree of disagree with this statement? Provide evidence to support your answer.

FIGURE 6–29 David Oppenheimer (third from right) taking civic dignitaries on a tour of Vancouver Harbour, around 1890. How does this family's success reflect the overall development of British Columbia?

The Chinese

The largest group of non-European immigrants to British Columbia in the 19th century were the Chinese. They also faced some of the most brutal forms of discrimination.

The first Chinese immigrants to North America came to California in the 1850s, and like so many others, they moved north in response to news of the Fraser River Gold Rush. As in California, they faced discrimination from other miners. Realizing that their opportunities were limited, Chinese miners started by reworking claims abandoned by European and American miners. Such claims were less expensive to buy, and if worked patiently, usually produced a reasonable amount of gold. By the 1870s, most of the small claims still being worked in British Columbia were operated by Chinese miners.

FIGURE 6–30 A street scene in the Chinese section of Victoria in 1886. Did immigration to British Columbia help the local economy? If so, why would any group have been prevented from entering the province?

Other Chinese immigrants helped develop the economy of the province by starting service industries—stores, restaurants, and laundries—in frontier mining towns. They also operated vegetable farms both in the interior and near coastal communities.

The Railway Builders

Part of the railway in British Columbia was built by an American named Andrew Onderdonk, who was under contract with the CPR. The line through the Fraser Canyon was incredibly difficult and expensive to build, and by 1881, Onderdonk was short of both money and workers. He solved his problem by hiring Chinese men at low wages. Between 1881 and 1885, more than 17 000 Chinese immigrants came to British Columbia to work on the railway. They were paid just a dollar a day, less than half the rate paid to European workers. They generally lived in separate camps and paid for food and lodging. Their work was dangerous and difficult; it is estimated that more than 600 Chinese workers lost their lives through accident and illness. According to some sources, the number of deaths reached 1200.

When the railway was completed in 1885, many Chinese workers could not afford to travel back to China, as they had originally planned. They had been misled about deductions from their wages and the cost of their food and equipment. Most moved to Vancouver and Victoria in search of work.

During the second half of the 19th century, living conditions in southern China were harsh. The land was overcrowded, and farmers were heavily taxed. Most families struggled to survive. In the 1850s and 1860s, political turmoil in China made matters worse.

Chinese farmers began to hear rumours of the riches to be made on the "Golden Mountain." Thousands journeyed across the Pacific to seek their fortunes and to find a better life. The reality, however, was quite different from the stories they heard.

It was mostly young Chinese men who immigrated to British Columbia at this time. They hoped to support their families back home. For many years the Chinese community was largely made up of young men. What effect did this situation have on society?

The conditions of the railway camps were basic, with only tents or wooden shacks for shelter. Chinese workers found British Columbia very cold. Snow was a new experience for many. The weather, along with poor food and living conditions, caused outbreaks of illness. What kinds of living conditions can you see in this image? What would living here be like in winter?

The mountainous landscape meant that using explosives was the only way to build the railway. The blasts threw rocks and debris into the air and caused landslides. Without warning, workers were hurt or killed. The CPR estimated that four Chinese workers were killed for every mile of track (1.6 km). What types of jobs are this dangerous today?

Wooden trestles were built to span rivers, ravines, and valleys. Many Chinese workers built these vital trestles without safety procedures or proper equipment. How is this type of work different today? How is it similar?

Some Chinese workers spent years on the railway. Unfortunately, when they collected their wages, they found themselves with much less than they expected. Deductions from their wages included fees for travel, food, clothing, housing, and tools. How might the workers respond to this treatment? What would workers do today?

FIGURE 6–31 This 1879 editorial cartoon shows a confrontation between Amor De Cosmos and a "heathen Chinese." Examine it carefully. Try to assess the cartoonist's point of view. Is the cartoonist anti-Chinese, or is he objecting to De Cosmos' behaviour?

Discrimination

As more Chinese immigrants came to British Columbia, discrimination against them also increased. The Knights of Labour, for example, pressed the government to have all Chinese people removed from Vancouver; some of their members physically forced Chinese residents out of town. Businesses selling to Chinese customers often found themselves targets of boycotts.

Chinese workers usually performed heavy manual labour. They were often hired by an English-speaking Chinese contractor who would bid on a job (e.g., land clearing or road building) and then recruit workers. To increase profits, most contractors cheated the Chinese workers. In 1900, the combined fortunes of the two largest Chinese contractors, Loo Gee Wing and Sam Kee, approached $1 million.

By 1900, the ethnic composition of British Columbia was changing. Most newcomers to the province were British, and they wanted to create a British society. Non-Europeans were depicted as being inferior and dangerous. Amor De Cosmos openly stated that he believed Chinese people were a threat because they "did not assimilate."

After a Royal Commission on Chinese Immigration, the government legalized discrimination. In 1885, with the railway finished, Canada no longer needed Chinese labour, so the government decided to limit Chinese immigration. Each Chinese immigrant was required to pay a $50 head tax for entry to Canada, and ships were allowed to carry only one Chinese passenger per 50 tonnes of cargo. As most ships could carry about 2000 tonnes, no more than 40 Chinese immigrants per ship could enter the country at a time. These provisions slowed Chinese immigration and made it almost impossible for families to come to Canada together.

ACTIVITIES

1. Hawaiian and Black immigrants arrived early in the development of British Columbia, yet they do not form distinct communities today. Explain.

2. Create a map depicting the immigration routes of British Columbian immigrants from 1800–1900. Include information for the major groups explaining how each contributed to the development of the province.

3. Read the Window on Canada (pages 236–237). Using the photos as evidence, write a "story" for each image.

4. Examine the editorial cartoon in Figure 6–31. Create a political cartoon that counters the message you think the artist is making.

Explore the Big Ideas

The development of British Columbia in the 19th century was driven primarily by the exploitation of natural resources, especially furs and gold. In the 1850s and 1860s, the impact of the gold rushes included political changes and the founding of communities. When the gold ran out, the resulting political crisis led to the creation of the province of British Columbia. As the 19th century ended, British Columbia became home to a population of British immigrants. The province also experienced an upsurge in racial discrimination.

1. Who or what created British Columbia? Was the development of the province a result of individuals, groups of people, or factors like geography? How are these components related to each other? Use the following chart to track the causes and consequences of events taking place in British Columbia during the 19th century. Consider the suggested topics below.

   Individuals: James Douglas, Matthew Begbie, Amor De Cosmos, Cxpentlum (Spintlum)

   Groups: First Nations, immigrants, gold miners, confederationists

   Factors: Oregon Territory, gold rush, smallpox, railway

Cause	Immediate Consequence	Later Consequence Connections to	Other Events

1. Assess the contributions of James Douglas to the creation of British Columbia.

2. Use the chart above to discuss the impact of the gold rush on the people and the land of British Columbia.

3. Hold a class debate to discuss how societal attitudes of the time influenced events during the smallpox epidemic and the gold rush.

4. Why is Victoria the capital of British Columbia? Relate your answer to political and geographical factors.

5. How would you characterize the relationships between First Nations of British Columbia and government leaders during the 19th century? Explain your thinking using specific examples from that time period.

6. a) Investigate the history of the community you live in today. How, when, and why was your community founded? Are the current economic activities of your local region the same as they were in the past? Why or why not?

   b) Visit your local museum, or invite a historian to speak to your class. Create displays to raise awareness of the importance of local history.

Cause and Consequence

7. Do some research to discover how the Canadian government was able to pass restrictive legislation regarding Chinese immigration. Describe the consequences of this act today.

Chapter Outcomes

In this chapter, you will focus on the dramatic changes that occurred in Canada between 1896 and 1914. By the end of the chapter, you will

- analyze the factors leading to the growth of a Canadian identity

- assess factors that led to the economic expansion of Canada

- describe significant events and trends affecting immigration to Canada, and evaluate changes to Canada's immigration policy

- describe the contributions of immigrants to Canada's development

- evaluate the impact of social change on workers, women, Aboriginal peoples, ethnic minorities, and immigrants

- describe the struggle for greater equality and human rights

- evaluate the impact of technological change

- describe the contributions of specific individuals to the arts in Canada

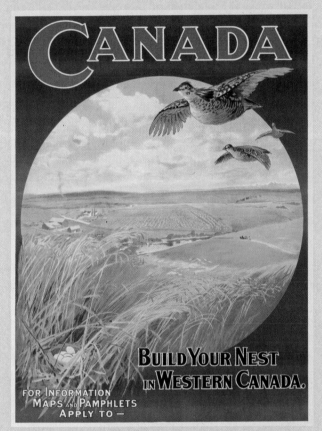

Have you ever moved from one country to another? What could you learn about the new country before you left your old home? The Canadian government used posters like the one above in Europe to advertise the West. Do you think the poster is accurate? Compare it to the image of a prairie farm on the opposite page. What does this poster and the quote below show about Canadian government policy at the time?

How did Canada change during the Laurier years?

In the two decades between 1896 and 1914, dramatic changes took place in Canada. The promise of Confederation was fulfilled with the completion of the railway, immigration to the West, and the creation of new provinces. Industry and technological change brought prosperity to some, while minority groups fought for equality against powerful forces. Canadians were struggling with a new sense of their own identity.

Key Terms

compromise	suffragist
patriotism	restorative justice
imperialist	capital
mother country	labour unions
homestead lands	
markets	
open-door policy	

Agriculture is the foundation of all real and enduring progress on the part of Canada... The possession of a... rural population having the virtues and strength of character bred only among those who follow agricultural life, is the only sure guarantee of our national future.

—Clifford Sifton, former Minister of the Interior, 1910

Laurier Is Elected

▶ **How were the domestic and international issues Laurier dealt with related to the development of a Canadian identity?**

TIMELINE

1896	Wilfrid Laurier becomes prime minister
1897	Yukon Gold Rush begins
1898	First automobiles are imported into Canada from the United States
1899	South African War breaks out
1901	First wireless message is sent across the Atlantic
1903	Alaska Boundary Dispute settled
1905	Alberta and Saskatchewan become provinces
1907	Vancouver riots
1908	*Anne of Green Gables* is published
1909	First airplane flight in Canada
1911	Robert Borden defeats Laurier in the federal election
1912	Coal miners strike on Vancouver Island
1913	Nisga'a First Nation takes their land claim to the British Privy Council
	400 870 immigrants arrive in Canada
1914	First World War begins

compromise settling a difference by each side giving up something

What event during your lifetime do you think was a turning point in Canadian or world history? The election of 1896 is considered to be a turning point in Canadian history. Twenty years of Conservative rule had come to an end with the election of a Liberal majority. The Liberal leader, Wilfrid Laurier, was Canada's first French-Canadian prime minister.

Laurier wanted to promote national unity in Canada and to protect Canada's interests in the world. However, since the Northwest Uprising of 1885 and the execution of Louis Riel, tension between English and French Canadians had grown. As a French Canadian, Laurier had to be careful when dealing with issues of language and religion. French and English Canadians also disagreed about Canada's relations with Britain and its empire. Yet despite these challenges, Laurier had confidence in his country's future and was convinced that "the 20th century belonged to Canada."

The Manitoba Schools Question

When Manitoba joined Canada in 1870, equal rights were given to English-language Protestant schools and French-language Roman Catholic schools under the Manitoba Act. However, during the 1880s, the arrival of English-speaking immigrants created an English-speaking majority in the province. Pressure was placed on the goverment to review its language laws. The result was the Manitoba Schools Act, which removed government support from Roman Catholic schools. Francophones across Canada were outraged.

The Liberals had won the support of Quebec voters on a promise to protect the French language and Roman Catholic rights. Laurier believed in solving problems by **compromise**, so with Manitoba's premier, Thomas Greenway, Laurier worked out the following solution:

- Upon request, French instruction would be allowed in any school that had a minimum of 10 French-speaking students.

- There was to be no government funding for a Catholic school board.

- Catholic religious instruction would be allowed for a half-hour at the end of the school day.

Laurier's compromise left French Catholics feeling that they had given up far more than English-speaking Manitobans. For Laurier, it was a lesson in how difficult it was to govern Canada.

CRITICAL INQUIRY Evidence

Wilfrid Laurier believed in people coming to a reasonable agreement when they had a difference of opinion. He had to convince people that this was the best way to solve problems.

In Laurier's time, politicians relied on their speeches to convince people of their points of view. Skilled public speakers used persuasive techniques to grab the audience's attention and influence its thinking:

- repetition

- literary devices such as simile (a comparison using "like" or "as"), metaphor (a direct comparison without "like" or "as"), and personification (comparing a thing or animal to a person)

- strong, emotional language

- rhetorical questions

In the speech shown here, Laurier's mention of a coat, wind, and sun would have been familiar to his audience as a reference to a fable by Aesop, a writer from ancient Greece. In the story, the gentle warmth of the sun is more effective at getting a person to remove his coat than the raging wind, which only makes him pull it tighter around himself.

*Well, sir, the governments are very windy. They have blown and raged and threatened but the more they have raged and blown, the more that man Greenway [the premier of Manitoba] had stuck to his coat. If it were in my power, I would try the sunny way. I would approach this man Greenway with the sunny way of **patriotism**, asking him to be just and to be fair, asking him to be generous to the minority, in order that we may have peace between all the creeds and races which it has pleased God to bring upon this corner of our common country. Do you not believe that there is more to be gained by appealing to the heart and soul of men rather than by trying to compel them to do a thing?*

—Wilfrid Laurier in 1895

- What point of view on the Manitoba schools issue is Laurier putting forward in this speech?

- Find evidence of Laurier's skills as a convincing speaker in this speech. Identify examples of three persuasive techniques he uses.

- What does this source suggest about Laurier? About Canada at that time?

- Find a speech by a modern politician and compare its style and content with that of Laurier's speech.

patriotism love of one's country

FIGURE 7–1 What clues does this photo give you about Wilfrid Laurier's skills as a public speaker?

Imperialism: A French–English Split

For Laurier, Canada's relationship with Britain was a difficult problem. Most English Canadians were proud of being in the British Empire. Supporters of the Empire were known as **imperialists**. French Canadians, on the other hand, felt little pride in Canada being part of the British Empire, even as a self-governing colony.

Canada's involvement in the South African War, also known as the Boer War, split the country along French–English lines. In 1899, Britain controlled much of Africa. Because of newly discovered gold and diamonds in South Africa, Britain attempted to extend its control of the region. Descendants of early Dutch colonists, called Boers, resisted the British advance, leading to war in 1899.

The British government called on its colonies for support. Most English Canadians supported sending Canadian troops to help Britain. French Canadians sympathized with the Boers. They did not think Canada should get involved in an unjust imperialist war. Laurier compromised: Canada would equip and transport only volunteers. Still, English Canadians thought Canada should do more to help the **mother country**. French Canadians pointed out that Canada was getting involved in a place with no real connection to Canada.

imperialist someone who practises or supports imperialism, the policy of one nation acquiring, controlling, or dominating another country or region

mother country a term describing the country immigrants came from

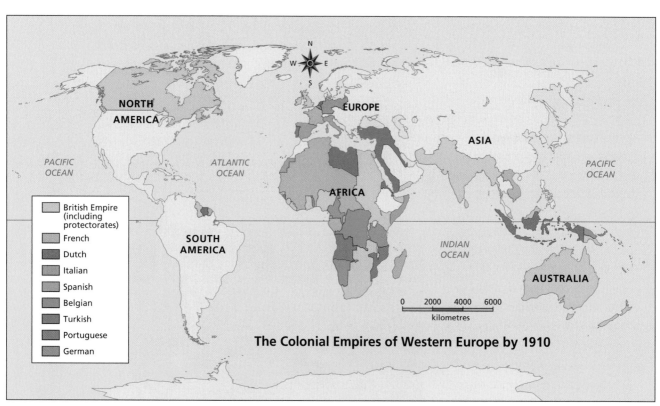

The Colonial Empires of Western Europe by 1910

British Empire (including protectorates)
French
Dutch
Italian
Spanish
Belgian
Turkish
Portuguese
German

FIGURE 7–2 Of the European powers, Britain had the largest empire in land and population. Many residents of imperialist nations believed themselves to be superior to the people they had colonized. How was this view reflected in Europeans' attitudes and behaviour toward Canada's Aboriginal peoples? What attitude do you think most Canadians have toward imperialism today?

Henri Bourassa, a French-Canadian politician, had resigned from Laurier's cabinet in protest over the South African War. He clashed with Laurier again over the Naval Issue. Canada had been asked to give Britain money to help build warships. English Canadians were in favour, but French Canadians wanted Canada to have a navy of its own. As usual, Laurier looked for a compromise.

In 1910, Laurier set out the Naval Service Act, which stated that Canada would have a navy of its own that could be turned over to the British in the event of an emergency. Both English and French Canadians opposed Laurier's plan. English-Canadian imperialists joked about Canada's insignificant "tin-pot" navy. Quebecois, led by Bourassa, feared involvement in wars that were unrelated to Canada's security.

> *I gave you the names of the wars which Great Britain has conducted during the course of the last century. It's on average, a war every four years... by the will of Sir Wilfrid Laurier we will be at war every time England is attacked or causes a conflict to arise at any point whatever on the entire globe...*
>
> —**Bourassa, writing about the Naval Issue in 1910**

> *If we were disconnected with Britain, we would have less occasion of conflict with Europe... if the British connection has some disadvantages... it has advantages that far outbalance the objections. We are all the same a nation... and we have to assume the duties and responsibilities of a nation. Part of these duties is the keeping of some armed force, both on land and at sea.*
>
> —**Laurier in a letter to a friend in 1909**

WHAT DO YOU THINK?

1. On what point did both Bourassa and Laurier agree? On what point did they disagree?

2. Why would Laurier's letter be unsatisfactory from an English-Canadian perspective?

3. What is historically significant about the Naval Issue? What "big story" is it part of?

The Giant Next Door

Britain was not the only country getting Laurier's attention. Canada, next door to the rapidly expanding United States, felt threatened by the growth of its powerful neighbour. This feeling united Canadians. When Laurier dealt with the American government over the new border between Alaska and northwest British Columbia, Canadians were united behind him. This issue became known as the "Alaska Boundary Dispute."

Few had been concerned about the exact location of the border, until 1897, when the discovery of gold brought more than 100 000 miners into the Yukon. This prompted a struggle by hopeful prospectors to get themselves and their equipment to the Yukon as quickly as possible, as you can see in the Window on Canada following this page.

A storyboard is like a graphic organizer that can be used to sketch out the action of a cartoon, television show, or movie. It can be drawn by hand or on a computer, and can be in colour or black and white, such as the storyboard that follows. Details in a storyboard are up to the artist, but they usually include arrows or notes to indicate the movement of the camera during the shot.

"The Lure of Yukon Gold" is a television show that tells the fictional story of a young man, Brendan Byrne, who sets out in 1898 to make his fortune in the Klondike. These selected storyboard scenes show some of his adventure as he makes his way to Dawson City.

Panel 1 "At last, Chilkoot Pass—the so-called Golden Stairs! I hope I can get these packs up there. But I've already come 1000 km. I can't stop now."

Panel 2 "It's going to be worth it, hauling these packs! Flour is more than $6 a sack in Dawson!"

Panel 3 "Sometimes I think we were crazy to come North in the winter. At least it's downhill from here to Lake Bennett."

Panel 4 "You'll be OK here, son. There are 200 of us in the territory, and Sam Steele makes sure there's no lawlessness.

Panel 5 "Don't wear yourself out!"
"I need to get onto the Yukon River before the spring thaw." "

Panel 6 Brendan and Dorothy join the two other miners to build a boat to use on the Yukon River after the ice breaks up in the spring.

Panel 7 "I can't believe I'm finally here."
"Nearly 200 000 people are here now!"

Panel 8 Brendan walks with other miners as they pass casinos, saloons, and hotels advertising steam baths, running water, electricity, and telephones. They also see banks, a hospital, and a school.

Panel 9 "I thought Dawson was a roaring boom town!"
"It must be Sunday. Sam Steele locks the place up tight from midnight Saturday to Monday morning. You can't even cut firewood on Sunday."

Panel 10 "It's so expensive here… I'm going to the goldfields, but I guess I'd better look for a job and leave the gold for now. But I'll get to the gold. No matter how long it takes."

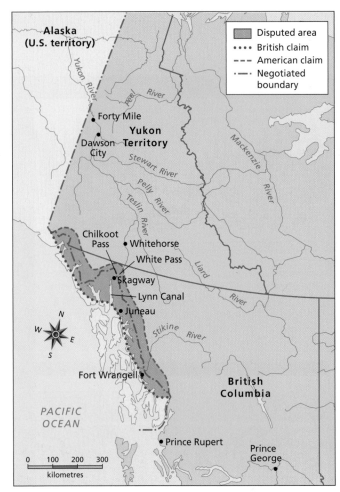

FIGURE 7–3 Canada wanted the boundary measured from the mountains nearest to the ocean, giving Canada access to the Pacific Ocean. The American president threatened military action when he heard the plan. What difficulties would people in northwestern British Columbia and the Yukon face without access to the sea?

Access to the Yukon goldfields by the easy sea route was only possible by crossing American territory. This was clearly a problem for Canada.

The strip of coastline extending south from Alaska was called the Alaska Panhandle. Everyone, including Canadian police, had to ask American permission to travel through ports such as Skagway. To solve the boundary dispute, Laurier agreed to an international tribunal—three judges from the United States, one from Britain, and two from Canada.

International politics decided the outcome. American President Theodore Roosevelt made it clear he wanted a result that favoured his country. Britain, already involved in border disputes in South America, did not want to anger Roosevelt. The British judges voted in favour of a boundary line that cut off half of British Columbia's coast from the sea. Canadians were outraged.

Canada was in a terrible position: it could not make its own international treaties, and it clearly could not rely on Britain to look after its interests. "Canada's Hands Are Now Tied," proclaimed the *Victoria Daily Colonist* on October 24, 1903. The same theme was echoed from coast to coast and in the House of Commons by Prime Minister Laurier.

ACTIVITIES

1. Why did English Canadians and French Canadians disagree on a) the South Africa War and b) the Naval Issue? Explain how Laurier's decisions on these issues had an impact on national unity.

2. Compare and contrast the Alaska Boundary Dispute with the present boundary problems in the Arctic.

3. What problems still exist for British Columbia as a result of the boundary settlement of 1903?

4. How might the Alaska Boundary Dispute have contributed to Canada's emerging identity as a nation independent of Britain?

Patterns and Change

5. How successful was Laurier's policy of compromise? In your evaluation, consider the impact on French–English relations.

"The Last Best West"

▶ **How did government policy shape immigration to the West?**

The booming economy of Canada during the Laurier era attracted thousands of immigrants, and the main destination was the Canadian West. The growing world demand for wheat and the end of free **homestead lands** in the United States made Canada an attractive destination.

From 1896 until 1914, the Canadian government actively encouraged people to come to Canada. Clifford Sifton, Laurier's Minister of the Interior until 1905, was a westerner who was committed to bringing settlers to the Prairies. How would he get the word out to the world?

homestead lands public lands granted by governments on the understanding that they be turned into farms

The Power of Advertising

Canada's Immigration Department attracted tens of thousands of settlers to the Canadian West by offering free homestead lands. Clifford Sifton set up a recruitment program to encourage immigrants from Europe and the United States to settle on the Prairies instead. Millions of pamphlets, newspaper ads, public lectures, posters, and bonuses for promoters were used. Sifton hired agents to distribute posters and pamphlets advertising "The Last Best West." All references to cold and snow were banned.

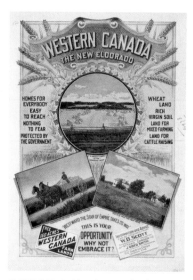

FIGURE 7–4 Why do you think readers in Europe might have been persuaded by these images? What was the purpose of this poster? What details in the poster support that purpose?

> [The] advertising that is done by the department in the United States is pretty extensive. We have advertised in over 7000 American newspapers having a circulation of about 7 000 000 and the states we have advertised in are [a list of twenty states follows]. In the United States, we also have a system of sending [American] delegates to inspect Manitoba and the Northwest and to make their report to the section of the country from which they come. These delegates... are chosen by a meeting of farmers called together by one of the agents [at the immigration department... the Canadian Pacific Railroad gives these delegates free transportation.
>
> —Superintendent of Immigration, 1909

Canada's immigration policy from 1896 to 1914 was successful because of "push-pull" factors. Vast migrations occur for two reasons: a need to leave one's homeland (push factor) and/or the attraction of opportunity in another country (pull factor). Push and pull factors often work together.

People looked to Canada as a place where they could improve the quality of their lives (pull factor). Some were fleeing harsh governments, discrimination, and poverty (push factor).

Push and pull factors also worked together for the Doukhobors, a group of Russians who left their homeland because service in the army was against their religious beliefs (push factor). They were also in search of free land (pull factor). Canada exempted them from military service and assisted their passage to the Prairies, where they were granted nearly three-quarters of a million acres of land. By 1899, more than 7000 Doukhobors had settled in Saskatchewan.

- Identify economic, social, and geographic factors that led to immigration to Canada.

- Which push-pull factors attract immigrants to Canada today? Explain how they are similar and different from those shown on the map below.

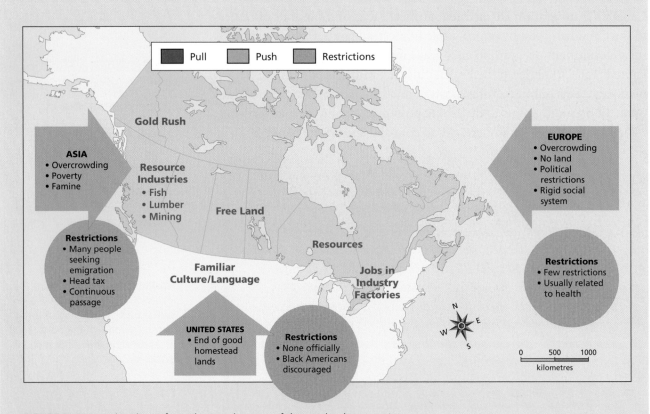

FIGURE 7–5 Vast migrations of people occur because of the need to leave one's homeland and/or the attraction of another country. Today Canadian immigration policy favours highly skilled immigrants, many of whom are from less developed countries. What is your opinion of this policy?

An Open-Door Policy

There were three main sources of immigrants during the Laurier era: Britain, the United States, and Europe. Sifton was criticized for encouraging immigrants from eastern and central Europe, but these farmers had the advantage of coming from an ecosystem similar to that of the Prairies. They were used to the climate and understood **dryland farming** methods. However, some Canadians were **prejudiced** against people whose language and customs differed so much from their own. As a result of Sifton's **open-door policy**, settlers on the Prairies came from many countries, including Russia, Poland, and Ukraine.

Britons also arrived during these years, making up one-third of all immigrants. However, those who did not come from farming backgrounds often failed as farmers. British immigrants were mostly working-class people from cities who were not used to the hardships of life on the Prairie.

American migrants were much more successful. They blended easily into Canadian society, some with knowledge of prairie farming and more money than the average European. American settlers favoured Alberta to such a degree that, by 1914, the province's population was overwhelmingly American.

dryland farming farming methods practised in regions with limited rainfall

prejudice dislike or distrust of a person or group; forming a judgement before knowing the facts

open-door policy an immigration policy that puts no restrictions on who can immigrate

DID YOU KNOW...

The average American coming to the Prairies brought $1000 and farming equipment. The average European immigrant brought $15.

FIGURE 7–6 Thousands of British children were sent to Canada as "home children." Many had lived in orphanages, and it was thought that farms in Canada would provide good homes for them. Farmers adopted some of the children, but others were used as cheap labour and lived in harsh conditions. How does the story of the home children tie in with the "big story" of immigration at this time?

Population Growth, 1891–1921						
Year	Manitoba	Saskatchewan	Alberta	B.C.	Yukon	Canada
1891	152 506	—*	—*	98 173	—*	4.83M
1901	255 211	91 279	73 022	178 657	27 219	5.37M
1911	461 394	492 432	374 295	392 480	8512	7.21M
1921	610 118	757 510	588 454	524 582	4157	8.79M

This table shows the rapid growth of population in western Canada during the Laurier years. Examine the table and make a statement about the rate of population growth on the Prairies. What reasons can you give for some provinces growing faster than others?
* Separate 1891 data for Saskatchewan, Alberta, and the Yukon are not available.

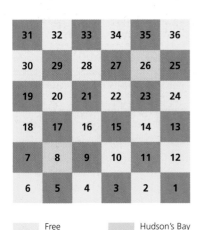

31	32	33	34	35	36
30	29	28	27	26	25
19	20	21	22	23	24
18	17	16	15	14	13
7	8	9	10	11	12
6	5	4	3	2	1

☐ Free homestead ☐ Hudson's Bay Company
☐ School ☐ Railway

FIGURE 7–7 Most land in the West was surveyed in a grid system of 10 km square blocks. How might this affect the shape of communities in the West?

Adjusting to Life on the Prairies

Once Canadian settlers claimed their land, they had to adjust to a new life. Each family was granted a quarter-section of 160 acres (64.75 hectares). Their first task was to raise at least $500 to outfit their homestead with the basics: a plow, a wagon, a horse, and a milk cow. Working on other farms, or in lumber or mining camps, was the typical way to make start-up money.

For the homesteading family, living conditions were primitive. Hardships included long, cold winters, a boring diet, mosquitoes, and natural disasters such as drought, hail, and swarms of grasshoppers. Families lived in tents until they could build housing. Their homes were usually made of local materials: wood, or sod.

Sod was typically the first choice of building material on the Prairies. To build their "soddies," homesteaders cut slabs of sod from the prairie ground. The tough roots of grasses held the sod together. Walls were built by stacking the slabs of sod. Doors and windows were covered with sacks, and the roof was thatched. Inside was a dirt floor. Soddies were usually cramped, malodorous, and damp. Eventually, the soddie would be replaced by a more permanent home, once the family could afford to ship in building materials.

> ...then the inside. That was boards and blankets laid out along them so to make little rooms. One for my mother and father. One for us. A kitchen. I think we had a toilet, which just meant digging another hole in the ground every month. [Felt cloth] was pinned to the sod with wooden pegs... to make you think you weren't living in a sod house.
>
> —a Prairie immigrant

FIGURE 7–8 How do the quote and this image of a soddie work together to give a picture of life in the past? What would a picture of your home tell future historians about your life?

Since the arrival of newcomers, human activity has dramatically altered the prairie ecosystem. Other than the temporary effects of drought, fire, and overgrazing, the prairie grasslands had remained in a state of natural balance. With the coming of settlement, everything changed.

In Canada and the United States, Aboriginal peoples did little to alter the ecosystem. They lived almost entirely on the bison, and the natural grasslands were unchanged. As you read in Chapter 5, factors such as the opening of the West to European settlement brought the bison close to extinction.

A prairie free of bison was a prairie wide open to farming and ranching. Cattle ranching on the western Prairies replaced the bison herds and, in some areas, led to problems of overgrazing.

Newcomers also introduced cereal farming, particularly wheat, to the Prairies. Natural prairie grasses were plowed under. Diversity within the ecosystem was lost when the many species of grasses were replaced with new, hardy strains of wheat.

The loss of variety in plants also changed the nature of the soil. Wetlands were lost, and runoff from farms and feedlots polluted the rivers and lakes.

FIGURE 7–9 Projects to bring back native species to the Prairie, such as the bison, are part of restoring the original Prairie grasslands. The effects of the bison's grazing, for example, are a vital component in restoring a grasslands ecosystem which once included a large variety of plants and animals. Other species supported by conservation programs include the pronghorn antelope, the burrowing owl, and the swift fox. Research a project that is dedicated to bringing back original Prairie grasslands, and explain how this work may affect the people, animals, and birds of the Prairies.

WHAT DO YOU THINK?

1. Make a two-column list of the positive and negative effects of agricultural development on the Prairies. Do the positive effects outweigh the negative? Explain.

2. Why was the loss of the bison critical to the Prairies and those who lived there? Research at-risk species today that are vital to the survival of ecosystems and people.

3. Using the chart you created for question # 1 and the information you researched, write a paragraph discussing how human action had consequences for the geography and ecosystems of the grasslands.

Railways to Everywhere

As more people settled on the Prairies, the demand for new rail lines and faster travel for people and goods increased. Prairie farmers complained about the monopoly of the CPR and the high freight rates it charged. Two rival companies asked for federal and provincial government aid to build new rail lines. The Macdonald government had built one transcontinental railway; the Laurier government would better it by building two.

The Canadian Northern Railway used government **subsidies** to extend lines it was building on the Prairies east to Quebec and west to the Pacific. Investors such as William Mackenzie and Donald Mann received more than $200 million in subsidies and land grants from the British Columbia government to expand their business empire from rail lines to mining and shipping.

The Grand Trunk Railway also went from coast to coast. The Laurier government even agreed to build railways in eastern Canada to service areas not covered by the CPR. In the west, the Grand Trunk Pacific went through the Yellowhead Pass to Prince Rupert.

However, the First World War stopped both the flow of immigrants and capital for industry. The new railways were no longer profitable and faced bankruptcy. The government joined all railways that did not belong to the CPR to form the Canadian National Railways, which was "to be owned by the people of Canada."

subsidies financial support to businesses to encourage projects considered to be in the public interest

DID YOU KNOW...

Towns along the new rail lines on the Prairies and in British Columbia were named starting with A and going through the alphabet to Z as many times as necessary. Towns were spaced every 18 km.

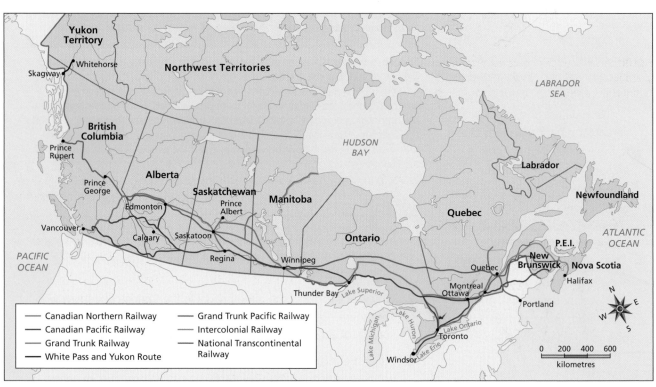

FIGURE 7–10 By 1914 new railways allowed settlers to move away from the CPR's southern route. What might be the consequences for an already established community if it were bypassed by the new rail lines?

In February 2008 the United Nations released a report that co tained a momentous milestone. It stated that during 2008, for the first time in history, the proportion of the world's population living in urban areas would reach 50 per cent. Globally, the level of urban ization is expected to rise from 50 percent in 2008 to 70 percent in 2050.

What is the significance of this trend? Cities will become even more influential in the global economy as centres of business trade, and investment. However, urban areas will still depend on rural areas and rural people to produce the resources that urba dwellers need. Food, water, mine als, forest products, and even clean air are produced in rural areas. Governments will need to enact policies and practices that revitalize rural areas. Nowhere is this more important than in the **Pacific Rim**.

Urban growth is occurring at faster pace in the Pacific Rim than anywhere else in the world Many Pacific Rim cities in Asia and the Americas—Beijing, Hor Kong, Kuala Lumpur, Mexico City, Santiago, Seoul, Singapore Shanghai, Taipei, Tokyo, and Vancouver—will create global connections and become impor tant players in the global econo These cities have invested in ne infrastructure, invited foreign investors, promoted new archite tural styles, and recruited profes sionals to help make their cities modern, world-class, cosmopol

Railway Cities

Many large cities in western Canada exist because of the railways. They often began as small fur-trade centres whose locations were originally chosen because of their **site** or **situation**.

Saskatoon, Edmonton, Prince George, and Prince Rupert were selected as divisional points on the Grand Trunk Pacific Railway. They all grew into major centres as a result of the coming of the railway. The rail yards and station became the hub from which the city expanded. However, when the automobile became more popular, the railway lost its central position.

site the features of the land on which a settlement is built, such as elevation or landforms

situation the position of a settlement in relation to its surrounding area, including its relationship to other settlements and routes

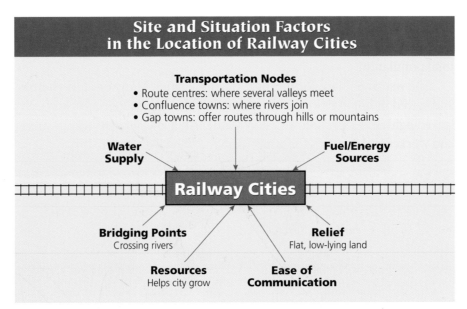

FIGURE 7–11 Cities grow because of the location factors shown above. Use an atlas to locate a railway city in British Columbia. How many of these factors can you identify within the community? Which of them would you consider to be the most important? Why?

ACTIVITIES

1. **a)** State three reasons for the rapid growth in immi-gration to Canada after 1896.

    b) List three problems resulting from the arrival of so many immigrants.

2. How accurate was it to call western Canada the "Last Best West"? Explain your answer.

3. What push and pull factors would apply to each of these immigrant groups: Americans, Asians, Britons, and Europeans?

4. Imagine you are an immigrant to Canada in the Laurier era. Write a letter home describing your experience homesteading on the Prairies.

5. Why do you think more immigrants continued to prefer the United States to Canada? To what extent is this still true today?

6. Why was there a rush to build so many railways during the Laurier period? Were all railways needed? Explain your answer.

7. Why did the government step in to create the Canadian National Railways? Find recent examples of governments stepping in to assist private companies. What do you think of this use of tax revenues?

urban in a town or city as opposed to the country

ghetto an area of a city inhabited by a minority group, usually with substandard housing, power, and sewage systems

WEB LINK

For more information about Canada's population history, visit the Pearson Web site.

FIGURE 7–12 In 1912, this family lived in one room in Winnipeg. Crowded, unsanitary conditions were common for working-class families. Women and children often took jobs and worked long hours to make ends meet. Where in Canada would you find conditions like these today?

Nellie McClung: Suffragist and Reformer

One important Canadian suffragist was Nellie McClung (1873–1951). Raised in Manitoba, she became a teacher and well-known author who published many articles and books, including her autobiography. McClung began promoting women's suffrage as a way to improve the working conditions for women in Manitoba. McClung was an effective speaker and often used wit and humour to win over an audience.

Devoted to many reform issues concerning women, McClung worked especially hard to win suffrage for the women of Alberta. In the excerpt below McClung's words are typical of the suffragist argument that if given the vote, women would change the world for the better.

FIGURE 7–18 Nellie McClung was a member of the "Famous Five," a group of Canadian women who in 1927 petitioned the British government to declare Canadian women "persons" under the law.

> *The real spirit of the suffrage movement is sympathy and interest in other women, and to make the world a more homelike place to live in. Women must be made to feel their responsibility. All this protective love, this instinctive mother love, must be organized in some way, and made effective. There [is] enough of it in the world to do away with all the evils that war upon children, undernourishment, slum conditions, child labour, drunkenness. Women could abolish these if they wanted to.*
>
> —Nellie McClung, Canadian suffragist and author

VOTE FOR WOMAN'S FREEDOM

THE WOMEN OF BRITISH COLUMBIA WANT THEIR POLITICAL FREEDOM BECAUSE

1. IF WOMAN HAS TO OBEY THE LAWS IT IS ONLY JUST THAT SHE SHOULD HAVE A VOICE IN MAKING THEM.
2. WOMAN'S INFLUENCE WOULD BE INCREASED AND LAWS FOR WOMAN'S PROTECTION WOULD BE MORE EASILY SECURED.
3. AS POLITICAL RIGHTS MAKE MAN NOBLER, SO THEY WOULD MAKE WOMAN NOBLER ALSO.
4. THE BALLOT IS AN EDUCATOR. WOMAN NEEDS THE EDUCATION OF THE BALLOT; THE WORLD NEEDS THE EDUCATION OF THE WOMAN'S BALLOT.
5. WOMAN CAN BETTER PROTECT HER HOME INTERSTS.
6. WOMAN HAS BORNE HER SHARE OF THE TOIL, SUFFERING AND LONELINESS IN THE PIONEER WORK OF THIS PROVINCE AND SHE OUGHT TO HAVE A VOICE IN HOW IT IS GOVERNED.

WOMEN ARE FREED FROM POLITICAL SLAVERY IN NORWAY, SWEDEN, FINLAND, NEW ZEALAND, AUSTRALIA, TASMANIA, ISLE OF MAN, UTAH, WYOMING, COLORADO AND IDAHO, WITH THE RESULT THAT THE LAWS ARE BETTER AND CONDITIONS IMPROVED.

GIVE THE WOMEN THE BALLOT

FIGURE 7–19 This handbill was circulated by the Women's Equality League in British Columbia. Women could not vote in British Columbia until 1916, a right which was at that time still denied to Asian and Aboriginal peoples. Today, you must be a resident of your province and be at least 18 years of age to vote. Should the voting age be lowered? Explain.

The Rights of Aboriginal Peoples

As you read in Chapter 5, the Canadian government did not always live up to the terms of treaties negotiated with Aboriginal leaders. First Nations farmers on the prairies were frustrated by the attitudes and policies of government employees such as Hayter Reed, and Aboriginal farmers were denied proper machinery, stock, and seeds. Even when Aboriginal farmers managed to overcome these difficulties and harvest crops, their efforts were often sabotaged by government agents who would deny them the passes they needed to leave the reserve and market their crops.

The myth that Aboriginal peoples were not suited to farming on the Prairies was soon widely believed, which allowed the Canadian government to displace them in favour of new settlers. As more immigrants continued to arrive in the West, the government allowed sections of reserve land to be transferred to homesteaders or to mining companies. Protests from Aboriginal leaders had little effect. In British Columbia, the same policies of seizing Aboriginal lands and ignoring protests were being followed.

WEB LINK ● ·

Find out more about Canada's residential schools on the Pearson Web site.

Residential Schools

Land loss was not the only problem faced by Aboriginal peoples. As you saw in Chapter 2, the Canadian government believed that Aboriginal children were the key to assimilation, so it established a system of residential schools. The government hoped that by removing Aboriginal children from their families and communities, they would lose their culture and identity and become part of the dominant culture.

It was a national policy of cultural extinction. By 1910 more than 60 government sanctioned and supported residential schools had been established. Over 150 000 Aboriginal and Métis children were forced to attend these schools.

Did You Know...

Aboriginal children were the only children in Canadian history who, because of their race, were forced by law to live in institutions for years.

FIGURE 7–20 Some non-Aboriginal settlers complained that it was unfair that they should have to compete with Aboriginal farmers to sell their crops. What might have caused them to feel this way?

FIGURE 7–21 The first-known residential schools were set up by Roman Catholic missionaries in the 1600s. Nuns and priests continued to be administrators and teachers at the schools; this photo was taken in 1900. Why might religious organizations have been interested in this work?

Young children were removed from their homes and families by police or Indian agents and transported hundreds of kilometres away to the frightening, unfamiliar boarding schools operated by strangers. The children had no contact with their families for up to 10 months at a time.

In the face of harsh physical discipline, the children were forbidden to speak their language or practise their culture. Overcrowding and unsanitary conditions caused outbreaks of tuberculosis and other infectious diseases, and many students were physically and sexually abused. In some schools, more than 50 percent of the children died as a result of the terrible living conditions, poor diet, and inadequate medical care. The discovery in 2008 of many unmarked graves around the former schools is a testament to the tragedy of these lost children.

I knew I couldn't stay home. I knew that. But the times that really, really get to the bottom of my soul: the first day back [after being home for the summer holidays]... You're feeling pretty lonesome, suddenly go to bed and in the morning, you wake up and you see this white ceiling. You may as well have a knife and stab me through the heart... You know where you are and you got to survive and you just cover it over, seal it up for ten months.

—a residential school survivor

Truth and Reconciliation

On June 11, 2008, Prime Minister Stephen Harper offered an apology to all Aboriginal peoples in Canada on behalf of the Canadian government.

> *I stand before you today to offer an apology to the former students of Indian residential schools. The treatment of children in Indian residential schools is a sad chapter in our history... The burden of this experience has been on your shoulders for far too long. The burden is properly ours as a government, and as a country.*
>
> —Prime Minister Stephen Harper

Assembly of First Nations Chief Phil Fontaine replied, "Our peoples, our history and our present being are the essence of Canada. Attempts to erase our identities hurt us deeply. But it also hurt all Canadians and impoverished the character of this nation."

In 2008, the Canadian government formed the Truth and Reconciliation Commission (TRC). The goal of the commission was to give anyone affected by residential schools a chance to share their experiences and create a historical record. The TRC practises **restorative justice**. By exposing the truth about this tragic part of Canadian history, the nation can work toward a stronger and healthier future.

Many Aboriginal peoples argue that the journey to an equal and fair relationship between Canada and Aboriginal peoples has a long way to go. The refusal of the federal government to sign the United Nations Declaration on the Rights of Indigenous Peoples in 2007 and the delay in settling land claims are two issues that show just how much has yet to be done.

restorative justice a process that focuses on healing relations between the victims and the accused rather than finding fault

FIGURE 7–22 Chief Phil Fontaine (wearing headdress) and residential school survivor Mike Cachagee react to Prime Minister Harper's 2008 apology in the House of Commons.

Land Claims in British Columbia

DID YOU KNOW...

According to the 2006 census, Canada's Aboriginal population has grown faster than the non-Aboriginal population. Between 1996 and 2006 it increased 45 percent, nearly six times faster than the 8 percent rate of increase for the non-Aboriginal population. Aboriginal peoples make up nearly 4 percent of the Canadian population.

Aboriginal peoples in British Columbia were in a special situation. The isolation of the province had delayed large-scale settlement, which allowed Aboriginal peoples to retain their lands longer than those in eastern Canada and the Prairies. The question of land in British Columbia was further complicated by the fact that the federal government looked after Aboriginal affairs while the provincial government controlled reserve lands.

As you learned in Chapter 6, the first governor of British Columbia, James Douglas, recognized Aboriginal ownership of the land. He had negotiated treaties with a number of groups. When immigrants began to flood into British Columbia during the Laurier era, issues of land and title became more urgent. The federal government wanted to settle all land issues by establishing reserves by treaties or special arrangement. By 1900, only 15 treaties had been made with the province's 200 distinct Aboriginal groups. These treaties covered only a small area of British Columbia.

Aboriginal groups in British Columbia united to press for Aboriginal title to the land. In 1911, Aboriginal leaders from across the province presented the provincial government with claims regarding land title, treaties, and self-government. The federal and provincial governments could not agree on how to respond to these claims.

The Banning of the Potlatch

The Aboriginal peoples of British Columbia had another problem with the federal government. The cornerstone of their culture was the potlatch, a ceremony that served many social functions.

Potlatches involved elaborate feasts to celebrate special occasions, such as the naming of a child, a marriage, or a burial. It showed the power of leaders and provided a way to share wealth throughout the community. Hosts gave away much of their possessions to their guests and later received gifts themselves.

Because the potlatch preserved important Aboriginal customs, the federal government thought that it slowed down the process of assimilation. In 1884, the government banned potlatch ceremonies. In 1914, the ban was extended to include a prohibition of appearing in "Aboriginal costume." However, the isolation of some villages allowed the potlatch to secretly continue.

FIGURE 7–23 This button blanket was once given away at a potlatch. It was not until 1951 that the federal government removed the anti-potlatch sections from the Indian Act.

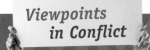

Aboriginal Rights or Assimilation?

The Nisga'a were the first Nation in British Columbia to use the political system to fight for their ancestral lands in British Columbia's Nass River valley. Here are some highlights of their struggle:

1887 Nisga'a leaders lobby the provincial government for a treaty. Premier Smithe turns them down.

1907 The Nisga'a form the Nisga'a Land Committee and protest government surveys that mark off reserves in their territory. They argue that they have not signed a treaty with the provincial government, so the concept of a reserve is invalid.

1910 Laurier encourages the Nisga'a Land Committee to take its case to the Privy Council in London. The British government decides that the claim must first be heard in a Canadian court.

1949 Nisga'a leader Frank Calder is elected to the British Columbia legislature.

1998 The Nisga'a sign a historic treaty with the federal government giving them land, self-government, and a cash payment.

2006 The Final Agreement, a full and final settlement of Nisga'a Aboriginal rights, is signed by Nisga'a and federal and provincial governments.

> *We are not opposed to the coming of the white people into our territory, provided this be carried out justly and in accordance with the British principle... in the Royal Proclamation... What we don't like about the government is their saying: "We will give you this much land." How can they give it when it is our own?... If therefore the aboriginal rights which we claim should be established by the decision of His Majesty's Privy Council, we would be willing to take a moderate and reasonable position. In that event, while claiming the right to decide for ourselves the terms upon which we would deal with our territory...*
>
> —1913 petition of the Nisga'a Land Committee to the Privy Council

> *In appraising the Indian title we should go back to the times when the lands were a wilderness, when we find a wild people upon an unimproved estate... cession [surrender] of Indian territory has always preceded the settlement of a country and whatever has been granted for the transfer has represented the good will of the Crown...*
>
> *I want to get rid of the Indian problem. I do not think as a matter of fact, that the country ought to continuously protect a class of people who are able to stand alone... Our objective is to continue until there is not a single Indian in Canada that has not been absorbed into the body politic and there is no Indian question and no Indian Department.*
>
> —Letter from Duncan Campbell Scott, Deputy Superintendant of Indian Affairs 1913–1932

WHAT DO YOU THINK?

1. Compare the perspectives on Aboriginal territorial rights revealed in these two sources. How do you account for the differences between them?

Closing the Door on Immigration

What factors might lead a country to close its doors to immigrants? The people of Canada were split in their reactions to Clifford Sifton's open-door immigration policy. Business owners tended to support the growth of immigration because the arrival of so many people gave them a cheap pool of labour, as well as markets for their products. However, many groups of Canadians began to resent the increasing numbers of immigrants during these years. There were four main reasons for their objections:

- Some labour unions saw unskilled immigrant workers as a threat to their members' jobs and livelihoods.

- Some British Canadians feared that immigrants from eastern, central, and southern Europe would change the British character of the country.

- Some French-Canadians feared that their culture would decline as they became a smaller percentage of the population.

- Racial prejudice was also widespread. People of African or Asian origin were not accepted by many Canadians.

British Columbia and Immigration: A Difficult Issue

Immigration policy was an especially difficult issue in British Columbia. Employers in the mines, forests, and canneries encouraged the arrival of hard-working Asian immigrants who were willing to accept less pay, sometimes as low as half, compared to other workers. However, many British Columbians felt their jobs were threatened by Clifford Sifton's open-door policy. They demanded the federal government restrict Asian immigration.

In 1905, Frank Oliver replaced Sifton as the federal Minister of the Interior. He agreed with those who wished to reduce the number of non-white immigrants. Oliver brought in a more selective immigration policy that was particularly aimed at Asian immigrants. Both the federal and provincial governments began to restrict Chinese, Japanese, and South Asian immigration.

British Columbia Population by Ethnic Origin, 1901–1921			
Year	British	European	Asian
1901	106 403	21 784	19 524
1911	266 295	69 799	30 864
1921	387 513	72 743	39 739

How does the increase in British population compare with the other two groups?

The "Golden Mountain"

Chinese immigrants were the largest single group of Asians in British Columbia. As you read in Chapter 6, the Cariboo Gold Rush and the construction of the Canadian Pacific Railway lured many Chinese people to British Columbia. By 1891, 9400 Chinese immigrants were living in the province. Most of them intended to return to their families in China when they had made enough money. Immigration from China continued despite the **head tax**, an extra charge for entry into Canada that was levelled against Chinese immigrants. Many Chinese workers lived in isolated "Chinatowns" in Vancouver, Victoria, Nanaimo, and New Westminster.

Most of the Chinese workers were employed in the salmon canneries and in the coal mines of Vancouver Island. When councils representing labour unions complained that the Chinese workers took the jobs of their members, labour organizations called for laws to restrict the number of Chinese people entering Canada.

Opponents of Asian immigration in British Columbia formed the **Asiatic Exclusion League**. In 1907, they protested against the Lieutenant-Governor's refusal to sign a bill excluding Japanese immigrants from entering Canada. The protest turned into a riot, and a thousand demonstrators left a trail of destruction through Chinatown and the Japanese section of the city.

head tax a tax paid only by Chinese immigrants to Canada; it started at $50 in 1885, was raised to $100 in 1900, and then went up to $500 in 1903

Asiatic Exclusion League an organization with an agenda to prevent Asian immigration

FIGURE 7–24 Debbie Yam holds the head tax certificate of her grandfather, Won Bing Yam, who immigrated to Canada in 1923. Beginning in the 1980s, Chinese Canadians fought for recognition and compensation from the Canadian government. In 2006, the government offered both an apology and compensation to those who had paid the tax and to their families. How did Chinese Canadians respond?

FIGURE 7–25 The mob from the Asiatic Exclusion League rampaged through the Chinese and Japanese sections of Vancouver during the riot of 1907. Many people had to find shelter in their homes and shops, some of which, like this store, were damaged. Fortunately, no lives were lost. Are there groups today that wish to restrict immigration? What are their reasons?

TIMELINE
The Asian-Canadian Experience

1872 ● Voters Act denies Chinese people the right to vote in B.C.

1885 ● Head Tax imposed

1902 ● Royal Commission recommends an end to Chinese immigration

1907 ● Anti-Asian riots in Vancouver

1908 ● Continuous Passage Act

1914 ● *Komagata Maru* incident

1947 ● All Asians except Japanese given right to vote

Continuous Passage Act a law passed in 1908 that allowed entry into Canada only to immigrants who had arrived by a single direct route

The riot brought international attention to Vancouver, much to the embarrassment of the federal government. Because Japan was an ally of Great Britain, Prime Minister Laurier apologized to the Japanese government. He also formed a Royal Commission to look into the riot and compensate Japanese and Chinese people for damage to their property. Nevertheless, in that same year, the Canadian government set an annual limit of 400 male Japanese immigrants.

By Continuous Passage Only

Laurier's Minister of Labour, William Lyon Mackenzie King, led the Royal Commission to investigate the Vancouver riots. He was also asked to find out how workers from Asia had been "enticed" to come to Canada. Since 1904, for example, CPR agents based in Hong Kong had encouraged East Indians to emigrate to Canada. As they were also subjects of the British Empire, it was difficult to restrict their entry into Canada.

The federal government decided to pass the **Continuous Passage Act**, a law that required all immigrants to come to Canada by a non-stop route. However, direct or "continuous" passage from countries such as India was impossible, since no steamship companies would offer such a route. The government thought it had solved the "problem" of Asian immigration.

This policy was challenged in 1914, when a Sikh businessman, Gurdit Singh, chartered a steamer called the *Komagata Maru*. It transported 354 Sikh immigrants from Hong Kong to Vancouver. The ship was put in quarantine, so the passengers could not land. The people on board nearly starved to death. Finally, the *Komagata Maru* was escorted out of Vancouver Harbour by the Royal Navy cruiser HMCS *Rainbow*.

FIGURE 7–26 The Punjabis aboard the *Komagata Maru* spent two uncomfortable months in Vancouver harbour while their fate was decided. How might Canadian government officials have explained the need to turn away the passengers on the ship? What arguments might members of the Canadian Sikh community have made to allow the ship to land?

On May 23, 2008, the British Columbia legislature voted unanimously to extend an apology for the *Komagata Maru* incident.

> *The House deeply regrets that the passengers, who sought refuge in our country and our province, were turned away without benefit of the fair and impartial treatment befitting a society where people of all cultures are welcomed and accepted.*
>
> —**Resolution of the British Columbia Legislature**

ACTIVITIES

1. Why did the suffragists believe that giving the vote to women would make the world a better place? Do you agree or disagree?

2. Explain the policies of the federal government toward Aboriginal Canadians during the Laurier era. Organize your response in a graphic organizer providing details for each of the policies.

3. Who was in opposition to Asian immigration, and why were they opposed? Was there any group that welcomed Asian immigrants? Explain.

4. **a)** Do you agree with present-day governments apologizing for past wrongs? Explain.

   b) Are Truth and Reconciliation Commissions the best way to deal with historic injustices? Explain.

5. Research immigration to Canada in the last ten years. What trends do you see? Investigate any opposition (government or popular opinion) to Canada's immigration policies and share your findings.

Evidence

6. Research the terms of the Nisga'a Treaty and compare it to one of the numbered treaties negotiated during the late 1800s.

Prosperity and Innovation

▶ **How did economic prosperity encourage technological change?**

Laurier had won the election of 1896 at the same time as a worldwide depression was ending. The next 20 years were prosperous for Canada. The economy grew as industry and transportation expanded, helped by rapid growth in immigration. Still, Canada's growth was largely based on its resources. Is this still the case today?

The Laurier Boom

The Yukon Gold Rush stimulated the Canadian economy. The gold helped provide a flow of **capital**, which was used to expand industries and buy equipment. A growing world economy meant rising prices and expanding **markets** for Canadian products, and demand for Canadian resources such as lumber and minerals was increasing. As you read earlier, this demand helped lead to the expansion of Canada's railway network.

In British Columbia the mining, forestry, and fishing industries grew. Railways expanded into the Kootenay along the Crowsnest Pass, allowing for a dramatic growth in forestry. Ease in getting harvesting rights and the nearby ocean transport led to a cutting bonanza. Easy water access also led to the building of a number of pulp mills along the coast.

Rising world prices also increased agricultural production in Canada, which encouraged farmers to expand their operations. As the population of the Prairies grew, that region became one of the main grain-growing areas of the world. As a result, manufacturing in the East expanded to supply the growing West. Now, the eastern industries needed electric power, which led to the development of hydroelectric dams.

Prime Minister Laurier benefited from this prosperity and won three more elections in 1900, 1904, and 1908. He lost the election of 1911, in part over his attempt to negotiate a reciprocity agreement with the United States. The agreement would allow western farmers to buy cheaper American goods, but in Ontario, industry owners were opposed and turned the province against Laurier.

capital money that is used by a company to increase production by investing in equipment, seeking new markets, and other strategies

markets a place or group demanding goods or services; also where goods are bought and sold, for example, the world market for wheat or oil

FIGURE 7–27 Logging at Powell River on British Columbia's coast began in 1908. Four years later the new pulp and paper mill, at one time the largest in the world, produced the first newsprint in Western Canada. What is the state of this industry in Powell River today?

A Transportation Revolution

At the turn of the 19th century, Canadians knew they lived in an exciting age, and they marvelled at the new technological developments. These "wonders of the age" promised speedy travel by car and by plane, rapid communication with the amazing wireless radio, and a new view of the world in "moving pictures."

The Arrival of the Car

In 1901, an automobile appeared for the first time on the cover of the Eaton's catalogue. As they became increasingly affordable, more cars appeared on Canadian roads. Many were produced in the United States, but Canadian companies such as the Canadian Cycle and Motor Company (CCM) quickly went into production.

Although some people complained about cars, most reactions were positive. Soon doctors, politicians, businesses, and the well-to-do were using cars. Lengthy trips in cars, such as from Victoria to Port Alberni and back, became a favourite pastime on Sundays. Cars were found mainly in the southern populated parts of British Columbia, where roads were generally in better condition.

> **DID YOU KNOW...**
>
> In 1908, Prince Edward Island banned cars after complaints that they tore up the roads and frightened children and livestock.

Zoom In ⊘ Canada's First Gas Station

The first gasoline-powered cars began to appear in British Columbia in 1904. They cost about $200 each. The number of cars in British Columbia doubled every year, creating the need to open Canada's first gas station in Vancouver in 1907.

Before that time, gasoline for cars in Vancouver was supplied from pails dipped into a wooden barrel for 20 cents a gallon (4.5 litres). Some bicycle shops were also selling gasoline at 40 cents a gallon. This method was considered unsafe and inefficient. A 60-litre hot-water tank was then used to store the gasoline, with a rubber hose attached to it. Later, as the photo shows, a more efficient system was installed.

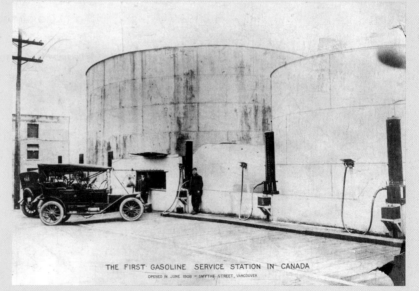

THE FIRST GASOLINE SERVICE STATION IN CANADA
OPENED IN JUNE 1908 — SMYTHE STREET, VANCOUVER

FIGURE 7–28 The first gasoline station in Canada, on Smythe Street in Vancouver. Why were oil companies initially unprepared to service cars? How has the system changed since then? How might it change in the future?

It took much longer for airplanes to become as widely accepted as automobiles. Early planes were held together by wire, and most pilots did their own repairs. The first successful flight in Canada took place in 1909 in Baddeck, Nova Scotia. The airplane flew 9 metres above the ground for a kilometre and a half at 65 km/hour.

A Communications Revolution

Canadians were quick to use the new communications technologies of the age. More than 300 000 telephones were in use in Canada in 1911, and Canadians became the greatest users of telephones in the world. Working conditions were hard for telephone operators, most of whom were women, and the pay was low.

In 1901, Canada also led the way when Guglielmo Marconi received the first wireless telegraph communication from Wales on Signal Hill, in St. John's, Newfoundland. Soon the Marconi Wireless Telegraph Company was accepting messages from the public for transmission to Britain at a rate of 15 cents a word. In 1907, Canadian inventor Reginald Fessenden transmitted the world's first radio broadcast of music and voice. This new medium was slow to catch on. People continued to listen to sound recordings on cylinders, a method introduced in the 1890s.

Perhaps even more exciting than the telephone or wireless telegraph was the new moving picture show. The first public screening of a moving picture in Canada was in 1896. Viewers paid 10 cents to crowd into a hall in Ottawa to see several one-minute films showing people performing everyday tasks. As films became more popular, the price was reduced to 5 cents, leading film theatres to be called "nickelodeons."

FIGURE 7–29 The novelty of airplane flight is shown in this program for a flying demonstration at Minoru Park in Richmond, British Columbia. What present-day event might match the excitement and glamour of these airplane demonstrations?

FIGURE 7–30 Guglielmo Marconi began to investigate long-distance radio waves around 1900. He believed it was possible to send signals across large distances, without having to rely on physical telegraph cables. How might past events in Canada have been different with wireless communication?

Enjoying Life: Arts and Leisure

The growth of towns and cities led to the growth of spectator sports and outdoor recreation. Paying spectators watched Babe Ruth's first home run at Hanlan's Point, Toronto. The first Grey Cup football game was also held in Toronto in 1909. In 1912, 75 000 people watched the parade that kicked off the first Calgary Stampede. Owning a car meant people could pursue recreation farther from home, so skiing, hiking, and camping became popular pastimes in Canada.

During the late 1880s and early 1900s, many Canadians became world champions in sports. George Dixon, of Halifax, won a world boxing championship. In rowing, oarsman Ned Hanlan of Toronto took part in more than 300 races and became world champion. In 1908, Canada sent its first team to the Olympics.

Canadians' tastes in food also began to change. The invention of refrigerated rail cars made a greater variety of food available. By 1910, processed foods such as Heinz ketchup were common, and the first 5-cent chocolate bars went on sale. The soft-drink craze sweeping the United States also came to Canada. Coca Cola, first promoted as a medicine, was now marketed as a soft drink. In Toronto, a pharmacist developed Canada Dry Ginger Ale, a brand now recognized around the world.

FIGURE 7–31 Tom Longboat, from the Six Nations Reserve in Ontario, was one of the world's greatest distant runners. He won the Boston Marathon in 1907. During the First World War, he served as a dispatch runner in France.

Poets, Writers, and Artists

Canadian poets, writers, and artists began to find wider audiences at this time. In British Columbia, artist Emily Carr was developing her unique style of painting. She also supported herself by working as a cartoonist for a weekly Victoria newspaper. Soon she started taking trips to the Queen Charlotte Islands, now called Haida Gwaii. First Nations villages and the landscape of British Columbia gave her the inspiration for some of her well-known paintings.

In Prince Edward Island, Lucy Maud Montgomery wrote *Anne of Green Gables* in 1908, and her books remain very popular. In Ontario, humorist Stephen Leacock wrote *Sunshine Sketches of a Little Town* in 1912, making gentle fun of small-town life. In the north, poet Robert Service brought the Yukon Gold Rush to life in his writing with poems such as "The Cremation of Sam McGee." All of these writers and poets represent the beginning of a growing national literature in Canada, and each had a distinct point of view of Canadian life.

THE EARLY STUDENT ENJOYS THE FOUL, THE LATE ONE GNAWS THE BONES.

FIGURE 7–32 Although Emily Carr is best known for her paintings of British Columbia's natural environment, she also produced many newspaper cartoons. How does this example provide us with information about Victoria's society at that time?

Pauline Johnson was born in 1861 on the Six Nations Reserve in Canada West. She was the daughter of a Mohawk father and an English mother.

Johnson began writing for magazines and newspapers such as the *Globe* and *Saturday Night* for a living, but poetry was her real passion. She wrote in the style of the British and American poets she admired. Her first poems were published in 1884, and her work was included in one of the first anthologies of Canadian poetry.

In 1892, Johnson began her career as a performer, and her poetry readings were popular in the United States and Europe.

When Johnson retired, she moved to Vancouver and wrote stories told to her by her friend Joe Capilano, a Squamish chief. She died in 1913.

- What evidence can you find in this poem of Johnson's values and her purpose in writing?

- How did her work contribute to a new Canadian identity?

FIGURE 7–33 Pauline Johnson adopted the name of her great-grandfather, Tekahionwake, and wore traditional Mohawk clothing for her appearances. Why do you think her performances were so popular?

The Corn Husker

Hard by the Indian lodges, where the bush
Breaks in a clearing, through ill-fashioned fields,
She comes to labour, when the first still hush
Of autumn follows large and recent yields.

Age in her fingers, hunger in her face,
Her shoulders stooped with weight of work and years,
But rich in tawny colouring of her race,
She comes a-field to strip the purple ears.

And all her thoughts are with the days gone by,
Ere might's injustice banished from their lands
Her people, that today unheeded lie,
Like the dead husks that rustle through her hands.

ACTIVITIES

1. Give two reasons why telephones became more popular in Canada than in any other country.

2. What other new technologies excited people in the Laurier era? How did these technologies affect Canadian leisure activities?

3. Choose three new technologies from today that you think will have as great an impact as did those described in this chapter. Support your choices with a least two reasons.

4. Research one of the athletes or artists discussed in this section. Develop a Facebook-type profile of this person in print form or electronically.

Explore the Big Ideas

In the two decades before the First World War, Canada experienced remarkable changes. Wilfrid Laurier skillfully guided Canada through 15 years of prosperity, as well as political and social upheaval. Immigration transformed Canada into a truly transcontinental nation with growing cities and industries. Agriculture and manufacturing prospered. New technologies changed social and cultural habits. However, not all Canadians were part of the new positive outlook. Aboriginal peoples, immigrants, women, and workers struggled for their rights. By 1914, Canada was beginning to resemble the country we live in today.

1. **a)** At the time, all Canadians were affected by these changes with both favourable and unfavourable results. Complete the organizer below to identify which changes affected each group either positively or negatively.

   b) After completing the organizer, write a paragraph stating which group gained the most, and which group lost the most as a result of these changes.

Group	Positive	Negative
Aboriginal peoples		
English Canadians		
French Canadians		
European immigrants		
Asian immigrants		
Women		
Industrialists		
Workers		

2. Laurier needed to follow a path of compromise to govern Canada. Make a list of issues facing Canada today. Look at different areas, such as the economy, social and cultural developments, regional differences, and human rights. Speculate how Laurier would deal with these issues and how his approach would compare to the approach of the current prime minister.

3. Working with a partner, assume the roles of two people living in Canada with opposing viewpoints on one of the following topics: Aboriginal rights, women's rights, the labour movement, settlement of the Prairies, supporting Britain overseas.

   a) Make a list of facts and opinions to back up the point of view you are supporting. You may need to do research to gather information.

   b) Consider what arguments your opponent might make and how you will respond.

   c) Perform your dialogue for the class.

4. Canada began on the road to multiculturalism during the Laurier era. Today we are one of the most multicultural countries in the world.

   a) Make a list of changes in Canadian society that were influenced by immigration.

   b) Who might see these changes as progress? Why?

5. Identify and show how various elements contributed to an emerging Canadian identity during the Laurier era.

8 | The Changing Canadian Economy

Chapter Outcomes

In this chapter, you will learn about key economic concepts, the economic regions of Canada, and the Canadian economy within North America. By the end of this chapter, you will

- analyze economic factors that led to the development of Canada and its regions

- describe Canada's economic sectors and economic regions, along with their activities and environmental challenges

- explain how geography influences economic development in regions of Canada

- evaluate the sustainability of various economic sectors and economic activities in Canada

- analyze the influence of resource development and decline on Canada's economy

- identify technological changes and their impact on Canada's economy

- discuss Canada's place in the North American economy, including trade agreements and disputes

Significance | Patterns and Change

Judgements | **CRITICAL INQUIRY** | Evidence

Cause and Consequence | Perspectives

Almost 100 years before Paul Martin made the statement below, Wilfrid Laurier declared that "Canada shall fill the 20th century." The images on these pages show two distinct parts of Canada's economy—the fishery and high technology. Use these images to develop your own statement on Canada's economic future.

How has the Canadian economy changed over time? What will be your role in the modern economy?

Canada has moved from a resource- and manufacturing-based economy to one that relies far more on service industries. Every region of Canada has had to diversify in order to remain prosperous. How is Canada facing the challenges of a world that is steadily moving in the direction of free trade and globalization?

Key Terms

global economy
trend
goods
services
laws of supply and demand
business cycle

economic region
rural–urban migration
outsource
NAFTA
free trade
fair trade

And so, let us come together—all of us—and make a pledge of common purpose: that we will do everything in our power today so that the generations of tomorrow are able to say not only that Canada belongs to the twenty-first century, but that the twenty-first century belongs to Canada.

—Finance Minister Paul Martin, 1999

Economic Essentials

▶ What factors influence the economy of a country?

The Canadian economy has changed dramatically during the 21st century. You are probably aware of some of these changes. Maybe a family member has lost a job, or someone you know has started a business. You may be wondering where you fit into the **global economy**. How can you prepare yourself for a job market that seems as changeable as the economy?

In the first decade of the 21st century, a boom in resource-based industries benefited provinces such as British Columbia, Alberta, Saskatchewan, and Newfoundland and Labrador. However, the downturn in the market economy led to a decline in the manufacturing sector in Ontario and Quebec. Changes like these are examples of **trends**. Some trends are easy to understand, but others are complex and require critical analysis. Basic economic principles are helpful tools in understanding how these trends affect Canada.

The Study of Economics

When you think of economics, you probably think of money. Economics does study the production, exchange, and consumption of **goods** and **services**, all of which involve the flow of money. But economics is also about deciding how to meet the basic needs and desires of individuals, businesses, and nations.

The biggest problem in economic decision making is the issue of scarcity. For example, you may want to buy a new computer game. Perhaps you also need to pay back a friend. What is the key issue? You do not have enough money to do both. That is what scarcity means in personal terms. In the same way, a society's needs and desires often exceed its resources, so it has to decide how those resources will be used. On a government level, the challenge to balance needs with resources drives economic policy making. Determining policy is the source of heated debates among members of political parties and those following diverse economic theories. These debates show the struggle between different beliefs and values. In fact, economic policies can reveal what a country stands for.

The Laws of Supply and Demand

Early European contact with Canada was based on the need for goods. For example, Samuel de Champlain viewed his settlement at Quebec as a trading venture. His purpose was to find a good supply of beaver pelts, for which there was a high demand in the fashion industry in France.

TIMELINE

1930	The Great Depression begins
1935	Most-favoured-nation trade agreement between Canada and the United States
1947	Leduc oil field opens
1965	Canada–U.S. Auto Pact is signed
1980	Prime Minister Trudeau introduces the National Energy Program (NEP)
1982	Softwood Lumber Dispute begins
1984	Prime Minister Mulroney dismantles the NEP
1989	Canada–U.S. Free Trade Agreement begins
1991	Economic recession in Canada
1994	North American Free Trade Agreement begins
2006	Seven-year Softwood Lumber Agreement is signed
2008	Global economic crisis

global economy international business and trade

trend the general direction in which something is moving

goods products that can be sold

services a system of supplying a public want or need (e.g., banking, transportation)

Canada's economy and welfare has always been affected by the prices Canada can set for goods and services in the world market. When the prices paid for Canadian exports are high, the economy booms. For example, the resource-based industries of western Canada benefit from increased demand and high prices for goods such as grains, potash, oil, natural gas, coal, and other minerals.

The reverse is true when global prices decrease, or when demand goes down. In the early 2000s, the rising cost of gasoline affected the makers of SUVs and trucks in Ontario. Consumers began buying more gas-efficient cars, and thousands of Ontario auto workers lost their jobs when the SUV and truck plants closed down. In this way, the **laws of supply and demand** directly affected the livelihood of Canadians.

laws of supply and demand economic laws about the relationship between the available amount of a product (supply), the number of people who want the product (demand), and the price of the product

 Zoom In > **How Does Supply and Demand Work?**  **Patterns and Change**

Supply

The law of supply applies to the producer side of the market:

- When prices are high, producers of goods and services usually increase production.

- When prices are low, producers tend to cut back on production.

By controlling supply, producers hope to keep prices high. If the price of a product is low, the producer might cut back on production, creating a shortage. If demand for the product remains the same, the price will go up.

Supply can affect prices in other ways. A coffee-crop failure in Central America would lead to a worldwide shortage in coffee beans. If the demand remains the same, there would be an increase in the price of coffee. On the other hand, if there was a bumper crop of wheat around the world, then wheat prices would fall because of the surplus supply.

Demand

The law of demand applies to the consumer side of the market:

- When the price for a product or service goes down, demand goes up.

- When the price increases, demand falls.

This happens for a simple reason: not all consumers can afford high prices. When the price of a product or service is lowered, it becomes more affordable for more people.

Demand also affects prices. When demand goes up, it pulls up the price of the product or service. However, when demand decreases, the price of the product or service goes down.

For example, in late January, clothing stores want to get rid of their winter stock to make room for their new lines of spring and summer clothing. Winter clothes are marked down, and the new spring and summer clothing is introduced at full price.

- How could government regulation change the pattern of supply and demand? Think of circumstances in which this change might be necessary.

FIGURE 8–1 Demand for a product can be increased through advertising and marketing, which can result in higher prices. How does advertising affect your choices?

Three Basic Economic Questions

Economics is about making decisions. Producers of goods and services must ask and answer three basic questions whenever they need to make an economic decision. At the core of each question is the issue of how best to use available resources. Consider these examples:

- **What is to be produced?** A farmer must decide whether to grow wheat or canola. A provincial government with a limited budget must choose between increasing funding for health care or education.

- **How is it to be produced?** A farmer needs to consider what technology is needed to produce and process the crop. A provincial government needs to determine whether additional funding for education will come from tax revenue or from cutting funding somewhere else.

- **For whom is it to be produced?** A farmer needs to determine if the crops will be sold within Canada or be exported. If a provincial government decides to increase the education budget, it has to determine where the funds should go—to elementary and high schools or to post-secondary education.

Resources

Companies, organizations, and business owners must also consider laws and regulations, which can affect their business decisions. Environmental regulations, for example, are becoming stricter. A business such as the Lehigh-Hanson cement plant, shown in Figure 8–2, represents a huge investment of resources, but faces an uncertain future as tougher environmental regulations drive up costs.

When a farmer decides which crop to grow, or a government decides which service to fund, both must assess available resources. As always, scarcity is an issue. If there is not enough of one type of resource to produce a good or service, steps must be taken to increase the resource, or that choice is eliminated. Resources are generally grouped into three categories, as shown in the chart below.

FIGURE 8–2 Lehigh-Hanson's cement plant in Delta, British Columbia, is British Columbia's third-largest emitter of greenhouse gases. How will environmental concerns affect the economic decisions made by this company?

Defining Resources	
Land resources	all natural resources that may be used to produce goods and services, such as land, water, fish, forests, and minerals
Human resources	people to produce goods and services, including fishers, forestry workers, store owners, educators, research scientists, and many others
Capital resources	money and human-made goods (also known as capital goods), which are used to produce other goods and services, such as transportation infrastructure, technology, and research and educational facilities

Economic Sectors

Economic activities are classified into four sectors: primary, secondary, tertiary, or quaternary. Look at the images below. How many sectors can you connect to yourself, your family, or your community?

Most Canadians are employed in the tertiary, or service, sector. Many people your age find their first job in the service industry. In most urban regions, particularly in southern Ontario and Quebec, many still work in manufacturing. However, Canada is usually described as having a **resource-based economy**. Primary activities such as forestry, fishing, and farming account for the greatest percentage of the national income.

A sector showing rapid growth in Canada is the quaternary sector. More and more Canadians are involved in research and development in various industries, from inventing telecommunications systems to designing interactive computer games.

resource-based economy an economy that relies on the extraction and/or primary processing of raw materials

FIGURE 8–3 Primary activities involve collecting, harvesting, or extracting resources. These workers are packing salmon for export. The fishing industry is a primary activity.

FIGURE 8–4 Secondary activities refer to the processing or manufacturing of goods. These workers are involved in construction, a key industry in the secondary sector.

FIGURE 8–5 Tertiary activities involve services. This sales team is part of the retail industry, a major component of the tertiary sector of the economy.

FIGURE 8–6 The creation and transfer of ideas and information is the quaternary sector of the economy, where these medical researchers work.

In Chapter 7, you used statistics to gain an understanding of the past. Economic statistics can help us understand the impact of economic changes. They can also be used to assess the present and prepare for the future by predicting trends.

Before analyzing and evaluating economic statistics, it is important to understand the business cycle (Figure 8–8). Regional, national, and even world economies go through cycles of expansion and contraction. These are caused by factors such as wars, technological change, and fluctuation in prices.

An expanding economy means prosperity: business grows, unemployment is low, and people invest and spend money. Contraction of the economy results in a recession or depression: high unemployment, the closing of businesses, and low consumer spending. Depressions are far more serious and long lasting. In the last year of the Great Depression, 30 percent of the Canadian workforce was unemployed. During times of recession and depression, governments generally take action to stimulate the economy.

Examine the tables and graphs on these pages. How can statistics be used to understand the past and predict future trends?

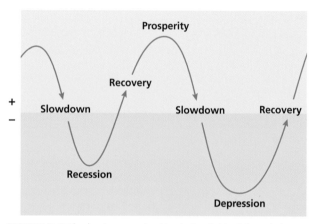

FIGURE 8–8 The business cycle. At what point in this cycle is today's economy?

FIGURE 8–9 Many Canadians had no work, and little hope, during the Great Depression of the 1930s.

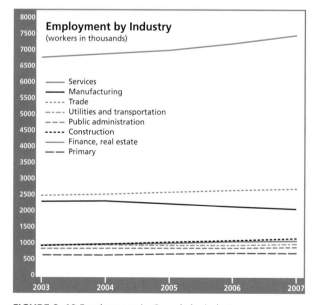

FIGURE 8–10 Employment in Canada by industry

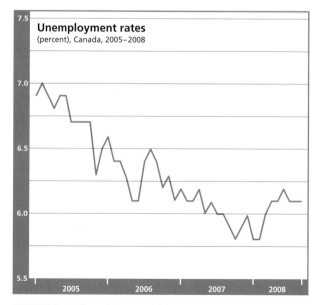

FIGURE 8–11 Canada's unemployment rate

Canada's Real GDP During the Great Depression		
Year	**Constant (1986) dollars, in millions**	**Annual change (percentage)**
1929	52 997	0.9
1930	51 262	–3.3
1931	45 521	–11.2
1932	41 032	–9.3
1933	38 331	–7.2
1934	42 318	10.4
1935	45 357	7.2

Canada's Real GDP (2003–2007)		
Year	**Constant (2002) dollars, in millions**	**Annual change (percentage)**
2003	1 174 592	n/a
2004	1 211 239	+3.1
2005	1 246 064	+2.9
2006	1 284 819	+3.1
2007	1 319 680	+2.7

APPLY IT

1. Compare the tables showing changes in Canada's GDP for 2003–2007 and during the Depression to the chart of the business cycle (Figure 8–8). Based on your observations, is a depression an inevitable consequence of an economic slowdown? Explain.

2. Examine the chart in Figure 8–10. What industry has shown the greatest growth in the number of people it employs? What industry consistently employs the lowest number of workers? After assessing the current economic situation in Canada and using the data shown in the graph, predict future employment trends.

3. Some economists conclude that unemployment is a constant in modern society. Use information from Figure 8–8 and Figure 8–11 to either support or contradict that conclusion.

4. Look at Figure 8–9. How does it illustrate the economy of that time? Imagine that you are a photographer who has been assigned to capture images that show the current state of the economy in your region. Focus on different segments of the economy that are experiencing both growth and decline. Describe the photos you might take.

▶ **What factors have played a part in the economy of each of Canada's major economic regions?**

As you saw in Chapter 1, Canada has a variety of landscapes and climates. It has mountain ranges, tundra, rain forests, prairie, farmland, and a mineral-rich Shield. Its peoples and cultures are equally varied. Canada's economy naturally reflects this diversity.

Just as we have used physical regions to study Canada's geography, we can use **economic regions** to study the country's economy. Economic regions can be seen in different ways, ranging from the business district of a city to several provinces. The economic regions discussed here follow the physical regions of Canada (pages 16–24), making the link between geography and human activity. The Cordillera region and the economy of British Columbia will be discussed in Chapter 9.

economic region an area defined by common economic activities

The Atlantic Region

The Atlantic region is dominated by the Appalachian mountain range and the Atlantic Ocean. It includes New Brunswick, Nova Scotia, and Prince Edward Island, as well as Newfoundland and the Gaspé region of Quebec. With thousands of kilometres of coastline, the region has many natural harbours. Halifax Harbour, for example, is well situated for trade with Europe and the eastern seaboard of the United States.

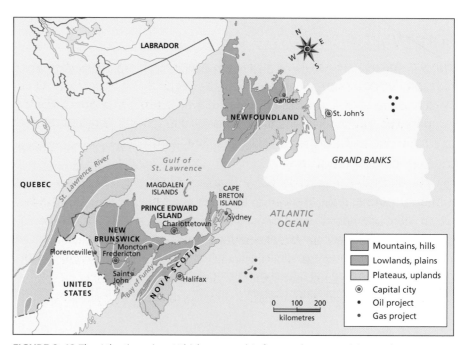

FIGURE 8–12 The Atlantic region. Which geographic factors shown on this map have most affected the economic development of this area?

Economic Development

The Mi'kmaq, Maliseet, and Beothuk of the Atlantic region hunted, trapped, fished, and farmed. After John Cabot arrived in Newfoundland in 1497, the plentiful fish of the Grand Banks drew fishers from England, Portugal, and France. Fishing was a major activity in the region for hundreds of years. European settlement remained relatively low in Newfoundland, with most fishers staying only during the summers. The fertile land and moderate climate in the southern areas of the Atlantic region encouraged quick growth of European settlements.

Agriculture, started with the First Nations and the Acadian settlers of the 17th century, remains a key industry in parts of the region today. Agricultural products include potatoes, corn, dairy products, and fruit.

At the time of Confederation, Halifax and Saint John had important dockyard and building facilities for wooden ships. Advances in steam technology and the building of iron ships in the 1890s, however, brought the wooden ship industry to a close. In Cape Breton, coal mining was a major industry, with the area once producing two-thirds of Canada's coal. Steel manufacturing was also a profitable industry in the area. Unfortunately, the manufacturing of steel heavily polluted the local environment. While steel production was shut down in 2001, environmental concerns such as the Sydney Tar Ponds, a hazardous waste site within Sydney's city limits, remain. The Atlantic region also had a financial sector based on trade with Britain and the United States.

After Confederation, the region's mining, financial, and manufacturing industries became secondary compared with those in central Canada. Changing markets and technology as well as depleted natural resources led to the region's economic decline, relative to the rest of Canada. **Regional disparity** became a chronic issue, which continues today.

The Region Today

The economy of the Atlantic region is changing. The collapse of the cod industry devastated entire communities, but there is still hope that cod stocks may recover. The agricultural industry has prospered. For example, by 2008, McCain Foods Ltd. employed more than 20 000 people in an operation that included not only farming but also frozen-food processing, trucking, and manufacturing.

The oil fields off the coast of Newfoundland represent tremendous economic potential for the region. Hibernia itself produces over 200 000 barrels of crude oil per day. The Sable Project, near Sable Island, began producing natural gas in 1999. Even though the entire Atlantic region stands to benefit from the oil and gas industries, there are concerns about these offshore sites. There have been accidents in the past, such as oil spills, and some fishers worry about possible damage to the fishing grounds.

FIGURE 8–13 The pulp and paper industry is a major employer in the Atlantic region. What changes might this industry face in the future?

regional disparity different levels of income among regions

FIGURE 8–14 The Hibernia oil platform was first developed in 1997. Is development of the oil industry a good direction for the Atlanic region to take? Why or why not?

The Great Lakes–St. Lawrence Region

The Great Lakes–St. Lawrence region is Canada's smallest economic region, occupying less than 2 percent of the nation's total land area. It includes the southern strip of Quebec, the St. Lawrence River, and the southern region of Ontario, surrounded by Lake Erie, Lake Ontario, and Lake Huron.

Economic Development

The Great Lakes–St. Lawrence region has fertile lowlands formed during the last ice age, a mild climate, and access to fresh water. These factors attracted Aboriginal peoples, such as the Haudenosaunee, to the region, where they farmed and hunted. The St. Lawrence River and the Great Lakes proved to be valuable waterways, and European explorers made their way through the Great Lakes. Water transportation routes connected communities and allowed raw materials and goods to be transported in and out of the region. This travel increased after the St. Lawrence Seaway, a series of canals and locks, was built in 1959, connecting western Canada with the Atlantic.

By the time of Confederation, manufacturing—iron, steel, clothing, lumber, and beer—had become a major part of the region's economy. Once it was linked by rail to the Atlantic and the West, the region had easy access to foreign markets and advantages for industrial development. As you learned in Chapter 3, opponents to Confederation feared that their own regions would be weakened if central Canada gained more economic power. The amount of wealth concentrated in the Great Lakes–St. Lawrence region still creates tensions across Canada today.

By the early 20th century, the region was known as Canada's **industrial heartland**. It had also become the country's financial centre, and today, most of Canada's banks, trust companies, and insurance firms have head offices in this region.

WEB LINK • • • • • • • •
Building the St. Lawrence Seaway was a major undertaking that affected many people in this region. Read more about it on the Pearson Web site.

industrial heartland the most developed industrialized area in Canada

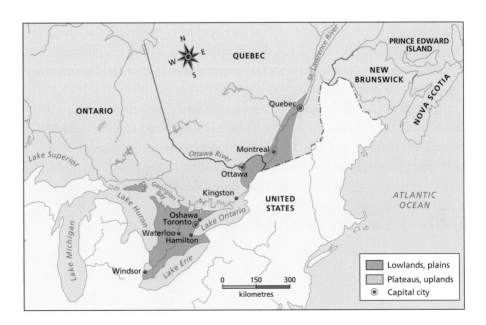

FIGURE 8–15 The Great Lakes–St. Lawrence region. Using what you learned in earlier chapters, discuss how the waterways in this region influenced European settlement and economic development.

The Region Today

During the beginning of the 21st century, high-tech industries expanded the economy of the Great Lakes–St. Lawrence region. In fact, the Ottawa Valley is now known as Silicon Valley North. Ontario's Technology Triangle in the Waterloo region has also experienced a surge in high-tech development.

With more than half of Canada's population, this region is the largest consumer market in the country. Skilled workers, high-tech resources, finance, and transportation infrastructure allow the region to maintain its status as the economic engine of Canada.

However, the manufacturing sector has to constantly adjust to stay competitive and sustainable. There are also environmental concerns. Most of the region is industrialized and densely populated. Pollution has resulted in industrial waste, smog, and acid rain. Sustainable practices and green policies will be needed to protect the environment and allow for continued prosperity.

The Shield Region

The Shield region is Canada's largest economic region. It extends east and south from Great Bear Lake in the Northwest Territories, through the northern Prairie Provinces, most of Ontario and Quebec, all of Labrador, and the eastern tip of Baffin Island. The Shield was once a volcanic mountain range, worn down by glacial activity. The rock left behind is rich in nickel, copper, gold, silver, lead, and zinc. Although the region's thin soils support boreal forests, agriculture is limited. Water is abundant.

Economic Development

The Aboriginal peoples of the Shield region, such as the Cree and Anishinabé, hunted, gathered, and fished. After European contact, the fur trade became the dominant economic activity. Later, forestry and the pulp and paper industry became important.

FIGURE 8–16 The city of Toronto planned to recycle 70 percent of its garbage by 2010. However, the economic crisis in 2008 decreased demand for products, including those made from recycled materials. Toronto must decide what to do with the recyclable material. What solutions can you suggest?

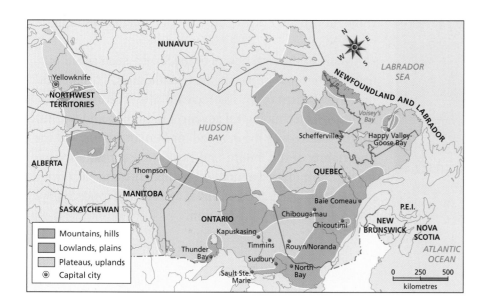

FIGURE 8–17 Using this map of the Shield region, assess how the landscape might have affected its economic development.

smelter a place where ore is melted in order to separate the metal from the ore

tailings waste left over after the mineral is removed during mining or smelting

commodity a raw material or partially processed product that can be bought or sold

Mines and **smelters** have been critical to the region's economy since the early 20th century. In Sault Ste. Marie, Algoma Steel has dominated the local economy since 1901, when the company built its first ironworks there and began the manufacture of steel rails in 1902. The region's heavy dependence on mining has led to major environmental and economic concerns. Mines have produced dangerous stockpiles of **tailings**, and refining operations have produced high levels of sulphur dioxide and nitrogen oxides, leading to acid rain that affects water systems, plants, and wildlife.

Other environmental issues surround hydroelectric developments, such as Hydro Quebec's James Bay project, which have flooded watersheds and threatened the way of life of Aboriginal peoples. Governments have responded by imposing environmental reviews and Aboriginal consultations, but the issues are far from being resolved.

The Region Today

Heavily dependent on natural resources, the Shield region's economy is sensitive to international prices. The minerals and metals produced are **commodities** that fluctuate in value according to global supply and demand. As a result, the region's economy can be bumpy as it rides through boom-and-bust cycles. Prices fluctuate, and resources eventually run out or become uneconomical. When a mine closes, the community around it dies or struggles to survive. For example, the Iron Ore Company of Canada closed its operation in Schefferville, Quebec, in 1981 when prices for iron ore were too low for the company to make a profit. More than 4000 people left the isolated town, but mining operations are expected to begin again in 2011.

Other attempts have been made to break the resource-town cycle. A current approach to mining means that newly developed mines are not supported by nearby towns; instead, the mining company flies employees and equipment into the mine site from other areas. Workers stay in temporary camps for two- or three-week work periods. If the mine is shut down, the temporary camp is simply removed.

Many of the larger cities in the Shield, such as Sudbury, have taken steps to diversify their economies. This includes the development of tourist, recreation, and retirement facilities. As technological advances in mining and smelting continue to reduce the demand for human labour, and the uncertainty of the "boom-and-bust" cycle continues, the need to shift toward a more diversified, sustainable, environmentally friendly economy is an ongoing concern for urban areas in the Shield region.

FIGURE 8–18 A glowing stream of slag in Sudbury. This smelting by-product is an environmental issue. How would this affect people in the local community, many of whom may also work at the mine?

The North Region

The North region reaches from the Yukon, across the Northwest Territories, Nunavut, and northern Manitoba and Ontario, to the northwestern tip of Quebec and the Arctic islands. The region consists of mountains, plateaus, lowlands, and highlands. Much of the landscape is stark, and the climate is extreme. In the past, most of the waterways were frozen almost all year. Winter months are typically cold and dark.

Economic Development

The Aboriginal peoples of this northern region, including the Inuit, hunted, trapped, and fished to sustain themselves. Along the coast, they hunted seals and whales. Early European contact was based on the fur trade, and on whaling and sealing. The search for the Northwest Passage brought more European contact.

Gold discoveries in the late 1800s encouraged European settlement and exploration. During the 1930s, interest from Canadians in the south led to increased mineral exploration. Geologists found rich deposits of copper, gold, silver, and radium. Lead and zinc deposits were uncovered, as well as deposits of oil and natural gas.

Environmental damage, however, has always been a concern in the North region. Leaks from oil pipelines, and refuse and pollution from mining activities have caused irreparable damage to the sensitive ecology of the region. Some mining operations have had problems containing spills of toxic materials, such as arsenic, and have also had difficulties storing tailings.

The Region Today

In the 1980s, **kimberlite** deposits containing diamonds were discovered in the Lac de Gras region of the Northwest Territories. After five years of environmental impact and economic studies, the Ekati mine began

FIGURE 8–19 The Inuit maintain many of their thousand-year-old traditions, but also use modern technology. What other factors might be changing their traditional way of life?

kimberlite a rare igneous rock that sometimes contains diamonds

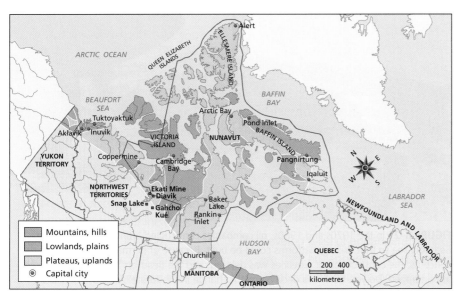

FIGURE 8–20 The North region. How has latitude defined economic activities in this region?

The Prairie Region

The Prairie region includes sections of the Yukon, the Northwest Territories, British Columbia, Alberta, Saskatchewan, and Manitoba. It consists primarily of rolling hills and flat plains, lakes and rivers, and sections of boreal forest and woodland. Deposits of fossil fuels and minerals such as potash have enriched the region's economy.

Economic Development

The Aboriginal peoples of the Interior Plains hunted the massive herds of bison that roamed the plains. Changes began with European contact and the fur trade. After Confederation, waves of immigrants transformed the Prairies. Forestry became an important activity in northern areas, while in the south, much of the natural grasslands were plowed under, to be replaced by crops and cattle ranges. The region became a leading world exporter of wheat.

The petroleum industry has had an even bigger economic impact on the region. Oil was discovered as early as 1914 in the Turner Valley. The turning point came in 1947 with the rich Leduc oil field. Oil sand deposits, particularly the Athabasca oil sands near Fort McMurray, are a major part of the Alberta economy. However, there is much controversy about the petroleum industry. Environmental issues are a concern, and some people worry that much of the Alberta oil industry is owned and controlled by foreign companies.

FIGURE 8–23 The drought of the 1930s was a severe blow to the agricultural industry in the Prairie region. What challenges might this industry face today?

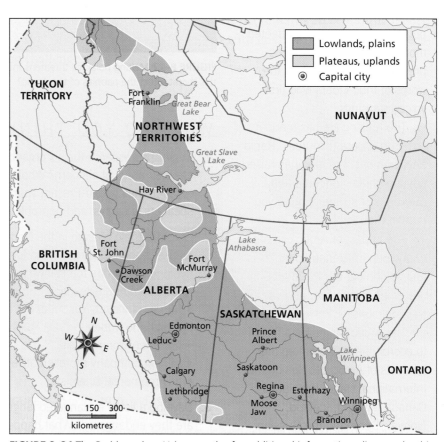

FIGURE 8–24 The Prairie region. Using an atlas for additional information, discuss why this region became known as the "breadbasket" of Canada.

The Region Today

More than 80 percent of Canada's farmland is located in the Prairie region. In 1995, the federal government ended a rail-freight subsidy that lowered transportation costs for farmers. Freight rates soared, forcing many farmers to end their dependence on a single **cash crop**. They began growing barley, oats, corn, and **canola**. Some began raising bison, emu, and ostrich instead of cattle. In 2007 and 2008, global demand for wheat, barley, and corn rose sharply when demand for wheat grew in China and India, and the **biofuel** industry raised the demand for corn. This boom saved many farmers from bankruptcy.

The Prairie region now has a number of growing urban areas such as Edmonton, Regina, and Winnipeg. However, urbanization has affected rural lifestyles, leading to the consolidation of small farms. Towns that serviced rural areas struggle to survive as rural residents migrate to cities.

While Alberta has seen tremendous growth in its manufacturing sector, the region's economy is still largely resource based. Continuing investment in other sectors holds the promise of economic stability. Nevertheless, environmental issues remain.

cash crop a crop produced only for sale, usually export

canola a plant that produces oil, usually used in cooking

biofuel fuel produced from organic matter

FIGURE 8–25 Another major player in the Prairie region's economy is potash mining. Potash is used for fertilizer, feed supplements, and glass making. Worldwide demand for potash has seen the price rise to almost $1000 a tonne, largely because of the expanding need for fertilizer in markets such as China and India.

ACTIVITIES

1. **a)** In small groups, complete an analysis of sustainability from an environmental perspective for one of the five economic regions of Canada.

   b) Discuss your findings. Through consensus, organize your conclusions in order of importance.

2. Summarize how each of the five economic regions relies on its natural resources and what the environmental concerns are for each.

3. Which economic regions of Canada are the most diversified? Which are the least? Support your opinion with details from the text.

4. Explain how geography has influenced economic development in each of the five economic regions.

5. An Aboriginal perspective on development considers the impact of their decisions on seven future generations. How might considering this perspective affect present-day policy in resource development? Give examples.

The Changing Canadian Economy

▶ **What factors have brought about the greatest changes in the Canadian economy?**

Do you live in a rural or an urban area? Which do you think offers people more economic opportunity? In Canada, the trend of people leaving rural areas and moving to cities has gone on for more than a hundred years. As you read in Chapter 7, this **rural–urban migration** started as Canada began to industrialize. At the end of the 19th century, two out of three Canadians lived in rural areas. By the end of the 20th century, the situation had reversed—three out of four Canadians lived in urban areas.

rural–urban migration the moving of people from rural areas into cities

People were attracted to cities for a number of reasons. Cities offered employment and better business prospects. They provided access to better education, recreation, and health care. As people left for the cities, services were cut back in rural areas and small towns, which in turn encouraged more and more people to leave.

City limits expanded with the arrival of more people, leading to urban sprawl. In cities such as Toronto, Montreal, and Vancouver, small towns on the outskirts were absorbed into the metropolitan area. Surrounding areas, sometimes good farmland, were transformed into business parks and suburbs. Larger roads and highways were built so that people living in the suburbs could commute to the city. This new infrastructure attracted not only more people but business and industry as well.

FIGURE 8–26 In Vancouver, entrepreneurial immigrants have invested heavily in real estate. The Concord Pacific development on Vancouver's False Creek, shown here, was built by Hong Kong billionaire Li Ka-Shing and his son Victor Li, a Canadian citizen. The project revitalized nearby neighbourhoods. What are the local economic results of such developments?

Immigration and Urban Growth

In the 2006 census, Toronto and Vancouver were home to a majority of Canada's visible minorities—43 percent and 42 percent respectively. South Asians were the largest visible minority group in Toronto, and Vancouver had a large Chinese population. Montreal also saw a growing visible minority population in 2006, but Montreal's new Canadians were typically from Africa, the Middle East, the Caribbean, and Europe.

The new ethnic makeup of Canada's major cities provide opportunites for greater global connections in trade and commerce. For instance, many Canadians of Chinese heritage maintain a network of relatives and work associates in China, Hong Kong, Taiwan, and Singapore. This alliance, referred to as the "guanxi network," brings real benefits to Canadian businesses in the new global economy.

Technology and Mass Production

At the beginning of the 21st century, Canada's economy rebounded from a downturn that had lasted throughout the 1980s and 1990s. However, not all industries recovered. Atlantic Canada's fishing industry remained in trouble. It was devastated when a **moratorium** was placed on the cod fishery in 1992. Cod stocks were depleted to dangerously low levels, mainly due to overfishing made possible by modern technology, such as larger boats and nets. Foreign fishing fleets contributed to the decline in the cod stocks.

Technology also had an impact on the industrial heartland of southern Ontario and Quebec. Technological breakthroughs in the 1980s and 1990s led to increased automation and mass production. These innovations increased productivity and efficiency, and reduced the costs of production. However, tens of thousands of Canadian workers lost their lifetime employment as their jobs were replaced or became unnecessary. **Structural unemployment** became a major concern in the final decades of the 20th century.

These developments reflect the cycle of the modern Canadian economy. Some economists describe Canada's resource-based economy as a boom and bust cycle. They recommend that the profits gained during the boom periods be invested in the economy to soften the blow when the bust occurs. As a result, many governments and businesses have invested in transportation, energy generation, and manufacturing. Experts also believe new investments and innovations in product design and mass production will help keep the manufacturing industry alive.

Employment Issues

Four types of unemployment are common in Canada:

1. *Cyclical unemployment* refers to work shortages that are affected by the business cycle. During recessions, many workers are laid off. When the economy recovers, most of these workers are re-employed.

2. *Seasonal unemployment* refers to workers who do not work year-round because of the nature of their jobs. For example, fishers must follow regulated seasons in fishing areas.

3. *Frictional unemployment* generally means that workers are only temporarily unemployed. They may be between jobs or just entering the labour force.

4. *Structural unemployment* is caused by the closing of an industry or a permanent decline in an economic sector. Those jobs may be lost forever.

FIGURE 8–27 In the Atlantic cod fishery, larger boats and nets meant that more fish could be caught. Did new technology benefit this industry in the long run? What could have been done differently?

moratorium a temporary enforced suspension of an activity

structural unemployment unemployment caused by changes in the economy that affect an entire industry or replace labour (e.g., robotics)

DID YOU KNOW...
In 2008, the federal Department of Fisheries and Oceans announced that the Atlantic cod stocks had not rebounded as expected. The total extinction of the local cod population is considered a real possibility.

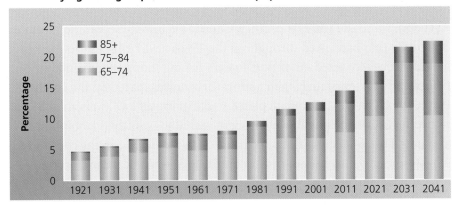

Seniors by age sub-groups, as % of the total population, Canada, 1921–2041

FIGURE 8–28 What patterns are evident in this graph? What might be some of the economic consequences of these trends?

Demographics

demographics population statistics that show age, income, etc.

Employment in Canada has also been affected by major shifts in **demographics**. After the Second World War, Canada experienced a population and economic boom, and 1946 to 1965 came to be known as the "baby boom" era. By the early 2000s, many baby boomers were retiring or preparing to retire. This trend promised to open up job opportunities for succeeding generations.

However, experienced workers are not easy to replace. Some industries began to have shortages, and retirees were asked to return to the workforce. Retiring baby boomers, who made up a significant part of the workforce, were losses that could only be resolved with training younger workers.

New Opportunities and New Training

underemployed employed in a job below a worker's skill level, or employed only part-time

The changing economy has created new job opportunities in the high-tech and information sectors of the economy. However, these sectors demand skilled and educated workers. While young Canadians may need to spend more time in school, older Canadians have difficult choices. They may go back to school, or take lower-paying jobs in the service sector. Workers in the service sector may need more than one job to maintain a decent standard of living. As a result, some Canadians may become **underemployed**.

Employers now seek people with varied backgrounds, who can be flexibile and creative. Lifetime security at one job is now usually a thing of the past; in the new job market, people are often hired on contract. Employers still need traditional literacy and numeracy skills, but new workers also have to be computer literate. Most importantly, employers are looking for workers with creative-thinking skills.

FIGURE 8–29 As the workplace changes, training programs may have to change as well. Will programs that offer training for work in primary and secondary sectors be eliminated in the future? Why or why not?

Many options for the new economy revolve around technology and production. General Motors of Canada's Autoplex plant in Oshawa, Ontario, is an example. In the 1980s, GMC began an $8 billion program designed to develop a high-tech, synchronized manufacturing complex. This was a radical change. In traditional mass production, cars move along an assembly line, and workers complete specific tasks until the vehicle is finished. In the new system, auto frames are moved to different work areas. Parts for individual vehicles are then assembled at each station. Robotic systems deliver parts to each section so that each car can be built to customer specifications.

Another advantage for GMC is that parts do not have to be produced or stored at the Autoplex, since they are made by other companies and delivered to the assembly plant. This shift resulted in increased productivity, efficiency, and quality. It created new high-tech jobs. However, the system is vulnerable, especially when parts are not delivered on time. The system has seen the loss of traditional assembly line jobs, which increased during the economic crisis of 2008–2009.

Canadian companies that are able to adapt to changing times and improve their technological capacity and mass production techniques can compete in the global economy. They can offer high-end products built by a well-educated and productive workforce. Those businesses unable or unwilling to undergo the necessary changes may not survive.

• In Chapter 7, you read about advances in communications and transportation during the Laurier era. Compare them with modern technological advances. How have things changed?

FIGURE 8–30 GMC's high-tech Autoplex plant in Oshawa, Ontario

FIGURE 8–31 An automobile assembly line in Tokyo, Japan.

The Effects of Globalization

As a result of globalization, some Canadian companies closed their factories and relocated in the United States and Mexico. These companies were attracted by lower labour costs and weaker labour and environmental regulations. Producers also took advantage of open trade agreements and innovations in communication, transportation, and manufacturing.

These changes were happening worldwide. Competition increased among developed and developing nations, and among businesses. In order to survive, many smaller companies **merged** with larger corporations. Some firms disappeared altogether. Globalization was used to justify corporate downsizing and the reduction of full-time jobs. People lost jobs, whether on the factory floor or in management offices.

merge to join companies together, usually resulting in job losses

Opposition to Globalization

> We must ensure that the global market is embedded in broadly shared values and practices that reflect social needs, and that all the world's people share the benefits of globalization.
>
> —Kofi Annan, secretary general of the United Nations, 2000

What does Kofi Annan's statement mean to you? Those who oppose globalization say it has a negative effect on economies, jobs, and the economic independence of countries. They also voice concern about global environmental and labour issues.

Many serious questions about globalization have yet to be answered: How can Canadian governments enforce laws protecting the environment and human rights if multinational businesses can pack up and move at the flick of a switch? If globalization continues, what role will national governments play? Will corporations have more power than governments?

FIGURE 8–34 More than 20 000 anti-globalization protesters gathered in Quebec City in 2001 to demonstrate against a proposed Free Trade Area of the Americas. As you read in Chapter 2, the right to peaceful protest is guaranteed by the Canadian Charter of Rights and Freedoms. Do you think mass protests are an effective way to promote change? Explain.

ACTIVITIES

1. Use the laws of supply and demand to explain the rise and fall of the Canadian production of trucks and SUVs.

2. A developer buys farmland in order to create a high-tech business park.

   a) List the economic benefits of the development.

   b) Explain why local farmers, environmentalists, and other citizens would oppose the plan.

3. Produce a chart listing the advantages and disadvantages of the GMC Autoplex from the perspective of a) the company; b) the workers; and c) consumers.

   Patterns and Change

4. In what ways has globalization been an example of progress? How has it brought about decline?

Canada in North America

> How has being the neighbour of the United States affected Canada's economic development?

> *Living next to you [the United States] is in some ways like sleeping with an elephant. No matter how friendly and even-tempered the beast, if I can call it that, one is affected by every twitch and grunt.*
>
> —Prime Minister Pierre Elliott Trudeau, 1969

bilateral between two nations

NAFTA a trilateral trade agreement between Canada, the United States, and Mexico

trilateral between three nations

What is your response to Trudeau's description of Canada's relationship with the United States? The United States has had an overwhelming economic influence on Canada. Canada's **bilateral** relationship with its neighbour has always been rooted in an awareness of the size and power of the U.S. As Trudeau's statement suggests, the influence of the U.S. is felt in almost every facet of Canadian life, especially economics. It is an influence that has grown since the North American Free Trade Agreement (**NAFTA**) which was launched in 1994. Canada, the U.S., and Mexico became partners in a **trilateral** arrangement that further changed the Canadian economy. Together they made up the world's largest free trade area.

A Branch-Plant Economy

In the 19th century, Canada was still a young, sparsely populated country. Investment capital was needed for further economic development, and British investment was crucial for Canadian businesses at that time. British investors lent money to Canadian entrepreneurs who, though indebted, became owners of their businesses.

As British investment and involvement in Canada diminished in the early 20th century, American investment increased. However, Americans invested in Canada by buying out Canadian businesses or opening their own enterprises. As a result, many businesses were neither owned nor controlled by Canadians.

By setting up branch operations in Canada, American multinationals could get around the high tariffs that John A. Macdonald's National Policy had placed on American products to guard the Canadian market. As companies operating within Canada, they could produce and sell their goods and services to Canadian consumers.

This trend resulted in a **branch-plant economy** in Canada. American multinationals continued to set up more factories, offices, and stores in Canada. The National Policy and the branch-plant economy co-existed without much challenge until the late 1960s and early 1970s.

DID YOU KNOW...

In 1968, the federal government established the CRTC, the Canadian Radio-television and Telecommunications Commission. Its purpose was to promote Canadian content in broadcasting and to preserve and nourish Canadian culture. By 1970, the CRTC issued its first Canadian-content regulations. Do you think the CRTC has been successful?

branch-plant economy an economy that has a high percentage of factories, offices, and stores owned by foreign interests

FIGURE 8–35 Prime Minister Jean Chrétien pays a visit to American President Bill Clinton in this editorial cartoon from *The Globe and Mail*. What point is the cartoonist making by showing the switching of the maps?

sectoral belonging to a distinct area of economic activity

managed trade a trade relationship that has built-in protection if one partner does not meet negotiated terms

WEB LINK • • • • • • • • • • • • • • •
Watch a multimedia presentation about the Auto Pact on the Pearson Web site.

Sectoral Free Trade and the Auto Pact

Sectoral free trade was a popular economic policy in the 1960s, when Canada and the United States entered into numerous trade agreements. One example of sectoral free trade is the Canada–U.S. Auto Pact, which was signed in 1965. At that time, Canada's car manufacturing industry was struggling. Assembly plants produced limited quantities of cars and trucks for the Canadian market. Production costs were high, and Canadian consumers paid the price. Something had to change.

The Auto Pact guaranteed freer trade between the two countries in auto parts and vehicles. A clause in the agreement ruled that North American-based manufacturers, such as Ford, had to assemble one automobile in Canada for each new car bought in Canada.

The Auto Pact was an example of **managed trade**. Canadian production rose and branch plants began to build models for the entire North American market. By 1968, 70 percent of vehicles made in Canada were being exported to the United States. The auto industry became a leader in the Canadian economy. However, the branch plants were still owned by American companies. This had significant effects on the Canadian manufacturing sector during the economic crisis of 2008–2009.

Economic Nationalism

Canadians had welcomed American and other foreign investment during the economic boom after the Second World War. Most Canadians were also pleased with the nature of sectoral free trade with the United States. However, some Canadians started to worry about the long-term consequences of a branch-plant economy and dependence on the United States as a trade partner. Often American multinationals sent American managers to run their branch-plant operations in Canada rather than hire Canadians. They also tended to spend little money on research and development in Canada. In a phenomenon known as the **brain drain**, many educated young Canadians migrated to the United States where they could work in research and development or move up the corporate ladder. In addition, the profits from the branch plants tended to flow back to the United States to be used to finance the company's projects in other countries.

In the early 1970s, Prime Minister Pierre Elliott Trudeau developed programs to monitor and control the growth of foreign investment. The government's objective was to protect the Canadian economy from domination by the U.S. and other foreign investors. The Canada Development Corporation (CDC) was the result. It was designed to promote investment and development in Canadian-controlled companies. The Trudeau government clearly had a nationalist economic agenda. In 1980, it introduced the National Energy Program (NEP). This program was designed to make Canada self-sufficient in its oil supply and to increase Canadian ownership in the energy sector.

These programs significantly reduced Amercian domination in the Canadian economy; however, many Canadian business leaders were critical of the measures and the government's increased regulation of the economy. The American government also complained, threatening to retaliate against Canadian firms operating in the United States.

FIGURE 8–36 Petro-Canada was created in 1975 as a Canadian-owned presence in the oil and natural gas industries. How would this company benefit Canadians? Find out what its position is in the world today.

brain drain the emigration of people with technical skills and knowledge to a country with greater employment opportunities

countervailing tariff a special tax that protects domestic products from subsidized foreign imports

anti-dumping duty a special tariff imposed on imports being sold at unreasonably low prices

softwood lumber wood such as pine and spruce that is used in building

Protectionism

Many Canadians became alarmed when they heard protectionist rhetoric from members of the U.S. Congress. When a series of **countervailing tariffs** and **anti-dumping duties** were slapped on Canadian products entering the U.S., trade conflicts between Canada and the U.S. became common. The most famous and longest lasting of these was the **softwood lumber** dispute.

Continentalism

The governments of Pierre Trudeau and John Turner, from 1968 to 1984, promoted more sectoral free-trade agreements. Then a major policy change occurred when Brian Mulroney became prime minister in 1984. There was an immediate shift in Canada's economic direction.

continentalist supporting further integration of the North American economies

The Mulroney government had a **continentalist** attitude, one which favoured less government interference in the economy and freer markets in North America. Shortly after taking office, Mulroney gave a speech in New York City where he told American business leaders that Canada was "open for business." Shortly after this, the National Energy Program ended and Investment Canada was created, an agency that was friendly to American and foreign investment. Then, rather than promoting sectoral trade, the Mulroney government went much further. It proposed that Canada negotiate a free trade-arrangement with the United States.

Zoom In ⊙ The Softwood Lumber Dispute

 CRITICAL INQUIRY Judgements

The Softwood Lumber Dispute, a trade conflict between Canada and the United States, has lasted for decades. There have been numerous renegotiations and partial agreements over the years.

At the centre of the dispute is the American objection to Canadian stumpage fees, which forestry companies must pay to gain rights to harvest trees. Since provincial governments own much of the forested land in Canada, they determine the fee.

American groups said the fees were too low, creating a subsidy for Canadian foresters. Calling this unfair competition, they lobbied their government to impose tariffs on softwood lumber entering the U.S. from Canada. This was a huge blow to Canadian forestry companies, costing them billions of dollars and putting hundreds of people out of work.

To compromise, the Canadian government agreed to collect an export tax on softwood lumber. This tax raised the cost of Canadian lumber, but at least the tax money stayed in Canada. However, many felt that this decision gave the U.S. influence over

Canadian tax policies, putting Canadian sovereignty at stake.

In 2002, the World Trade Organization ruled that it was wrong for the U.S. to impose punishing duties on Canadian softwood. Later, a NAFTA panel also ruled in favour of Canada. But some foresters believed that the U.S. was willing to ignore international laws. The Americans were still collecting tariffs, now numbered in billions of dollars, and

Canadian mills were still closing. In 2006, another agreement was reached. The U.S. would pay back 80 percent of the money it had collected, and Canadian lumber would take up no more than 34 percent of the American market.

- How can the history of the softwood lumber dispute influence the judgements of the Canadian government and businesses in the future?

FIGURE 8–37 Protesters in the softwood lumber dispute march in Vancouver in 2001. How did this dispute affect people in British Columbia?

Political cartoons are a useful source of information about historical or current issues. They present strong viewpoints that either praise or criticize current situations and ongoing public issues. Cartoonists use their drawings to try to convince their readers to see an issue in a specific way.

Political cartoons expose the unsettling and unflattering side of politics and politicians through satire and humour. Cartoonists use caricatures, or exaggerated drawings, to represent well-known individuals and iconic symbols that depict nations or interest groups. By identifying these caricatures and symbols, the reader can understand the message of the cartoon.

Look at the following political cartoons. Decipher the symbols being used and the cartoonist's message, and consider the validity of the content. Ask yourself:

1. What is the cartoon about?

2. Who appears in the cartoon?

3. If you cannot identify everyone, can you guess who they might be or represent?

4. Did you find the cartoon effective, funny, or both? Think about why.

• How is each cartoon biased? Provide examples to explain your answer.

• To what extent has analyzing these cartoons changed how you understand and view the Softwood Lumber Dispute?

• Draw your own cartoon on this issue from an American perspective. Share your cartoon with a partner and then with the class.

FIGURE 8–38 How is American big business depicted? How is the United States government depicted? What point is the cartoonist making?

FIGURE 8–39 This 2006 cartoon uses symbols to represent the United States and Canada. Why are they used? What is the message of the cartoon? Is the cartoonist supportive of the Softwood Lumber Agreement?

Freer Trade

fair trade the removal of trade barriers such as tariffs, quotas, and regulations

freer trade a trade relationship that has reduced its protective measures, but not entirely

marketing boards an association of food producers that control the marketing and pricing of their product

In the last decades of the 20th century, many trade barriers in North America were removed under "free trade" agreements. **Free trade** means the complete removal of all trade barriers. In reality, free trade is difficult to achieve, so these agreements were actually "*freer* trade" agreements. **Freer trade** is a compromise, involving the removal of some trade barriers but still allowing protective measures.

The Canada–United States Free Trade Agreement

In 1985, Prime Minister Mulroney and President Reagan began talks to arrange a free trade agreement between Canada and the United States. Public reaction was passionate and divided in both countries. In Canada, those who opposed the agreement feared that it would allow American businesses to exploit Canada's economy. Those who supported free trade argued that without it, Canada's economy would decline and become uncompetitive globally. Critics on both sides of the border criticized the talks for not promoting **fair trade**.

Nonetheless, an agreement was reached and on January 1, 1989, and the Canada–U.S. Free Trade Agreement (FTA) came into effect. The agreement covered every economic sector and included the following features and terms:

- No export subsidies were permitted.

- Canada's restrictions on foreign ownership were reduced.

- All restrictions on energy exports and imports were removed.

- The Auto Pact and Canada's agricultural **marketing boards** were maintained.

- Canada's cultural industries—publishing, television, cable, satellite broadcasting, movies, music, and radio—were exempt.

- Trade barriers were reduced, but both nations could, and did, impose measures if they felt trading practices were unfair. The dispute over softwood lumber is one example. The Free Trade Dispute Panel worked, but often slowly. Still, within five years, trade between the two nations increased greatly, and Canada enjoyed a large trade surplus.

For many Canadians, the big concern about the FTA came down to the sheer size and power of the American economy compared with Canada's. They complained that because American lobby groups were so powerful, the U.S. was favoured in trade disputes. However, Americans complained that Canadian industry was unfairly subsidized by Canadian government programs. These disputes are ongoing and not easily resolved.

FIGURE 8–40 A Mexican corn farmer holds a poster that reads, "No country without corn." Mexican farmers compete with American farmers, who get billions of dollars in subsidies from the U.S. government. Would a protective tariff be justified in this situation?

The North American Free Trade Agreement

On January 1, 1994, a new era in North American trade began when the North American Free Trade Agreement (NAFTA) came into effect. NAFTA expanded the existing Canada–United States free trade area to include Mexico and set out a schedule to reduce tariffs over a ten-year period.

Canada's membership in NAFTA and its trade agreements with Chile, Costa Rica, Peru, and Colombia brought Latin American issues to the forefront. Canadians became more aware of human rights concerns, environmental problems, and labour issues in this region of the world. Some Canadian groups argued that safeguards were needed.

Critics of NAFTA were concerned about the human rights of Mexicans in the southern province of Chiapas. They believed that people were being exploited for the sake of the new global economy.

Environmentalists worried that Canadian mining companies operating in Latin America would cause increased ecological damage. Canadian companies might also add to rain forest depletion and land pollution.

Many Canadians also feared that jobs could be lost if companies moved to Latin America to exploit cheaper labour, particularly child labour. It is estimated that one in five children in Latin America—about 15 to 18 million children—work on a daily basis. Many of these children work under conditions that do not meet Canadian standards. In urban areas, children—including those escaping the poverty of the countryside—are often employed in manufacturing. For example, in Mexico, some **maquiladoras** along the U.S. border have become notorious for exploiting impoverished girls who work long hours for low wages.

International and regional organizations are working hard to assist homeless children, eliminate child labour, and fight poverty, but progress has been slow.

- Should safeguards regarding the environment, human rights, and labour issues be added to the trade agreements between Canada and Latin America? Why or why not?

- With a partner, conduct a Web search about maquiladoras in Mexico. One partner should look for material that promotes maquiladoras from the viewpoints of economic growth and profit. The other should search for information about labour conditions and environmental impact. Pool your findings and write a summary report of your discoveries.

maquiladora a Latin American factory run by a foreign company and exporting its products to the country of that company, often exploiting cheap labour

FIGURE 8–41 A woman assembles American auto parts at a plant in a maquiladora near the Mexico–U.S. border. Why might companies be attracted to maquiladoras? Why would people be willing to work there?

As you learned in Chapter 3, the colonies of Canada, New Brunswick, and Nova Scotia joined together in a political and economic union in 1867. Why did New Brunswick and Nova Scotia join, even though Canada had the potential to dominate the new economic relationship? Some people asked a similar question when Canada and Mexico joined with the United States in NAFTA.

New Brunswickers and Nova Scotians in the 19th century were probably more familiar with free trade and economic unions than Canadians in the 20th century. From 1794 to 1846, the British North American colonies enjoyed preferential tariffs (such as the Corn Laws) when trading with Britain. These gave the colonies an edge over their American competitors. When Britain repealed the tariffs in 1846, the British North American economy fell into a depression. Colonial governments began to look for alternatives, such as the Reciprocity Treaty with the United States, which lasted less than 10 years. Once again, colonial leaders in New Brunswick and Nova Scotia looked for economic alternatives. One option was Confederation with Canada.

Many New Brunswickers and Nova Scotians opposed the plan, seeing that Canada would be the dominant partner in the economic union. Indeed, New Brunswick and Nova Scotia would become resource-based economies that supplied raw materials to the industrial heartland—central Canada. Central Canada's manufacturing industries then sold their finished goods back to the other regions. This practice has been an issue since 1867.

When Canada joined NAFTA in 1994, there were bitter debates about the long-term consequences of joining a partnership with a dominant United States. Supporters of free trade said that Canada and Mexico had to join the United States to counteract the worldwide trend toward trade blocs. Their rationale was that if Canada and Mexico did not join, both would be left behind in the global economy.

Trade and investment did increase tremendously. Trilateral trade between the "three amigos" more than doubled in the first 12 years of the agreement. But critics point to the increased corporate power exercised by American-based companies and American dominance in the energy and commodities sectors.

- What other correlations can you draw between Confederation and NAFTA? Are there any historic patterns that may provide some clues to future trends? Explain.

Hup~ two~three ~four !

FIGURE 8–42 The large figure wearing the striped pants is Uncle Sam, a symbol of the United States. How does this image reflect a viewpoint of NAFTA? Draw an editorial cartoon that would show a critical viewpoint of the economic consequences of Confederation between Nova Scotia, New Brunswick, and Canada.

The Canadian Perspective on NAFTA

For Canada, NAFTA's provisions were mostly carry-overs from the 1989 Canada–U.S. Free Trade Agreement. However, there were additions and changes. The Auto Pact, for example, was preserved, but the North American content requirement was raised. Canada's marketing boards for eggs, poultry, and dairy products were left untouched, but tariffs on all other food products had to be removed by 2009.

Canada also agreed to share available energy sources with the United States when and if that country experienced a shortage. This development completely undercut the goals of the National Energy Program. Canadian nationalists viewed this as a threat to the future of Canada's energy supply.

Some Canadian industries fully supported NAFTA. Telecommunications and transportation companies expected to increase business in Mexico, as did banks. Those in favour of NAFTA argued that Canada must adapt to the global economy by forging stronger international trade links.

An End to NAFTA?

In 2008, there were calls to renegotiate or even cancel NAFTA. The analysis of NAFTA's impact on the economies of Canada, Mexico, and the United States seems to depend on the perspective of the analyst: most labour-union organizations, nationalist groups, and human rights advocates are critical of NAFTA, while most corporations, trade groups, and government organizations support NAFTA.

> **DID YOU KNOW...**
> Under NAFTA, Canada also agreed to share bulk water supplies with the United States if that country were to experience serious water shortages. This provision provoked an outcry from environmentalists as well as nationalists.

FIGURE 8–43 American interest groups often successfully persuade their government to impose trade measures against Canadian products, such as lumber, beef, steel, and wheat. While Canadian lawyers can appeal, the process takes a long time. How might this aspect of free trade affect Canadian farmers and ranchers?

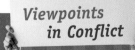

Canadians hold strong opinions about free trade and NAFTA. For some, it was a logical step in Canada's historic trade relationship with the United States and Mexico. For others, it was a blow to Canadian sovereignty. Many Canadians fall somewhere in between these two points of view.

> *Globalization and free trade do spur economic growth, and they lead to lower prices on many goods.*
>
> **—Robert Reich, American economist and former secretary of labour in the Clinton administration, 2005**

> *We're doing massive trade with the U.S., so there's no question in my mind that whatever the weaknesses might be, the general relationship has been an astounding success.*
>
> **—Simon Reisman, chief Canadian negotiator for the FTA, quoted in 1997**

> *I always felt Canadians would get a lot more self-confidence when they listened to all those doom and gloom stories and then realized this thing they feared for 100 years [free trade] turned out to be a modest step in the right direction.*
>
> **—Richard Lipsey, Canadian economist, 1997**

> *We are progressively moving towards American standards whether you look at the erosion in health care or the erosion in education or unemployment insurance. We were promised this agreement would bring us a better economy, a better standard of living... it has brought us none of these things.*
>
> **—Mel Hurtig, economic nationalist and publisher, 1997**

> *NAFTA was supposed to unleash a flood of foreign investment—boosting our industrial capacity and productivity. Instead... more than 95 percent of direct foreign investment has been used to buy up Canadian companies. Head offices and research and development money has headed south, and Canada has seen a steady decline in manufactured goods as a percentage of its GDP for the past ten years.*
>
> **—Murray Dobbin, columnist for online magazine *The Tyee*, in *The Globe and Mail*, March 5, 2008**

WHAT DO YOU THINK?

1. Analyze the different points of view. Classify them according to whether they favour free trade, oppose free trade, or fall somewhere in between. Are any of the viewpoints biased? Explain.

ACTIVITIES

1. Why do economic nationalists worry about foreign investment? Does it matter that Canada has been described as having a branch-plant economy?

2. What are the consequences of the Softwood Lumber Dispute for British Columbia? Do you believe the Softwood Lumber Agreement of 2006 resolved the issues?

Judgements

3. Look again at the primary sources in this section and analyze what they are saying about the relationship between Canada and its North American trading partners. Have these sources influenced your opinon about this issue? Explain.

Explore the Big Ideas

Will the 21st century "belong to Canada?" The answer may not be simple. Canada has become more urbanized, and its economy more concentrated in service industries. Many traditional economic activities have proved unsustainable. Technological innovations led to a more globalized economy, and the movement to freer trade led to trade agreements with the United States and Mexico. Some Canadians benefited from this, while others experienced negative consequences. One thing is clear: every region in Canada must continue to change, adapt, and diversify in order to sustain its economy, environment, and quality of life of its citizens.

1. Complete a table like the one below by providing information about every topic for each region.

	Atlantic Region	Great Lakes–St. Lawrence Region	Shield Region	North Region	Prairie Region
Aboriginal economy					
Natural resources					
Major economic activities					
Economic challenges					
Environmental challenges					

2. Given what you have learned about the changing Canadian economy, how might this influence your decision about potential careers? Consider factors such as supply and demand, "boom and bust" cycles, sustainability of resources, technological changes, and the impact of globalization.

3. Debate the following resolution: Canada should renegotiate NAFTA. The debate should have speakers for and against the resolution, opening statements, rebuttals, and closing statements. Find quotes, graphs, and tables, and other primary sources that you can use to support the side you are arguing.

4. Choose one of the companies mentioned in this chapter. Conduct an Internet research project updating information about the current status of the company. Has the company prospered or experienced some difficulties? Explain in detail and include proper references to the Web sites that you visited.

5. Based on what you have learned in this chapter, make predictions about Canada's economic future. Will Canada be able to sustain its economy and environment and society in the 21st century? Why or why not?

6. Public opinion is still divided regarding free trade. Why is free trade an ongoing issue? Provide details to support your conclusion. Which side of the issue do you support? Why?

9 | The Economy and Environment of British Columbia

CRITICAL
INQUIRY

Significance

Patterns and
Change

Judgements

Evidence

Cause and
Consequence

Perspectives

While the port of Vancouver connects British Columbia to the rest of the world, the mountains are often seen as a barrier between B.C. and the rest of Canada. These geographical features help determine the identity of British Columbians. For painter Emily Carr, whose painting *Totem Forest* is shown here, the appeal of British Columbia lay in its "power and intensity everywhere." What is your response to the views of Bruce Hutchison (below) and Emily Carr?

How have the physical landscape and resources of British Columbia affected the province's economy? How has economic growth had an impact on the environment?

British Columbia faces many changes in the 21st century. Dwindling fish stocks, a reduced supply of timber, and fewer opportunities for mining have underscored the shift from abundance to scarcity. A changing economy, a growing population, and an increasingly fragile environment are some of the challenges people face as they look to the future of British Columbia.

Key Terms

renewable

non-renewable

stewardship

value-added

allowable
annual cut

silviculture

Agricultural
Land
Reserve (ALR)

diversification

arable

carbon tax

multiplier effect

Crossing the Rockies, you are in a new country, as if you had crossed a national frontier. Everyone feels it; even the stranger feels the change of outlook, tempo, and attitude.

—Bruce Hutchison, British Columbian journalist and author

British Columbia's Economy and Resources

TIMELINE

1912 ● British Columbia passes first Forest Act

1913 ● Last year of the great salmon runs on the Fraser River (38 million sockeye)

1914 ● Rock Slide at Hell's Gate partially blocks the Fraser River

1945 ● Hell's Gate Fishways is opened to help salmon bypass the Fraser River rapids

1947 ● Forest Act is revised

1973 ● Agricultural Land Commission is formed

1987 ● United Nations Report of the World Commission on Environment and Development

1990 ● Salmon fishery and mining in B.C. decline

1995 ● Forest Practices Code created

1996 ● Federal government cuts B.C. salmon fleet

2000 ● Mountain pine beetle is recognized as a threat to forests

2008 ● Carbon tax introduced

2010 ● Vancouver/Whistler host the Winter Olympics

▶ **How have British Columbia's resources determined the type of economy that has developed there?**

British Columbia has a vast and varied landscape and coastline. Its 952 263 square kilometres include mountains, plateaus, plains, valleys, and coastal islands. Canada's third-largest province is nearly three times the size of Japan and four times the size of Great Britain.

British Columbia's size and physical diversity have influenced the province's economy in many ways. From the earliest times, people have drawn on the land's natural resources—fish, furs, metals, and timber. Although the province's dependency on forestry, fishing, and mining is decreasing, much of its wealth still comes from these primary industries.

Today, the service sector is a significant part of the economy, a trend seen in many industrialized countries. Tourism and filmmaking, along with other service industries, are growing at an impressive rate. Another area of growth is high technology, in both development and information. As you learned in Chapter 8, many changes have taken place in the Canadian economy. The economy of British Columbia is no exception.

British Columbia's top 12 industries by percent of labour force in 2006

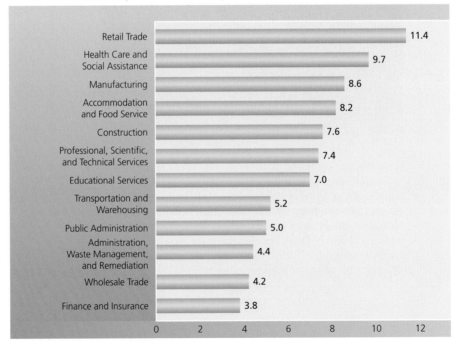

FIGURE 9–1 From these statistics, what two generalizations can you make about future trends in British Colombia's economy?

Boom and Bust in a Global Economy

Modern resource-based economies like British Columbia's depend on global customers, and these economies are therefore affected by the ebb and flow of global demand. For example, the commodities boom at the beginning of the 21st century turned into a bust when worldwide demand declined rapidly as a result of a global recession in 2008–2009. Commodity prices fell, as did the Canadian dollar.

Provincial and federal governments have little power or influence to manage this aspect of the resource-based economy. They can predict future trends and prepare resource-based industries for disruptions, but ultimately, the globalized nature of the modern resource-based economy makes provincial and federal policies and practices susceptible to surprises.

Look at the map below, which shows the Cordillera economic region. Which regions do you think might be most vulnerable to booms and busts in the global economy?

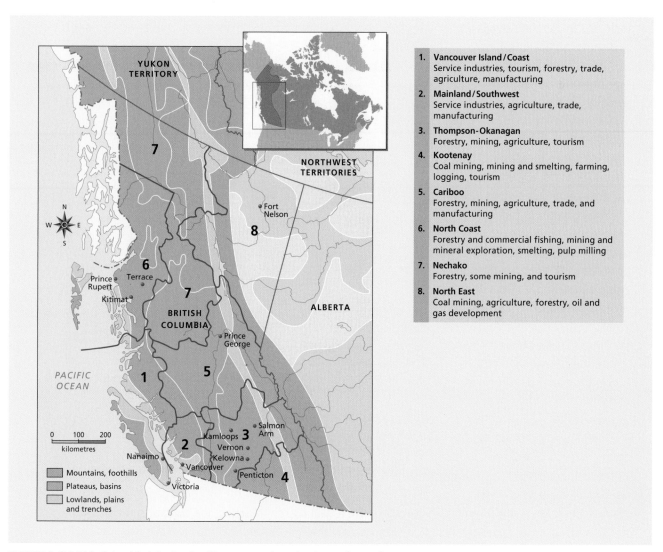

1. **Vancouver Island/Coast**
   Service industries, tourism, forestry, trade, agriculture, manufacturing

2. **Mainland/Southwest**
   Service industries, agriculture, trade, manufacturing

3. **Thompson-Okanagan**
   Forestry, mining, agriculture, tourism

4. **Kootenay**
   Coal mining, mining and smelting, farming, logging, tourism

5. **Cariboo**
   Forestry, mining, agriculture, trade, and manufacturing

6. **North Coast**
   Forestry and commercial fishing, mining and mineral exploration, smelting, pulp milling

7. **Nechako**
   Forestry, some mining, and tourism

8. **North East**
   Coal mining, agriculture, forestry, oil and gas development

FIGURE 9–2 British Columbia is in the Cordillera economic region (part of Canada's economic regions, as you studied in Chapter 8). B.C. can also be divided into small, diverse economic regions, shown here. How would physical features, geology, distance from the coast, and climate help determine the economy of these regions?

British Columbia has had a long history of connections with the **Asia Pacific** region. Most of British Columbia's exports go to the United States or within Canada, but more and more raw materials are being shipped across the Pacific Ocean to Asian nations.

Although Japan remained British Columbia's leading Asian trade partner at the beginning of the 21st century, there were increases in commodity exports to other Asia Pacific nations.

China, in particular, created high demand for natural resources, which resulted in a global commodity boom. Canada benefited from this trend. However, when the demand for commodities decreased, the Canadian economy slowed down.

The economy of Canada experienced other consequences due to exploding economic activity in Asia. For example, cheaper manufactured goods from Asia entered the Canadian market, creating challenges for Canadian producers. Some Canadian companies outsourced their production to the cheaper labour pools of Asia, creating unemployment in Canada.

Nonetheless, Canada has been proactive in its dealings with Asian countries. Canada and British Columbia have made efforts to increase their presence in Asia-Pacific trade. The federal government approved a Foreign Investment Protection and Promotion Agreement with India

in 2008, and has been actively negotiating a Free Trade Agreement with South Korea. Some economic and international business experts have also recommended that Canada try

to open free trade negotiations with Japan.

Asia Pacific a sub-region of the Pacific Rim; includes nations with Pacific coastlines on the western Pacific plus nations that have close political and economic connections with those countries

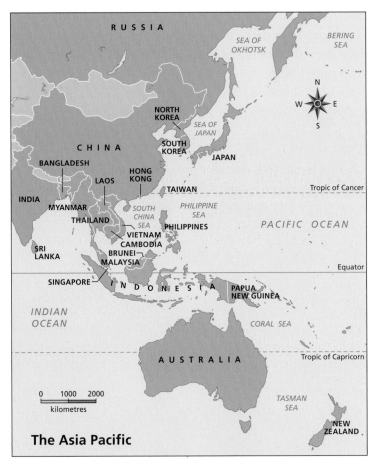

The Asia Pacific

FIGURE 9–3 Do you think Canada should have a free trade agreement with countries in the Pacific Rim? Explain.

WHAT DO YOU THINK?

1. Are you interested in working in the Asia Pacific in the future? Explain why or why not.

2. Complete a Web search to explore the cultural and economic connections between British Columbia and the Asia Pacific.
    a) Is commodity trade still booming? Explain.
    b) Is Asian immigration to Canada continuing? Why or why not?
    c) What conclusions can you draw from these trends?

British Columbia's Resources

With its varied physical geography and climate, British Columbia has incredibly diverse ecosystems. Differences among regions within the province has affected how people work and live in a resource-based economy. Although the economy has recently become more diversified, with the tertiary sector playing a greater role, exports from the province are still largely resource based, both **renewable** and **non-renewable**.

Abundant forest and Pacific fish stocks have made forestry and fishing major renewable resource industries in the province. Hydroelectric power is another growing renewable resource, and many other forms of renewable energy, such as solar and wind power, are being developed. The sustainability of these resources is affected by many forces, such as overharvesting, pollution, climate change, and urban growth. Increasingly, people are recognizing the need for stewardship and sustainability of these resources. Look at the graph below. What does it tell you about the role of the forestry industry in British Columbia? How might concerns about sustainability affect this industry in the future?

Oil, natural gas, and minerals are B.C.'s main non-renewable resources. They owe their existence to the region's complex geology. The rise and fall in world demand for these resources has played a major role in the boom-and-bust nature of the British Columbia economy.

renewable resources that can be replaced, for example, trees or fish

non-renewable resources that cannot be replaced, for example, mineral deposits or fossil fuels

FIGURE 9–4 Gasoline prices in Canada hit a record high in the summer of 2008 when the world price for crude oil skyrocketed. By late November, the average price of a litre of gas had fallen to $0.83. In what ways might high gas prices affect British Columbia's economy?

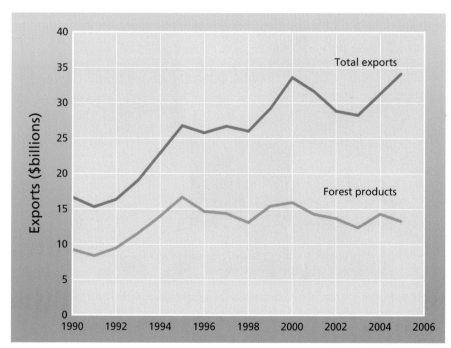

FIGURE 9–5 Forest products, which include wood and paper, are British Columbia's most important export commodity. However, they account for a decreasing share of total international shipments.

Sustainability and Stewardship

As British Columbia's population and economy have grown, so too have demands placed on the land and on the resource base. Today people are beginning to realize that there are limits to resource development. Increasingly, people question uncontrolled exploitation of resources and its impact on the environment. Sustainability seeks a balance between a sound economy and concern for the environment. Balance is maintained when a resource is not used faster than the time it takes to replace it. We no longer see ourselves as simply consumers of resources. We are also the managers, or stewards, for future generations.

Stewardship assumes a respect for the earth and its resources and a commitment to protect the environment. The British Columbia Ministry of Environment and most other ministries have an environmental stewardship division. Thinking about sustainability and stewardship forces us to think about how the environment might provide for all species, today and in the future. Some environmentalists argue that we need to go much further in our thinking. They say that we need to acknowledge that our practice of overconsumption and its effect on the environment cannot be labelled sustainable by any measure. According to David Suzuki, "Our personal consumer choices have ecological, social, and spiritual consequences. It is time to re-examine some of our deeply held notions that underlie our lifestyles."

stewardship cooperative planning and management of environmental resources with the goal of sustaining those resources

FIGURE 9–6 What statement about our rate of consumption does this photo make?

FIGURE 9–7 What solution to our consumption of natural resources does this photo suggest?

ACTIVITIES

1. What is the difference between renewable and non-renewable resources? Is one type of resource better than the other? Explain.

2. Which economic regions of British Columbia do you think are most affected by a drop in the export market? Explain.

3. Examine a recent example of the effect of globalization on your community. Consider cost and availability of items, employment and labour issues, and any other relevant factors.

4. Explain the relationship between British Columbia's natural resources and a "boom and bust" economic cycle.

Forestry in British Columbia

▶ **Can the forestry industry in British Columbia be sustainable?**

Forests cover about 60 million hectares in British Columbia. Approximately 49.9 million hectares are considered productive forest land, and 48 million hectares are provincial Crown land, managed by the Ministry of Forests. How do you think B.C.'s forests should be used?

Since the late 1800s, wood products from British Columbia have been shipped around the world. Although its dominance of the economy is in decline, foresty remains the mainstay of B.C.'s exports. Logging and the manufacture of forest products provide more employment and contribute more **value added** than any other industrial sector in British Columbia. In 2008, more than 80 000 jobs relied on the forest industry. Outside of the lower mainland and Victoria, forestry is an important source of income for many communities.

value added economic value added to a product at each stage of its production

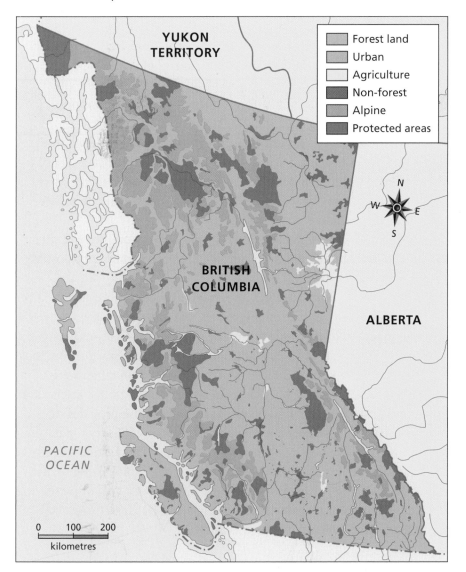

Legend:
- Forest land
- Urban
- Agriculture
- Non-forest
- Alpine
- Protected areas

YUKON TERRITORY

BRITISH COLUMBIA

ALBERTA

PACIFIC OCEAN

0   100   200
kilometres

FIGURE 9–8 Forests cover two-thirds of British Columbia's landscape. Urban and agricultural areas make up only about 2 percent of the province. The rest consists of mountain and alpine areas and glaciers. Based on information provided by this map, what conclusions can you draw about British Columbia's economy?

However, concern is growing about the sustainability of the forest industry. People have looked for new, creative ways to add value to harvested wood. The industry is also affected by ups and downs in the global economy. Workers are laid off when the demand for forest products goes down, and they are rehired when demand goes up. More and more, people are recognizing the necessity of thinking about the industry and the forest itself in the long term.

The United Nations Intergovernmental Panel on Climate Change (IPCC) emphasized the importance of forests in ensuring our economic well-being and in reducing the effects of climate change.

mitigate to reduce in force or intensity

allowable annual cut the number of trees that can be legally cut down in a year

silviculture nurturing tree growth from seed to maturity

> *...a sustainable forest management strategy aimed at maintaining or increasing forest carbon stocks, while producing an annual sustained yield of timber... will generate the largest sustained **mitigation** benefit.*
>
> —IPCC, 4th Assessment Report, November 2007

Forestry Practices

The expansion of Canada's railway system benefited the lumber industry in British Columbia, and settlement of the Prairies provided new markets for lumber as British Columbia's trade shifted east-west after Confederation. Investment in the forest industry in 1900 was about $2 million. Only 10 years later, it had grown to $65 million.

During these years of expansion, uncontrolled cutting and wasteful logging practices went unmanaged by the provincial government. Public pressure forced the government to establish a Royal Commission on Timber and Forestry. This led to the 1912 Forest Act, which established a forest service to enforce new regulations.

In 1947, the Forest Act was revised. Logging companies were limited to an **allowable annual cut**—only as much timber could be cut as could be replaced by new growth.

More recently, **silviculture** has improved the yield of forests. Attention is paid to replanting, clearing undergrowth, and spacing the trees. In 1995, the Forest Practices Code was introduced, enforcing regulations for planting and reharvesting. In 2004, the Forest and Range Practices Act took effect to maintain environmental standards. Forestry companies were required to prepare stewardship plans, ensuring reforestation, conservation of soils, and protection of habitats and watersheds. It also provides rules for the construction, maintenance, and deactivation of forestry roads.

Finding a balance between protecting ecosystems and economic development is difficult, especially given the number of people relying on the forest industry. In 1992, the provincial government set a goal of preserving 12 percent of British Columbia forest as parkland. By 2007, protected areas covered 13.8 percent of British Columbia.

FIGURE 9–9 Today leaving a stump this high would be viewed as a wasteful forestry practice. When do you think this picture was taken? Explain why forestry practices have changed over the years.

FIGURE 9–10 Clear-cutting, when all the trees in an area are removed at the same time, is probably one of the most controversial forest practices. Today, clear-cutting is less common in response to pressure from environmentalists and consumers.

FIGURE 9–11 Selective logging, which is more expensive than clear-cutting, does less harm to the forest floor. Should companies' ability to make a profit affect sustainable practices? Explain.

Forest Industries in British Columbia

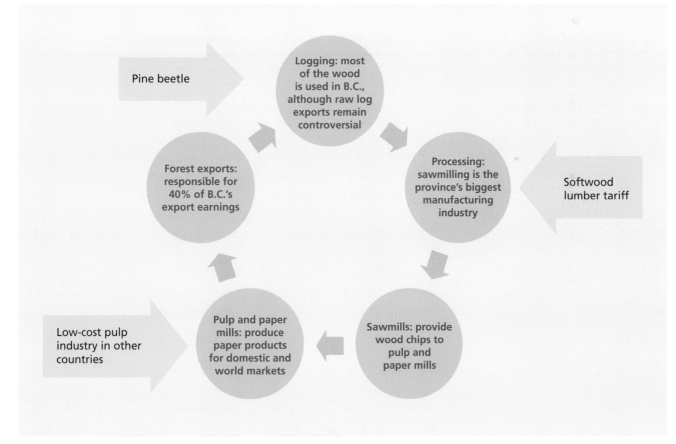

Pine beetle

Logging: most of the wood is used in B.C., although raw log exports remain controversial

Forest exports: responsible for 40% of B.C.'s export earnings

Processing: sawmilling is the province's biggest manufacturing industry

Softwood lumber tariff

Low-cost pulp industry in other countries

Pulp and paper mills: produce paper products for domestic and world markets

Sawmills: provide wood chips to pulp and paper mills

FIGURE 9–12 The yellow arrows in this diagram show some of the influences on the forest industry. Explain why all parts of the forestry industry are connected. Give an example of what might happen if one part of the industry experienced a downturn.

The Value of Old-Growth Forests

Old-growth trees can be from 120 to 250 years old. How much of British Columbia's old-growth forests need to be preserved to protect the forest ecosystem?

Old-growth forests are a unique resource, and not everyone views them the same way. Environmentalists say that old-growth forests help protect watershed ecosystems by anchoring topsoil, preventing erosion. Forest companies point to the economic value of the forest industry to the province. They argue that further restrictions on old-growth cutting will have a negative effect on the economy. For Aboriginal peoples, old-growth forests play a central role in their cultures, providing building materials for canoes and totem poles as well as sites for ceremonies. The recreation industry sees the growing popularity of ecotourism in wilderness areas, and says that old-growth forests offer a special opportunity for visitors.

A 2008 study by Simon Fraser University suggests that old-growth forests play a complex role in the environment, and that leaving old-growth forests standing may make more economic sense than cutting them down. In this case, conservation may win out over logging when forests are valued for their role in capturing carbon from the atmosphere, protecting species, and providing jobs in recreation.

FIGURE 9–13 Old-growth trees can be as high as 100 metres and provide organic material for a complex ecosystem in the trees and on the forest floor. What value of old-growth forests is suggested by this photo?

One of the most controversial forestry practices in British Columbia is the exporting of raw, or unprocessed, logs. While there is no ban on raw-log exports, there are restrictions on sales outside the province. The export of logs from private lands—a little over 10 percent of the total volume of timber—is under federal government control and can only take place if no buyer can be found in the province.

Timber harvested from Crown land must be used within British Columbia; exports are prohibited. However, an exemption is possible if the timber is part of a surplus (more than British Columbia facilities can handle), or if it cannot be processed economically near the harvesting area or transported economically to another facility.

According to the government, log exports make up a small percentage of British Columbia's total harvest; 95 percent of logs harvested are processed within the province. Opponents to raw log exports argue that when timber is not processed in British Columbia, jobs are lost and the value added of forestry products goes down. They believe that keeping timber processing within the province will keep the entire industry alive. Unions point out that exporting raw logs means exporting jobs, and other opponents say that companies use exemptions unfairly.

> *Log exports play an important role in the coastal economy by providing jobs in the logging and transportation sectors. Before logs can leave the province, exporters must prove that logs are surplus to domestic needs... Exporters must pay a "fee in lieu of manufacture" on logs they export from Crown land. Effective February 1, 2008, export fees on timber from Crown lands in the southern coastal region will be linked to the export tax on softwood lumber products shipped to the U.S.*
>
> —B.C. Ministry of Forests and Range

> *...B.C. has seen a dramatic fall in forest-sector employment because, despite government and industry claims to the contrary, log exports equal job losses. It simply stands to reason: With fewer logs to process in B.C. sawmills and less wood for value-added plants, we have seen about 50 major wood-processing facilities close their doors for good... That's why B.C. has lost more than 20 000 good-paying jobs since 2001.*
>
> —Bob Matters, United Steelworkers Wood Council Chair, *Vancouver Sun*, August 25, 2008

FIGURE 9–14 Anti-logging protesters. What could be the short-term and long-term consequences of ending all export of British Columbia logs?

WHAT DO YOU THINK?

1. How do you account for the opposing points of view expressed by these two sources?

2. What improvements to the restrictions set by the government on log exports would further protect the forest industry in British Columbia?

The Mountain Pine Beetle

It is hard to believe that an insect the size of a grain of rice can cause such devastation to the forests of British Columbia. The mountain pine beetle threatens dramatic environmental, economic, and social upheaval.

The pine beetle infestation began around the year 2000. The infestation grew rapidly for several reasons. Warmer winters meant that the beetle could survive in areas that had previously been inhospitable. Forest management geared to limiting forest fires resulted in large stands of mature lodgepole pines, the ideal food supply for the beetles. As well, fewer natural forest fires meant that infestations would not be destroyed. This also allowed for fewer opportunities for new pine to grow. Eighty percent of British Columbia's mature pine forests are expected to be killed by pine beetles, a catastrophe that will significantly reduce the province's wood supply by 2013. Only cold winters and a lack of food will stop the progress of the infestation.

The spread of the pine beetle has a profound effect on the environment. Forests act as carbon sinks, absorbing and storing carbon dioxide. Dead trees stop storing carbon—they actually begin to release the stored carbon back into the atmosphere. Not all the dead trees can be harvested, which adds to the risk of uncontrollable wildfires.

The pine beetle moves with the wind, from west to east. By 2008, it had firmly taken root in the pine forests of northern Alberta. This has raised fears that global warming may allow the insects to survive in the jackpine of the boreal forests all the way to Labrador.

FIGURE 9–15 The mountain pine beetle, which is about the size of a grain of rice, tunnels through tree bark to lay its eggs.

FIGURE 9–16 The red trees in this image are in the first year of a pine beetle attack. When beetles first attack a tree, they release a fungus that stains the wood. The wood remains structurally sound and can still be used. Can you think of uses for beetle-stained wood that take advantage of this effect?

After the Beetle

For communities in British Columbia's interior, the mountain pine beetle infestation is a natural disaster. Forest-dependent communities must deal with the economic, environmental, and cultural effects of the infestation.

The B.C. government's Mountain Pine Beetle Action Plan allows an increase in annual cuts, which is a measure to salvage as much beetle-killed wood as possible. The government also encourages clear-cutting of pine forest in an attempt to stop the spread of the beetles. Environmentalists have criticized this practice, pointing out that it threatens surviving species of other trees in the infected areas. The clear-cutting has also had serious consequences for salmon populations. The removal of trees and the shade they provide along the banks of waterways has raised water temperatures, resulting in disease, parasites, and even death for cold-water species like salmon. Other effects include greater runoff into streams, erosion, and damaged steam channels. Areas of the interior that depend on forests face economic collapse because of the pine beetle. A 2008 strategy report predicted that some communities will face severe and complex challenges as the pine forests die:

> Without external assistance to encourage economic growth and **diversification**... forest-sector job losses will lead to significant numbers of displaced workers and their families leaving the region.
>
> —Cariboo-Chilcotin Beetle Action Coaliton final report, Mountain Pine Beetle Strategy, 2008

The beetle infestation has also changed the lives of First Nations living in affected areas. People are concerned about jobs and keeping remote communities together. There is also the threat of fire from the dry, dead trees. First Nations culture has been seriously affected. Clear-cutting has made hunting more difficult. Berries and herbs no longer grow in dead or cleared forests. Some trees were marked generations ago to show territorial boundaries or traditional camping sites, and the loss of these trees will affect the cultural history of First Nations of the interior.

DID YOU KNOW...

Damage caused by the pine beetle also includes increased flooding in British Columbia's rivers. More snow accumulates beneath the dead trees, which then melts more quickly in the spring because of a lack of shade. Water from melted snow then becomes runoff, ending up in rivers and streams.

diversification having a number of economic activities to avoid dependence on one industry

WEB LINK • • • • • • • • • • • • • • • • •

Read the British Columbia government's Mountain Pine Beetle Action Plan on the Pearson Web site.

ACTIVITIES

1. Why is forestry so important to British Columbia's economy? In what ways has the forest industry changed since the 19th century?

2. What industries in British Columbia would be affected by a downturn in the forestry industry? Give at least three examples.

3. Create a timeline to summarize how forestry practices have changed in British Columbia over the past century. Note what you think marks the most significant changes and explain your thinking.

4. Explain how the mountain pine beetle has affected the forestry industry. What do you think is the most important consequence of the infestation?

CRITICAL
INQUIRY Cause and Consequence

HORIZONS online

home   news   blogs   photos   e-mail to a friend   print

Students plan a future in forestry

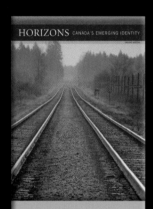

HORIZONS CANADA'S EMERGING IDENTITY

SEE ALSO
- Summer jobs in B.C.
- Web courses now offered at UNBC
- Challenges in environmental studies

LINKS
- UNBC Web site
- Ministry of Forests and Range

Jennifer Spencer and Kirsty Mills are students at the University of Northern British Columbia (UNBC) in Prince George. Both are interested in resources management.

Spencer grew up in Vancouver, although she was born in Prince George. In recent years, something has drawn her back to the North. "I wanted a smaller university," she explains. "UNBC offered the courses I wanted—resource tourism and forest management. Something I would have to come out of the city to study."

Mills is a native of Fort St. James. She credits UNBC for giving her the chance to continue her studies. "Some say that people from the interior don't think beyond Grade 12," she says. "And that we just count on forestry or mining for work, without a thought for sustainability. That's not true for me at all."

Mills has spent summers tree planting—and has the scars to prove it. Her plans lie in silviculture and sustainable forest practices. "Tree planting is the kind of job that will help me pay for university," she says. "But studying resource management is about the future."

Mills and Spencer both acknowledge that it is silviculture, forest renewal projects, and multiple uses for forest products that will help long-term stability of the forestry industry in British Columbia. "Keeping the industry strong, but also preserving habitats and recreational space—it's a tall order," Spencer says. "But forests should still be a part of B.C.'s economy in the future."

Fisheries: A Dwindling Resource

What is the future of the fishing industry in British Columbia?

The fishing industry of British Columbia has been facing hard times. Although herring, cod, and other species are part of the yearly catch, the west coast salmon runs have always been the backbone of the industry. In 1990, salmon represented 55 percent of the total value of the commercial catch. By 2005, salmon made up just 10 percent of the total value of the catch.

Fishing has been an economic mainstay in British Columbia for thousands of years. The First Nations of the coast depended on fish, particularly salmon, which was caught with spears, hooks, dip nets, and **weirs**. As Europeans began to settle on the coast, a commercial fishing industry grew. The first salmon cannery was opened on the Fraser River in the 1870s. Fishing became an important part of the economy, and growing fleets of trawlers used large nets to catch as many fish as possible.

Today, everyone agrees that salmon stocks are dwindling, yet few can agree on the cause. Overfishing and the destruction of habitats, spawning areas, and migration routes have certainly played a role.

WEB LINK

For more information about the fishing industry in British Columbia, visit the Pearson Web site.

weir an enclosure of stakes and nets in a stream or river

DID YOU KNOW...

Dams, pollution, soil erosion, and overfishing have reduced the survival rate of spawning salmon to as little as 1 percent in some rivers.

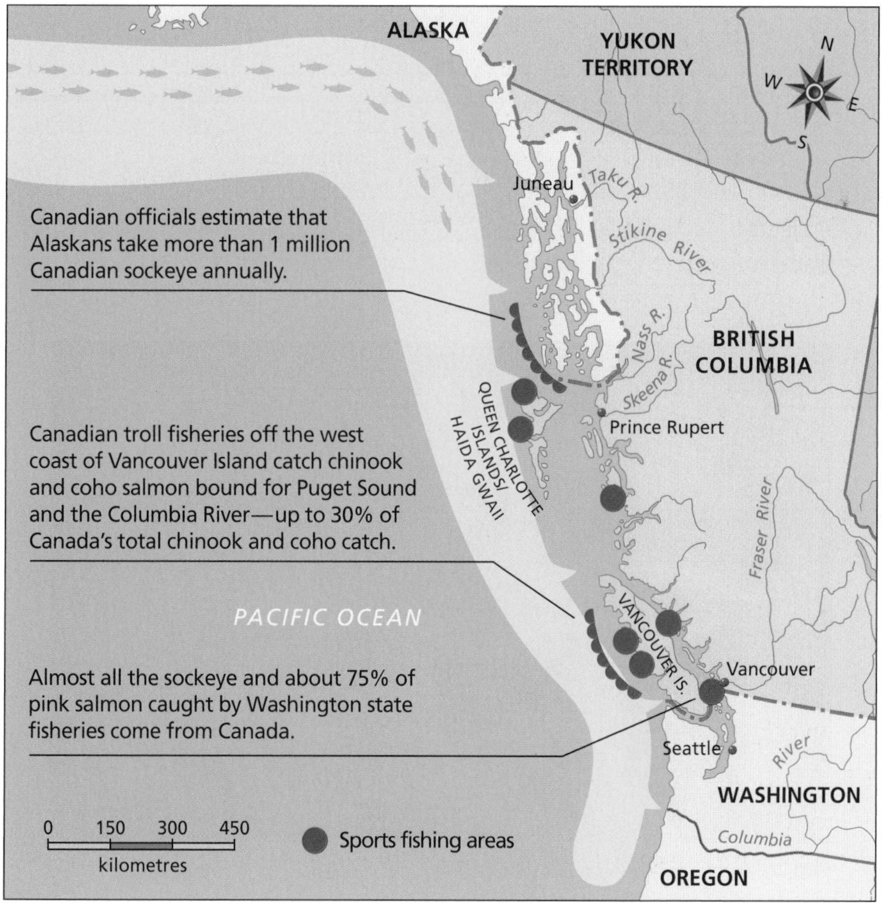
ALASKA
YUKON TERRITORY
N
W
E
S
Juneau
Taku R.
Stikine River
Nass R.
Skeena R.
BRITISH COLUMBIA
Prince Rupert
QUEEN CHARLOTTE ISLANDS/ HAIDA GWAII
Fraser River
VANCOUVER IS.
Vancouver
Seattle
Columbia River
WASHINGTON
OREGON
PACIFIC OCEAN
Canadian officials estimate that Alaskans take more than 1 million Canadian sockeye annually.
Canadian troll fisheries off the west coast of Vancouver Island catch chinook and coho salmon bound for Puget Sound and the Columbia River—up to 30% of Canada's total chinook and coho catch.
Almost all the sockeye and about 75% of pink salmon caught by Washington state fisheries come from Canada.
0 150 300 450
kilometres
Sports fishing areas

FIGURE 9–17 Decisions about sharing the salmon stocks between Canada and the United States are regulated by the Pacific Salmon Commission. What clues does this map give you about why this is necessary?

Aboriginal Fisheries

What rights do Aboriginal fishers have? It took Canada's Supreme Court almost 20 years to answer this question. The most important decisions were *Sparrow* and *Kapp*.

subsistence the production of enough food to feed oneself and one's family, without surplus for trade

- In the *Sparrow* decision (1990), the Supreme Court ruled that members of the Musqueam band had the right to fish for "food, social, and ceremonial" purposes. **Subsistence** fishing by Aboriginal peoples became a priority, after conservation requirements. Aboriginal fishers must also be consulted when their fishing might be affected.

- In the *Kapp* decision (2008), non-Aboriginal commercial fishers protested against the federal Aboriginal Fisheries Strategy that allowed First Nations to fish exclusively on certain days during the salmon season, arguing that this violated their equality rights. The Supreme Court ruled that a policy that improves conditions for a group that has been historically disadvantaged is allowable.

WEB LINK ●

For more information about the *Sparrow* and *Kapp* decisions and Aboriginal fisheries, visit the Pearson Web site.

These two decisions have done much to spell out Aboriginal fishing rights. As treaties continue to be negotiated, there will be further clarification of the fishing rights of individual First Nations.

Zoom In ⊜ Eulachon: The Little Fish That Matters

In recent years, the supply of eulachon along the coast has collapsed. This small fish, a type of smelt, is about 20 cm long. Nearly 20 percent oil, a eulachon will burn like a candle if dried and strung on a wick.

For First Nations communities, the decline of the eulachon has been devastating. Coastal First Nations people have traditionally harvested the eulachon. The oil, sometimes called t'lina, was part of their diet and served important social and ceremonial purposes. It is commonly given away at potlatches. Historically, the oil was a valuable trading commodity. Mountain passes travelled during this trade were called "grease trails."

In the last big spawning runs of the early 1990s, millions of eulachon turned the rivers black.

By 2008, fishers, seals, birds, and sturgeon waited in vain for the eulachon to return.

Aboriginal leaders are urging governments to begin restoration projects to bring back the little fish so important to their culture.

- What are the consequences of the decline in the eulachon stocks?

WEB LINK ●

To see a virtual exhibit of t'lina making, visit the Pearson Web site.

FIGURE 9–18 Another name for eulachon is "candlefish." What other uses for the eulachon can you discover?

There are few topics in British Columbia that create a more emotional response than the discussion of wild versus farmed salmon (aquaculture). British Columbia is the fourth-largest producer of farmed salmon in the world after Norway, Chile, and the United Kingdom. Approximately 80 sites are in operation at one time.

Farmed salmon is British Columbia's largest agricultural export. The industry argues that salmon farming is an alternative to declining wild stocks and creates much-needed jobs. Farmers say they have addressed environmental concerns by making changes to their operations.

Environmentalists, commercial fishers, tourism operators, and many Aboriginal communities oppose salmon farming.

Their concerns include fish escaping from salmon farms, spreading lice and disease to wild salmon. Sea lice are larvae that attach themselves to salmon, often causing death. Pollution from the farms—everything from chemicals to fish waste—can also affect the surrounding waters. Opponents add that farmers feed their fish meal made from overfished species.

> *Both salmon farming and commercial salmon fishing have an impact on ecosystems, but that of salmon farming pales in comparison. In my view, British Columbia could largely abandon the commercial fishery, and with only a modest expansion of salmon farming, bring more fish to market, increase rural employment and contribute more revenue to the provincial economy. And, most important, runs of wild salmon, unmolested by gillnetter and seiner, would recover, bears would gorge, rotting fish carcasses would fertilize trees... The industry should grow slowly, and in conjunction with careful environmental assessment and government regulation.*
>
> **—Cameron MacDonald, a Vancouver college instructor and writer**

> *In recent years, wild salmon stocks in British Columbia have declined. Our ability to harvest and earn a living from fishing has likewise declined.*
>
> **—Robert McKamey, Fraser River Gillnetters Association**

WEB LINK • • • • • • • • • • • • • •

Read more opinions about salmon farming on the Pearson Web site.

WHAT DO YOU THINK?

1. Where do you stand on salmon farming? Why?

2. What steps should the government take to ensure that concerns about salmon farming are addressed?

ACTIVITIES

1. **a)** What are the possible causes for the decline of the west coast fishing industry? Rank the top three in terms of their impact. Justify your ranking.

   b) What are the consequences of the declining catch?

2. Speculate on the state of the fishing industry in British Columbia 20 years from now. Support your conclusions.

3. Do the economic benefits of aquaculture outweigh the concerns of those opposed to fish farming? Explain and support your point of view.

Both private and public lands may fall within the ALR, and they may be forested, farmed, or unused. The ALR also protects land that has the *potential* for use as farmland. This means that land-use decisions in the future will be affected as new methods of irrigation, pest management, and fertilization are developed.

Under the act, farmlands can be converted to other uses, such as golf courses, and still remain in the ALR. In this case, it must be shown that the land can eventually be used again for farming. Some people oppose this measure, seeing it as a weakening of the act.

Today, the Georgia Basin and the Okanagan Valley are among the fastest-growing regions in Canada. The Georgia Basin makes up only 3 percent of British Columbia's land area, but more than two-thirds of its population lives there. Mountain slopes, water, and border lines restrict expansion in these areas. This places increasing pressure on land that is being used for agriculture, and harder decisions will have to be made in the future.

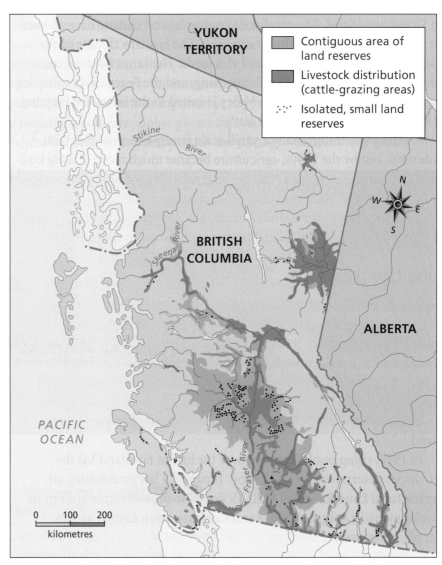

FIGURE 9–23 The Agricultural Land Reserve (ALR) covers more than 4.7 million hectares. Some ALR blocks cover thousands of hectares, while others are small areas. How might the ALR affect the growth of urban areas in the future?

Municipal Governments and Land-Use Decisions

Municipal governments are very concerned with land use issues. As their communities grow, elected officials must monitor and regulate land used for homes, businesses, or farming.

While the Agricultural Land Commission is responsible for the administration of the ALR, municipal governments must make decisions regarding agricultural land use and growth within their communities. Changes in policies are often led by the mayor, an elected official who serves a term of three years.

Working with the Commission, municipal governments process all applications affecting agricultural lands. These applications may include requests to take away soil, or to use the land for non-farming activities, such as recreation. Applications must be made first through the municipal government, which will review the application. If the application goes againts local **bylaws**, this must first be considered. Land development and zoning in municipalities is controlled by bylaws. They can be adopted or changed by the municipality's council through a procedure of readings, discussions, and votes. If it is a land-use bylaw, there must also be a public hearing.

bylaw a law made by a municipal government, rather than by the legislature

FIGURE 9–24 Farmland in the Okanagan Valley faces increasing pressure from population growth and development. What evidence can you find in this image that shows the geographical restrictions on farmland in this area? Is this typical of British Columbia?

ACTIVITIES

1. What changes in agriculture have occurred in British Columbia in the past 50 years? What changes can you see occurring in the next 50 years? Explain.

2. Farmers' markets have grown in British Columbia in response to the demand for more local and organic produce. How do these markets benefit the farmer and the local community?

Judgements

3. British Columbia's Environmental Farm Plan (EFP) supports farmers in the sustainable use of land and water. Should the government make programs like EFP compulsory for those involved in agriculture? Explain.

4. Find out the status of the ALR in your region. Have any lands been removed? If so, for what purpose?

Mining and Energy

▶ **How can we lessen the impact of using non-renewable resources?**

Mining

unprocessed in raw form, without value added

labour intensive requiring a lot of people to do the job

open-pit mining the process of uncovering mineral deposits by scraping off surface layers of rock

Mining has always been an important part of British Columbia's resource-based economy. Aboriginal peoples mined copper before the arrival of Europeans, and coal mining on the east coast of Vancouver Island started around 1850. Gold prospecting along the Fraser River and in the Cariboo region, which you read about in Chapter 6, expanded mining to the mainland. This led to the development of the colony and province of British Columbia. In the later 1800s, mining began in the Cassiar and Omineca goldfields in the northwest corner of the province, and mining of copper, zinc, and lead started in the Kootenay region of the southeast.

British Columbia's mining economy is heavily dependent on export sales. Most exported minerals are **unprocessed** and their value is determined by shifting world prices and demand. Twenty-five years is the average lifespan for a producing mine, and as mine locations in British Columbia close down, the community built around them may close as well. Mining ghost towns in British Columbia include Barkerville (see Chapter 6) and Britannia Beach.

Until the 1950s, most mining in British Columbia was underground. Underground operations give miners access to high-grade ores but are **labour intensive**. Large-scale production of lower-grade ores was made possible through the development of **open-pit mining**. These vast operations require major capital investment and fewer workers, and they are safer than the underground operations.

Today, geological maps are used to determine the bedrock in an area, and remote-sensing devices can identify some minerals through aerial survey. Before any mine can begin operating, a profitability study is undertaken and then lengthy environmental assessments are conducted.

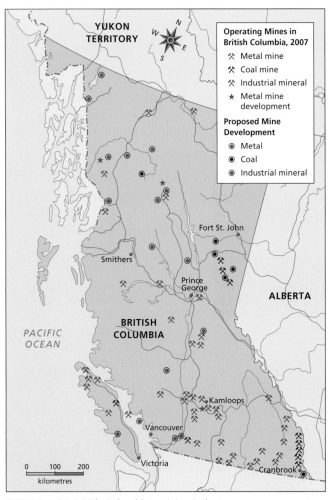

FIGURE 9–25 British Columbia's mining industry covers every part of the province. How many products in your home have mineral content?

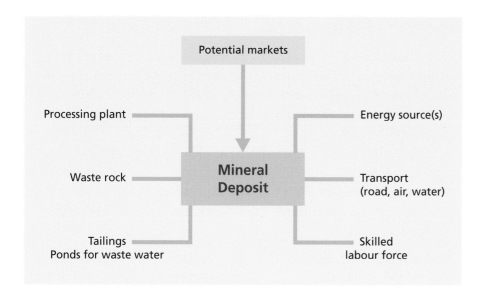

FIGURE 9–26 Although markets are available, many promising mineral deposits in British Columbia remain undeveloped. This diagram shows the factors that affect mining operations. Environmental factors are shown on the left, and the economic factors are on the right. Discuss how these factors may affect the decision to open a mine.

Environmental Considerations

Most environmental damage from mining results from disturbing the site during the exploration period and from developing the mine itself. Open-pit mines leave behind bare rock faces and large residues of waste rock. Acid rock drainage occurs when sulphuric minerals in rock are exposed to air or water, resulting in the formation of acid. Although this process occurs in nature, it is accelerated by mining activity, which exposes more rock. As water comes into contact with mine waste and re-enters streams, lakes, and rivers, it can have a significant impact on water quality and damage aquatic ecosystems.

According to the Ministry of Environment, none of the province's coal mines and only six of the metal mines generate acid rock drainage, and those mines are taking steps to eliminate it. However, acid rock drainage continues in some abandoned mines.

WEB LINK

For more information about mining in British Columbia, visit the Pearson Web site.

FIGURE 9–27 The British Columbia government now requires mining companies to post a bond to make sure they return mining sites to their original condition. Based on the information in this photo, which shows a copper mine on Vancouver Island, do you think it is possible for the mining companies to achieve this requirement?

Energy: Old and New

British Columbia's energy resources include crude oil, natural gas, and hydroelectric power. The province is committed to the continued development of fossil fuel reserves, but declining world reserves of crude oil and the effects of carbon emissions on the environment have created interest in alternative energy sources.

In 2007, the provincial government introduced the BC Energy Plan, setting targets to reduce greenhouse gas emissions. The plan encouraged innovative clean-energy projects. It also required BC Hydro to get 50 percent of its energy needs through conservation by 2020. Other commitments include:

- all existing plants and new electricity projects developed in British Columbia will have zero net greenhouse gas emissions by 2016

- clean or renewable electricity generation will continue to account for at least 90 percent of total generation

Alternative Energy Sources

Many of the sustainable energy sources available could lessen our dependence on fossil fuels. Some of the power sources that could be harnessed in British Columbia include wind, solar, tidal, and geothermal, which uses heat stored underground. Although these alternatives have drawbacks, they do not produce the harmful emissions associated with fossil fuels.

The main drawbacks of alternative energy sources include high set-up costs and, in some cases, conflicts over where they are placed. Some sources can also have a negative impact on the environment. For example, tidal power requires a generating system that can harm the plants and animals in a marine environment.

A company called Ballard Power has been developing hydrogen fuel cells in British Columbia. The high cost of the technology in automobiles has slowed its development, but the company has turned to small-scale uses in homes and in equipment such as forklifts.

FIGURE 9–28 Critics have objected to modern wind farms covering wide areas because of noise pollution and the appearance of turbines. To solve this problem, some farms are located offshore. Are wind farms a good alternative source of energy for all, or some parts, of British Columbia? Explain.

In 2008, the British Columbia government committed to cutting greenhouse gas emissions by 33 percent by 2020. To meet this goal, the government introduced a **carbon tax**, the first of its kind in North America. The carbon tax applies to all fossil fuels.

The goal of the tax is to discourage the use of fossil fuels, which cause greenhouse gas emissions. Drivers pay an extra 2.4 cents a litre at the pump for gasoline in the first year. By 2012 this amount will rise to 7.2 cents.

This revenue will be returned to British Columbians. Business and income taxes will be reduced and some residents will receive an annual climate-action credit of $100 per adult and $30 per child.

Interior and northern communities have objected to the tax, claiming that they face a challenge heating their homes and must drive farther, since they cannot opt to use mass transit.

An alternative to the carbon tax is a cap-and-trade system, which the Western Climate Initiative, whose members include British Columbia, Ontario, Quebec, and Manitoba, plans to bring into effect in 2012. This system puts a ceiling on emissions from companies operating in a particular region. Companies going over the limit must buy permits on a "carbon market" from companies staying under the allowable limit.

carbon tax a tax on energy sources that emit carbon dioxide, such as fossil fuels

- What other actions could the government take to discourage the use of fossil fuels? What results might these actions produce?

Fossil Fuels in British Columbia

The Peace River region of British Columbia has seen growth in its petroleum industry, and the economic benefits have led the government and the oil industry to suggest that other oil and gas resources in the province be developed. An energy source favoured for development is coalbed gas (CBG), which is found in almost every coalfield across the province. The British Columbia government views CBG as a clean energy source because it needs little processing. It hopes that CBG will bring increased economic activity and job opportunities.

However, there is opposition to harnessing CBG in many rural communities. Opponents argue that water sources may become contaminated by chemicals and waste water used in the extraction process, and that the building of new roads, pipelines, and compressor stations will damage the environment and reduce property values.

ACTIVITIES

1. Why is the mining industry in British Columbia so dependent on world prices and markets?

2. Do the economic benefits from mining and the use of fossil fuels outweigh environmental concerns? Explain your thinking.

3. Why might the government wish to support both a reduction in fossil fuel emissions and the development of fossil fuel energy?

Manufacturing and Service Industries

▶ **How do manufacturing and service-based economies compare with a resource-based economy?**

The trend in the British Columbia economy is growth in service industries. As you saw in Figure 9–1 on page 322, almost four out of five people in the labour force work in a service industry. With the decline of resource-based industries and the growth of information technology, this trend will likely continue into the future.

Manufacturing industries are those that take raw materials and make them into new products. Wood, paper, and food make up over 50 percent of manufacturing in British Columbia. Because markets in Canada are limited, manufacturers must look to export markets to prosper.

The High-Tech Revolution

Although it makes up only a little more than 6 percent of the provincial economy, high technology is one of the fastest-growing sectors in British Columbia. In 2006, the total number of people employed in high-tech industries exceeded that of forestry and mining combined. Four out of five workers in the sector work in service industries, such as computer design, engineering, telecommunications, and film and video production. Their activities range from designing a bridge to analyzing a blood sample. Many of the companies in the industry are small.

FIGURE 9–30 MacDonald Dettwiler in Richmond, B.C., develops some of the most advanced communications and control equipment and software for use on earth and in space. Most of the non-military earth observation systems in the world contain hardware and software developed by this company. Why might this industry be growing?

Computer service is by far the largest part of the information technology industry. It includes computer consulting, processing, programming, systems analysis and design, and multimedia applications. Other companies in this sector specialize in communications, satellite parts and components, and recording instruments. British Columbia leads Canada in the number of companies that are developing products in the field of satellite, mobile, and microwave communications.

Tourism, Recreation, and Entertainment

British Columbia's provincial motto, "Splendour Without Diminishment," is well deserved. The province's diverse geography and breathtaking scenery, have become a resource of increasing economic value. Nowhere is this more apparent than in two of the fastest-growing industries—tourism and recreation, and television and film production.

British Columbia is a worldwide destination for tourism and recreation. From whale watching to skiing, the province's many attractions draw large numbers of tourists. Promoting British Columbia's recreational areas has been a primary goal of the provincial government.

The completion of the Canadian Pacific Railway established tourism in British Columbia. To provide accommodation for its passengers, the CPR built hotels in scenic areas such as Banff, Lake Louise, and Victoria.

A few decades later, increasing use of the automobile encouraged touring. The impact of the automobile continued to grow as the highway system expanded. For example, when the Coquihalla Highway opened in 1986, it made the Okanagan Valley more accessible to people from the lower mainland.

The waters of the west coast have also attracted sightseers from around the world. In the early 20th century, tourists were content with day trips from Vancouver to the Gulf Islands. Today, luxury cruises to Vancouver, whale watching excursions, and trips to remote lodges for fishing and recreation are common. The marine parks system is expanding to meet the needs of kayakers and boat owners. Hiking on the West Coast Trail and ecotourism in remote regions of British Columbia have also become popular as more people seek out the dwindling number of natural and unspoiled places on the planet.

Winter sports are one of British Columbia's success stories, particularly the ski industry. Led by the first-rank facilities at Whistler and Blackcomb, this province has become an international ski destination. An estimated 60 alpine ski areas operate in the province, with huge resorts on Vancouver Island, the Thompson Okanagan, and the Kootenays. Awarding the 2010 Winter Olympics to Vancouver/Whistler brought a boost to tourism in British Columbia. This opportunity will generate a legacy of world-class recreation and training facilities.

FIGURE 9–31 In the past, Vancouver was the departure point for Canadian Pacific Steamships bound for Asia. Sightseers were encouraged to travel across Canada on their way to Asia. Today the direction of tourists has been reversed as many people from Asia choose Canada as a holiday destination. Where else do tourists to British Columbia come from today?

Population and Environment

WEB LINK

For more information about interactive maps and population statistics for British Columbia, visit the Pearson Web site.

▶ **What is the relationship between population growth and the environment in British Columbia?**

Since the 1980s, the Georgia Basin has become the centre for new employment opportunities in the province. Communities in both the interior and the north have experienced job losses because technology has reduced the number of workers needed in the primary industrial sector. These trends are clear in unemployment data. In 2008, Vancouver and Victoria had unemployment rates of just under 4 percent, while North Coast and Nechako had rates of 8 percent, and the Cariboo region's rate was almost 6 percent. These figures in the interior and north are likely to rise as communities begin to feel the effects of the pine beetle infestation.

DID YOU KNOW...

People in the Georgia Basin generate an average of 1000 kg of solid waste per person. A little over 40 percent of it is recycled.

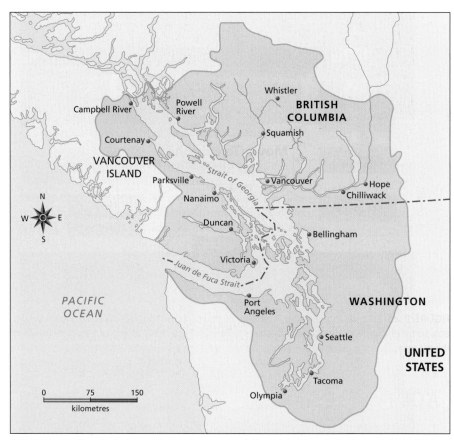

FIGURE 9–36 The shaded area shows the extent of Canada's Georgia Basin and the United States' Puget Sound. As tourism increases, the quality of the environment is taking on greater economic importance. The increasing population of the region puts added pressure on the quality of the land, air, and water. If you live in, or have visited the Georgia Basin, what evidence have you seen of damage to the environment?

The Georgia Basin makes up only 3 percent of British Columbia's total area, but it is home to nearly two-thirds of the province's population. According to the 2006 census, more than 3 million people live in this broad, sheltered basin that includes the Strait of Georgia, the lower Fraser Valley, the Sunshine Coast up to Powell River, the Gulf Islands, and the eastern side of Vancouver Island. Over the past 25 years, the population of the Georgia Basin has doubled. People are drawn to the region by its mild climate and the diverse natural environment of sea, islands, and mountains. Relative job abundance and many cultural and educational facilities also attract people to this area.

It is projected that in the next 20 years the population of the lower mainland and southern Vancouver Island will grow by up to 40 percent. The environmental damage that is already evident in the area will only worsen if restrictions are not enforced. Smog from Vancouver can be detected as far north as Texada Island, 120 km away. At one time, pulp mill pollution was a serious problem. However, this source of pollution has been brought under control by strict government regulations.

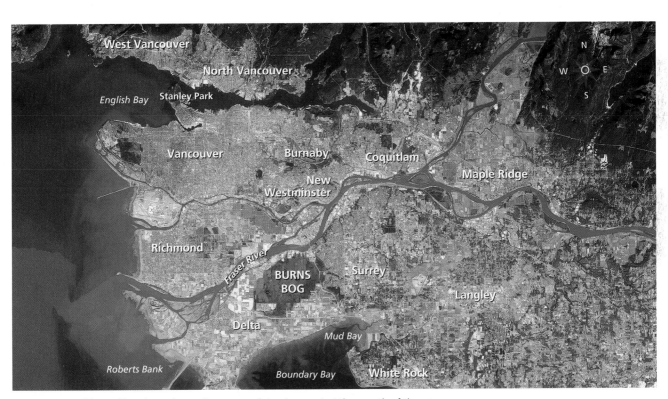

FIGURE 9–37 This satellite photo shows the extent of development at the mouth of the Fraser River. Encroaching urban sprawl can be seen in Richmond, Delta, and Surrey. Burns Bog is particularly threatened. The bog has been called the "lungs of the lower mainland" because of its ability to convert carbon dioxide into oxygen. It also purifies water, reduces and controls water flow, and provides habitat for wildlife. What steps would you suggest to protect areas like Burns Bog?

FIGURE 9–38 Many communities have stream stewardship programs in place to protect local waterways, particularly salmon spawning streams. How are streams protected in your community? If they are not, what can you do about this issue?

Many activities are altering the landscape of the Georgia Basin. Urbanization and development, forestry, agriculture, recreation, and the creation of new transportation corridors all affect the environment of the region. As cities expand, they encroach on streams, rivers, and coastal zones such as marshes and wetlands. Preserving and sustaining natural systems under these conditions is almost impossible. Too often the environment takes second place to development.

Rising gasoline prices have put more emphasis on finding ways to reduce our dependence on the automobile. This trend may slow the spread of suburbs as the cost of commuting becomes too expensive. A migration of people back into city centres might make other means of travel more popular. An expert on habitats and cities says that the challenge will be to create something more meaningful than urban sprawl:

> *The chief challenge of the coming decades will not be to control sprawl but rather to add to it the ingredients of urbanity: density, walkability, and variety. The key to a successful urban environment is to create what real estate developers call a 24-hour place, combining residential, office, retail and entertainment uses in relatively close proximity... This is what makes downtown Vancouver... so attractive.*
>
> —Witold Rybczynski, author and professor of urban studies

The Coast Salish

The geographic area of the Georgia Basin and Puget Sound closely corresponds to the traditional territory of the Coast Salish, who call the area *Sqelatses*, meaning "home." The Coast Salish exercised stewardship over the land and resources of this ecosystem millennia before Europeans arrived.

Contact with Europeans brought smallpox epidemics, dramatically reducing a once thriving population. Today the Coast Salish, along with other First Nations in British Columbia and Canada, are seeing their numbers grow faster than the general population. The 2006 census listed over a million Canadians reporting themselves as having Aboriginal identity. British Columbia has the second-largest Aboriginal population in Canada, after Ontario.

The Coast Salish First Nations of the Georgia Basin are in treaty negotiations with the provincial government. By 2008, a number of treaties had been ratified, including a treaty with the Tsawwassen First Nation.

In 2008, a landmark treaty with the Tsawwassen First Nation was ratified by the Parliament of Canada after 15 years of negotiations. Some terms of the treaty are controversial. For example, 207 hectares are to be added to Tsawwassen First Nation land from the Agricultural Land Reserve. The Tsawwassen will also receive $20.7 million.

Supporters say that the treaty will finally give the Tsawwassen control of their own destiny. Opponents within the Tsawwassen First Nation are concerned because they believe that more safeguards should be in place to control the use of the money. Other Coast Salish communities object to the settlement because of overlapping claims.

Some also say the treaty does not go far enough in recognizing Aboriginal title to land and resources. Municipal councils in the region and environmental groups object to the removal of land from the ALR.

> *In my view... this treaty achieves a new relationship between the Tsawwassen First Nation, British Columbia and Canada. It achieves reconciliation... To me, reconciliation signifies real action and tangible change. Consider a clause in our treaty that stipulates the transfer of 207 hectares to us from the Agricultural Land Reserve... we made it clear that we needed those lands to grow, to set up businesses and build houses. No other aspect of our treaty resulted in so much controversy... Critics choose to ignore Tsawwassen's history of being victims of industrial and urban development to the benefit of everyone but us.*
>
> —Tsawwassen Chief Kim Baird

> *...we're going to see a large chunk of our farmland cemented over. This is ground zero for a major change of life here. I think the biggest problem is people are loathe to speak out because it's a First Nations agreement. What the... governments have done is to use the treaty... to get around the agricultural land commission and have the largest chunk of farmland removed in recent history in one swoop. There could be hundreds of hectares more farmland removed from the ALR as roads are built. It's going to be a massive change in our region and I think it's... wrong-headed.*
>
> —Joe Foy, Western Canada Wilderness Committee

WHAT DO YOU THINK?

1. Do you agree with Chief Baird that agreements such as the Tsawwassen Treaty are the way to achieve reconciliation? Why or why not?

2. Do you think the removal of land from the ALR is justified in the case of the Tsawwassen Treaty? Explain your position.

ACTIVITIES

1. Summarize the major trends in British Columbia's population growth. What concerns do these trends raise?

2. Provide three reasons for the growth of the population in the Georgia Basin.

3. Make a two-column chart of the positive and negative outcomes of the rapid population growth in the Georgia Basin region. Identify and explain what you believe to be the most significant benefit and the most significant drawback of the growth.

4. Research programs in your community designed to protect or restore a waterway, landscape, or wetland.

Understanding how causes, effects, and results are related to one another can help you determine how and why things change. It can show not only how something happened, but *why*. For example, if you were relating the story of your family's move to a new home, you would probably tell the story in a certain order, and relate events (parent's new job) to their results (a move closer to work). Of course, things do not always move in a clear, logical order, and sometimes what seems like a small event can bring about dramatic results further into the future.

Historians and geographers look for a chain of events leading to change. This can be called the **cause-effect-results chain**. The links of this chain can be defined this way:

- **Cause**. An incident or event that leads to a follow-up event or events.

- **Effect**. The short-term consequence, or set of consequences, that comes from such a cause.

- **Result**. The long-term consequence, or set of consequences, that develops from cause and effect.

It is important to remember that cause, effect, and result are not just a simple chain with three links. A cause might have more than one effect. A result might come from a variety of causes.

Cause → Effect → Effect → Result ← Effect ← Cause

APPLY IT

1. Keep cause, effect, and result in mind as you study patterns and change, as well as cause and consequence. In the examples below, identify (a) cause, (b) effect, and (c) result.

Confederation
Meetings take place to discuss joining all colonies in a federation
Pressure on politicians to find a solution
Economies of Canada East and West in trouble

2. Pick one of the topics below and browse through the chapter associated with it. List one example of the topic's (a) causes, (b) effects, and (c) results.

- The CPR extends across Canada

- The Treaties of the 1870s and the Indian Act of 1876

- The Colony of British Columbia is formed

The Internet has made it much easier to find up-to-date information on many topics, and along with books and other resources, it is an excellent place to do research. However, keep in mind that there is no agency to control what is put on the Internet, and that some Web sites are not reliable sources of information. Here are a few tips to help you critically assess Web sites.

- **Authority**. Are the authors identified, and do they have qualified expertise in the subject area?

- **Accuracy**. Do the authors provide source references for their information? If not, how can you measure the accuracy of what they say? How does the information compare with other sources?

- **Bias**. Are the authors arguing on behalf of a particular point of view? Is more than one point of view presented? Is the difference between facts and opinions clear?

- **Style**. Is the writing casual or full of grammatical errors, or does it seem thorough and well written?

- **Currency**. Is the information up to date? Are the links to other sites current?

- **Usability**. Is the material presented in a way that is clear and easy to use?

Another way to help determine the reliability of a Web site is to look at the type of Web site it is. Clues can be found within the domain names (although styles can vary from country to country).

- .com or .ca indicates a commercial site

- .org indicates an organization, usually non-profit

- .edu indicates an educational institution

- .gov indicates a government agency (.gc in Canada)

- the tilde (~) usually indicates a personal Web site

If you find two or more sites on the same topic that give conflicting information, use these steps to determine which site may be the most reliable. Remember to always record the Web site address and refer to it when you use the information in an essay or presentation.

APPLY IT

1. Choose one of the people profiled in *Horizons*. Check the Internet to find more information on that person, using the steps above as a guide.

   a) What information in the text is confirmed by the Web site?

   b) What information in the book is called into question by a Web site?

   c) What new information is available on the Web site?

Recognizing, Evaluating, and Using Sources

Name a famous person you admire—a current TV or film star, an athlete, a politician, activist, or scientist. How can you find out more about that person? You could watch a TV or magazine interview with the person. Perhaps he or she is involved with a certain charity, and a co-worker has written about what it is like working with this person.

Historians use the same methods to study people they are interested in. Historians ask questions such as:

- What does the person say and do?

- What do other people say about that person?

To answer those questions, historians seek out sources. How these sources are used tells us what type they are. **Primary sources** are items that have survived from the past. They can be written items such as letters and diaries, or visual items such as photographs, paintings, blueprints, and drawings. They are used to gain a first-hand account of people or events in the past. For example, a historian writing about Mary Ann Shadd might read her articles to learn what Shadd thought about the social or political issues of the time.

Artifacts, which are objects from the past, are also primary sources. Clothing, tools, furniture, or jewellery are examples of artifacts. A historian writing about mapmaker David Thompson might examine his sextant to determine the mapmaking technology of the time.

Secondary sources are accounts of the past written sometime after the person lived or the event happened. This social studies textbook is an example of a secondary source. However, it also contains some primary sources. It is also possible that in the future a historian may examine this text as a primary source—an example of textbooks at this time. It is important to know what kind of source you are using. This can help you determine the reliability of the source, and also decide if it is a source you need to use.

Check the Origin of the Source

- If it is a book, examine the front pages, which usually contain its publication information. Who is (are) the author(s)? When was it published?

- If it is another type of written source (for example, a newspaper or magazine) find publication information about it.

- If it is an artifact, try to find who made it and when.

- Find out anything you can about those who created the source and why they did so.

- If it is an electronic source (like a CD-ROM or a Web site), try to find out who compiled the information and when. Ask, is this material borrowed from another source, or is it original to this source?

Look for Clues Within the Source

- Sources usually use quotation marks or special formatting when they borrow primary material from another source. (See pages 32 or 205 for examples in this book.)

- Secondary sources normally contain a credit line or footnote, telling the reader where the material came from.

- Secondary sources are normally written in the third person and use formal language.

- Primary sources sometimes come from an earlier time. They may use old-fashioned language or technical terms.

- Some primary sources, like letters or journals, have a personal feel to them, using words like "I" or "we."

Evaluate the Source for Point of View

All authors, speakers, or artists have a point of view about a subject. In studying history, you will find that people can often have very different evaluations of the same event—even when they have the same facts and evidence to work with. Those evaluations are based on point of view. (Refer to Exploring Points of View, on page 360 to review this topic.) When using and evaluating sources based on point of view, ask these questions:

What?	What is the source? What is the point of view of the author? What was the purpose of the material?
Who?	Who wrote or created it? How can you be certain it was really that person?
When?	When was it created? How can you tell its age?
Where?	Where was it created?
Why?	Why did the person create this material?
So what?	What interpretation of the person or event can be made from the primary source?

APPLY IT

Choose one of the following topics:

- British North America in 1860

- the culture and lifestyle of the Métis

- earthquakes in Canada

- James Douglas

1. Use the library and Internet to find at least one primary source and one secondary source for your topic. Examine both sources. Are they reliable or unreliable? Why?

2. How does each source contribute to your understanding of the person or topic you chose to research?

In the summer of 2006, there was a war in Lebanon. During the war, Reuters, an international news service that sells photographs to media all over the world, fired one of its photographers when he was caught adding smoke to an image of a fire caused by Israeli bombing. Why might the photographer have done this? Why do you think Reuters fired him?

Like the media, this textbook uses many different types of visuals to relay information. They can give you as much information as the text that you read, but remember that every image is biased in some way. This means that it represents a certain point of view.

Identify the Image

There are many types of images. Each has a different purpose.

- Paintings, photographs, or posters are artistic expressions that contain a message or information.

- Cartoon series or editorial cartoons convey a message using humour.

- Drawings or diagrams are illustrations that simplify or explain a topic.

- Maps, aerial photographs, or satellite images show geographic information.

When you see an image, read the title and caption that goes with it. See if you can find out when the image was created, by whom, and for what purpose.

Read the Image

A useful way to look at images is to identify what is in the foreground or the centre. This is probably the main subject, and the most important part. Next, examine the background or the edges of the image. This tells you the setting or context. Reading foreground and background will help you draw information from the image. Think as well about what may not be in the image. A photograph, for example, can be cropped to emphasize a particular part of the image. An artist depicting a scene in a painting may have left out part of what he or she saw if it does not add to the message they wish to give.

Analyze the Image

You have gathered information about the image and its content. Now you can ask yourself some questions in order to determine what the creator's point of view might be.

- What does the image show?

- Who created the image, and why?

- When was the image created?

- What is the artist's message? How does he or she make this message clear?

- What is the artist's point of view about the topic? In what way is he or she trying to show a certain point of view?

- What was the purpose of the image: to entertain, to inform, or to persuade?

- Are there symbols being used? What are they? What is their usual meaning, and how are they being used here?

Evaluate the Image

To evaluate something means to judge or assess it. Ask these questions to evaluate the image.

- Is the message easy to understand or difficult to identify?

- Is the artist's point of view current or out of date? Do you agree with it or not?

- Would another type of image have been as effective, or perhaps even better?

Identify
This painting, *Canoe Manned by Voyageurs Passing a Waterfall*, was created by Frances Anne Hopkins in 1869.

Read
At the centre of the image are two passengers.

Analyze
Voyageurs and their canoe are iconic symbols; the artist may intend to use these symbols to represent Canada.

Evaluate
This seems to be a romanticized view of voyageurs.

This painting was based on sketches made by Frances Anne Hopkins while she travelled with her husband, who was a Hudson's Bay Company official. She and her husband appear in the painting.

APPLY IT

1. Use the notes surrounding the image as an example to make your own observations about this painting. Organize your notes under *Identify*, *Read*, *Analyze*, and *Evaluate*.

2. How does the caption help with understanding the image? Describe the steps you might take to identify the image if the caption was not present.

3. What is the artist's message? Identify the point of view.

4. How effectively is the message presented? Does it create a response in the viewer? What other type of image could have been used instead? Why?

Researching a Topic

Take a look at the Chapter Outcomes for Chapter 2 (page 42). One of the outcomes reads, "Describe the roles and daily activities of men and women in colonial society." That seems interesting, but what is missing? What if you wanted to know more about the lives of children in colonial times? How could you find out more? You might do some research. Here are some guidelines to help your approach to a research project.

Ask Research Questions

Be clear about the questions you want to answer and the information you want to find. This often involves narrowing things down. Even if all of the information is available you, you will probably not have the time to find out everything. You will want to have a focused research question. Look at the chart below for an example.

Find Out What You Need to Know

Now that you have a focused question, you will need to address three key components of research.

- **What do I already know about the question?** You might be surprised by how much you already know from your textbook, previous studies, or other sources. Start by making a list of what you already know.

- **What do I need to find out?** In this case, you might want to find out about important aspects of a teenager's life: school, chores, family, etc.

- **Where can I find what I need to know?** Make a list of sources that might help you find the answers you need. These could be primary or secondary sources.

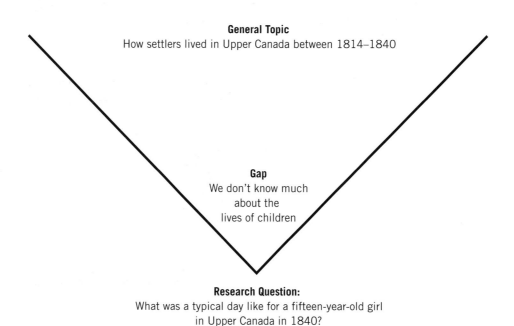

General Topic
How settlers lived in Upper Canada between 1814–1840

Gap
We don't know much
about the
lives of children

Research Question:
What was a typical day like for a fifteen-year-old girl
in Upper Canada in 1840?

Gather Information

Begin to gather your sources and read them for information. Information can be gathered from books, articles, documents, photographs, the Internet, and many other sources. These can be found in your school, museums and historic sites, libraries, and archives. Many of these organizations make some of their collections available online. You might check out the Libraries Without Walls site from the government of B.C. or for this project, the Archives of Ontario Web site.

Assess and Evaluate Sources

All sources, whether they are primary or secondary, have points of view. You will need to assess how accurate their material is. Use the guidelines in the Skill on pages 364–365 to review how to assess primary and secondary sources. Keep in mind that while something may be accurate in one situation, it may not be accurate in all situations. A child's diary, for example, may report that a teacher used a cane to strike students in school. That may be accurate for that school and teacher, but it does not mean that it was for *every* school and teacher. Ask yourself how the information in the source fits with information from other sources.

Organizing Information

There are many ways to organize information—file cards, written notes, or diagrams. Try to find the method that works best for you. One way to organize information is shown below.

Presenting Information

An organizer like the one shown here can form the basis for presenting your material. For example, if you were going to write an essay, the central box provides your introduction, where you outline what you plan to show. The other boxes provide a framework for the paragraphs or sections of the essay. If you wanted to do a poster or other visual presentation, you could also use the graph to organize slides or visual material.

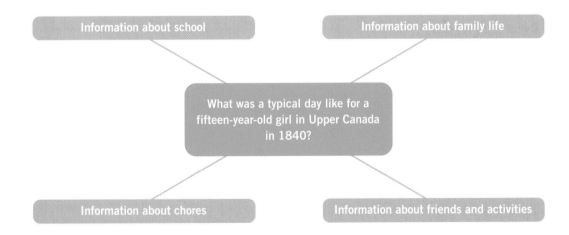

Think of the last time you made a presentation. Were you prepared? Were you comfortable and confident? Did you have everyone's attention from start to finish? What worked, and what did not work? As experience may tell you, the key to a successful presentation is being organized. Here are some guidelines to help organize your next presentation.

Establish Your Content

- Research your topic (see pages 368–370).

- Decide on what information you will talk about and the order you will present it in. What will go toward a catchy introduction and an informative conclusion?

Make Use of Multimedia

- Use video or DVD material to support your presentation.

- Write a script and record a dramatic piece to present as video or audio, or prepare a dramatic presentation such as a short play, newscast, or recitation.

- Design a Web site on your topic, including a home page, links to useful research sites, and selected text, photos, and sound or video clips.

- Use a program such as PowerPoint or AppleWorks to create a slide show to display text with sound and graphics.

Prepare

- Write up an outline of your presentation. Include cues for multimedia elements. If you make changes, make sure they are clean and easy to read.

- If needed, write a script, making sure that the content and language are appropriate for your audience and topic.

- Rehearse, rehearse, rehearse!

Presentation Dos and Don'ts

- **Do** make eye contact with the audience.

- **Do** use a hook—an interesting image, story, or question at the beginning of the presentation that will draw your audience in.

- **Do** speak loudly and clearly, at a medium speed.

- **Don't** simply read your entire presentation.

- **Don't** sit or lean on a desk.

APPLY IT

1. Look back at presentations you have done recently and consider how you might have used multimedia to improve them. List your ideas. How can multimedia help you explain your topic and engage your audience?

Glossary

Words that appear in blue are your chapter Key Terms.

abolition putting a legal end to slavery

Aboriginal title the claim by Aboriginal peoples that they have ownership of the land because they were the first to occupy it

absentee landlord a person who owns and rents out a property, but does not live in the region

Agricultural Land Reserve (ALR) an act that provides for protection of farmland

allowable annual cut the number of trees that can be legally cut down in a year

American Civil War also called the War Between the States, it began in 1861 and ended in 1865. The industrialized North fought the agricultural South. A divisive issue was slavery, which the South supported.

annex to take over a territory and add it to the territory of another country

annexation the act of adding another territory to one's own

annexationist someone in favour of annexation with the United States

anti-confederationist someone opposed to joining Confederation

anti-dumping duty a special tariff imposed on imports being sold at unreasonably low prices

antiseptic something that kills and prevents the spread of bacteria

aquifer an underground source of water in saturated sand and gravel deposits

arable capable of being used for agriculture

Asia Pacific a sub-region of the Pacific Rim; includes nations with Pacific coastlines on the western Pacific plus nations that have political and economic connections with those countries

Asiatic Exclusion League an organization with an agenda to prevent Asian immigration

assimilate to join another culture and to give up one's own language and traditions

asylum a hospital that treats people with mental illnesses

autocrat a person who rules like a dictator

band an Aboriginal community recognized by the government as an administrative unit

bannock a simple bread, fried or baked, consisting of flour, baking powder, and salt

barter economy an economy based on trading services and products instead of using money

beam the most extreme width of a vessel, usually at the mid-point

bias strongly favouring a point of view to the point of misrepresenting other views

bilateral between two nations

biofuel fuel produced from organic matter

bison also called buffalo; large grazing animals that travel in herds

blight a disease caused by mold, fungus, or bacteria that can kill plants

boom and bust words used to describe a healthy (booming) economy and/or one that is failing (bust)

brain drain the emigration of people with technical skills and knowledge to a country with greater employment opportunities

branch-plant economy an economy that has a high percentage of factories, offices, and stores owned by foreign interests

buffalo runners small horses specially trained to be used during the buffalo hunt

business cycle alternating periods of ups and downs in economic activity

bylaw a law made by a municipal government, rather than by the legislature

Canadas, the Canada East and Canada West, within the Province of Canada

Canadian Pacific Railway (CPR) Canada's first transcontinental railway

canola a plant that produces oil, usually used in cooking

capital money that is used by a company to increase production by investing in equipment, seeking new markets, and other strategies

carbon tax a tax on energy sources that emit carbon dioxide, such as fossil fuels

cash crop a crop produced only for sale, usually export

celibacy refraining from sexual relations

census an official count of a population, often including information such as age, language, and work

Château Clique the wealthy elite who controlled Lower Canada, mostly made up of English-speaking merchants

class system a society in which those born into privileged groups have rights and advantages that others do not

clergy people ordained for religious service

climate the temperatures, humidity, rainfall, and atmospheric conditions of a region over long periods of time

coalition in politics, when one or more political parties or interest groups work together to achieve a common goal

coffin ship a death ship; disease and death were common on cargo vessels used to carry passengers at this time

colony the overseas possession of another country that governs and uses it for its own purposes

commodity a raw material or partially processed product that can be bought or sold

compromise settling a difference by each side giving up something

confederationist someone in favour of joining Confederation

constituency a district that is represented by an elected person

constitution the document that describes the powers and responsibilities of the government and its parts, and the rights of citizens

consumer price index a measure of price changes for standard goods and services

continental climate the climate of a continent's interior

continentalist supporting further integration of the North American economies

Continuous Passage Act a law passed in 1908 that allowed entry into Canada only to immigrants who had arrived by a single direct route

co-opt to win over or to bring someone into a group by capitalizing on their strengths, even if they disagree with the group

Corn Laws laws which protected agriculture in the British Empire by limiting the import of grain from other countries

corruption in politics, taking bribes or using one's influence to gain an unfair advantage

countervailing tariff a special tax that protects domestic products from subsidized foreign imports

cultural genocide the act of completely destroying the culture of a people

cultural landscapes landscapes that have been changed by human societies

culture the behaviour, arts, beliefs, and institutions of a particular community or population

deficit a situation where there is more spending than income

demographics population statistics that show age, income, etc.

dictator a ruler with unrestricted power, without any democratic restrictions

diversification having a number of economic activities to avoid dependence on one industry

dry forbidding the selling or drinking of alcohol

dryland farming farming methods practised in regions with limited rainfall

economic depression a period of low economic activity marked by high unemployment

economic region an area defined by common economic activities

ecosystem an ecological community of plants and animals together with its environment, extending over an area

Elders people respected for their wisdom and understanding of traditional knowledge

electorate the group of persons entitled to vote

elite a group of persons enjoying superior social or economic position

enfranchisement granting someone the rights and protection of a citizen of a particular country

estate a tract of land often covering thousands of hectares, owned by one person

evaporite a type of sedimentary deposit resulting from the evaporation of seawater

factor an agent who conducts business on someone's behalf

fair trade the removal of trade barriers such as tariffs, quotas, and regulations

Family Compact the small group of wealthy elite who controlled government in Upper Canada

federation a union of provinces, each of which keeps certain powers but gives up other powers to a central, national government

feedlot an enclosed area where large herds of cows are fed and raised

flume an artificial water channel

fold mountains mountains formed by sedimentary rock being pushed together by forces within the earth and folded into mountains and valleys

fossil fuel a natural fuel formed by geological forces from the remains of living organisms

Francophone a French-speaking Person

free trade a system of trade that is not fully regulated by government control

freer trade a trade relationship that has reduced its protective measures, but not entirely

Gatling gun a large, rapid-fire weapon with multiple rotating barrels, cranked by hand

gentry the upper class in Britain

Geographic Information System (GIS) an information system that stores, analyzes, and presents geographic data

geographic perspective a way of looking at and understanding the world

geology the study of the earth's crust to learn its origin, history, and structure

ghetto an area of a city inhabited by a minority group, usually one with substandard housing, power, and sewage systems

global economy international business and trade

globalization the process of economic, technological, political, and cultural forces creating a single, global society

Global Positioning System (GPS) a system of satellites and portable receivers able to pinpoint each receiver's location anywhere on earth

gold rush a period of intense migration of people to an area where gold has been discovered

goods products that can be sold

habeas corpus requiring that the lawfulness of a person's arrest or detention be investigated by a judge or court

head tax a tax paid only by Chinese immigrants to Canada; it started at $50 in 1885, was raised to $100 in 1900, and then went up to $500 in 1903

hivernants employees of the NWC who lived in the Northwest year-round

homestead lands public lands granted by governments on the understanding that they be turned into farms

huckster a person who usually uses aggressive selling tactics to make a profit

Hudson's Bay Company (HBC) the oldest commercial corporation in North America; once a major player in the fur trade, it is still in business today as a department store retailer

igneous rock rock formed from molten material, such as lava

imperialist someone who practises or supports imperialism, the policy of one nation acquiring, controlling, or dominating another country or region

implicit something that is implied, and not openly expressed

impropriety improper activity or conduct

incentive something that encourages action or greater effort

Indian Act an act created to regulate the lives of the First Nations of Canada

industrial heartland the most developed industrialized area in Canada

infrastructure the roads, canals, sewers, public services, and transportation networks that allow a community to function

insurrection taking up arms against the government

intensive farming achieving a high yield from a small growing area

Kanaka a person of Hawaiian descent who immigrated to British Columbia to work; many were contracted to work with the HBC

kimberlite a rare igneous rock that sometimes contains diamonds

knave an untrustworthy person

labour intensive requiring a lot of people to do the job

labour unions an organization representing workers in dealing with employers

land speculators those who buy property at a low price and sell it at a higher price, usually without spending much of their own money

latitude the distance of any point north or south of the equator, measured up to 90 degrees

laws of supply and demand economic laws about the relationship between the available amount of a product (supply), the number of people who want the product (demand), and the price of the product

leisure travel travelling just for the fun of it, to get away for a holiday

liberal democrat in the 19th century, someone who fought for the rights of the poor and underprivileged

longitude the distance of any point east or west of the Prime Meridian, measured up to 180 degrees

Lower Canada British colony "down" the St. Lawrence, mostly French speaking

Loyalist Americans who did not support the American Revolution, many of whom moved to the British colonies

magistrate an officer with limited authority to administer and enforce the law

managed trade a trade relationship that has built-in protection if one partner does not meet negotiated terms

Manifest Destiny an American idea that it was the fate of the United States to control all of North America

maquiladora a Latin American factory run by a foreign company and exporting its products to the country of that company, often exploiting cheap labour

maritime climate a coastal climate

marketing boards an association of food producers that control the marketing and pricing of their product

markets a place or group demanding goods or services; also where goods are bought and sold, for example, the world market for wheat or oil

materialistic valuing material possessions and physical comfort above all else

mercantilism an economic system based on colonialism, in which the home country uses raw goods imported from the colonies to manufacture goods

merge to join companies together, usually resulting in job losses

metamorphic rock rock changed from its original form through heat and pressure

Métis a person of both Aboriginal and European descent

Métis Bill of Rights a document that outlined grievances of the Métis and others in the North-West Territories

middle class at the time, a social class that had very wealthy members without aristocratic heritage

militia civilians with military training who are called to service in times of war or unrest

mitigate to reduce in force or intensity

moratorium a temporary enforced suspension of an activity

mortgage to use something as security for a loan

mother country a term describing the country immigrants came from

multinational having offices or factories in many different countries

multiplier effect the ripple effect as money from one sector works its way through the economy

muzzle loaders any firearm loaded through the muzzle (open end of a firearm)

NAFTA a trilateral trade agreement between Canada, the United States, and Mexico

nationalism devotion to the support of one's culture and nation, sometimes resulting in the promotion of independence

National Métis Committee an organization formed to support Métis rights in the Red River Valley

National Policy a mainly economic program introduced by the Macdonald government in 1879

non-renewable resources that cannot be replaced, for example, mineral deposits or fossil fuels

North West Company (NWC) the HBC's main rival in the fur trade; based in Montreal

North West Mounted Police (NWMP) Canada's national police force, now called the Royal Canadian Mounted Police (RCMP)

Northwest Uprising a series of battles in 1885 between the Métis and the Canadian forces, brought about by the Métis' attempts to gain recognition of their land rights

oligarchy rule by a small, select group of people

open-door policy an immigration policy that puts no restrictions on who can immigrate

open-pit mining the process of uncovering mineral deposits by scraping off surface layers of rock and creating a hole that becomes wider and deeper as each layer is removed

oral tradition a way of remembering the past through stories and spoken explanation, rather than in writing, although objects to aid memory were also used

orator an eloquent public speaker, able to inspire an audience

Oregon Territory an area in the Pacific Northwest occupied by both British and American colonists, also called the Columbia District by the British

outsource to export a job to another region or nation where labour costs are lower

Pacific Rim the region of the world that borders on or is connected economically and culturally to the Pacific Ocean and the Pacific Basin

paramilitary a force that operates like the army but is not part of it

parley a discussion under truce, sometimes to discuss peaceful alternatives to battle

paternalistic an attitude based on a family hierarchy—the "father" makes decisions on behalf of the "children"

patriotism love of one's country

pemmican dried meat pounded to a paste and mixed with melted fat and berries

Pemmican Proclamation issued in 1814 to prevent the export of pemmican from the Red River Valley

plate a slab of the earth's crust; plates are underneath all continents and oceans, regularly moving away from and toward each other

plate tectonics forces and movement within and on the earth's crust that form its features, such as mountain ranges and ocean basins

plunder to rob someone of goods or valuables by force

portage to carry boats and goods around dangerous parts of a river

precipitation climate rain, snow, hail, and fog

prejudice dislike or distrust of a person or group; forming a judgement before knowing the facts

prohibition the banning of the sale and consumption of alcohol

prospecting searching for gold

provisional government a temporary government

Rebellion Losses Bill a bill promising compensation to people of Canada East who suffered property damage during the Rebellions of 1837

reciprocity an agreement that provided for free trade between the United States and the British colonies

Red River carts two-wheeled carts used on the Prairies

Red River Resistance events leading up to the Métis' attempt to achieve recognition of their rights and self-government; also known as the Red River Rebellion

regional disparity different levels of income among regions

renewable resources that can be replaced, for example, trees or fish

representation by population a form of proportional representation in government; areas with higher populations have more elected officials in government

representative government a government made up of officials elected to office by the people

reserves land set aside by governments for the use of First Nations

resource-based economy an economy that relies on the extraction and/or primary processing of raw materials

responsible government a government subject to the votes of the people

restorative justice a process that focuses on healing relations between the victims and the accused rather than finding fault

Richter scale a measure of the power of Earthquakes

Royal Proclamation of 1763 a British declaration confirming Aboriginal title to lands west of the Mississippi River

runoff pesticides, herbicides, and other materials that drain from fields into rivers, lakes, and groundwater

Rupert's Land a territory consisting of the drainage basin of Hudson Bay

rural–urban migration the moving of people from rural areas into cities

sanctity considered sacred

scrip a piece of paper that could be used to certify possession of land or be exchanged for money

secede to formally withdraw from an alliance or a federal union

sectoral belonging to a distinct area of economic activity

sedimentary rock rock made up of layered deposits that have fused together

seigneurial system the system of landholding in New France; seigneurs were given estates and responsibilities to settle the land and oversee its administration

seismic relating to earthquakes or other vibrations of the earth's crust

Selkirk Settlement also called the Red River Colony; a settlement organized by the Earl of Selkirk in what is now southern Manitoba

sentimentalize to appeal to emotion rather than reason

services a system of supplying a public want or need (e.g., banking, transportation)

silviculture nurturing tree growth from seed to maturity

site the features of the land on which a settlement is built, such as elevation or landforms

situation the position of a settlement in relation to its surrounding area, including its relationship to other settlements and routes

smelter a place where ore is melted in order to separate the metal from the ore

softwood lumber wood such as pine and spruce that is used in building

sovereign rights the right to form a government or country

squat to settle on unoccupied land without legal title and without paying rent

stake a claim declare mining rights in a specific area

steerage the area below decks on a ship, used to store cargo

stewardship cooperative planning and management of environmental resources with the goal of sustaining those resources

structural unemployment unemployment caused by changes in the economy that affect an entire industry or replace labour (e.g., robotics

subduction zone a long region with a trench, where a descending tectonic plate is pushed down into the earth

subsidies financial support to businesses to encourage projects considered to be in the public interest

subsistence the production of enough food to feed oneself and one's family, without surplus for trade

suffragist a person who advocates extending the right to vote, especially to women

sustainable an activity that maintains an ecological balance by avoiding the depletion of a natural resource

syndicate a group of people who combine their resources to conduct a business together

tailings waste left over after the mineral is removed during mining or smelting

tariff a duty, or charge, that must be paid on an imported item

tenant farmer someone who farms land owned by someone else, keeping part of the produce as payment

threshing the process of separating grain from stalks or husks; the steam-powered threshing machine saved time and labour

topography the shape and structure of the surface features of a place or region

transnational extending beyond national boundaries

trend the general direction in which something is moving

trilateral between three nations

turn off to leave behind a Métis wife and children or to replace a Métis wife with a European wife

underemployed employed in a job below a worker's skill level, or employed only part-time

unprocessed in raw form, without value added

Upper Canada British colony "up" the St. Lawrence, mostly English speaking

urban in a town or city as opposed to the country

urbanization the process of becoming an area with a large, concentrated population

value-added economic value added to a product at each stage of its production

veto to stop with authority

Victorian of or pertaining to the reign of Queen Victoria; also someone who shares the values of that period

voyageur someone hired to transport goods by canoe from one trading post to another

ward a minor under the care of a guardian; in this

weir an enclosure of stakes and nets in a stream or river

whip the person who is responsible for ensuring discipline and solidarity within a political party

whist a card game for four players divided into two teams

Index

Credits

The publisher would like to thank the following people and institutions for permission to use their © materials. Every reasonable effort has been made to find copyright holders of the material in this text. The publisher would be pleased to know of any errors or omissions.

Photo Credits

bg/i: background/inset
t/c/b/l/r: top/centre/bottom/left/right

viii tl (1) Goodshoot Image/Jupiter Unlimited Images; (2) Comstock Images/Jupiter Unlimited Images; (3) Stockxpert Images/Jupiter Unlimited Images; (4) Henrik Andersen/Shutterstock Images; (5) © **Nruboc** <http://www.dreamstime.com/Nruboc_info> /Dreamstime.com; (6) © **Alptraum** <http://www.dreamstime.com/Alptraum_info> / Dreamstime.com; **bl** (1) Pardi/Dreamstime.com; (2) Brand X Pictures/Jupiter Unlimited Images; (3) © **Jbatt** <http://www.dreamstime.com/Jbatt_info> / Dreamstime.com; (4) scyther5/Shutterstock Images; (5) © **Tupungato** <http://www.dreamstime.com/Tupungato_info> / Dreamstime.com; (6) © PSL Images / Alamy; **x** Photos.com/Jupiter Unlimited Images; **xi** © Robert W. Ginn/Alamy; **2** iStockphoto; **3 t** Yves Marcoux/First Light; **3 bl** McCord Museum VIEW-1803; **3 br** Romilly Lockyer/Getty Images; **4** Comstock Images/ JupiterImages Unlimited; **5** Greg Locke/First Light; **6** Courtesy of Public Works and Government Services Canada; **8** JupiterImages/First Light; **10 t** Photo Courtesy of Wap Sigatgyet, School District 52; **10 b** © WorldFoto/Alamy; **11** © NASA/Corbis; **13 l** © Gavin Hellier/Alamy; **13 r** © Mark Tomalty/Alamy; **14** Image courtesy of Forest Analysis and Inventory Branch, BC-MOFR; **15 tl** Stockxpert Images/JupiterImages Unlimited; **15 bl** © North Wind Picture Archives/Alamy; **15 tr** © image100/Alamy; **18 t** Sean White/All Canada Photos/Getty Images; **18 b** Photos.com Images/ JupiterImages Unlimited; **19 l** Toronto Star Syndicate[2003] all rights reserved/Canadian Press; **19 r** Photos.com Images/JupiterImages Unlimited; **20 l** Photos.com Images/JupiterImages Unlimited; **20 r** Philippe Henry/First Light; **21 l** © Janusz Wrobel/Alamy; **21 r** Photos.com Images/Jupiter Images; **22 l** Don Johnston/All Canada Photos/Getty Images; **22 r** Photos.com Images/JupiterImages Unlimited; **23 l** Canadian Press/Jonathan Hayward; **23 r** Russ Heinl/All Canada Photos/Getty Images; **24** © Gunter Marx / Alamy; **27 t** CP Photo/Medicine Hat News/Dave McCord; **27 b** Courtesy of Environment Canada/National Oceanic and Atmospheric Administration (NOAA); **28** Stuart McCall/Photographer's Choice RF/Getty Images; **30** Stockxpert Images/JupiterImages Unlimited; **31** Canadian Press/Larry MacDougal; **33** Jan Martin Will/Shutterstock Images **34** © imac/Alamy; **35** © All Canada Photos/Alamy; **36** Revised from original, courtesy of Hudson's Bay Company Archives and the Archives of Manitoba; **38** CP Picture Archive/Nick Procaylo; **40** Maun-gua-daus Collection/Library and Archives Canada/PA-125840; **41 t** www.canadianheritage.ca, ID #23233, Philip John Bainbrigge, National Archives of Canada, C-11811; **41 bl** Government of Ontario Art Collection, 621229; **41 br** Library and Archives Canada/C-000733; **42** Library and Archives Canada/C-102463; **43** © The Three Robinson Sisters, George Theodore Berthon, 1845, courtesy AGO/T-216; **44** www.canadianheritage.ca, ID #23233, Philip John Bainbrigge, National Archives of Canada, C-11811; **45** Library and Archives Canada, Acc. No. 1981-55-6; **46 l** Taken from James Patrick Howley, *The Beothucks, or Red Indians, the Aboriginal Inhabitants of Newfoundland* (Cambridge: University Press, 1915. Courtesy of Dr. Hans Rollman; **46 r** Courtesy of Murray Hudson, Halls, Tennessee; **47** The Village of Secoton, from 'Admiranda Naratio…', published by Theodore de Bry (coloured engraving) by Bry, Theodore de (1528-98), after White, John (d. 1593) © Service Historique de la Marine, Vicennes, France/Lauros/Giraudon/ The Bridgeman Art Library; **48** Library and Archives Canada, Acc.

No. 1946-131-1, Gift of Mrs. J.B. Jardine; **49** Peter Mintz/First Light; **50** © Stephen Saks Photography/Alamy; **51** Painting by Carson Waterman, Permission by Rod Dowling; **52** Library and Archives Canada/C-17; **53** Library and Archives Canada/C-12649; **54** James B. Wandesford/Portrait of Col Thomas Talbot/nd watercolour on card 67.3 x 49.5 cm Collection of McIntosh Gallery, The University of Western Ontario, London Ontario Canada, Gift of Judge Talbot MacBeth, 1941; **55 l** Library and Archives Canada, Acc. No. 1970-188-2092 W.H. Coverdale Collection of Canadiana; **55 r** Stockxpert Image/JupiterImages Unlimited; **56** Canadian Press/AP Photo/NZPA, Malcolm Pullman; **58** www.canadianheritage.ca, ID #20089, National Archives of Canada, C6556; **60** © Bettmann/CORBIS; **62** Library and Archives of Canada/C-029977; **63** Mary Evans Picture Library/The Image Works; **64** Archives of Ontario, F 1077-11-0-5-2; **65** Government of Ontario Art Collection, Archives of Ontario, 619857; **66** Courtesy of the Archives of Ontario, S 2123; **67** Queen's University Archives, watercolour, 1830 by F.H. Consett; **71** Artist: Alexander Charles, Title: Manifestation des Canadiens contre le gouvernement anglais, à Saint-Charles, en 1837, dit aussi L'Assemblée six comtés, 1891 [Rally of the Canadians against the English Government, Saint-Charles, 1837], Medium: Huile sur toile, Dimensions: 300 X 690 cm, Collection: Musée national des beaux-arts du Québec, Accession no.: 37.54, Photographer: Patrick Altman; **72** www.canadianheritage.ca, ID #10231, Rare Book Collection, National Library of Canada/ Collection des livres rares, Bibliothèque Nationale du Canada/NL-18299; **73** © The Print Collector/Alamy; **74** Government of Ontario Art Collection, 621229; **77 t** Courtesy of photographer William Dutfield; **77 b** Hulton Archive/Getty Images; **78** © Alan King engraving/Alamy; **82** McCord Museum VIEW-1032.1; **83** Courtesy of Parks Canada, Confederation House Charlottetown PEI and artist Dusan Kadlec; **84** Canadian National Exhibition Archives; **85 l** Library and Archives Canada—Canadian Illustrated News, Vol. XII, No. 23, Dec. 4, 1875, p. 361; **85 r** Archives of Ontario, F 4356-0-0-0-2; **86 l** Courtesy of Dick Hemingway photographer; **86 r** L. Tom Perry Special Collections Brigham Young University; **87** © Bettmann/CORBIS; **88 t** © Bettmann/CORBIS; **88 b** McCord Museum II-180990.0; **89** Archives of Ontario, S 17839, Acc. 2802; **90** Glenbow Archives NA-265-10; **91** Canadian Illustrated News - Come to Stay by Henri Julien, vol. XXII, no.7, 97, August 14, 1880/Library and Archives Canada; **92** © Culver Pictures Inc./Super Stock/Maxx Images; **93** Maun-gua-daus Collection/Library and Archives Canada/PA-125840; **95** CP Photo/Tom Hanson; **96 t** Library and Archives Canada/PA-147585; **96 b** www.canadianheritage.ca, ID #20052; **97** Library and Archives Canada/PA-042133; **98** La scie, Quebec, Quebec: L-P, Normand, 1863-1865, Vol. II, no. 2, 2 December 1864/Library and Archives Canada; **102** McCord Museum M930.51.1.52; **103** McCord Museum M11588; **104** www.canadia heritage.ca, ID #21943; **107 l** Accession no. 1989-565 CPA, Library and Archives Canada; **107 r** Hunter & Co./Library and Archives Canada/C-009553; **108** Aaron Lynett/Toronto Star; **111** Library and Archives Canada, Acc. No. 1946-35-1; **112** Topley Studio/Library and Archives Canada/PA-025486; **116** Library and Archives Canada/C-000733; **118** Courtesy of BC Archives C-06116; **122** Canadian Pacific Archives A.6116; **123 t** Glenbow Archive NA-1039-1; **123 bl** Paul Kane (1810–1871) Metis chasing the Main Buffalo Herd (detail) 1846, watercolour on paper 5 3/16 x 9 inches (13.2 x 22.9 cm) Stark Museum of Art, Orange, Texas 31.78.127, PWC 16; **123 br** McCord Museum 93015015; **124** © Stan Zack/Alamy; **125** © Rubens Abboud/Alamy; **126** Courtesy of Hudson's Bay Company Archives and the Archives of Manitoba; **127** © Bill Brooks/Alamy; **129** Archives of Ontario, F 443, R-C (U), AO 1541; **130** Glenbow Archives NA-4201-1; **133** CP PHOTO/Montreal La Presse-Andre Forget; **134 t** www.canadianheritage.ca, ID #10043, National Archives of Canada/PA-44566; **134 b** McCord Museum M10399.1-2; **139** Glenbow Archives NA-1905-20; **140** Paul Kane (1810–1871) Metis chasing the Main Buffalo Herd (detail) 1846, watercolour on paper 5 3/16 x 9 inches (13.2 x 22.9 cm) Stark Museum of Art, Orange, Texas 31.78.127, PWC 16; **141 t** With permission of the Royal Ontario Museum © ROM; **141 b** © JupiterImages/Photos.com/Alamy; **143** © Illustrated London News Ltd./Mary Evans;

145 Courtesy of Hudson's Bay Company Archives and the Archives of Manitoba; 146 Courtesy of Hudson's Bay Company Archives and the Archives of Manitoba; 148 Glenbow Archives NA-2617-48; 149 Archives of Ontario, F 431, G-361; 150–151 Natural Moments/Darwin Wiggett/First Light; 153 t Photograph of a miniature portrait of Frances, wife of Governor George Simpson, undated. HBCA Album 10/82; 153 b Courtesy of Hudson's Bay Company Archives and the Archives of Manitoba; 154 Photos.com/Jupiter Images; 155 Glenbow Archives NA-933-1; 157 Glenbow Archives NA-1039-1; 159 Glenbow Archives NA-1406-71a; 160 Courtesy of Hudson's Bay Company Archives and the Archives of Manitoba; 164 McCord Museum II-306116.0; 165 Canadian Pacific Archives A.6118; 167 Glenbow Archives NA-2839-4; 170 t Glenbow Archives NA-1063-1; 170 b Library and Archives Canada, Acc. No. 1970-188-1064 W.H. Coverdale Collection of Canadiana; 172 Glenbow Archives NA-354-30; 174 Glenbow Archives NA-550-11; 175 CP PHOTO/Winnipeg Free Press-Ken Gigliotti; 176 Winnipeg Art Gallery G-72-75; 177 Saskatchewan Archives Board R-B2837; 179 Glenbow Archives NA-127-1; 181 Glenbow Archives NA-1472-7; 182 University of Saskatchewan Libraries Special Collections, 24215; 183 CP Photo/Tom Hanson; 184 © Bill Brooks/Alamy; 186 l O.B. Buell/Library and Archives Canada/C-001875; 186 c www.canadianheritage.ca, ID #20752, Duffin & Co./National Archives of Canada/C-17430; 186 r CP Photo 1999 (Library and Archives Canada/ Alexander J. Ross) PA-134918; 187 O.B. Buell/Library and Archives Canada/ PA-118759; 188 O.B. Buell/Library and Archives Canada/C-001879; 189 O.B. Buell/Library and Archives Canada/C-006688b; 193 t CP PHOTO/Winnipeg Free Press-Joe Bryksa; 193 b Glenbow Archives NA-1480-19; 194 © Bettmann/CORBIS; 197 McCord Museum MP-0000.809.5; 198 t Glenbow Archives NA-3080-4; 198 b Glenbow Archives NA-967-12; 200 Glenbow Archives NA-3082-4; 201 t www.canadian heritage.ca, ID #20745, Library and Archives of Canada/C-4634; 201 b CP PHOTO 1998 (Library and Archives Canada) C-003693; 202 CP Photo 1998 (Library and Archives Canada) C-011371; 204 McCord Museum 93015013; 205 Library and Archives Canada C-114507k; 208 Courtesy of Vancouver Maritime Museum; 209 © CORBIS; 211 t © BC Archives, Royal BC Museum A-01228; 211 b © BC Archives, Royal BC Museum H-04909; 214 © BC Archives, Royal BC Museum D-06815; 215 British Columbia Photos; 217 McCord Museum 1323007; 218 t © BC Archives, Royal BC Museum A-00347; 218 b Glenbow na-674-44; 220 Library and Archives Canada C-001572k; 222 © Andre Jenny/Alamy; 223 © Douglas Lander/ Alamy; 225 © BC Archives, Royal BC Museum A-01751; 227 © BC Archives, Royal BC Museum G-03061; 228 © Chris Howes/Wild Places Photography/ Alamy; 229 Volodymyr Kyrylyuk/Dreamstime Images; 231 City of Vancouver Archives, A32533; 232 Salt Spring Island Archives; 233 t © BC Archives, Royal BC Museum C-06124; 233 b City of Vancouver Archives, 677-441; 234 City of Vancouver Archives, BO P56; 235 Library and Archives Canada A-053604; 236 l Library and Archives Canada C-064764; 236 r Library and Archives Canada C-021990; 237 tl Canada Science and Technology Museum, CN000401; 237 tr © BC Archives, Royal BC Museum I-33036; 237 b © BC Archives, Royal BC Museum D-07548; 238 © BC Archives, Royal BC Museum PDP01873; 240 Library and Archives Canada/C-085854; 241 t Canadian Press/Bayne Stanley; 241 b Canadian Press/J.P. Moczulski; 242 Glenbow Archives NA-3961-31; 243 Library and Archives Canada/C-126302; 245 Library and Archives Canada/C-463; 251 Library and Archives Canada/C-085854; 253 Isaac Erb/Library and Archives Canada/PA-041785; 254 Glenbow Archives NA-1255-31; 255 © Design Pics Inc./Alamy; 258 Lewis W. Hine/Library and Archives Canada/ C-30937; 259 t © Richard T. Nowitz/CORBIS; 259 b © Yang Liu/CORBIS; 262 l Paula Cobleigh/Shutterstock; 262 r Glenbow Archives NA-4061-54; 263 Canadian Press/AP Photo/Eugene Hoshiko; 264 © BC Archives, Royal BC Museum e_02631; 265 Hulton Archive/Getty Images; 266 t Cyril Jessop/Library and Archives Canada/PA-030212; 267 Glenbow Archives NC-5-6; 268 Glenbow Archives NA-3482-8; 269 Canadian Press/Tom Hanson; 270 © BC Archives, Royal BC Museum 12923; 273 CP Photo/ Toronto Star/David Cooper; 274 Library and Archives Canada/C-023555; 275 Library and Archives Canada/PA-034014; 276 Harry Rowed/National Film Board of Canada/Library and Archives Canada; 277 Glenbow Archives IP-12-1-1; 278 t Western Canada Archives; 278 b © Bettmann/CORBIS; 279 t Charles A. Aylett/Library and Archives Canada/C-014090; 279 b © BC Archives, Royal BC Museum PDP06149; 280 Cochran/Library and Archives Canada/C-085125; 282 © Lloyd Sutton/Alamy; 283 CP PHOTO/Richard Lam; 285 © Bob Pardue-Lifestyle/Alamy; 286 CP Photo/Adrian Brown; 287 tl Al Harvey/The Slide Farm Inc.; 287 bl Creatas Images/JupiterImages Unlimited; 287 tr Photos.com Images/JupiterImages Unlimited; 287 br iStockphoto; 288 © Douglas Lander/Alamy; 289 Courtesy of Merle Tingley Collection, Western Archives, University of Western Ontario; 290 (C) Toronto Star Syndicate [2003] all rights reserved; 293 t David Nunuk/First Light; 293 b CP Photo/Jonathan Hayward; 295 CP Photo/Kevin Frayer; 296 Grant Black/First Light; 297 B & C Alexander/First Light; 298 © Toronto Star Syndicate [2003] all rights reserved; 299 © Tim Davis/CORBIS; 300 Glenbow NA-1308-20; 301 © Craig Ellenwood/Alamy; 302 © Rich Iwasaki/Alamy; 303 © Jean Guichard/Sygma/Corbis; 304 © Keith Dannemiller/Alamy; 305 t © J.P. Moczulski/Reuters/Corbis; 305 b © David Ball/Alamy; 306 Canadian Press/J.P. Moczulski; 307 Canadian Press/AP Photo/Katsumi Kasahara; 308 CP PHOTO/Tom Hanson; 310 Courtesy of Brian Gable and The Globe and Mail; 311 CP PHOTO/Don Denton; 312 CP PHOTO/Richard Lam; 313 t Courtesy of Roy Peterson/Vancouver Sun; 313 b Courtesy of Roy Peterson/Vancouver Sun; 314 Canadian Press/AP Photo/Eduardo Verdugo; 315 Canadian Press/AP Photo/L.M. Otero; 316 Courtesy of Roy Peterson/Vancouver Sun; 317 © Chris Cheadle/Alamy; 320 © Imre Cikajlo/iStockphoto; 321 Emily Carr, Totem Forest, 1930, oil on canvas, 128.6 x 92.0 cm, Collection of the Vancouver Art Gallery, Emily Carr Trust, VAG 42.3.3, Photo: Trevor Mills, Vancouver Art Gallery; 325 Steve Bosch/The Vancouver Sun; 326 l Masterfile Royalty Free; 326 r © Tony Freeman/PhotoEdit; 328 City of Vancouver Archives A-08077; 329 l © Joel W. Rogers/CORBIS; 329 r © Lloyd Sutton/Alamy; 330 Dale Wilson/ Masterfile; 331 CP PHOTO/Halifax Daily News-Paul Darrow; 332 t © jack thomas/Alamy; 332 b © Tracy Ferrero/ Alamy; 334 tl Albert Normandin/ Masterfile; tr © Lloyd Sutton/Alamy; b Andrey Armyagov/Shutterstock; 336 © Steve Kaufman/CORBIS; 338 Courtesy of Independent Power Producers Association of BC, www.ippbc.ca; 339 © Technology And Industry Concepts/Alamy; 340 Canadian Press/AP Photo/Laura Rauch; 341 © McCanner/Alamy; 343 © All Canada Photos/Alamy; 345 © Gunter Marx/Alamy; 346 CP Photo/Larry MacDougal; 350 Courtesy of NASA; 351 Canadian Pacific Archives A.6118; 352 t © Mike Dobel/Alamy; 352 b Canadian Press/Bayne Stanley; 353 © 20th Century Fox Film Corp. All rights reserved/Courtesy Everett Collection; 356 Courtesy of Henry Stanski

Literary Credits

32 Mikisew Cree First Nation, Government and Industry Relations Department; 99t "The botheration scheme," Halifax Morning Chronicle, January 11, 1865. © Public Domain; 99b 'Confederation Day!,' The Globe, July 1, 1867, vol. 24, no. 56, supplement, p. 4. © Public Domain; 112 "The botheration scheme", Halifax Morning Chronicle, January 11, 1865. © Public Domain; 125 Reprinted by permission of Mark McCallum; 175 Alexander Morris (1826-1889), The Treaties of Canada with the Indians of Manitoba and the North-West Territories (Belfords, Clarke, Torono: 1880) October 20, 1876; 195 Reprinted with permission from the estate of Pierre Berton; 172 (both quotes) CBC.CA, Canada: A People's History. Reprinted by permission of CBC; 259 Source Article: UN says half the world's population will live in urban areas by end of 2008, Magazine: The Associated Press, February 26, 2008. Reprinted with permission; 269 Text of the apology, Canwest News Service, Vancouver Sun, Wednesday June 11, 2008. Reprinted with permission from The Vancouver Sun; 275 Excerpt from Votes and Proceedings related to the Komagata Maru, from: http://www.leg.bc.ca/38th4th/votes/v080520.htm. Reprinted by permission of the Office of Speaker of the Legislative Assembly of British Columbia; 331 Source: Russia sees what B.C. doesn't: Raw log exports cost forest industry jobs, Bob Matters, The Vancouver Sun, August 25, 2008. Reprinted with permission from The Vancouver Sun; 339 A Million Points of Pollution, Mark Hume, The Vancouver Sun, May 30, 1995. Reprinted with permission from The Vancouver Sun; 348 B.C. Oil could ease crisis, Peter O'Neil with files from Kelly Sinoski, The Vancouver Sun, July 14, 2008. Material reprinted with the express permission of: "CANWEST NEWS SERVICE", a CanWest Partnership.